BRITISH NON-BANK FINANCIAL INTERMEDIARIES

D.J. Goacher

P.J. Curwen

Sheffield City Polytechnic

WITH

R. Apps · P.F. Cowdell

Sheffield City Polytechnic

J.G. Boocock · L. Drake

Loughborough University

London
ALLEN & UNWIN
Boston Sydney Wellington

Allen & Unwin, the academic imprint of
Unwin Hyman Ltd
PO Box 18, Park Lane, Hemel Hempstead, Herts HP2 4TE, UK
40 Museum Street, London WC1A 1LU, UK
37/39 Queen Elizabeth Street, London SE1 2QB, UK

Allen & Unwin Inc.,
8 Winchester Place, Winchester, Mass. 01890, USA

Allen & Unwin (Australia) Ltd,
8 Napier Street, North Sydney, NSW 2060, Australia

Allen & Unwin (New Zealand) Ltd in association with the
Port Nicholson Press Ltd,
60 Cambridge Terrace, Wellington, New Zealand

First published in 1987

British Library Cataloguing in Publication Data

British non-bank financial intermediaries.
1. Financial institutions – Great Britain
I. Apps, R.
332.1'0941   HG2986
ISBN 0-04-332109-7
ISBN 0-04-332110-0 Pbk

Library of Congress Cataloging-in-Publication Data
British non-bank financial intermediaries.
Bibliography: p.
Includes index.
1. Financial institutions – Great Britain.
2. Finance – Great Britain. I. Apps, R.
HG186.G7B73 1987 332.1'0941 86-32146
ISBN 0-04-332109-7 (alk. paper)
ISBN 0-04-332110-0 (pbk.: alk. paper)

Set in 10 on 12 point Palatino by Columns of Reading
and printed in Great Britain by
Billing & Sons Limited, Worcester.

Contents

CONTENTS

CONTENTS

CONTENTS

CONTENTS

Tables

Figures

Preface

Since 1980 the financial services sector has been one of the few areas of economic activity in the UK to have experienced persistent and, at times, rapid growth. In terms of its contribution to the national product, its generation of employment and its influence on the day-to-day activities of the majority of the population, the importance of the financial services sector is unquestionable. However, with only a small number of exceptions, the component parts of the financial services sector have tended to receive very limited attention in the academic literature, and much of that has been directed towards the specialist economist or investment analyst. Furthermore, the traditional demarcation lines drawn between financial institutions have often led to the examination of their activities in isolation, thus distorting the perception of their true significance within an increasingly integrated financial system.

The operations of the banking institutions have been heavily researched and catalogued, and their position in relation to the implementation of government monetary controls has ensured the widespread recognition of their roles. In recent years increasing attention has also been paid to the building society sector. The growing areas of overlap between the operations of building societies and those of the clearing banks, and the resultant impact upon the degree of competition, have almost inevitably placed them in the spotlight both for academic analysis and for discussion in the financial press. However, the institutions operating in the other areas of the financial sector have received very mixed treatment in the literature. The academic debate has often focused upon rather esoteric technicalities of their operations, whilst the financial press and several textbooks have offered their readers little more than investors' guides to the relevant financial services provided by the institutions. It has been rare to find a coherent analysis of the broader implications of ongoing developments in the financial services sector, and even more unusual to have the veil lifted from the 'back-room' activities of the non-bank institutions. The major purpose of this book is to make a modest contribution to filling this obvious gap in the literature.

The nature of the UK financial services sector today is so complex, and its recent evolution has been so rapid, that within the space available in this book we are able to examine only one broad category of financial services institutions in depth. We have chosen the non-bank financial intermediaries for two reasons. First, as mentioned above, the banking institutions have received more than their fair share of attention in the literature, and with the growing importance of the non-bank intermediaries it would appear fitting to redress the balance somewhat. Secondly, it is in relation to the activities of the non-bank financial intermediaries that the most fundamental and pervasive developments have occurred in recent years. However, our enforced acceptance of the conventional financial services dichotomy should not be interpreted as giving support to the view that it is correct for analytical purposes to separate financial intermediaries into distinct categories. Indeed, recognition of the diversification and overlaps in the operations of UK financial intermediaries forms a central theme of our discussion. Our approach merely accepts the practical reality that in order to explain the key issues and problems it is necessary to group institutions according to their dominant characteristics. Hence, for example, just because a bank makes mortgage loans to personal customers does not mean that it should also be classified as a building society. Nevertheless, as the demarcation lines between financial institutions became increasingly blurred, questions can be expected to arise over the appropriateness of classifications. At that stage there may be no alternative but to shift the basis of academic discussion to the provision of types of financial services irrespective of the precise form of institution providing those services.

The second major limitation of this book as a text on the financial services sector is that we deliberately concentrate purely upon the institutions offering some form of financial intermediation service. We do not consider institutions involved exclusively in the provision of fund management services, financial consultancy, broking activities and the like. Neither do we examine the structure of the financial markets within which many of the financial intermediaries operate, although, in so far as it is necessary for a complete understanding of the activities of the non-bank financial intermediaries, the relevant financial markets are introduced into the discussion.

One obvious difficulty in preparing this book was the need to cover a wide range of intermediaries, since the major criticism of existing books in the field is that their authors appear to lack detailed up-to-date knowledge across the board. It was therefore decided to utilize a number of different authors, each covering the operations of specific non-bank financial intermediaries, with one author having particular responsibility for Chapters 1 to 3, 11 and 12, which attempt respectively to outline the theoretical framework of financial intermediation and to provide an overview of the broader evolution of the UK financial system. Furthermore, a separate person was assigned the task of editing the individual components into a cohesive whole. We believe that this approach has produced a text which not only has a satisfactory breadth and depth of coverage, but also embodies a style of presentation manageable to the non-specialist reader.

Whilst this book should prove to be invaluable to university and polytechnic students taking one of the rapidly increasing number of courses devoted to the activities of UK financial institutions, the nature of its subject matter and its style of exposition should also make it of great use to practitioners in the financial services sector itself, and especially to those who are about to enter, or who have recently entered, the sector. For such individuals it is often difficult to appreciate the relative position and significance of their own institutions within the rapidly changing financial services environment, and we hope that this book will prove to be a useful guide.

Sheffield City Polytechnic   David Goacher
September 1986   Peter Curwen

CHAPTER ONE

The Theoretical Basis of Financial Intermediation

The Nature of Financial Intermediation

The process of financial intermediation involves the channelling of funds between those who wish to lend and those who wish to borrow; that is, between people and institutions with budget surpluses and people and institutions with budget deficits. Financial intermediaries are normally thought of as comprising banks, building societies and the like, but it is important to appreciate that the intermediation activity stretches well beyond these widely known components of the financial system. In fact, whenever an individual or institution (irrespective of its size) channels funds between lenders and borrowers by way of a business venture, then the process of financial intermediation occurs. In the UK, in addition to the banks and building societies, the major financial intermediaries include the National Savings Bank, finance houses, unit trusts, investment trust companies, pension funds and insurance companies.[1] There is also a host of less widely recognized institutions involved in somewhat more specialist forms of intermediation, often relating to the particular financial needs of the business community, and including, for example, the venture capital companies such as 3i, which space does not permit us to discuss in this text.

The structure of the modern financial system is extremely complex, and hence, as might be expected, there are many

1

variations on the basic financial intermediation activity. For example, some intermediaries, mainly within the banking sector, channel funds almost exclusively between other financial intermediaries and thus facilitate the working of the financial system as a whole, rather than interacting directly with ultimate lenders and ultimate borrowers. Discount houses, for example, operate in this way, channelling wholesale (large-volume) short-term funds between commercial banks, and between the latter and the Bank of England's Banking Department. There are also institutions which obtain all, or nearly all, of their funds from other financial intermediaries for the purpose of on-lending outside the financial sector. Some UK finance houses operate in this way. However, the majority of financial intermediaries, at some stage of their operations, raise funds from and/or lend funds to the domestic non-bank private sector, although even in this respect there may be differing balances between personal and corporate sector activity, and between domestic and overseas activity.[2]

Irrespective of the precise form of financial intermediary, the intermediation activity will always lead to the creation of new financial assets and liabilities. The funds originally held by the ultimate lender will be transformed into a financial asset which is the liability of the financial intermediary. This type of asset, which is usually interest-bearing, is often referred to as a secondary (or indirect) security, as it constitutes a claim on the financial intermediary rather than on an ultimate borrower. The financial intermediary will normally utilize a large proportion of the funds deposited with it to purchase interest-bearing (or at least income-earning) financial assets, which are the liabilities of ultimate borrowers, and which are often referred to as primary securities. Thus, for example, an individual may deposit cash into a share account at a building society. This act leads to the creation of interest-bearing building society shares, which are an asset of the shareholder and a liability of the building society. Some or all of the money (depending upon the building society's reserve position)[3] may be on-lent to an individual wishing to borrow funds in order to purchase a dwelling. Thus, an interest-bearing mortgage loan is created

2

which is an asset of the building society and a liability of the borrower. Clearly, the process of financial intermediation has led to the creation of additional amounts of two financial assets matched by equal amounts of financial liabilities. Where ultimate lenders provide funds directly to ultimate borrowers, additional pairs of assets and liabilities will always be created, but these are purely in the form of primary securities; there are no indirect securities created. The existence of financial intermediaries leads to a multiplication of the financial claims generated. There is always at least one additional pair of assets and liabilities (indirect securities) flowing from a transaction where financial intermediation is involved, relative to the situation where the ultimate lender provides funds directly to the ultimate borrower.

A less obvious example of financial intermediation is where an individual contributes (often through his employer) to a pension fund, in order to 'purchase' a claim to a stream of income after retirement. With the contributions received the pension fund is likely to purchase fixed interest securities and equity shares, and thereby hold claims against the government and company sectors with the view to earning sufficient income and realizable capital gains in future periods to be able to meet its financial liabilities (to pay pensions) as they fall due. Therefore, the pension fund acts as an intermediary between ultimate lenders (those saving for retirement) and ultimate borrowers. It makes little difference to the parties concerned whether the funds are on-lent to the government or company sector directly via the purchase of newly issued securities, or indirectly via the purchase of pre-existing securities. In the latter case the pension fund merely takes over a claim on the ultimate borrower from some other institution or individual wishing to make a portfolio reallocation.[4]

The Assets Created by the Financial Intermediation Process

The form of assets (and hence liabilities) created by the financial intermediation process will depend largely upon the type of financial transaction undertaken. For many individuals, perhaps the most familiar financial asset, after cash itself, is the bank deposit or building society deposit (or share).[5] Quite simply, funds are deposited with an intermediary on the understanding that they may be withdrawn either on demand or after some minimum period of notice of withdrawal, and that the financial intermediary will either pay interest periodically on the funds or will provide some service to the depositor in return for the use of the funds. Where the financial intermediary does not pay interest on deposits, it is almost invariably the case that money transmission services will be offered to the depositor, involving the provision of cheque book, standing order and direct debit facilities and so on. These services will either be free of charge, or offered at a price below cost. However, a large proportion of deposits with banks, and all deposits with other financial intermediaries, do attract interest payments which tend to be related to the nominal period of notice required for withdrawal. In general, within any particular institution, the rate of interest paid on deposits will be higher the longer is the period of withdrawal notice required, although it is common for financial intermediaries to waive the formal period of notice and merely to deduct an appropriate amount of accrued interest in lieu.

A second important form of financial asset which may be created by the financial intermediation process is the marketable security. In this instance, the lender of the funds effectively purchases a document which constitutes a legal claim upon the financial intermediary and which is negotiable (tradable in a secondary market). This type of financial instrument may be issued and redeemed at par (face) value, and will attract interest, either to be paid periodically or at the time of maturity. Alternatively, the instrument may be issued at a discount on its par value but redeemed at par value, and thus technically provides the holder with a yield on his asset rather than an interest payment in the strict sense. Examples of the former type of assets are government gilt-edged securities and bank certificates of deposit. Instruments issued at a discount include Treasury bills and commercial bills. An important advantage of marketable securities to the lender is that, irrespective of their original or residual maturity, they may be sold prior to maturity to some other individual or institution, and thus the lender may attempt to realize his investment at a time of his own choosing. However, although financial claims in the form of marketable securities are transferable, there is no guarantee that a buyer will be found for the securities in the secondary market at any particular time.

In practice, the marketability of any instrument will depend upon its nature in terms of the associated interest payments and its residual maturity, as well as the credit-worthiness of the issuer of the instrument. The less creditworthy is the issuer, the riskier is the asset, and hence the lower is the price that it is likely to realize for any given interest payment. Similarly, an instrument paying an interest rate on par value which is low relative to the ruling market rate of interest is also likely to trade below its par value. Therefore, whilst the holding of marketable securities may enhance the overall liquidity of an assets portfolio, there is also the risk that a capital loss may accrue if realization of the securities is desired prior to their maturity.

The nature of the return on marketable assets will have an important influence on the associated risk. For example, a commitment to fixed nominal interest payments means that the lender may find that he holds an asset offering a relatively poor yield should market rates of interest subsequently rise; conversely, a reduction in market rates of interest will enhance the attractiveness of the asset. If inflation rates should exceed those which were expected when the asset was initially purchased then the real return on the asset may prove to be disappointingly poor. An index-linking agreement may overcome this particular uncertainty for the lender, but will mean that the borrower has to make an open-ended commitment to nominal interest payments. To neutralize the effect on the capital value of the asset flowing from changes in the market rate of interest, the asset may offer a floating rate of interest, itself linked to market rates. Once again, the nature of the risks to be accepted by both the borrower and the lender are altered. Furthermore, a large body of marketable securities, referred

5

to as equities, involve no specific commitment to pay interest (fixed or otherwise). Instead the issuing company allots some portion of its profits to be distributed amongst its equity shareholders. Here, the return received by the shareholders (and ultimately the capital value of the shares) will depend crucially upon the success of the operations of the company. In addition, in normal circumstances, equities are not redeemable, and hence the existence of a ready market in these instruments is extremely important to the potential investor.

Finally, it should be noted that some securities, issued as the counterpart to the borrowing of funds, are non-marketable. National Savings certificates and bonds, and certificates of tax deposit fall into this category. To a large extent these instruments are very little different from ordinary term deposits. Technically the lender is obliged to hold the debt until it matures, whereupon the funds will be repaid. However, facilities are sometimes offered for the early redemption of such securities, although this may involve some form of interest penalty. Where this does not occur, and to the extent that there is a significant period of time until maturity, the lender holds an illiquid asset. Therefore, if funds are required urgently the holder of the non-marketable security may himself be forced to borrow funds, perhaps using the security as a form of collateral. Clearly, once again the lender must be willing to accept a degree of risk in addition to that normally associated with default.

The Interest Rate Paid on a Financial Asset

Implicit in the above discussion are the three related reasons as to why nominal interest rates are positive. First, the lender requires compensation for giving up current con-sumption possibilities, since basic human nature prefers consumption in the current period thereby generating a positive time preference in most individuals. Secondly, the lender requires compensation for giving up liquidity as a result of exchanging funds (immediately available spending power) for some other form of financial asset. Thirdly, the lender requires a positive return for accepting the risk attached to lending. However, the actual rate of interest established on a borrowing/lending transaction will be determined by the combined characteristics of the transaction, as these characteristics will affect the supply of, and the demand for, the type of funds implicit in the transaction, and hence will affect the price of the asset created. Moreover, the pattern of interest rates established in the economy will be determined by the relative supplies of, and demands for, the various types of financial assets available.

The major characteristics of a financial transaction which will ultimately determine the rate of interest established may be summarized as follows:

(1) *Risk* In addition to the possible losses which may accrue on marketable securities, there is the more extreme risk that the borrower may either default on the interest payments on a loan or on the repayment of the principal. Indeed, if the risk is thought to be unacceptably high there will be no rate of interest which will offer sufficient compensation to the lender, and hence the loan will not be made. Similarly, there is the risk that a company in which equity shares have been purchased will prove to be unprofitable, or perhaps even go bankrupt with insufficient residual assets to cover even the normal creditors of the business.

(2) *Time to maturity* In general, other things being equal, the longer is the term to maturity of a loan, the higher will be the interest rate desired by the lender. This reflects the underlying liquidity preference of the lender and the increasing uncertainty surrounding transactions as time passes. It is only where there are sufficiently strong expectations of interest rate reductions that rates on longer-term debt may fall below those on shorter-term instruments.[6]

(3) *Marketability of the asset* The easier is access to an active market in securities, the lower will tend to be the rate of interest which the securities will attract,

other things being equal. This characteristic relates to the liquidity of the asset in the broadest sense.

(4) *Type of loan* In relation to banks, funds may be lent through normal term loans (on which interest must be paid irrespective of whether or not the funds are actually used by the borrower) or through overdraft facilities (where only the portion of the funds actually used by the borrower attracts interest). With fixed-maturity debt there may also be some form of agreement on rolling-over facilities.

(5) *Absolute size of the transaction* Unit administration costs will tend to be lower the larger is the amount of funds borrowed/lent, and thus a financial intermediary will often be willing to pay a higher rate of interest for large (wholesale) deposits than smaller (retail) deposits. In addition, the added risk for the lender of reduced portfolio diversification, arising from the making of a relatively small number of large loans (as opposed to a large number of small loans) may tend to promote higher rates of interest on wholesale loans. However, in respect of on-lending activities of financial intermediaries, the reduced unit administration costs arising from economies of scale in operations will tend to counteract the pressure for higher rates of interest as a result of the limited portfolio diversification implied by wholesale activities.

(6) *Expectations of inflation* These are likely to differ between individuals, and certainly they will vary over time within society as a whole. Thus, the nominal rates of interest acceptable to lenders for any given underlying desired real rate of interest will tend to vary both at a point in time within society, and over time.

(7) *Market imperfections* Concentration of financial power with individual participants in particular sectors of financial markets, or the existence of legal constraints on financial activities, may cause segmentation of markets, leading to interest rates being established which may appear to be inconsistent with the general pattern of interest rates according to normal market

8

criteria. In addition, the lack of reliable financial information may allow interest rate structures to become distorted.

(8) *Tax-treatment* The tax positions of the borrower and lender, as well as tax concessions available in respect of specific forms of debt instruments, are likely to affect the structure of interest rates established.

(9) *Management policy of the financial intermediary* It may be the case that specific intermediaries are willing to set interest rates with the view to maintaining customer loyalty, and hence longer-term profitability or organizational stability, rather than with the aim of maximizing short-term profitability. However, the extent to which individual institutions are able to allow their interest rates to deviate from the general market levels is probably quite limited, unless, of course, the institution is willing to risk severe dislocation of its funds flows.

(10) *Official intervention in financial intermediation activities* For reasons of monetary or banking/financial regulatory controls, intermediaries may be limited in their operational freedom. To the extent that official intervention imposes costs on institutions, the level of interest rates is likely to be affected. Furthermore, where controls are imposed in a discriminatory manner, interest rate differentials may be distorted relative to their free market structure.

As time passes, one or more of the above-listed factors may change in respect of any particular type of financial transaction, and hence the interest rate generated by that transaction may alter. The combined movements of these factors will determine the evolution of the pattern of interest rates within the economy. It should also be recognized that on some occasions major changes in the determinant factors may effectively cancel each other out, and thus leave a fairly stable set of interest rates. On other occasions a modest shift in one determinant may be sufficient to cause substantial upheaval to the structure of interest rates. The potential implications of changes in interest rates for the activities of financial intermediaries cannot be overemphasized.

Financial Intermediation as a Business Activity

Almost invariably the profit motive lies behind the financial intermediation operations of individuals and private sector institutions. Their activity is undertaken in the expectation of generating a surplus over and above the costs incurred. If total costs are not covered, then it would seem reasonable to suggest that the financial intermediation service would cease to be provided, at least through the private market mechanism. As mentioned above, financial intermediaries are in general committed to providing some form of income to the supplier of funds or to providing money transmission services which are likely to involve substantial costs for the intermediaries. Also, operating costs must be borne in the form of salaries of employees, the purchase or rental of premises and equipment, and so on. For successful intermediation, the sum total of these costs must at least be covered by the income earned through interest payments on funds on-lent, or through dividends paid on equities held. Intermediaries may also be able to realize capital gains on holdings of marketable assets.

Where financial intermediaries are involved in the straightforward on-lending of funds (as opposed to the purchase of equity shares), the setting of a wider margin between the rate of interest paid on deposits and the rate of interest charged on funds on-lent does not necessarily imply a greater level of net profit. This is because a lower deposit rate will tend to reduce the inflow of funds to the financial intermediary, whilst a higher loan rate will tend to depress the demand for borrowed funds. Thus, even if the deposit and loan rates are adjusted so as to maintain a balance between the flows of deposits and loans, turnover is likely to be reduced by the setting of a wider margin, and this may be sufficient to outweigh the effect on total profits of a greater net profit per unit of turnover. Further to this, since certain operating costs such as rents and rates on premises are likely to be fixed in the short term, unit operating costs may be raised as turnover falls, and hence the net benefit to unit profits from widening interest rate margins will tend to be less than the raw increase in the differential between deposit and loan rates.

Where the intermediary does not guarantee a specific return to investors, but rather offers a share in the net profits generated by the assets of the business, the immediate financial pressures are clearly not as great as when fixed interest commitments have been made. However, if the actual or expected returns to be provided to investors prove to be below the returns offered by comparable institutions, it is likely that the longer-term growth of the intermediary will be adversely affected. In other words, the competitive pressures within the specific financial sector, and indeed between financial sectors, will tend to restrain the excesses of bad management and will help to hold down unit administration costs. Unfortunately, the relatively long term nature of investments held in pension funds, life insurance companies, and the like may make it difficult to obtain meaningful performance data which might be used as the basis for comparison between intermediaries. Consequently, the investor may be obliged to choose between intermediaries on the basis of limited information, and hence the market check on these intermediaries may not be particularly effective in the short run.

A financial intermediary may attempt to improve its profitability by diversifying the range of indirect securities which it is willing to offer to prospective lenders, as well as by diversifying the range of primary securities which it is willing to 'purchase' from ultimate borrowers. The undeniably heterogeneous nature of financial requirements in the modern economy allows considerable scope for an intermediary to build up asset and liability portfolios to satisfy its perceived commercial needs. In addition, many financial intermediaries offer non-intermediation services to their customers, such as investment advice, currency exchange facilities and so on. To the extent that these services generate a return over costs, a loss on the financial intermediation activity need not necessarily mean that the institution makes a loss overall. Nevertheless, in the absence of expectations of improvement in the returns from the financial intermediation activity, it seems probable that the institution would withdraw from the latter unless, of course, it was deemed to be inseparable from the package of financial services offered in the sense of being necessary to attract customers in the first instance.

The range of activities which might be undertaken by the modern financial intermediary means that today, for many institutions, the intermediation process is only one of several activities pursued. The precise package of financial services offered may be unique to any given institution. Indeed, the nature of the non-intermediation services provided is likely to be strongly influenced by the institution's longer-term objectives in relation to the growth of the intermediation business.

The Relevance of Financial Intermediaries in the Financial System

Financial intermediaries constitute an extremely important element of Western financial systems, and the substantial profits which are often earned imply that they provide a valued service to both ultimate borrowers and ultimate lenders. Nevertheless, the question still arises as to why borrowers and lenders do not simply bypass intermediaries and come together directly. In fact substantial direct borrowing and lending does occur, but in the modern economy the bulk of borrowed funds pass through intermediaries. Indeed, it is often the case that the differences between the financial requirements of prospective borrowers and those of prospective lenders are so great that the direct transfer of funds is effectively precluded.

Before making the choice of assets to hold the prospective lender will usually consider their characteristics, as outlined above, and particular importance will be placed upon the expected return on the funds, the risk associated with lending, the liquidity of assets purchased, and the transactions costs related to buying and selling the assets. The expected return is obviously a crucial factor, and it may be the prospect of future income receipts which motivates the desire to save in the first instance. However, potentially higher returns are often associated with greater risks, and the higher returns may be seen as the necessary prerequisite for the holding of higher risk assets. At the extreme there is always some risk of default on interest payments and/or principal, although for British government securities and deposits with major clearing banks and building societies this risk is negligible. With fixed coupon marketable assets (such as government gilt-edged securities) there is the less extreme risk of capital loss resulting from an increase in the level of market rates of interest. Similarly, when interest and principal are measured in money terms, there is the danger that the rate of inflation will prove to be higher than was originally expected, and thus that the real return on the assets purchased will turn out to be smaller than expected (and perhaps even negative). Finally, there is also the risk that the choice of assets will prove to be poor in the sense that other assets rejected at the initial portfolio selection stage may ultimately generate greater returns than the assets actually chosen. This issue relates to the problem of portfolio diversification, and the assessment of the risk and return attached to available assets.

An equally important consideration is that of the liquidity of the asset portfolio. Strictly, the liquidity of an asset is measured in terms of the length of time taken for the holder to realize the asset (for cash or bank sight deposits) without any capital loss being incurred. However, liquidity is often taken to encompass the marketability of the asset prior to its maturity date, despite the possibility that some degree of capital loss may result if market conditions are unfavourable at the time of a 'forced' sale. Technically, a non-marketable asset is quite illiquid, in the sense that it must be held by the original lender until the date upon which the funds are to be repaid according to the contractual agreement with the borrower, although some non-marketable assets allow for repayment of funds after a period of formal notice has been given by the holder.

Finally, there may be substantial transactions costs related to the purchasing of assets which will influence lenders' portfolio choice. These costs include the time and effort required to seek out and evaluate alternative uses for surplus funds, as well as any brokerage costs, commissions and fees which must be paid to professional agents and advisers. The ease with which marketable assets may be sold is also likely to be a relevant factor. In addition, there are often minimum fees or charges which must be paid for access to financial services or information, and these costs may appear to be prohibitive where only relatively small amounts of funds are involved, thus effectively excluding certain types of assets from portfolios below a specific size. Obviously, the lender will attempt to minimize these costs within the constraint of obtaining the quantity and quality of information and assistance which is thought to be necessary for the making of a reasoned portfolio choice.

The prospective borrower will wish to obtain a specific amount of funds on a particular date, and to have possession of these funds for a desired minimum period of time. Also, the borrower will inevitably attempt to minimize interest costs, and obtain the most flexible arrangements for repayment or rolling-over of debt at any given interest cost. These requirements may, of course, conflict, in the sense that most lenders will require a greater compensation for the uncertainty generated by giving the borrower increased discretion over repayment conditions on a loan. The borrower will also incur transactions costs, relating mainly to the accquisition of information on the availability and nature of sources of funds, and often there will be commissions and fees payable to professional intermediaries and agents in respect of sales of debt instruments. Furthermore, the borrower also incurs risk due to the possibility either that funds may not be available (or known about) when required; or that the lender may be unwilling to extend the term of a fixed period loan; or that (where permitted by the legal contract underpinning the transaction) the funds may be recalled by the lender at short notice. In addition, the borrower might find that his financial requirements alter after funds have been obtained, and hence he might have to seek extra funds, perhaps on less favourable terms than those obtained on the original loan. Alternatively, he might find that he no longer requires all the fixed-term funds obtained and may not be able to earn sufficient interest from on-lending to cover his own interest payments.

Therefore, given the wide variety of factors influencing the decisions of prospective lenders and borrowers, even at an aggregated level it is most improbable that their financial requirements will match. The true magnitude of the problem becomes apparent once it is recognized that individual lenders and borrowers may be located in different parts of the country; indeed, potential partners may be located in different countries. Furthermore, even if the parties to a prospective transaction are able to achieve contact, the amounts of funds which individual lenders have available are often smaller than the amounts which individual borrowers wish to take up; the time period of loan desired by lenders is often shorter than that desired by borrowers; and the conditions of repayment desired by lenders are often less flexible than those desired by borrowers. In addition, the interest payments required by lenders in the light of the risks perceived to be attached to particular transactions may be much greater than the level which borrowers are willing to pay; in fact, it is possible that lenders and borrowers will hold different perceptions on the risk factor itself. Nevertheless, the accommodation of lenders' and borrowers' requirements might be brought about through the adjustment of the intererst rate.

If the rate of interest is raised, other things being equal, the prospective lender may be willing to provide funds for a longer period of time; be more flexible on repayment conditions; accept a higher level of risk; or perhaps provide a larger amount of funds (the opportunity cost of current consumption being raised). Moreover, the prospective borrower may be encouraged to cut back on the volume of funds required or to bring forward the desired repayment date. In order to avoid paying a higher rate of interest he might also be willing to accept less flexibility in relation to repayment conditions, or might offer a higher quality of collateral to the lender. However, it is quite conceivable that there may be no rate of interest which is mutually acceptable to both borrower and lender in respect of a particular financial transaction, and it is in this context that the real value to society of financial intermediation becomes apparent. The intermediation process involves far more than merely matching individual borrowers and lenders. Indeed, given the above-mentioned (often conflicting) financial requirements of borrowers and lenders, it is probable that the opportunities for matching users and providers of funds are extremely limited. Thus, the major operations of financial intermediaries may be seen in terms of the maturity transformation of funds, the pooling of financial risk, and the reduction of transactions costs associated with borrowing and lending.

Maturity Transformation of Funds

The assets of a financial intermediary are often less liquid than its liabilities. In other words, the average ultimate lender holds a claim on the financial intermediary which is more liquid than the claim which the financial intermediary holds on the average ultimate borrower. Underlying the financial intermediary's ability to remain solvent in such circumstances is the operation of the law of large numbers. This natural statistical phenomenon is only relevant where the intermediary obtains funds from a large number of ultimate lenders, and hence it may be fairly confident that on any given day the maximum percentage of deposits (in net terms) likely to be withdrawn is relatively small. This implies that by holding just a small proportion of its assets in the form of cash or other liquid assets, the intermediary will be able to fulfil its obligations to its suppliers of funds whilst utilizing the bulk of its funds for longer-term on-lending, and yet will maintain its solvency.

Substantial maturity transformation of funds can only occur where there is a sufficiently large base of suppliers of funds to allow the law of large numbers to be effective, and hence to keep the risk of a miscalculation of required liquidity tolerably low. Also, it is important that confidence is maintained in the operations of the intermediary by its suppliers of funds, and ideally that the intermediary should be able to adjust its liquidity position if required, perhaps by bidding for funds in the wholesale money markets. When an intermediary has only a relatively small number of depositors, the degree of maturity transformation which is expedient is also likely to be small. In this instance the intermediary may opt for a policy of matching assets with liabilities according to their term to maturity. The degree of mismatching, and hence maturity transformation under-taken, will depend upon the actual number of depositors involved; the distribution of deposits amongst depositors; the amount of risk which the intermediary is willing to accept; and the ease with which funds may be raised at short notice, especially in the wholesale money markets. Nevertheless, even where maturity transformation of funds is minimal, the other advantages of financial intermediation still provide sufficient cause for the institutions to exist. Indeed, in relation to the operations of intermediaries such as pension funds and life assurance companies, the maturity transformation issue is of only marginal relevance, despite the very large numbers of suppliers of funds to many of these organizations.

The Pooling of Financial Risk

Financial intermediaries are able to spread the risk related to on-lending between all of the individuals and institutions providing them with funds. Specific defaults or capital losses on assets purchased by a financial intermediary are not attributable to any single ultimate lender, and thus the fundamental nature of the risk faced by the ultimate lender is altered. Instead of bearing a small risk of losing all funds lent (which is always possible when direct lending takes place), the ultimate lender implicitly accepts the near certainty that a small proportion of his funds will be lost, as effectively a share is held in the diversified assets portfolio of the financial intermediary. Once again the law of large numbers is relevant to this risk transformation. Thus, so long as the financial intermediary is efficiently managed, and hence is unlikely to go bankrupt, the ultimate lender has little risk of losing all the funds invested. Furthermore, the rate of interest charged, or the level of return sought by the financial intermediary on investments made, will be set at a level which allows for the absorption of the defaulted loans or capital losses on assets, but still leaves sufficient return to cover operating costs and to pay a positive return to the depositors. Therefore, the ultimate lender will often be quite unaware that some of his funds have been 'lost' in loan defaults and the like; quite simply, the rate of return received will be somewhat lower than it would otherwise have been had the defaults by ultimate borrowers and the capital losses on investments not occurred.

A further benefit to the ultimate lender is that the financial intermediary often employs specialists in risk evaluation, and hence is probably better equipped than the average ultimate lender to avoid both lending to high risk borrowers, and purchasing high risk assets. In short, the average risk taken on by the intermediary may be somewhat less than the average risk existing in relation to all prospective borrowers in the economy as a whole. Nevertheless, large-scale asset holdings mean that extensive portfolio diversification into different types of assets is possible for the intermediary, thus allowing some risky ventures to be undertaken whilst still keeping the overall portfolio risk tolerably low. But beyond this the capital base (share-holders' funds) of the intermediary is also available to cover the repayment of deposits should an unusually high level of on-lending defaults and capital losses on assets occur.

Reduction of Unit Transactions Costs

The importance of economies of scale to the operations of financial intermediaries cannot be overemphasized. Not only are such institutions able to harness economies in the collection of financial data, but they may also employ specialist personnel capable of undertaking in-house analyses of creditworthiness or future prospects of potential borrowers, as well as sophisticated investment appraisal exercises. Also, where there are fixed overhead costs associated with the purchase or sale of financial assets (for example, in respect of brokerage commissions and professional fees), intermediaries are able to spread these over a large volume of transactions, thus reducing unit transactions costs relative to those which would be incurred by the ultimate lender should he choose to place funds directly with an ultimate borrower. Similarly, the paperwork related to the making of loans and the legal niceties of financial transactions will be routine, thus tending to make the associated unit administration costs relatively modest.

As the services offered by established financial intermediaries are likely to be widely recognized, and because they can afford to advertise their activities, search costs are reduced for both the prospective lender looking for a suitable repository for his surplus funds, and for the prospective borrower wishing to obtain funds. Indeed, as many prospective lenders often have only relatively small amounts of funds available, an important function of financial intermediaries is to bundle deposits into amounts which are of an appropriate size to meet borrowers' needs.

The Gains from Financial Intermediation

The foregoing discussion clearly underlines the benefits to be gained from efficiently managed financial intermediation activity. For the ultimate lender, the claim held against the financial intermediary is likely to be more liquid than if funds had been lent directly to an ultimate borrower, and there is a reduced level of risk related to the funds lent. Indeed, where the intermediary issues marketable debt instruments in exchange for deposits, the liquidity of the lender's asset portfolio is enhanced since the lender is endowed with the opportunity to sell his claim on the intermediary prior to its maturity. Furthermore, not only does the ultimate lender effectively purchase a share in a professionally managed diversified portfolio of assets which will tend to reduce the underlying risk involved with lending funds, but there is also often either an explicit or an implicit guarantee of a minimum positive nominal return on funds. Finally, the financial decision is simplified in the sense that the ultimate lender needs only to choose between competing intermediaries (and possibly the specific deposit facilities offered), rather than between the members of the much wider group of individual prospective ultimate borrowers.

In respect of the ultimate borrower, a major gain from financial intermediation is the greater probability that sufficient funds will be available from a single source at the time required, and almost certainly at a lower interest rate than would have to be paid if the funds had been borrowed directly from an ultimate lender. The risk spreading characteristic of financial intermediation activity is responsible for the latter phenomenon, and the ability of intermediaries to undertake maturity transformation of funds means that they will often be made available to the borrower for longer periods than would otherwise be feasible. Also, as mentioned above, the search costs incurred by the borrower are likely to be substantially reduced because of the existence of financial intermediaries.

In addition to the clear benefits generated for ultimate borrowers and lenders, it must not be overlooked that the process of financial intermediation generates important gains for society as a whole. It is generally agreed that by reducing the risks and transactions costs involved for the prospective lender, efficiently managed financial intermediaries encourage the lending of surplus funds in circumstances where this might not otherwise occur. Consequently, economic growth may be facilitated by making it easier for risky enterprises to obtain external funds, which may be crucial during the initial stages of expansion of existing businesses or indeed at the formative stages of new businesses. In short, the existence of financial intermediaries is not only likely to lead to a more efficient use of funds within the economy, but it is also likely to assist the longer-term growth prospects of the latter.

Notes

1 Companies which only provide general insurance cover for risks related to fire, theft, accidents and so on are not financial intermediaries in the normal sense of the term. They accumulate funds through premium payments by policyholders, and then stand ready to meet claims which fall within the scope of outstanding policies. However, whilst a significant proportion of premium payments are used by insurance companies to purchase income earning assets, it is the hope of the insured parties that no claims will have to be made, and hence, by implication, that no funds will have to be repaid. Thus the intention of the policyholder is clearly different from that of the individual who deposits funds with a financial intermediary with the view to generating a positive return on accumulated savings.

2 At the extreme, it might be suggested that the government acts as a financial intermediary to the extent that it runs a budget deficit (and hence has to borrow from the private sector) at the same time as it loans funds to private businesses. However, since it is not usual for the government to earmark specific borrowed funds for on-lending activities, the government itself is not classed as a financial intermediary, although certain government-backed financial institutions are usually recognized in discussions of specialist intermediaries.

3 It is usual for building societies, and indeed for most financial intermediaries, to hold back a percentage of the funds deposited with them in assets of very high liquidity. Usually, some of this liquid reserve will be held in the form of cash or bank sight deposits in order to meet claims from depositors for withdrawals in so far as this is allowed within the confines of the explicit or implicit contract of deposit.

4 The relevance of the primary (new issues) market and the secondary (pre-existing issues) market is discussed in Chapter 3.

5 The bulk of funds placed with building societies are technically in the form of purchases of shares rather than straightforward deposits. This division stems largely from the development of building societies as mutual institutions. But although there are differences between the legal rights of deposit holders and shareholders, in practice the distinction is very fine, and they tend to be spoken of synonymously.

6 If prospective lenders believe that interest rates are about to fall, it is probable that a larger number will wish to lend longer term and hence lock their funds into relatively high yield assets. To lend short term would necessitate reinvestment of funds in the

near future at an expected lower rate of interest. Conversely, prospective borrowers will probably be more willing to borrow short-term funds in the hope of being able to roll-over their debt at lower future rates. Thus, the expectation of lower future interest rates will tend to cause the supply of long-term funds to rise relative to demand, whilst simultaneously the demand for short-term funds will tend to rise relative to supply. If this effect is strong enough then long-term rates of interest may be pushed down to below short-term rates.

CHAPTER TWO

The Classification of Financial Intermediaries

Introduction

All financial intermediaries share the common central function of channelling funds between individuals or institutions
with budget surpluses and those with budget deficits.
However, intermediaries almost invariably specialize in the
provision of services to specific groups within society, and
often concentrate on taking up and on-lending specific
categories of funds. Thus, some intermediaries may operate
exclusively on a wholesale level, only being willing to deal
in sums greater than a very large laid-down minimum value,
whilst others may on-lend exclusively to retail customers.
Some intermediaries may emphasize longer-term investments, whilst others specialize in the purchase of primarily
short-term instruments. Furthermore, in addition to the
basic intermediation activity, institutions also often provide
various forms of non-intermediation services to their
customers, which further contribute to their distinctive
characteristics. However, whilst it is probably correct to
assert that in the modern financial system each financial
intermediary is almost unique in terms of the set of
functions which it performs, it is nevertheless necessary to
attempt to classify intermediaries in order that a general
analysis of their activities may be undertaken.

There are two broad approaches to the classification of
financial intermediaries which highlight different major

aspects of their operations. The first approach to be considered divides institutions into those which take deposits, those which are primarily involved with the accumulation of longer-term savings, and the specialist intermediaries. The alternative approach emphasizes the fundamental dichotomy between bank and non-bank financial intermediaries. However, it must be emphasized from the outset that neither of these categorizations is without ambiguity, and both are subject to some degree of criticism in respect of their institutional groupings. Nevertheless, they do provide an extremely useful conceptual framework for the development of a discussion on financial intermediaries in the UK.

Deposit-Takers, Non-Deposit-Takers and Specialist Intermediaries

Deposit-Taking Financial Intermediaries

In the UK the major deposit-taking institutions are the banks and the building societies, but this group also includes the National Savings Bank and the finance houses. The common characteristic of these institutions, as their collective name implies, is that they take deposits either from the general public or from other institutions. These deposits may often be withdrawn on demand or subject to only a short period of notice, and although some deposits are in the form of term deposits, the institutional conventions in the UK (which tend to allow premature withdrawal of funds, often at the cost of a financial penalty to the deposit holder) mean that the deposit liabilities overall are relatively liquid. However, whilst the liabilities of many deposit-taking institutions may be quite liquid, their assets are usually relatively illiquid. Certainly, to a greater or lesser extent, all institutions hold some liquid assets, but those engaged in retail activities rely in particular upon the operation of the law of large numbers and their high standing in the money markets to enable them to undertake a relatively high level of maturity transformation of funds. UK building societies

24

provide an excellent example of this form of financial intermediation. With few exceptions, their liabilities are short-term, yet the mortgage loans which dominate their asset portfolios normally have original maturities of between 15 and 25 years. A similar situation holds for UK retail banks, although their crucial role in the provision of money transmission services, and the highly liquid nature of their liabilities, means that they must hold significantly diversified asset portfolios which contain substantial amounts of liquid assets. Nevertheless, it is common for retail banks to hold over one-half of their assets in the form of advances, which are relatively illiquid assets.

It is generally agreed that retail funds flows for banks (and indeed for building societies) are fairly difficult to control with precision in the short term. When a large number of relatively small-scale transactions are involved, the administrative costs of frequent changes in interest rates may be prohibitive, and there are serious doubts over the wisdom of subjecting relatively unsophisticated retail customers to excessive changes in the terms and conditions of facilities. It may be argued that the longer-term profitability of the institution may be undermined by attempts in the short term to fine-tune flows of retail funds. It is for this reason that banks engaged in retail activities have always maintained fairly close links with the wholesale money markets, where funds flows are very sensitive even to fine changes in interest rates, and where the financial sophistication of participants allows institutions to adjust their liquidity positions without difficulty in accordance with their wishes. Indeed, in recent years a number of the larger UK building societies have begun to turn to the wholesale money markets for purposes of adjusting short-term funds flows, although the extent of this activity is still quite limited. In addition, it must be emphasized that on occasions wholesale funds may only be available at a high price, and thus retail institutions will have to balance the urgency with which liquidity is thought to require adjustment against the costs of achieving that adjustment.

Whilst most UK retail banks engage in some wholesale activities, there is a large group of banks which are almost exclusively concerned with such operations. The aggregate portfolios of these wholesale banking institutions are currently over three-and-a-half times the size of the corresponding portfolios of retail banks, and hence their importance within the UK financial system is unquestionable. However, since a large proportion of their assets and liabilities are denominated in foreign currencies, their direct relevance to the domestic banking activities of most individuals and companies is fairly limited. Nevertheless, wholesale banks exhibit rather interesting characteristics in respect of their financial intermediation activity. In particular, there is a clear emphasis on liability management. That is, the sensitivity of flows of funds to interest rate movements allows individual banks to bid for deposits to match requests for loans from customers. This activity takes place in addition to the more widely recognized financial intermediation role (referred to as asset management) which involves the seeking out of profitable uses for the funds which have been accumulated. Moreover, the sophisticated communications networks to be found within the UK financial sector sometimes make it extremely difficult in practice to separate the asset management from the liability management activities, and UK wholesale banks are often involved with extremely complex chains of on-lending which makes analysis of ultimate sources and uses of funds somewhat problematic. However, it should also be recognized that a large proportion of deposits with wholesale banks are term deposits which do not have to be repaid until their maturity date arrives, and hence asset liquidity does not hold the same relevance as it does for retail banks, although it will always be an important consideration in respect of portfolio selection.

The other deposit-taking financial intermediaries in the UK tend to limit the scope of their activities, and emphasize particular forms of deposit-taking and on-lending. For example, the National Savings Bank aims to raise its funds primarily from the personal sector through retail deposits, and its on-lending is exclusively to the British government through the purchase (either directly or indirectly) of gilt-edged and other securities. Similarly, until 1965, the trustee savings banks operated within a very restrictive framework which limited the nature of on-lending activity. In fact, it was not until the mid-1970s that the trustee savings banks began to make personal loans to customers. A further example relates to UK finance houses. These institutions take deposits from both the personal and the company sectors, but on-lend almost exclusively in the form of instalment credit, although the former emphasis on hire-purchase loans has long since given way to the provision of a more sophisticated array of financial services for its private sector customers.

Long-Term Saving Institutions

The major long-term savings institutions in the UK are the pension funds, life insurance companies, unit trusts, and investment trust companies. The common characteristic of these institutions is that they collect funds from individual savers and from other institutions wishing to amass financial claims, either through one-off investments or through regular payments on the basis of a contractual commitment. The funds are used by the intermediaries to purchase assets which it is hoped will generate income and/or realizable capital gains in a manner which will both meet their future commitments to the suppliers of the funds and also cover their management costs (including a profit element, where appropriate). The precise nature of the assets portfolio selected by any institution depends upon the form of the liabilities held. Thus, for example, as contributors to pension funds are unable to call upon their accumulated claims prior to reaching a certain minimum age, the liabilities of these institutions tend to be relatively stable and long-term. Consequently, assets may be chosen primarily for their long-term income and capital gains potential, and there is little pressure on fund managers to seek out short-term gains which might ultimately be detrimental to the long-term prospects of the fund. Indeed, there is little need for liquid assets to be held in order to cover unexpected withdrawals of funds, although at any given time some liquid assets are likely to be held merely in readiness for purchasing new long-term assets and as a result of realizations of existing holdings of assets. A similar position occurs in respect of life insurance companies, although the common facilities for the surrender of policies by contributors perhaps makes the liquidity issue somewhat more pertinent.[1]

Whilst contractual savings tend to dominate pension fund and life insurance company inflows of funds, it is lump sum savings which are particularly important for unit trusts and investment trust companies. These institutions are very similar in the sense that both types hold diversified asset portfolios comprising predominantly company equities. However, they are quite different in respect of their legal constitution and the nature of fund raising. Unit trusts sell 'units' to individuals and companies, and utilize the funds raised to purchase assets for their portfolios. The value of the units at any point in time will reflect the underlying value of the assets held by the trust, and the income earned will depend upon the earning power of the asset portfolio as a whole. However, a key characteristic of unit trusts is that they are obliged to repurchase units at their holders' behest, and thus funds may be withdrawn from the assets pool, causing the size of unit trusts' asset portfolios to contract. Clearly, it is desirable for unit trusts to maintain sufficient liquidity in their portfolios to be able to cover net withdrawals of funds without having to engage in sales of assets on grossly unfavourable terms. Investment trust companies, on the other hand, do not face this type of problem. These institutions have corporate limited liability status, and hence they obtain funds through the issue of equity shares to the public and by raising loans against debentures and the like. Therefore, these companies have a more stable base of funds than the unit trusts, as whilst loans will mature at some stage and hence funds have to be arranged in order to make repayment, their equity bases cannot be repaid (in normal circumstances). Thus if a shareholder in an investment trust company (that is, the saver) wishes to realize some of his accumulated savings, he must attempt to sell shares on the Stock Exchange. This secondary market activity has no direct implication for the funds flow of the investment trust company, and hence the requirement for liquidity in its asset portfolio pertaining to withdrawals of funds is limited to the out-standing loans base (which for some companies is very small).

The nature of saving with unit trusts and investment trust companies is such that they are naturally under greater pressure than life insurance companies and pension funds to produce shorter-term gains. Thus, whilst the manage-ments of both unit trusts and investment trust companies continually propound the longer-term benefits to savers of placing funds with their institutions, the prospect of with-drawals of funds (from unit trusts) and falling Stock Exchange share valuation (for investment trust companies) mean that assets may sometimes be selected for their short-term gains rather than for their longer-term prospects. In addition, by implication, the managers of unit trusts and investment trust companies are likely to be more sensitive to shorter-term market trends than the managers of insurance companies and pension funds, and hence the asset portfolio turnover of the former may be somewhat greater than that of the latter institutions. Nevertheless, irrespective of the investment philosophy followed by the managements of the longer-term savings institutions, there is no doubt that their investment behaviour has extremely important implications for the operation of the UK capital markets. In particular, the huge size of the investment portfolios of the life insurance companies and pension funds means that port-folio reallocation may have significant effects on the market prices of assets. The potential power of fund managers in respect of proposed company take-overs and the like can never be ignored.

Specialist Financial Intermediaries

In general, the UK's specialist financial intermediaries were established to cater for the specific financial requirements of particular categories of borrowers, predominantly within the industrial and commercial sectors. These institutions are often closely associated with other financial intermediaries, and they frequently obtain funds directly from the banking sector. Indeed, a number of the specialist intermediaries are wholly- or partly-owned subsidiaries of banks. However, their sources and uses of funds are quite varied, as are their internal management structures. They may raise funds both through the issue of equity shares and through the taking of term loans. Some are supported directly by public sector funding, with the conditions for repayment of principal and payment of interest/dividends depending upon the extent to which the institutions' activities are seen as having important social implications. Thus, some of the specialist intermediaries may not be driven by the profit motive, although there is almost always some form of financial target set.

One of the UK's best-known specialist financial intermediaries is 3i. Technically, this is the holding company for a number of closely related institutions involved in the provision of venture capital and similar types of funding to companies. Its equity is held jointly by the major UK clearing banks and the Bank of England, and it raises substantial amounts of funds on the wholesale money markets. Its overriding aim is to provide financial support to risky business ventures, but ones which are believed to have good longer-term prospects. The management philosophy is to avoid the pursuit of short-term gains at the expense of the longer-term returns on investments. As this institution was established as the result of official pressure to assist the development of the UK's industrial and commercial base during the postwar period, this approach to on-lending is largely to be expected. The newer breed of venture capital companies is somewhat different from 3i, their aims are much more openly commercial, and they are often willing to pursue short-term gains, with little apparent concern for the broader longer-term issues. At the other extreme, some government-sponsored intermediaries take a predominantly social view of their function, and provide finance for businesses in the hope of assisting depressed regions in the UK, with only a limited weight applied to the commercial aspects of projects to be supported. Clearly, the activities of the latter institutions are of only marginal relevance directly to the study of financial intermediaries, although it must never be forgotten that their presence is likely to have indirect effects on the nature of the services which may be offered by the more mainstream financial intermediaries.

Bank and Non-Bank Financial Intermediaries

In the course of the above discussion on deposit-taking financial intermediaries, the activities of banks were mentioned on the basis of the implicit assumption that there is some general agreement over which institutions are in fact banks. Unfortunately, this issue has for many years been the subject of considerable controversy, which may be considered within the context of an examination of the second broad classification of financial intermediaries. This classification is based on the division of institutions into bank financial intermediaries (BFIs) and non-bank financial intermediaries (NBFIs).

There are basically two approaches to formulating the BFI/NBFI classification. One approach takes the view that BFIs have liabilities which are spendable; that is, which are part of the money supply. The main problem here is in choosing the appropriate definition of money. If a narrow definition is used, which incorporates only immediate media of exchange such as cash and bank sight deposits, then this would probably lead to most, if not all, of the main UK clearing banks being classified as NBFIs, since a fairly large proportion of their liabilities are not included in the narrow measures of money. A better position may be to take a broader definition of money which includes bank time deposits. This would immediately bring into the BFI group all the clearing banks, but would still leave doubt over the position of 'banks' which hold a large proportion of their deposits in foreign currency denominations as these latter deposits are not included in the conventional measures of the domestic money supply. In addition, as no institution holds a liabilities portfolio which is comprised entirely of items included in measures of the money supply, even when there are no foreign currency items, the problem still remains of deciding what proportion of liabilities must be included in the money supply measure in order to allow an institution to be categorized as a BFI. In short, there are many ambiguities surrounding this particular basis for classification.

The alternative approach is based upon the criterion of whether the intermediary creates credit, or whether it merely passes on credit created elsewhere. When an intermediary unambiguously creates credit then it is included in the BFI group. In the case of clearing banks the creation of credit is synonymous with the creation of sight deposits, which happen to be part of the money supply according to all conventional measures, although using the credit creation basis avoids the problem of having to specify a precise definition of the money supply.[2] Where an institution relies entirely upon deposits of cash or transfers of bank sight deposits for its ability to on-lend, then that institution will be included in the NBFI group. However, this form of classification is not without controversy, for it is sometimes argued that whilst certain institutions cannot add to the volume of credit in the economy, they can add to the spending power available per period of time by acting to raise the velocity of circulation of money. Thus, for example, if building societies raise the rate of interest paid on share accounts, other things being equal, funds may be transferred by savers from bank time accounts to building society accounts. It is quite probable that, at least in the short term, building societies will pay those funds into their own bank accounts, and hence there will be no net effect on the level of bank deposits, and no effect on the money supply. As time passes, building societies are likely to make additional mortgage loans using their increased liquid reserves. Thus, so long as all transactions are financed by the transfers of bank deposits through the chequeing system, extra spending has been allowed to take place as a result of the actions of building societies in activating idle balances held in bank time deposits.

In view of the conceptual problems involved in finding a sound theoretical basis for the BFI/NBFI classification, it is normally thought to be appropriate for analytical purposes, to fall back on an operational classification based upon the broad nature of business activities undertaken by financial intermediaries. Thus, in the UK, BFIs may be defined to comprise the clearing banks, the Banking Department of the Bank of England, discount houses, accepting houses, and other wholesale banks. The NBFI group includes the building societies, most finance houses, National Savings Bank, insurance companies, pension funds, unit trusts, investment trust companies, and specialist financial intermediaries such as 3i. The NBFI group may be subdivided into deposit-taking institutions (that is, the building societies, finance houses and the National Savings Bank), and non-deposit-taking institutions (that is, the rest; the most important of these are the insurance companies and pension funds).

The structure of the remainder of this book is based upon this operational classification, which divides the UK non-bank financial intermediaries into the deposit-taking and the non-deposit-taking institutions. However, no meaningful discussion of the current activities and ongoing development of NBFIs can ignore the relevance of banking institutions. Increasingly, the operations of both groups of institutions are impinging upon each other's traditional areas of activity. As will be explained in later chapters of this book, competition and co-operation between banks and the non-bank deposit-takers in particular has played an extremely crucial role in the evolution of the UK financial system in recent years, and as time passes, it is likely that the operations of these institutions will become increasingly interdependent.

The Practical Significance of the Bank/Non-Bank Classification

It is not merely for purposes of academic analysis that a coherent classification of financial intermediaries is required. There are also important practical issues relating to the legal responsibilities of institutions and to the operation of official monetary controls. In particular, the Banking Act 1979 defined a bank in law (for the first time) in the UK, and placed upon the Bank of England the legal duty to execute supervision over the institutions falling within that definition. The Act also defined a further category of institutions referred to as licensed deposit-takers.[3] Thus the legislation has overridden the economists' debate on the concept of a bank in the UK for regulatory purposes. But it is most probable that those responsible for the drafting of the relevant legislation paid close attention to the flow of that debate.

The monetary control issue is, perhaps, somewhat more serious, in the sense that BFIs have often been forced to bear the brunt of official controls on account of their important role in the money creation process. However, institutions which might not yet be included in the BFI category might have liabilities which are regarded as being 'near-money' assets by the domestic private sector. If these near-money assets influence the level and pattern of expenditure within the economy in a similar way to the conventional money assets, then there would appear to be a strong case for extending the focus of monetary controls to at least some of the NBFIs. Alternatively, controls might be designed to influence the supply of particular types of instruments, irrespective of the institutions from which they originate. It is at this stage that the definitional problem becomes acute, for the authorities must be able to identify relevant groups of institutions if an efficient, effective and equitable control package is to be devised. Thus, as financial intermediaries continue to evolve, the pressure is likely to grow for the whole issue of financial intermediary classification for monetary control purposes to be thrown open to debate once again.

In recent years the classification problem has become more complex due to the increasing sophistication of the services offered by all manner of financial institutions. Diversification of the activities of institutions which previously fitted unambiguously into the NBFI group has caused particular problems. An increasing number of non-bank institutions are now performing functions which were previously the exclusive domain of the banking sector. Indeed, some institutions have linked with banks to offer money transmission and other services which are virtually indistinguishable from those offered by the banks themselves. Nevertheless, despite these recent developments, it must be acknowledged that a large proportion of UK financial intermediaries may still be placed into the BFI/NBFI framework without hesitation, their operations being predominantly banking or non-banking as the case may be. It is in the more rapidly evolving sectors of the financial system, and particularly in relation to the building society sector, that the real controversy exists and is likely to intensify in future.

Notes

1 It must be emphasized that general insurance activities are quite different from life insurance activities in terms of their fundamental rationale, and the former do not fall within the conventional interpretation of financial intermediary operations. Nevertheless, both forms of business may be undertaken by the same company, although general insurance places a much greater emphasis on liquidity in order to meet claims against policies as they arise.

2 As transfers of bank sight deposits, through the chequeing system, are generally acceptable in discharge of debt, banks are able to create money through a book-keeping exercise. When a bank makes a loan to a customer, it will merely credit the customer's sight account with the appropriate sum, and hence money is created. However, banks cannot create credit without limit as there is always the possibility that some deposits will be withdrawn in cash, or will be transferred, in net terms, to another bank, and therefore cash (or other liquid assets) must be held to cover this eventuality. Nevertheless, this credit creating power does mean that banks are able to go well beyond the basic pure financial intermediation role, which limits on-lending to no more than the volume of funds which is deposited with the intermediary.

3 It is the stated intention of the UK authorities to have just a single category of banks for supervisory purposes, and the Banking Act is expected to be amended to this effect.

CHAPTER THREE

Recent Developments in the British Financial System

Introduction

In order to understand the development of British financial intermediaries and to be able to assess the implications of the changing functions of those intermediaries, it is first necessary to consider the broad evolution of the British financial system as a whole. The nature and limits of activities within the various financial markets which comprise the financial system obviously have a very significant influence on the evolution of individual intermediaries, whilst the existence of the markets themselves depends upon the interaction of specific groups of intermediaries as well as other participants. Hence the developments of institutions and of markets are to a large extent mutually dependent, and the direction of cause and effect of observed changes in operations may be somewhat controversial. However, this particular analytical problem does not preclude consideration of the broader implications of identified changes in the activities of institutions, although it does add to the difficulty of determining the cause of those changes and hence of predicting likely future developments.

The opportunities offered by financial markets for particular financial intermediaries, and indeed the threats posed by markets to existing institutional activities, are strongly influenced by the regulatory framework within which the markets and institutions operate. Furthermore, the freedom of institutions to participate in market activities, and the forms of innovation allowed in respect of the services which may be offered to customers (in relation to both pure financial intermediation and other financial services in general) not only affect the scope for profitable business ventures for institutions choosing to participate in specific markets, but, to a greater or lesser degree, they also affect the activities of all financial intermediaries. The reason for this contention is simply that in the modern financial system no financial market is self-contained. Thus, new attractive opportunities offered in one market may cause some institutions to redirect the emphasis of their business, and flows of funds may be channelled away from existing groups of ultimate borrowers. Moreover, ultimate lenders may themselves redirect their surplus funds towards institutions active in new areas of operations which offer higher returns (or perhaps lower risks) on their funds, and this in turn will affect other institutions not directly concerned with the new activities.

The situation is made even more complex by the fact that innovation within the financial sector may be initiated by changes in the financial behaviour of other sectors of the economy. Changing requirements for borrowed funds from any particular sector, or possibly growing surpluses of funds in another sector, may offer the prospect for profitable financial intermediation between sectors. But it must never be forgotten that substantial borrowing and lending transactions may take place within sectors. Thus, for example, one group within the domestic personal sector may see the advantages of home ownership and their demand for long-term mortgage loans may rise significantly. At the same time the saving habits of another group within the personal sector may result in the accumulation of large volumes of funds which financial intermediaries may seek to tap for purposes of channelling to prospective mortgage borrowers. Of course, it is quite possible that initially an increase in the demand for mortgage loans may not be matched by larger financial surpluses, either elsewhere in the personal sector or in any other sector of the economy. In this instance the demand pressures placed on financial intermediaries will almost certainly initiate a round of competitive bidding for funds by institutions, which may cause a chain of adjustments to take place in the financial activities of prospective borrowers and lenders throughout the whole economy. It may be taken for granted that the price mechanism, as it operates through the level and structure of interest rates, will be crucial to the ultimate pattern of financial flows within the economy. Thus, so long as interest rates are not artificially constrained by official administrative edict, it is not simply the case that demands for additional borrowed funds will be frustrated if intermediaries are unable to attract sufficient inflows of funds; rather, the non-availability of funds implies upwards pressure on interest rates (for both deposits with, and on-lending by, intermediaries), and hence the underlying demand for funds is likely to be depressed and the supply of funds simultaneously stimulated, which will tend to push the markets for funds towards their equilibrium positions.

Therefore, to summarize, the operations of any particular financial intermediary are likely to be influenced as the structure of financial markets evolves within the context of the official regulatory controls in force. Changes in the financial behaviour of specific sectors of the economy will probably have repercussions throughout the financial sector as a whole, but the extent to which individual intermediaries react either to the opportunities offered or to the threats posed will ultimately depend upon their management strategies and their innate ability to cope with a changing environment. At the extreme, failure to adapt to the evolving financial environment may lead to the demise of particular institutions, perhaps with their business interests being absorbed by more dynamic competitors. However, at least in the past, the nature of financial evolution has usually led to a less dramatic, gradual erosion of institutions' relative positions in markets. Indeed, history has shown that on occasions whole groups of financial intermediaries have been left behind in the race for market shares, although during periods of market growth absolute positions have been maintained with ease. The real test of the commercial viability of financial operations comes when markets stop growing, and gains in market share for one institution consequently imply both relative and absolute losses in market share for at least one other institution. The contraction of a market merely exacerbates the problems facing individual institutions, and crucial decisions must then be taken as to whether competition should be intensified in the hope of taking a larger slice of the available business, or whether the pursuit of alternative lines of activities (involving either financial intermediation or the provision of other financial services) would be the better option.

Financial Markets

Financial institutions interact with each other and with ultimate suppliers and users of funds within financial markets. These markets form the basic building blocks of the financial system, and they may have quite varied organizational structures. At one extreme, there are the clearly identifiable tangible markets such as the Stock Exchange and Lloyd's, which deal in company and government securities and insurance underwriting respectively. At the other extreme are the money markets and foreign currency exchanges which have no physical form, but rather exist as integrated communications networks between market participants. Some markets are narrow in the sense that they deal with only a closely defined group of instruments; other markets cover a wide array of financial transactions, perhaps with only one key characteristic in common. The market for short-term borrowed retail funds is a good example of the latter form of market structure. Furthermore, the activities of markets will often overlap, and so not only may there be some ambiguity as to the ambit of particular markets, but there may also be doubt as to the practical relevance of precise definitions of certain markets. Indeed, as mentioned above, an important characteristic of the modern financial system is the interaction between markets, and the mutual dependence of many markets is of great importance. Nevertheless, the concept of the financial market does make a useful contribution to the analysis of the activities of financial intermediaries.

Formally, the term 'financial market' relates to the activities of suppliers and users of funds, intermediaries, brokers and agents in respect of their dealings in a particular financial instrument, or group of instruments. In this context the term 'instrument' is to be interpreted in its widest sense to encompass all pairs of assets/liabilities generated by a borrowing/lending transaction. In addition, financial markets may be divided into primary and secondary markets. Activities in the primary markets involve the supply of new funds to the borrower. For example, the provision of a personal loan by a bank comes within the scope of the primary market in retail funds as does a building society mortgage loan. Where the assets created by the financial transactions are non-negotiable only the primary market is of relevance. The holder of the asset is not able to trade the financial claim prior to the underlying debt being extinguished by the borrower. However, where the instruments are negotiable the activities of the secondary markets come into play. Participants in these markets deal in existing financial claims, and no new funds are channelled to ultimate borrowers. Nevertheless, the importance of these markets should not be underestimated, for their very existence allows marketable instruments to be issued where this would not otherwise be feasible. The more efficient and active are these markets, the greater will be the liquidity of marketable assets in the broadest sense. In some instances it is quite possible that funds will only be placed on primary markets because there is the prospect of the ultimate lender being able to retrieve his funds through a secondary market prior to the nominal maturity date of the assets.

Within the financial system the interest rate or return on assets traded in particular markets broadly directs funds to where the relative supplies and demands for funds dictate, although the adjustments of markets are made more complex by the provision of non-intermediation services by financial intermediaries which may make the assessment of returns on assets somewhat ambiguous. There may also be inertia in respect of market participants' behaviour; financial habits within some sectors of the economy are well established and tend to evolve only slowly. However, it is generally agreed that even in this context, in the longer term, market pressures will be felt and funds will be channelled as dictated by the price mechanism. The deliberate obstruction of market forces through collusion by powerful groups of intermediaries or other market participants may present a more serious threat to market efficiency, but as the collapse of the building societies' interest rate cartel in the early 1980s clearly demonstrated, competitive market forces will usually overcome artificial constraints in the end.

Not only does competition between intermediaries and between brokers and agents in markets serve to encourage the efficient operation of those markets, but it is also important that reliable and timely information on market opportunities is available to prospective providers and users of funds. Quite simply, in the absence of adequate intelligence of market opportunities, prospective participants in markets are unlikely to be able to assess accurately the true value of financial innovations. Consequently, alterations to the financial services offered by institutions may cloud the resource allocation problem rather than enhance the real choice for the user or provider of funds. Genuine improvements in facilities will always be welcomed by those market participants who gain, whether they are providers or users of funds or the intermediaries which experience increased turnover as a consequence. However, some alterations in financial products may be purely cosmetic and add little, if anything, to the value of products. In this instance it would seem reasonable to suggest that society as a whole loses, as there may simply be a redistribution of activity within markets, whilst financial decisions become harder to reach. Informed comments and analysis from independent observers of market conditions can help to minimize the potential distortion of participants' perceptions of available facilities, as well as perhaps draw attention to the broader social implications of specific investment decisions which might otherwise be ignored by participants. Of course, the role of advertising by commercially motivated intermediaries and other market participants must be viewed with caution, and the nature of official regulatory guidelines on persuasive

41

rather than purely informative advertising will be crucial. Indeed, in a competitive market regime an effective regulatory framework covering the fundamental aspects of participants' activities is likely to be vital to the stability of both individual markets and the financial system as a whole. In this respect, the long-term health of markets will depend upon a delicate balance being achieved between regulatory constraints and the operation of free market forces. On the one hand unfettered competition with no external independent supervision of standards may frighten away potential participants, whilst on the other hand excessive bureaucratic interference with transactions may merely stifle the growth of activity.

Finally, it should be recognized that whilst the operation of free markets within a sensibly structured regulatory framework may lead to an efficient allocation of resources from the point of view of those directly participating in the markets, there is no guarantee that the outcome of the financial intermediation process will be socially optimal. This is because the demand for funds reflects only the factors which are of direct concern to those wishing to borrow, whilst funds are supplied according to the factors of relevance to the suppliers which are mainly the commercial considerations of the level of return expected from, and the risk related to, lending. The price established for any particular type of funds is unlikely to be influenced systematically or significantly by social issues. Thus, for example, the supplier of funds may not bother to discover whether the funds are to be used to finance socially useful projects (in which case the total gains generated may go beyond the immediate commercial returns), or whether they are to be used to support activities which might raise moral issues or lead to excessive environmental damage. In the former case the rate of interest established by market forces may call forth insufficient funds from the social welfare point of view (although the amount may be optimal so far as private participants in the transactions are concerned). In the latter case the market may direct too great a volume of funds to a particular use as the full social costs are not reflected in the free market transaction.

Sectors of the UK Economy

For purposes of analysing the activities of financial intermediaries it is useful to divide the economy into broad
sectors and to examine the flow of funds between sectors.
The usual classification of sectors of the UK economy may
be summarized as follows:

(1) *Personal sector*: comprises all individuals resident in the
    UK, unincorporated businesses and non-profit-making
    institutions (including registered charities, friendly
    societies and trade unions).

(2) *Industrial and commercial companies*: comprises all private
    sector companies which are not defined as banking or
    other financial institutions. Subsidiaries and branches
    of overseas companies operating in the UK are
    included, but subsidiaries and branches of UK com-
    panies operating overseas are not included.

(3) *Public corporations*: these are the nationalized industries
    together with other state-owned commercial enter-
    prises.

(4) *Government sector*: this may be subdivided into the
    financial operations of the central government (exclud-
    ing those of public corporations) and those of the local
    authorities. Due to the nature of the financing arrange-
    ments of the government sector and public corporations
    it is often the case that their financial activities are
    consolidated into an aggregate public sector.[1]

(5) *Monetary sector*: this classification formally came into
    existence in August 1981, as the replacement for the
    banking sector. It comprises all banking institutions
    required to seek authorization from the Bank of
    England within the terms of the Banking Act 1979, the
    Bank of England's Banking Department, Girobank plc,
    TSB Group and any banks operating in the Isle of Man
    or Channel Islands which elect to join the Bank of
    England's cash ratio scheme.[2]

(6) *Other financial institutions*: comprise the building
    societies, finance houses,[3] National Savings Bank, unit

trusts, investment trust companies, life assurance companies, pension funds and the specialist financial intermediaries.

(7) *Overseas sector*: this relates to the financial transactions between domestic residents and overseas residents.

An important aspect of the analysis of financial intermediation relates to the flows of funds between sectors. Clearly, the level of aggregation of economic units chosen as the basis for formulating the sectors of the economy predetermines the extent of intermediation relevant in this context. However, it is reasonable to suggest that whilst intra-sector intermediation is undoubtedly of great significance for the operation of the economy, it is the inter-sector intermediation which is of the most fundamental importance in respect of the distribution of funds within the economy and hence the composition and level of demand for domestic output. Looked at from an alternative viewpoint, the nature of activities within the broad sectors of the economy, and consequently the financial deficits and surpluses generated by these sectors, will have a decisive effect upon the growth and development of financial intermediaries. Quite simply, specific forms of desired borrowing and lending within the economy will be more appropriate for some intermediaries than for others, and hence there may be differential effects on financial institutions as a result of particular changes in the nature of economic activity. Whilst some institutions may be favoured by certain economic developments, others may be forced to adapt their operations, perhaps fundamentally, if they desire to maintain their longer-term prosperity. Therefore, by implication, consideration of the changing pattern and composition of deficits and surpluses within the sectors of the UK financial system, as well as the absolute level of financial imbalances, may offer extremely useful insights into the pressures which have been exerted on UK financial intermediaries, and may provide at least a part of the explanation of the broad trends in institutional developments observed in recent years.

Sector Financial Deficits and Surpluses

Table 3.1 shows the pattern of financial deficits and surpluses by sector for the UK for the years 1977–85. Notwithstanding the large residual (unallocated) balances[4] in recent years, the major trends in net flows of funds are quite clear. Throughout, the personal sector has remained in substantial surplus. In other words, in aggregate the members of the personal sector have saved a larger proportion of their disposable income than they have invested in real capital assets, thus resulting in financial saving. Indeed, in every year from 1977 to 1985 the personal sector's surplus was considerably greater than the total domestic surplus which occurred in most of those years. This emphasizes the importance of the personal sector as a net provider of borrowed funds in the UK financial system. It also implies that the other elements of the domestic economy in aggregate have been persistently in deficit. However, whilst the public sector has been the major net borrower in recent years, the position of the industrial and commercial companies sector has been somewhat more variable, with significant deficits in 1979 and 1980 giving way to a generally upwards trend of net surpluses during the first half of the 1980s.

The overall domestic financial position has been one of substantial surplus in recent years, which implies that total domestic saving has exceeded total domestic capital investment. Theoretically, this surplus should be balanced by an equal deficit for the overseas sector, the value of which is the sum of the balance on the current account of the balance of payments plus net capital transfers (with the sign reversed). It is clear that the magnitudes of internal and external financial balances have not been compatible, but in general the direction of recorded flows has been in accordance with theory. Thus, between 1980 and 1985 the UK ran financial surpluses with the rest of the world, which reached a peak in 1981 but diminished through to 1984, reflecting in particular the steady deterioration in the UK current account balance on the balance of payments.

Table 3.1

UK Aggregate Financial Deficits and Surpluses by Sector, 1977 to 1985, in £ million

	1977	1978	1979	1980	1981	1982	1983	1984	1985
Personal sector	5,279	9,208	13,030	18,543	13,205	12,064	9,903	12,166	10,489
Industrial/commercial	486	1,960	−2,870	−1,371	1,724	1,896	4,934	7,752	6,204
Public sector	−5,926	−7,949	−8,271	−9,869	−8,320	−7,587	−11,343	−14,016	−10,300
All financial institutions	86	−1,081	−772	−2,164	−942	5	1,196	36	1,172
Total domestic	−75	2,138	1,118	5,139	5,667	6,378	4,690	5,938	7,565
Overseas sector	41	−1,018	853	−2,929	−6,226	−4,033	−3,164	−879	−2,952
Residual	−34	1,120	1,971	2,210	−559	2,345	1,526	5,059	4,613

Source: Bank of England Quarterly Bulletin, various issues.

Table 3.2

UK Aggregate Financial Deficits and Surpluses by Sector as a Percentage of Gross Domestic Product at Market Prices, 1977 to 1985

	1977	1978	1979	1980	1981	1982	1983	1984	1985
Personal sector	3.6	5.5	6.6	8.1	5.2	4.4	3.3	3.8	3.0
Industrial/commercial	0.3	1.2	-1.5	-0.6	0.7	0.7	1.6	2.4	1.8
Public sector	-4.1	-4.7	-4.2	-4.3	-3.3	-2.7	-3.8	-4.4	-3.0
All financial institutions	0.1	-0.6	-0.4	-0.9	-0.4	—	0.4	—	0.3
Total domestic	-0.1	1.3	0.6	2.2	2.2	2.3	1.6	2.0	2.2

Sources: Bank of England Quarterly Bulletin, various issues; National Income and Expenditure (Blue Book), 1985; Monthly Digest of Statistics, June 1986.

Table 3.2 shows the magnitude of domestic sector financial flows in aggregate as a proportion of gross domestic product at market prices for the years 1977 to 1985. It is interesting to note how sector imbalances overall tended to grow during the late 1970s relative to total domestic output, whilst since 1980 they have diminished somewhat. In particular, the behaviour of the personal sector reflects a marked increase in the savings ratio until 1980, after which time its value has diminished substantially. The downwards trend of the public sector deficit between 1978 and 1982 is quite in keeping with the government's policy in relation to public sector financing, although the more recent out-turn would suggest that the policy has been relaxed somewhat in practice, albeit not necessarily by intention. There would appear to have been no significant trend in the overall domestic balance during the first half of the 1980s in relation to gross domestic output.

Personal Sector

As the personal sector has been the major net provider of borrowed funds to the UK financial system in recent years, its aggregate financial account provides an extremely useful insight into certain aspects of financial intermediation in the UK. Table 3.3 shows the uses of surplus funds of the UK personal sector for the years 1977 to 1985. Between these years, the retail price index rose by approximately 108 per cent, which implies that the gross outflows of funds from the personal sector have risen substantially in real terms in recent years. Furthermore, whilst comparison of the funds flows in individual years has only limited relevance, the broad trends are unmistakable. For example, the total flow of funds into liquid assets was 151 per cent greater in 1985 than in 1977; the flow into life assurance and pension funds was 177 per cent greater; and the overall gross outflow of funds was no less than 225 per cent higher (that is, the 1985 value was approximately twice that in 1977 in real terms). During the first four years of the period covered by the data, the trends observed were underpinned not only by a rising level of personal disposable income, but also by a savings ratio rising to historically high values, reaching 15.6 per cent of personal disposable income in 1980.

In respect of holdings of liquid assets by the personal sector, the dominance of flows of funds into building societies is self-evident. It was only during 1979 that the flows of personal sector funds into bank deposits exceeded the flows into building societies. However, more than half of all funds flows have gone into non-liquid assets, and with the exception of 1985, flows into life assurance and pension funds have formed the largest single element. Indeed, the flows into pension funds and life assurance companies between 1977 and 1985 exceeded significantly the aggregate flow into banks and building societies.

Table 3.4 draws attention to a number of key trends in the flows of personal sector funds. An interesting occurrence has been the gradual reduction in the proportion of surplus funds flowing into liquid asset holdings since 1980. To a certain extent this pattern follows the trend of price inflation in the UK in recent years, and is compatible with the phenomenon observed during the 1970s in respect of the proportionately greater flows of funds into liquid assets at times of rising inflation rates. It is believed that part of the explanation for this occurrence relates to the concept of 'target saving' in respect of real liquid asset balances. Thus, as individuals perceive that the real value of their nominally denominated asset holdings is eroded by inflation, they are encouraged to top up their liquid asset holdings in an attempt to make good the effects of inflation. In addition, it has also been suggested that high and accelerating inflation rates imply uncertainty in respect of future macroeconomic developments. Hence individuals may wish to raise their balances of liquid assets for precautionary purposes, or they may wish to do so because the possible returns associated with non-liquid assets become more difficult to anticipate. In other words, the level of perceived financial risk is likely to play an important role in the personal sector's decision-making in respect of its funds flows into liquid assets, and hence this will be a significant factor influencing the relative growth rates of the financial intermediaries whose opera-

Table 3.3

UK Personal Sector: Uses of Funds, 1977 to 1985, £ million

	1977	1978	1979	1980	1981	1982	1983	1984	1985
Liquid assets									
Notes and coin	487	597	532	383	265	664	562	167	472
National Savings	1,290	1,525	1,063	1,378	4,182	3,522	2,911	3,317	2,543
Tax instruments	7	15	29	−3	12	18	24	22	10
Local authority temporary debt	−435	−67	312	67	74	−328	9	55	38
Deposits with banks	562	3,237	6,386	6,608	3,978	3,788	3,222	3,318	5,147
Deposits with building societies	5,932	4,849	5,833	7,175	7,082	10,294	10,250	13,249	12,938
Deposits with other financial intermediaries	577	592	945	808	297	—	—	—	—
Total liquid assets	8,420	10,748	15,100	16,416	15,890	17,958	16,978	20,128	21,148

Life assurance and pension funds	6,410	7,965	10,294	11,761	13,270	13,996	15,244	17,059	17,739
Company securities	−2,937	−1,669	−2,341	−2,359	−1,644	−2,514	−1,068	−3,053	443
British government securities	427	−25	1,917	1,914	2,047	1,100	1,463	2,113	1,594
Other public sector debt	322	12	−226	−187	147	464	−394	−262	−914
Investment in fixed assets and stocks	4,936	5,622	6,877	6,724	10,316	13,040	15,141	16,375	17,774
Capital transfers	765	752	897	1,022	1,041	1,197	1,303	1,446	1,814
Total asset purchases	18,343	23,405	32,518	35,291	41,067	45,241	48,667	53,806	59,598

Source: Financial Statistics, January 1983 and May 1986.
Notes:
(1) During the fourth quarter of 1981 the UK banking sector was redefined, consequently absorbing the 'other financial institutions' as relevant to the liquid assets section of the table.
(2) A small volume of miscellaneous asset purchases have been excluded from the table and hence from the total of identified asset purchases.

Table 3.4

UK Personal Sector: Uses of Funds, Proportionate Distribution, 1977 to 1985

	1977	1978	1979	1980	1981	1982	1983	1984	1985
Percentage of additions to liquid assets accounted for by:									
Deposits with building societies	70.5	45.1	38.6	43.7	44.6	57.3	60.4	65.8	61.2
Deposits with banks	13.5	35.6	48.6	45.2	26.9	21.1	19.0	16.5	24.3
National Savings	15.3	14.2	7.0	8.3	26.3	19.6	17.1	16.5	12.0
Percentage of additions to total assets accounted for by liquid assets	45.9	45.9	46.4	46.5	38.7	39.7	34.9	37.4	35.5
Percentage of additions to total assets accounted for by:									
Deposits with building societies	32.3	20.7	17.9	20.3	17.2	22.8	21.1	24.6	21.7
Deposits with banks	6.2	16.4	22.5	21.0	10.4	8.4	6.6	6.1	8.6
National Savings	7.0	6.5	3.3	3.9	10.2	7.8	6.0	6.2	4.3
Life assurance and pension funds	34.9	34.0	31.7	33.3	32.3	30.9	31.3	31.7	29.8
British government securities	2.3	-0.1	5.9	5.4	5.0	2.4	3.0	3.9	2.7
Fixed assets and stocks	26.9	24.0	21.1	19.1	25.1	28.8	31.1	30.4	29.8

Source: Financial Statistics, January 1983 and May 1986.

Note:
A small volume of miscellaneous asset purchases have been excluded from the table.

tions depend heavily upon the drawing of funds from the personal sector.

The dominance of the building societies, banks and National Savings in respect of flows of funds into liquid assets is unquestionable. Since 1977, in total they have accounted for at least 94 per cent of such flows in each year. However, the precise distribution of funds between these three forms of intermediaries has varied markedly over time. For example, 1977 was an extremely poor year for the banking sector in relation to personal sector funds flows, whereas the building societies accounted for 70.5 per cent of the total flowing into liquid assets. By contrast, only two years later the banks accounted for almost 50 per cent of total inflows of funds associated with personal sector liquid asset holdings, whilst the building societies' share was down to 38.6 per cent. Since 1982 the distribution of funds flows has been somewhat more stable, with building societies being the dominant intermediaries, although there has been a steady decline in the proportion of funds going into National Savings.

Looking at the distribution of funds flows as a whole, as would be expected in the light of the above comments the relative importance of the banks, building societies and National Savings in aggregate has declined quite significantly in recent years. Furthermore, whilst the flows of funds into life assurance and pension funds have been substantial in absolute terms, they too have experienced a slight decrease in their relative importance. The major beneficiary of recent trends has been purchases of fixed assets and stocks, of which a substantial proportion relates to investment in dwellings. This occurrence obviously has important implications for the growth of financial institutions willing and able to provide mortgage loans to the personal sector. It could, however, also be argued that competition between intermediaries wishing to enter this (at least hitherto) low-risk and variable-yield lending activity may itself have provided an important stimulus to the observed trends in asset holdings.

Since 1981, the upsurge of bank lending in the form of mortgage loans to the personal sector has been clear. As illustrated in Table 3.5 the building societies have been the dominant force in the making of loans for house purchase, although in 1982 their share of the market fell to 58 per cent. More recently, they have accounted for approximately 80 per cent of mortgage loans to the personal sector. Furthermore, given the high proportion of total personal sector borrowing accounted for by loans for house purchase, the effects of the banks raising their profile in this market are reflected strongly in the proportion of total personal sector borrowed funds drawn from the building societies. Thus, during 1981 and 1982, when the banks made substantial inroads into the mortgage market, the proportion of total personal sector borrowed funds derived from the building societies fell markedly. Indeed, it would appear that it has been the mortgage element of bank lending to the personal sector which has been the basic cause of the relatively high volatility of banks' share of total lending to the personal sector in recent years. By comparison bank loans for purposes other than house purchases have been a much more stable component of total flows of borrowed funds. The behaviour of banks in this respect has been criticized by some commentators as being the root cause of a destabilization of the mortgage market. However, whilst the extent of any destabilization is debatable, there is little disagreement that banks' aggressive competitiveness in respect of making loans for house purchase has had fundamental effects upon the operations of building societies in recent years.

Since 1977, there have only been relatively minor changes in the distribution of total outstanding holdings of liquid assets by the personal sector. As shown in Table 3.6, National Savings suffered a decline in its relative position in 1979 and 1980, but subsequently regained its lost ground and has taken approximately 15 per cent of the market for outstanding liquid assets since 1981. Building societies have experienced a gradual upwards trend in the proportion of liquid assets for which they are responsible, and in recent years they have accounted for approximately one-half of the total. However, whilst the banks accounted for roughly the same proportion of personal sector liquid assets in 1985 as they did in 1977, there was a marked growth in the

Table 3.5
UK Personal Sector: Sources of Funds, 1977 to 1985, £ million

	1977	1978	1979	1980	1981	1982	1983	1984	1985
Loans for house purchase									
Local authorities	4	−43	293	461	272	555	−305	−195	−475
Other public sector	18	17	74	247	353	351	21	−86	10
Banks	120	270	590	490	2,265	5,078	3,639	2,314	4,134
Building societies	4,100	5,112	5,269	5,715	6,323	8,133	10,904	14,530	14,234
Other	120	171	364	469	271	6	124	259	116
Other bank loans	1,126	1,503	2,718	2,975	3,990	4,980	4,891	4,173	6,604
Other borrowing	554	1,146	1,712	692	943	422	1,046	896	1,525
Total borrowing	6,042	8,176	11,020	11,049	14,417	19,525	20,320	21,891	26,148
Saving	10,352	14,537	19,731	25,082	23,302	24,549	23,779	27,032	27,770

Source: Financial Statistics, May 1986.

Table 3.6

UK Personal Sector: Selected Liquid Asset Stocks, end-year values, percentage distribution, 1977 to 1985

	1977	1978	1979	1980	1981	1982	1983	1984	1985
National Savings	14.5	14.5	11.7	11.3	14.8	15.4	15.6	15.7·	15.5
Building societies	47.4	47.5	46.4	46.2	45.3	47.6	49.1	50.9	51.4
Sterling bank sight deposits	15.5	15.6	14.4	13.0	13.9	13.8	13.7	14.0	16.1
Sterling bank time deposits	15.9	15.8	18.8	21.1	23.8	21.7	20.3	17.8	15.5

Source: *Financial Statistics*, May 1986.

importance of time deposits during the early 1980s, which was at least partly the result of the relaxation of direct monetary controls on the banking sector in 1980 and 1981.[5] After 1982, sight deposits began to reassert their importance, probably due to the increasing availability to interest-bearing sight deposits, offered as a response to the more aggressive competition from non-bank financial intermediaries in the retail deposits market.

If we now turn to personal sector financial asset holdings in total, irrespective of their liquidity, Table 3.7 illustrates that there have been a number of major distributional changes in recent years. The proportion of financial wealth held in the form of the component parts of £M3 (which comprises notes and coin and all sterling bank deposits) fell significantly between 1977 and 1985, reflecting the reduced importance of liquid assets within the financial assets portfolio in general. However, building society deposits and shares, and to a lesser extent National Savings instruments, have largely maintained their position within the aggregate portfolio. The reduced proportion of financial wealth held in £M3 form probably reflects the growing financial sophistication of private sector wealth holders and the easier access to credit facilities which tends to undermine the rationale for holding highly liquid assets in excessive quantities. Indeed, this trend was quite apparent even before the Stock Exchange boom of the early 1980s, which automatically inflated the relative importance of equity in insurance companies and pension funds (given the dominance of company securities in these institutions' own assets portfolios), giving them 40.7 per cent of personal sector financial wealth by the end of 1985.

Thus, the value of equity in insurance companies and pension funds (which amounted to approximately £249 billion at the end of 1985) has been boosted both by massive inflows of new savings from the personal sector and by the exceptionally good performance of the bulk of the assets held in their portfolios during the first half of the 1980s. On a much smaller scale, and for the same reasons, the relative importance of unit trusts has grown substantially during the same period. However, whilst investment

Table 3.7

UK Personal Sector: Selected Financial Asset Stocks, end-year values, percentage distribution, 1977 to 1985

	1977	1978	1979	1980	1981	1982	1983	1984	1985
Sterling M3	14.2	14.7	15.4	15.2	14.7	14.5	13.2	11.7	11.6
National Savings	5.1	5.3	4.4	4.1	5.5	5.4	5.2	5.0	4.9
Building societies	16.5	17.1	17.2	16.7	17.0	16.4	16.1	15.9	16.2
UK company securities	16.5	14.8	13.6	13.5	12.6	12.3	13.0	14.1	13.0
Unit trust units	1.1	1.0	1.0	1.0	1.0	1.1	1.4	1.4	1.5
Equity in life insurance companies and pension funds	29.6	31.3	31.6	33.6	34.4	37.4	39.1	40.0	40.7
Overseas assets	1.2	1.1	1.3	1.2	1.4	1.5	1.6	1.7	1.5

Source: Financial Statistics, May 1986.

in life insurance and pension funds is often made upon the basis of regular contractual contributions, unit trusts are often seen as repositories for lump sum investments which may be realized at relatively short notice.

An interesting phenomenon has been the decline in the relative importance of direct holdings of company shares by the personal sector, notwithstanding the small reversal of this trend in 1983 and 1984 (occurring largely as a result of the Stock Exchange boom during those years). Simultaneously, indirect holdings of equities through claims on financial intermediaries have grown substantially. The portfolio diversification and risk spreading characteristics of investment through financial intermediaries are extremely important in this context. However, it is reasonable to suggest that many individuals who contribute to life assurance and pension funds view them primarily as effective savings media which have often offered significant tax advantages. The fact that holdings of company securities have largely been the means through which these intermediaries have generated their returns has probably been merely incidental so far as the individual investor is concerned. It must be emphasized that whilst direct holdings of company shares are now much less important to the personal sector than they were in the mid-1970s, there has still been a substantial growth in the absolute value of share holdings. In fact, between 1977 and 1985, the value of company securities held rose by approximately 153 per cent. However, this value should be compared to the growth in financial wealth in aggregate which was 219 per cent over the same period, and the comparable growth in combined life assurance and pension fund claims of 339 per cent.

As mentioned above, a very large proportion of the funds borrowed by the personal sector are for house purchases. Table 3.8 shows how the non-bank financial intermediaries have dominated the provision of outstanding mortgage loans in recent years, with the building societies alone accounting for approximately three-quarters of the total. Furthermore, whilst there has been a slight increase in the proportion of mortgage loans owing to the monetary (banking) sector, this has largely been at the expense of

Table 3.8

UK Personal Sector: Selected Financial Liabilities, end-year values, percentage distribution, 1977 to 1985

	1977	1978	1979	1980	1981	1982	1983	1984	1985
Bank loans and advances (excluding housing)	13.3	13.6	14.8	16.0	17.4	19.9	19.8	19.5	20.0
Hire purchase and instalment	4.6	4.9	5.1	4.9	4.4	2.4	2.5	2.5	2.5
Loans for house purchase									
Public sector	6.2	5.3	4.8	4.9	4.8	4.8	3.9	3.2	2.6
Monetary sector	2.8	2.8	3.1	3.3	5.1	8.5	10.0	10.0	10.3
Building societies	48.5	49.2	47.5	47.3	46.2	45.3	45.6	47.6	50.0
Insurance companies and pension funds	2.9	2.5	2.4	2.3	2.1	1.8	1.6	1.5	
General creditors and accounts payable	16.0	15.6	15.5	14.2	13.4	12.1	12.0	11.7	11.1

Source: Financial Statistics, February 1986.

public sector provision of funds, which has declined absolutely in recent years. In addition, through housing finance alone, the building societies, insurance companies and pension funds have consistently provided about one-half of total funds borrowed by the personal sector. Nevertheless, it is interesting to note that the proportion of personal sector liabilities accounted for by bank loans and advances has risen steadily since the mid-1970s, whilst at the same time general creditors and accounts payable, as well as hire-purchase and instalment credit outstanding have diminished in proportionate terms by a similar amount in aggregate. The increasing flexibility of bank loans and overdraft facilities, as well as the growing popularity of the use of credit cards have probably been important determinants of this trend. These developments clearly increase the importance of financial intermediation to the financial activities of the personal sector.

Industrial and Commercial Companies

Table 3.9 shows the flows of funds in respect of financial asset holdings of UK industrial and commercial companies for the years 1977–85. It is clear that liquid asset holdings have been built up continuously throughout the period, although in 1979 there was a marked slow-down in the rate of accumulation. Moreover, as might be expected, bank deposits have dominated companies' liquid asset holdings since 1977.

These funds are held both as normal business transactions balances (which tend to be related to price level movements), and also for short-term investment purposes (especially given the more competitive rates of interest offered on bank deposits in recent years). In addition some companies have undoubtedly built up liquid balances in readiness for taking advantage of investment opportunities as they arise and in preparation for take-over activity. Building societies have traditionally played only a minor role in respect of company sector financial asset holdings, although since 1982 the amount of funds flowing into building societies from

Table 3.9

UK Industrial and Commercial Companies: Uses of Funds, 1977 to 1985, £ million

	1977	1978	1979	1980	1981	1982	1983	1984	1985
Liquid assets									
Notes and coin	498	608	265	341	320	−201	108	114	95
Market Treasury bills	−18	−167	70	16	16	83	−25	−64	−25
Tax instruments	566	247	−30	330	−193	1,008	−60	285	420
Deposits with banks	2,100	1,923	297	3,012	4,929	1,592	4,817	1,346	3,933
Deposits with building societies	167	−35	−42	−22	60	91	597	564	518
Deposits with other financial intermediaries	5	111	−47	−1	−21	—	—	—	—
Total liquid assets	3,318	2,687	513	3,676	5,111	2,464	5,437	2,245	4,941
British government securities	171	24	250	133	−350	459	439	−40	−248
Local authority and public corporation debt	−356	87	170	−48	−70	−268	−64	36	−15
Overseas company securities	418	941	762	1,403	1,848	711	1,086	1,288	1,188
Other overseas assets	−130	372	748	−328	2,702	2,639	3,319	5,927	3,260
Total funds	3,421	4,111	1,790	4,836	9,241	6,005	10,217	9,456	9,126

Source: Financial Statistics, January 1983 and May 1986.

industrial and commercial companies has increased significantly. Indeed, during 1984 approximately 25 per cent of the
additional liquid assets accumulated by companies were in
the form of building society deposits. This occurrence bears
witness to the increased competitiveness and flexibility of
facilities currently being offered by building societies.

Within the broader base of company sector financial
assets, banks have often been the single most important
repository of funds, but, as shown in Table 3.10, the relative
position of banks would appear to have been influenced
strongly by the flows of companies' funds to the overseas
sector. Since the late 1970s flows of funds into both overseas
company securities and overseas direct investment projects
have risen substantially, and this trend most probably
reflects the wider opportunities for portfolio diversification
offered to companies by the abolition of exchange controls in
the UK in October 1979.

The major sources of borrowed funds for the industrial
and commercial companies sector during the period 1977 to
1985 are shown in Table 3.11. Once again the dominance of
the banking sector in the provision of these funds is quite
evident. It was only in 1981 and 1982 that the banking sector
accounted for less than one-half of the funds borrowed by
companies, and in these years there were unusually large
contributions to company funding from sales of bills (a
substantial proportion of which were ultimately purchased
by the Issue Department of the Bank of England) and
through issues of company securities. Nevertheless, the
importance of bank funding is illustrated by the fact that
during the three years 1977 to 1979 total bank lending
amounted to more than the total net borrowing of the
company sector, which, of course, implies that companies
were running down some other forms of outstanding debt
and effectively replacing it by bank loans.

Table 3.12 illustrates the growth in importance of bill
financing to the company sector since 1980, and the implicit
downgrading of other financing modes. This change came
about largely as the result of alterations in the authorities'
approach to monetary control, beginning in November 1980.
In short, bill financing was made more attractive for

Table 3.10

UK Industrial and Commercial Companies: Selected Uses of Funds, percentage distribution, 1977 to 1985

	1977	1978	1979	1980	1981	1982	1983	1984	1985
% of liquid assets:									
Deposits with banks	63.3	71.6	57.9	81.9	96.4	64.6	88.6	60.0	79.6
Deposits with building societies	5.0	−1.3	−8.2	−0.6	1.2	3.7	11.0	25.1	10.5
% of total assets:									
Deposits with banks	61.4	46.8	16.6	62.3	53.3	26.5	47.1	14.2	43.1
Deposits with building societies	4.9	−0.9	−2.3	−0.5	0.6	1.5	5.8	6.0	5.7
Overseas assets	8.4	31.9	84.4	22.2	49.2	55.8	43.1	76.3	48.7

Source: Financial Statistics, January 1983 and May 1986.

Table 3.11

UK Industrial and Commercial Companies: Sources of Funds, end-year values, 1977 to 1985, £ million

	1977	1978	1979	1980	1981	1982	1983	1984	1985
Issue Department's transactions in bills	−304	−12	12	403	2,559	4,714	−725	3,062	1,129
Bank lending:									
Foreign currency	872	587	690	1,229	2,621	882	500	265	996
Sterling	2,142	2,352	4,082	5,566	667	967	1,784	3,838	4,437
Retail and trade credit	−97	−694	−416	−1,124	−569	611	−685	−680	766
Other public sector lending	186	−19	91	−76	−27	118	175	142	96
Loans for house purchase and other lending by other financial intermediaries	129	507	332	200	279	178	408	188	353
UK company securities	−181	96	−212	958	1,920	−297	1,442	−1,367	1,012
Total sources of funds	2,747	2,817	4,579	7,156	7,450	7,173	2,899	5,448	8,789

Source: *Financial Statistics*, January 1983 and May 1986.

Table 3.12

UK Industrial and Commercial Companies: Selected Sources of Funds, percentage distribution, 1977 to 1985

	1977	1978	1979	1980	1981	1982	1983	1984	1985
% of total sources:									
Bank lending:									
Foreign currencies	31.7	20.8	15.1	17.2	35.2	12.3	17.2	4.9	11.3
Sterling	80.0	83.5	89.1	77.8	8.9	13.5	61.5	70.4	50.5
Issue Department's transactions in bills	−11.1	−0.4	0.3	5.6	34.3	65.7	25.0	56.2	12.8
UK company securities	−6.6	3.4	−4.6	13.4	25.8	4.1	49.7	−25.1	11.5
Loans for house purchase and other lending by other financial intermediaries	4.7	18.0	7.3	2.8	3.7	2.5	14.1	3.5	4.0

Source: Financial Statistics, January 1983 and May 1986.

companies as the government's policy encouraged an increase in competition between banks in relation to short-term money market activities. The immediate effect of this was to ease pressure from the company sector for bank credit creation with a consequent limit upon the rate of growth of the money supply. Also, of course, it tended to depress the rate of growth of banks' assets relative to what it would otherwise have been. In addition it is interesting to note that in the years when bill financing was particularly high, funds provided in the form of loans from non-bank financial intermediaries were only of minor significance, whereas when bill financing was low or negative (meaning that a net reduction in the stock of outstanding bills occurred), loans from non-bank financial intermediaries often accounted for a very significant proportion of company sector borrowing. In the light of the available evidence, and recognizing that there is some uncertainty about the matter, it would seem reasonable to suggest that the nature of bill market activities, which have been strongly influenced by the Bank of England's monetary control activities, have had a significant effect upon the volume of funding sought by companies from the non-bank financial intermediaries.

Public Sector

From an analytical viewpoint it is sufficient to consider the public sector financial accounts in aggregate. Thus the data in Tables 3.13 and 3.14 relate to the combined accounts of central government, local authorities and public corporations, and intra-public-sector financial flows are consequently ignored. Given the persistent and substantial financial deficits recorded by the public sector in recent years, and the absence of any underlying motive for the long-term accumulation of financial assets, the focus of attention must be upon the sources of borrowed funds for the public sector. Indeed, the selection of funds flows related to public sector asset purchases shown in Table 3.13 largely reflects the financial implications of specific government policy actions, rather than the deliberate accumulation

Table 3.13

UK Public Sector: Selected Uses of Funds, 1977 to 1985, £ million

	1977	1978	1979	1980	1981	1982	1983	1984	1985
Issue Department's transactions in bills	−304	−12	12	403	2,559	4,714	−725	3,062	1,129
Official reserves	9,588	−2,329	1,059	291	−2,419	−1,421	−607	−908	1,758
Deposits with banks	467	−128	−32	387	109	496	104	696	686
Deposits with other financial intermediaries	−53	69	−124	—	—	906	—	−281	—
Loans for house purchases	22	−26	367	708	625	906	−284	−281	−465
Other lending	283	100	169	−42	107	287	399	285	197
Company securities	−437	459	121	206	478	−39	−549	−2,582	−2,283

Source: *Financial Statistics*, January 1983 and May 1986.

Table 3.14

UK Public Sector: Sources of Funds, 1977 to 1985, £ million

	1977	1978	1979	1980	1981	1982	1983	1984	1985
Market Treasury bills	790	−1,166	−125	355	−1,215	−346	32	71	43
Notes and coin	1,044	1,286	1,199	406	672	463	822	617	429
British government securities	7,291	4,939	10,228	10,672	8,117	6,434	9,468	8,583	9,554
National Savings	1,290	1,525	1,063	1,378	4,191	3,644	2,991	3,390	2,566
Tax instruments	711	306	204	266	−180	1,013	4	488	592
Net government indebtedness to Banking Department	−264	150	−251	−864	−309	156	−157	51	122
Local authority debt	821	132	1,552	2,095	1,173	−1,772	−2,399	−78	−2,613
Official foreign currency debt	2,379	−825	−581	−769	−1,375	−278	−36	−69	1,722
Public corporations' debt	1,265	−321	515	641	−148	−312	−133	487	−657
Retail and trade credit	−85	410	−575	1,260	666	−253	600	542	−1,140
Life assurance and pension funds	248	203	242	209	646	621	791	539	916
Other instruments	−102	−36	−94	−299	−35	135	−799	−706	−625
Total sources of funds	16,667	6,603	14,527	14,068	12,203	9,905	11,184	13,915	10,909

Source: Financial Statistics, January 1983 and May 1986.

of financial assets by the public sector. For example, the purchase of commercial bills by the Issue Department of the Bank of England is basically determined by the authorities' monetary control objectives, and since 1980 this has led to a substantial growth in bill holdings by the Bank. Loans made for house purchases relate mainly to the activities of local authorities and other publicly funded bodies providing long-term funding for housing projects and, more recently, for council house sales which are strongly influenced by the ruling official policy directives.

The composition of sources of borrowed funds for the public sector is shown in Table 3.14. Between 1977 and 1985 issues of marketable government securities covered approximately 70 per cent of public sector borrowing, with a substantial proportion of the remainder being covered through deposits with the National Savings Bank and sales of non-marketable National Savings instruments. Whilst the personal sector has taken up some of the government securities and the bulk of the National Savings debt, a high proportion of the marketable securities (and particularly gilt-edged securities) have been purchased by non-bank financial intermediaries. With the exception of the trustee savings banks, UK banks have tended to hold only relatively modest amounts of government securities in their portfolios, although they have often been willing to purchase local authority debt, either through the medium of marketable securities or through the provision of market loans. However, in more recent years the local authorities have been encouraged by the government to rein in their borrowing requirements, and where necessary to use central government sources of borrowed funds. This occurrence is reflected in the recent run-down of local authorities' debt to bodies outside the public sector. A similar trend has been visible in respect of public corporations' activities.

Since the mid-1970s the UK authorities have attempted to finance as large a proportion as possible of the public sector borrowing requirement through the issue of long-term gilt-edged securities and National Savings instruments to the non-bank private sector. The reason for this action has been to facilitate the control of money supply growth since such transactions neither have any direct implication for credit creation by the banking sector nor do they involve the creation of high-powered money (that is, notes and coin and bankers' balances at the Bank of England). By way of contrast market holdings of Treasury bills have diminished considerably, which is mostly of relevance to the activities of the banking institutions as these instruments were formerly important liquid reserve assets. Therefore, the public sector's financing policy has probably tended to favour the longer-term savings (non-bank) intermediaries and the general public purchasing assets directly through National Savings outlets. Without doubt the returns on many of the public sector's longer-term debt instruments have been extremely attractive in recent years since it is necessary for the authorities to achieve their financing targets in competition with the major financial intermediaries operating in the UK. Indeed, the authorities have ultimately raised large amounts of funds from certain of those intermediaries, and the volume of borrowed funds derived from life assurance companies and pension funds has grown substantially during the past decade, both absolutely and as a proportion of total public sector borrowing. Overall, the public sector's financing policy would appear to have favoured the non-bank intermediaries at the expense of the banks in recent years, which is largely to be expected given the overriding emphasis on monetary control by the Government.

Overseas Sector

Whilst there is no disagreement over the vital significance of overseas financial flows for the successful operation of the UK financial system, the direct relevance of the overseas sector for the activities and development of UK non-bank financial intermediaries is fairly modest. It is the banking sector which is of primary relevance to the overseas sector in terms of the provision of funds to UK financial intermediaries, and in this respect foreign currency transactions dominate. Thus, for example, during 1985 the overseas sector made foreign currency denominated net deposits with the UK banking sector of a value equivalent to £25,474 million, whilst net sterling deposits amounted to £4,159 million. By contrast, during the same year, the overseas sector undertook a net repatriation of funds from the non-bank financial intermediaries to the value of £19 million, having raised its claims by £31 million in the previous year. These relative magnitudes of flows of funds from the overseas sector are quite typical of those experienced in recent years, and thus it is quite clear that the dependence of the non-bank intermediaries on inflows of funds from abroad is of very little consequence.

A similar position holds in respect of direct lending to the overseas sector by UK financial intermediaries. Thus, during 1985 UK banks lent £19,546 million in foreign currencies, and £1,751 million in sterling, to the overseas sector, whilst by comparison direct lending by non-bank intermediaries was negligible. However, the overseas sector has obtained substantial amounts of funds from UK non-bank intermediaries through their purchase of overseas company securities, although even in this respect their net purchases have been somewhat smaller than those undertaken by banking institutions. Direct and other investment flows to the overseas sector from UK financial intermediaries have been rather volatile in recent years, with a modest repatriation of funds overall by both bank and non-bank intermediaries. These trends are illustrated in Tables 3.17 and 3.18. For the non-bank financial intermediaries in aggregate, the overseas sector has accounted for only 8 or 9 per cent of total annual uses of funds during the first half of the 1980s, and this represents a substantial increase over the flows experienced prior to the removal of exchange controls in 1979.

Financial Institutions

The dominant position of the personal sector in the provision of sterling funds to UK financial intermediaries, as described on pp. 48–61, is clearly reflected in the overall pattern of inflows of funds into these institutions. Table 3.15 shows the percentage distribution of inflows of funds into

Table 3.15

UK Non-Bank Financial Institutions: Sources of funds, percentage distribution, 1977 to 1985

	1977	1978	1979	1980	1981	1982	1983	1984	1985
Building society shares and deposits	45.2	33.0	31.7	34.1	31.2	38.7	37.4	37.0	33.3
Bank borrowing:									
Foreign currency	2.3	3.1	0.7	-0.5	0.6	2.5	3.3	11.4	1.7
Sterling	0.8	4.3	6.7	3.5	8.1	7.1	5.8	6.9	10.8
Unit trust units	0.2	0.7	-0.2	—	0.8	0.6	1.9	1.6	2.3
Capital issues	1.0	0.6	0.5	0.4	1.1	—	0.4	0.7	4.1
Life assurance and pension funds	45.8	53.1	55.2	55.1	55.1	49.7	46.8	42.4	41.6
Other	4.7	5.2	5.4	7.4	3.1	1.4	4.4	—	6.1

Source: Bank of England Quarterly Bulletin, various issues.

the non-bank intermediaries for the years 1977 to 1985. It may be observed that life assurance and pension funds took the largest share of funds, but despite a continual growth in the absolute flow of funds into these institutions their percentage share of the total inflows of non-bank inter- mediaries diminished significantly during the early 1980s. In contrast, after an especially good year in 1977, the building societies' share of inflows of funds settled down to around one-third of the total.[6]

Since 1981 unit trusts have attracted increasingly large volumes of funds from outside of the financial sector. However, the most significant change in the pattern of funds flows has possibly related to the growth in borrowing from the banking sector by the non-bank financial inter- mediaries. It may be observed that in 1984 this accounted for 18.3 per cent of total inflows of funds, although this diminished to 12.5 per cent in 1985. To a greater or lesser extent this form of borrowing has been undertaken by most of the non-bank financial intermediaries, and since 1982 a number of the larger building societies have become increas- ingly important in this respect. In addition, 1985 saw a massive increase in the aggregate capital issues of the non- bank intermediaries (amounting to about £1.7 billion). This occurrence was probably due to institutions taking advan- tage of the buoyant conditions on the Stock Exchange with a view to raising capital funds on relatively attractive terms. Also, some institutions will have been influenced in their actions by the unquestioned need for them to strengthen their capital bases following the recent rapid growth in their liabilities, and in readiness for expected future develop- ments within the financial system which are likely to require more highly capitalized institutions.

In recent years non-bank financial intermediaries have accounted for approximately two-thirds of total net inflows of funds to UK financial intermediaries, as illustrated by Table 3.16. However, whilst the banking institutions have obviously taken up the remaining one-third of funds flows, there have been significant fluctuations in the relative importance of the different forms of bank deposits. The importance of sterling sight deposits diminished markedly during the years prior to 1980, at which time they accounted for only 2.2 per cent of the total inflow of funds to UK financial intermediaries. However they have subsequently regained much of their earlier importance. The reasons for this trend are probably that the rate of inflation in the UK has diminished significantly since 1980, and hence the holding of zero-interest sight deposits entails a much smaller loss of real purchasing power than it did during the late 1970s and early 1980s when inflation rates were relatively high, and that an increasing proportion of sight accounts now pay interest at reasonably attractive rates. Thus, quite simply, it has become possible for wealth holders to maintain a higher level of liquidity in their asset portfolios without incurring the financial costs which were formerly associated with this option. Competitive pressures, both within the banking sector and between banks and the major deposit-taking non-bank financial intermediaries (especially the building societies and the National Savings movement) have undoubtedly been the main cause of this trend. The higher level of competition has itself been stimulated by the growing financial sophistication of both personal and corporate customers of the financial intermediaries. In the light of these developments it is perhaps to be expected that the relative importance of sterling time deposits has diminished somewhat in more recent times. In addition, the ability of banks to bid for interest-bearing deposits was severely constrained by official monetary controls until June 1980. Immediately after the abolition of these restrictive controls there was a massive portfolio adjustment on the part of banks which is clearly visible in the upsurge of time deposits in 1980, although soon afterwards the increasing attractiveness of sight deposits began to make itself felt on the growth of time deposits.

The structures of aggregate on-lending by the UK monetary (banking) sector and by the non-bank financial intermediaries for the years 1983 to 1985 are shown in Tables 3.17 and 3.18 respectively. For the banking sector normal lending to private (personal plus corporate) sector customers dominates activities, and has recently accounted for around 70 per cent of total uses of funds. In contrast, public sector

Table 3.16

UK Financial Institutions: Net Inflows of Funds, percentage distribution, 1977 to 1985

	1977	1978	1979	1980	1981	1982	1983	1984	1985
Non-bank financial intermediaries	66.0	75.4	64.1	64.4	68.3	69.2	70.6	69.8	64.6
Monetary sector:									
Sterling sight deposits	16.6	13.6	6.2	2.2	8.3	9.5	9.0	12.0	14.4
Sterling time deposits	-1.0	14.4	14.2	29.1	18.0	9.9	11.4	6.2	9.9
Foreign currency deposits	3.8	4.5	2.8	4.4	6.6	2.9	4.9	2.0	4.0
Other inflows	14.6	-7.9	12.7	-0.1	-1.2	8.5	4.1	10.0	7.1

Source: Bank of England Quarterly Bulletin, various issues.
Note: 'Other inflows' comprise changes in net external claims of banks, plus capital issues, accruals, and so on.

Table 3.17

UK Monetary Sector: On-Lending, 1983 to 1985, £ million and percentage distribution

	1983 £m	1983 £m	1983 %	1984 £m	1984 £m	1984 %	1985 £m	1985 £m	1985 %
Notes and coin	127			295			-164		
Market Treasury bills	-28			-2			114		
British government securities	235			183			309		
Local authority debt	-1,941			-115			-1,376		
Public corporations	-79			738			-647		
Other public sector	-238			86			117		
Total public sector		-1,924	-5.9		1,185	3.0		-1,647	-3.4
Loans for house purchases		3,639	11.2		2,314	5.9		4,134	8.5
Other private sector lending:									
Foreign currencies	17,561			14,266			23,548		
Sterling	10,820			15,168			16,300		
Total other private sector lending		28,381	87.6		29,434	74.9		39,848	82.2
UK company securities		133	0.4		-250	-0.6		-2,745	-5.7
Overseas company securities		2,962	9.1		7,983	20.3		9,003	18.6
Other overseas investment etc.		-786	-2.4		-1,384	-3.5		-95	0.2
Total on-lending		32,405	100.0		39,282	100.0		48,498	100.0

Source: *Financial Statistics*, May 1986.

Table 3.18

UK Non-Bank Financial Intermediaries: On-Lending 1983 to 1985, £ million and percentage distribution

	£m	1983 £m	%	£m	1984 £m	%	£m	1985 £m	%
Market Treasury bills	54			−7			−33		
British government securities	6,449			5,418			4,866		
Local authority debt	−28			201			−430		
Public corporations	−3			4			−10		
Other public sector	7			60			1,256		
Total public sector		6,479	24.1		5,676	16.3		5,649	15.8
Deposits with banks:									
Sterling sight	325			2,020			1,645		
Sterling time	2,053			2,069			5,063		
Foreign currencies	557			1,857			1,548		
Total bank deposits		2,935	10.9		5,946	17.1		8,256	23.0
Loans for house purchase		11,052	41.1		14,831	42.6		14,434	40.3
Other lending		1,029	3.8		547	1.6		965	2.7
UK company securities		2,586	9.6		3,701	10.6		5,522	15.4
Overseas company securities		3,492	13.0		1,625	4.7		4,637	12.9
Other overseas investments, etc.		−685	−2.5		2,507	7.2		−3,616	−10.1
Total on-lending		26,888	100.0		34,833	100.0		35,847	100.0

Source: Financial Statistics, May 1986.

indebtedness to the banking sector has actually fallen as outstanding debt has been run down. However, the most interesting trend in banking sector intermediation in recent years has been in respect of the growth of purchases of overseas company securities, since at a time when banks have been making net sales of UK company securities from their portfolios, holdings of overseas company securities have risen sharply. In 1985 purchases of such securities amounted to approximately £9 billion in value, and accounted for 18.6 per cent of total on-lending by banks. Without doubt the freedom over international capital movements offered by the ending of exchange controls in October 1979, as well as the unusually good performance of quoted securities throughout much of the Western world during the first half of the 1980s, have been largely responsible for this trend.

If we turn to the non-bank financial intermediaries, we find that the pattern of on-lending during the three years 1983 to 1985 was quite different from that of the banking sector. In particular, the on-lending was spread somewhat more widely between the other sectors of the economy, with loans for house purchases dominating throughout. The non-bank intermediaries have also purchased large volumes of government securities, and have consequently covered a significant proportion of the public sector's borrowing requirement. In addition, recent years have seen a substantial growth in the amount of on-lending to the banking sector. This trend has probably been encouraged by the banks' increased need to raise funds through the wholesale money markets, which, somewhat ironically, has been the result of the higher level of competition from the non-bank intermediaries in the markets for retail funds. In contrast to the banking sector, the non-bank intermediaries have also continued to purchase large amount of UK company securities as well as overseas company securities, although other overseas investment flows have been rather volatile in recent years with an overall net repatriation of funds under this head.

Table 3.19 shows clearly the growth in the financial strength of the major UK non-bank financial intermediaries

Table 3.19
Total Asset Holdings of the Major Groups of UK Non-Bank
Financial Intermediaries, end-year values 1978 and 1984
(in £ million) and percentage growth

	1978 £ million	1984 £ million	% growth 1978 to 1984
Building societies	39,723	103,345	160
Finance houses	4,300	16,325	280
National Savings	11,233	28,131	150
Insurance companies	46,829	132,867	184
Pension funds	31,346	130,858	321
Unit trusts	3,874	14,915	285
Investment trusts	6,677	15,655	134
Total non-bank intermediaries	143,683	442,096	208

Sources: *Financial Statistics*, November 1985 and January 1986; *Credit Quarterly Review*, FHA; Wilson Committee Report (1980), Appendices.
Notes:
(1) The value for finance houses' assets relates to the outstanding credit of members of the Finance Houses Association, and therefore somewhat understates the actual asset value of the complete group of finance houses.
(2) The figures for insurance companies, pension funds, unit trusts and investment trusts are net of short-term borrowing.

during the six years to the end of 1984, and since that time there has been no indication of any downturn in the fortunes of these institutions as a whole. At the end of 1984, the aggregate asset value of the non-bank intermediaries was almost three times the size of the corresponding value for UK retail banks (which stood at approximately £153 billion), and twice the size of the aggregate sterling assets of all institutions comprising the UK banking sector, although it was considerably smaller than the corresponding total asset value of the latter group, which, of course, includes very large amounts of foreign currency denominated assets.[7]

Within the non-bank intermediaries sector the most rapid growth in recent years has been experienced by the pension funds and the unit trusts, but all elements of the sector have exhibited quite substantial growth. Between the end of 1978 and the end of 1984, the aggregate assets' value of the major non-bank financial intermediaries rose by 208 per cent. During the same period the retail price index rose by 'only' 78 per cent, thus illustrating the significant real growth in asset holdings of these institutions. However, to put this event into perspective, it should be recognized that the corresponding growth of sterling assets of all UK banking institutions was approximately 185 per cent; and when foreign currency denominated assets are included the banking sector's growth was a phenomenal 243 per cent.

Notes

1 For statistical purposes the public sector includes a number of government-supported agencies which perform financial inter-mediary type operations, and which may be regarded as being specialist financial intermediaries. These include the Scottish and Welsh Development Agencies and the National Research Development Corporation. In addition, the Bank of England's Issue Department is included within the public sector's accounts.
2 The cash ratio requirement is part of the Bank of England's August 1981 monetary control provisions. All authorized banks must hold cash reserves with the Bank of England, but in return certain operating privileges are available in the UK.
3 A number of the larger finance houses are currently listed as licensed deposit-takers within the provisions of the Banking Act 1979, and are consequently included in the monetary sector. It is most probable that these finance houses will remain within the monetary sector even after the proposed amendments to the Banking Act are implemented, which it is expected will lead to the abolition of the two-tier categorization of banking institu-tions for regulatory purposes.
4 Assuming the absence of errors in, and omissions from, the statistics, the sum of deficits and surpluses of the personal sector, industrial and commercial companies, public sector, monetary sector, other financial institutions and overseas sector, should equal zero. This is because, by definition, a deficit in one sector must be matched by a surplus of equal value in some other sector(s) of the economy.
5 In particular, the abolition of the supplementary special deposits (corset) scheme in June 1980 allowed banks to compete freely once again for time deposits without the fear of incurring severe financial penalties from the Bank of England. In fact, large amounts of funds which had been the object of 'disinter-mediation' in order to avoid the official constraints on bank

deposit growth were drawn back into conventional banking channels.

6　The 1977 position was perhaps somewhat artificial in the sense that the building societies gained disproportionately from the rather strict controls being applied at that time to UK banks in respect of their sterling deposits. The controls effectively constrained banks' willingness to bid for sterling funds in both retail and wholesale markets.

7　It must be emphasized that the asset values quoted represent the aggregates for each group of financial institutions, and therefore the overall sums of assets for the non-bank intermediaries and for the banking sector include intra-sector borrowing and lending. Thus, for example, if an insurance company purchases units in a unit trust, this adds to the aggregate assets of the non-bank institutions, but this action does not raise the volume of resources made available to institutions or individuals outside of the respective sectors. However, the available statistics would appear to indicate that the volume of inter-bank funds (adding to the aggregate assets value for the banking sector) is considerably larger than the inter-non-bank financial intermediary funds, suggesting that the growth rate of the non-bank intermediaries relative to that of the banking sector (in terms of funds made available to borrowers outside of the respective sectors) has been even greater than might be implied by the raw asset values.

CHAPTER FOUR

Building Societies

The Origin and Structure of the Building Society Sector

The history of building societies in the UK may be traced back to the year 1775, at which time the first mutual fund was established (in Birmingham) for the specific purpose of financing the housing of its members. The need for various mutual and self-help organizations arose out of the enormous social and economic upheavals which took place in the eighteenth century. In particular, the industrial revolution caused high levels of migration from rural to newly urbanized areas where the social provision for the workforce was often grossly inadequate.

The fundamental concept of the mutual building society was that members would each contribute a regular subscription to a fund, which would then be used to finance the purchase or erection of a house to be allotted to a specific member. All members would continue to pay their subscription until houses had been acquired for them all, at which point the society would terminate. It was from the basis of these 'terminating societies' that the modern 'permanent societies' evolved. Quite simply, in order to speed up the provision of housing, societies began to offer interest payments to people who were willing to lend funds to them but who did not necessarily desire to purchase a house themselves. Simultaneously, of course, societies had to charge interest to their borrowers in order to cover the cost of raising funds. The first society with a proper permanent constitution was established in 1845, and as its title implies its operations were expected to continue indefinitely into the future, and specifically beyond the time at which all original members of the society had been housed.

It has been estimated[1] that between 1775 and 1825 around 250 terminating societies were established, mostly in the Midlands, Yorkshire and Lancashire, but by the late nineteenth century over 100 societies per year were being dissolved. In 1912 terminating societies accounted for approximately one-half of all societies; by 1932 this proportion had fallen to only 16 per cent. No new terminating societies have been formed since 1953, and the last one in operation was dissolved in 1980. Nevertheless, the concurrent growth of permanent societies ensured the continued expansion of the industry as a whole.

In 1890 there were 2,795 building societies operating in the UK, which in aggregate had 659,000 shareholders and held assets valued at £51 million. However, by 1895 the number of building societies had reached its peak at 3,642. After this time their number declined continually. In 1935 there were less than 1,000 societies in existence, and by July 1986 only 157 remained. Nevertheless, prior to the First World War the decline in the number of separate institutions in the building society sector was considerably slower than that taking place in the banking sector. It is probable that the legislative framework within which the building societies had to operate contributed to this slower decline in institutional numbers, for it was required that amalgamations and transfers of engagement could only take place with the consent of at least three-quarters of the society's members, holding at least two-thirds of the total value of outstanding shares. In fact prior to the 1940s, most of the decline in the number of societies could be attributed to the dissolution of terminating societies. Table 4.1 illustrates the average rates of decline in the number of building societies for each decade since 1900. It may be observed that these rates slowed markedly during the three decades 1930 to 1960, reflecting the reduced importance of terminating societies. However, since 1960 these rates have increased once again, mainly due to the growth in merger activity. During the decade 1953 to

Table 4.1
Rates of Decline in the Number of UK Building Societies,
1900 to 1985

Period	Average Annual Rate of Decline (%)
1900–10	2.8
1911–20	3.0
1921–30	2.1
1931–40	0.7
1941–50	1.5
1951–60	1.2
1961–70	4.0
1971–80	5.5
1981–85	9.0

Source: *BSA Bulletin*, October 1983 and April 1986.

1962 there were 138 transfers of engagements and 14 unions, whilst in the period 1963 to 1972 the figures were 183 and 28 respectively, and for 1973 to 1984 they were 228 and 23 respectively.

Transfers of engagement, which technically result in the closure of the transferor, are by far the most common form of merger between societies, and in general these have been the consequence of smaller societies transferring their engagements to larger societies. This is illustrated by Table 4.2 which shows the size distribution of the smaller societies involved in the 108 transfers of engagements which took place between 1979 and 1984. Nevertheless, the building society sector has also experienced a number of large-scale amalgamations, such as the merger between the Halifax Permanent Benefit and the Halifax Equitable Benefit (in 1928) to form the Halifax Building Society, which is currently the largest (by asset size) in the UK.[2] A more recent example is the merger between the Anglia and the London and South of England societies which in 1983 held 3.6 per cent and 0.7 per cent of the sector's assets respectively.

There are a number of reasons which can be advanced to

Table 4.2
Asset Distribution of Smaller Societies Involved in
Transfers of Engagements, 1979 to 1984

Asset Size	Number
Over £500m	2
Over £100m and under £500m	4
Over £10m and up to £100m	22
Over £1m and up to £10m	52
Over £100,000 and up to £1m	27
Under £100,000	2
Total	109

Source: *Building Society Fact Book*, 1985.

explain the tendency for smaller societies to transfer their engagements to larger societies, and to explain the increased number of amalgamations in recent decades. First, the increasingly competitive environment has tended to result in the smaller, less efficient societies being put under pressure to seek ways of reducing their unit operating costs. This trend is likely to continue with the demise of the building society interest rate cartel, which had previously set lending and borrowing rates to give margins conducive to the survival of the least efficient societies. Secondly, societies have faced increased administrative burdens, which again place particular pressure on the smaller institutions. Amongst the recent developments in this area were the introduction of MIRAS in 1983,[3] and the measures announced in the 1983 Budget which require societies to account quarterly rather than annually for income tax in respect of interest paid to investors. Thirdly, it has been argued, somewhat controversially, that large societies can benefit from economies of scale.[4]

Irrespective of the reason for merger activity, its occurrence obviously leads to an increasingly concentrated structure for the building society sector. Table 4.3 illustrates this trend very clearly. For example, in 1950 the largest 20 societies accounted for 62.5 per cent of the total assets of the sector (which amounted to £785 million); by 1984 that

Table 4.3

The Degree of Concentration in the Building Society Industry, 1930 to 1984

| Year | Largest 5 | | Next 5 | | Largest 10 | | Next 10 | | Largest 20 | | All societies |
	Total assets £m	Share of total %	Total assets £m	Share of total %	Total assets £m	Share of total %	Total assets £m	Share of total %	Total assets £m	Share of total %	Total assets £m
1930	145	39.1	53	14.4	198	53.4	43	11.6	241	65.0	371
1940	287	38.0	93	12.3	380	50.3	79	10.5	459	60.7	756
1950	469	37.3	145	11.5	614	48.9	170	13.6	785	62.5	1,256
1960	1,435	45.3	366	11.6	1,801	56.9	371	11.7	2,171	68.6	3,166
1970	5,416	50.1	1,539	14.2	6,955	64.3	1,414	13.1	8,369	77.4	10,819
1975	12,797	52.9	3,701	15.3	16,498	68.2	3,432	14.2	19,930	82.3	24,204
1976	15,144	53.7	4,257	15.1	19,401	68.8	3,943	14.0	23,344	82.8	28,202
1977	18,391	53.6	5,324	15.5	23,715	69.2	4,856	14.2	28,571	83.3	34,288
1978	21,489	54.4	6,412	16.2	27,901	70.6	5,319	13.5	33,220	84.0	39,538
1979	25,192	55.0	7,198	15.7	32,390	70.7	6,099	13.3	38,489	84.1	45,789
1980	29,798	55.4	8,419	15.7	38,217	71.0	7,157	13.3	45,374	84.3	53,793
1981	34,077	55.1	9,638	15.6	43,715	70.7	8,698	14.1	52,413	84.8	61,815
1982	40,665	55.7	12,663	17.3	53,329	73.0	9,733	13.3	63,062	86.3	73,033
1983	47,807	55.7	15,075	17.6	62,882	73.2	11,865	13.8	74,746	87.0	85,868
1984	57,845	56.3	17,707	17.2	75,552	73.6	14,507	14.1	90,059	87.7	102,689

Source: Building Society Fact Book, 1985.

proportion had risen to 87.7 per cent of total assets worth £90,059 million. The diversity in size of individual building societies is further demonstrated by the fact that at the end of 1984 the smallest 112 societies (representing 59 per cent of total institutions in the sector) held only 1.5 per cent of total sector assets in aggregate.

Despite a number of aborted merger plans involving several of the larger societies during 1985–6, many commentators believe that the trend towards higher concentration within the sector is likely to continue. For whilst the largest societies have not completed any mergers in recent years, they have exhibited some of the highest rates of internal growth within the sector. Nevertheless, in January 1985 alone there were five merger announcements where the smaller partners held assets in excess of £100 million each at the end of 1983, which compares to only four such mergers for the whole of the period 1979 to 1982 inclusive. Furthermore, as societies have tended to face increasingly severe competition for retail funds, both from other societies and from other financial intermediaries (notably from National Savings, but also from the major clearing banks in more recent years), they have viewed the wholesale money markets as providing a possibly cost-effective alternative source of funds. However, entry into the wholesale markets is only really viable for the larger societies, and hence a further incentive is provided for mergers, particularly between medium-sized institutions. Beyond this, the new legislative framework for building societies[5] is likely to provide a further catalyst to merger activity, as it would appear that some of the more innovative powers embodied in the legislation are only to be available to the largest twenty or so institutions.

The Legal Constitution of Building Societies

In 1836 building societies were given legal status for the first time, and the Certifying Barrister of Friendly Societies (subsequently the Chief Registrar of Friendly Societies) was appointed and charged with certifying the rules and regulations of savings banks and building societies. The 1874 Building Societies Act was, however, the first comprehensive legislation governing societies, and established them as distinct legal entities. This legislation, following the recommendation of the 1870 Royal Commission, formed the basic framework within which societies were to form their own rules. Although the Royal Commission had wanted to give the Chief Registrar wide discretion with respect to the certification of societies' rules, the 1874 Act did not provide for this. In fact, so long as 14 specified items were dealt with in the rules, for example relating to the provision for alteration of the rules and the investment of surplus funds, then the Chief Registrar was under an obligation to certify those rules.

It should be noted that the 1874 legislation applied only to those existing societies which chose to incorporate within its provisions and to any new societies which were formed after 1874. Those societies which chose not to incorporate, and which were mainly terminating societies, were catered for under the 1836 legislation. One of the major advantages to be had from incorporating under the 1874 Act was that societies no longer had to operate through trustees, but could themselves hold mortgage deeds and provide security for loans. The Act also provided for limited liability of society members. Those members without a mortgage advance had their liability limited to the amount they had paid (or were in arrears in the case of the subscription shares involving long-term saving), while those members with mortgages had their liability limited to the amount they owed under the terms of the mortgage. It was also under this Act that societies were permitted to raise funds through small denomination paid-up shares for the first time, rather than through subscription shares as was previously the case.

Although the 1874 Act did strengthen the position of societies, as implied above, it also provided for restrictions on the activities of societies, many of which were still operative until 1987, albeit in a modified form. Thus, under the 1874 Act both permanent and terminating societies were only permitted to borrow from depositors an amount up to two-thirds of the sum secured by mortgages. The alternative, open only to the terminating societies, was to borrow an amount not exceeding twelve monthly subscriptions. Societies were prohibited from building or owning land, except for the purpose of conducting their business. Furthermore, the surplus funds of societies could only be invested in mortgages, or alternatively in government securities. It was also the 1874 Act which placed restrictions on unions between societies. However, an important weakness of the Act lay in the limited powers it bestowed on the Chief Registrar. In short, the resulting lack of close supervision of building societies' activities enabled a series of major frauds to be perpetrated during the late nineteenth century. Indeed, because of the economic environment at that time many societies became involved with increasingly speculative lending, often backed by inadequate security. The problem came to a head in 1892 when the UK's largest building society (The Liberator) failed whilst carrying liabilities of £3.3 million.

New legislation (the Building Societies Act 1892) came into force in August 1894 giving the Chief Registrar greater powers. He was empowered to appoint an accountant to inspect and report on the books of a society at the request of a minimum of 10 of the members, and if one-tenth of the society's members so wished he could appoint an inspector to examine and report on the affairs of the society. Sections 6 and 7 of the 1892 Act provided that registrations could be cancelled or suspended, and in some cases that a society be dissolved if the Chief Registrar felt that violations of the Building Societies Acts had been made, or if it was felt that the society in question could not meet the claims of its members. These types of measures were introduced primarily to quell public concern over the possible mismanagement of societies' affairs. The legislation also tightened up the reporting requirements for all societies, which were now obliged to incorporate within the Act, as well as limiting certain forms of potentially suspect operational activities.

The final stage of legislation, prior to that which was recently introduced by the British government, came in 1960, and was the result of the activities of some so-called 'rogue' societies during the 1950s. These societies had effectively been circumventing the spirit, if not the letter of the 1892 Act, by lending substantial sums of money to individual companies, and by providing bridging finance without security (in the sense that the funds were released to the party buying the property before the property could legitimately be mortgaged as security for the loan). The precipitant event in this instance was the collapse of the State Building Society in 1959. This institution had advanced £3¼ million which was later to be secured by mortgages on acquired properties, but when the deal collapsed due to lack of bridging finance, the State was left with no security for its advance.

Many of the problems pertaining to the activities of the 'rogue' societies in the 1950s stemmed from the fact that existing legislation placed no restrictions on the types of property which societies could take as security for loans. Hence, the 1960 Act changed this by dividing building society lending into two categories, namely normal advances and special advances. Special advances were defined to be any advance to a limited company, any advance over £5,000 to an individual, or any additional advance to an individual which would result in that individual's total indebtedness exceeding this £5,000 limit. The Act prescribed that only 10 per cent of a society's advances in one year should be special advances. In addition to curbing the undesirable practices of the previous decade, this measure also ensured that most of the industry's lending business was directed to the growing demand for finance for owner occupation. The special advance limit has been raised many times since 1960 in order to reflect rising house values, and in 1986 it stood at £60,000. Furthermore, the Chief Registrar was given the power, under the legislation, to authorize a building society to exceed the 10 per cent limit on special advances for loans on newly constructed houses or flats to be let to tenants. His power was also increased to allow him to prohibit building societies from accepting potential investors' funds, to control the contents of advertisements from societies, and to make regulations concerning the way in which societies would be allowed to use their surplus funds.

The Building Societies Act 1962 merely consolidated the

existing legislation, and hence provided the framework within which societies operated for the following 24 years. The major aspects of that framework may be summarized as follows:

(1) Societies are mutual institutions, having no equity shareholders, and being owned by their investing and borrowing members.

(2) Societies can only lend on the security of freehold or leasehold estate, and furthermore, are restricted to lending on first mortgages (that is, where there is no loan from another lender already secured on the property).

(3) The amount which societies can lend to corporate bodies, or in large advances to individuals, is circumscribed by the special advances provision.

(4) Societies are required to value properties taken into mortgage.

(5) Societies hold some of their assets in liquid form, and the 1962 Act and various statutory instruments specify the form which these liquid assets can take. Very simply, surplus funds must be invested either in bank deposits or public sector instruments.

In addition, since 1981, the government's implementation of the EEC Directive has meant that societies have had to receive new authorization if they are to continue in business. To obtain this authorization they have had to convince the Chief Registrar of the adequacy of their reserves and the competence of their management.

The Regulation and Prudential Supervision of Building Societies Prior to 1987

A major role of the Chief Registrar of Friendly Societies was to undertake the prudential supervision of building societies, and hence to attempt to ensure that their financial integrity was maintained. Each society was required to make an annual financial return to the Chief Registrar, and he could request further information or conduct such investigations as were felt to be appropriate. Societies also had to provide a monthly financial statement to the Registry of Friendly Societies on a voluntary basis which provided it with up-to-date information about cash flows. In addition, with Treasury approval, the Chief Registrar was able to prohibit or restrict societies in respect of deposit-taking or advertising for new deposits. Under the 1962 Act a minimum of ten persons could form a building society if each of them was willing to put £500 into the society for a minimum of five years (although this figure was effectively raised to £5,000 by the 1981 Authorisation Regulations), and it was the function of the Chief Registrar's Office to scrutinize the proposed rules of the society to ensure that they conformed to statutory requirements. Once the Registry had been satisfied of the proposed society's constitutional structure, it issued a certificate of incorporation which endowed the society with legal status. The Chief Registrar was also responsible for authorizing unions and transfers of engagements between societies, as well as hearing disputes concerning Building Society Law, and granting or revoking trustee status for societies.

Liquidity Requirements

The Building Societies Act 1962 laid down no specific requirement for societies to hold liquid assets, although Section 58 of that Act states that a society shall not invest its funds except in a manner authorized by an Order made by the Chief Registrar of Friendly Societies. In this respect, societies were subject to the Building Societies (Authorised Investments) (No. 2) Order 1977, as updated by the subsequent Amendment Orders, culminating in that of 1983 which permitted societies to invest in bills of exchange and in certificates of deposit issued by other societies with assets of over £2,000 million.

The Authorised Investments Order set out a three-part schedule of investments as outlined by the following:

Part I   Investments:
    Cash and bank balances; bills of exchange; building

Society certificates of deposit; quoted government and government backed securities within five years of redemption; unquoted securities repayable within six months.

Part II   Investments:
Government and government backed securities with between five and fifteen years to maturity; unquoted securities repayable between six months and two years.

Part III   Investments:
Government and government backed securities with between fifteen and twenty-five years to maturity; unquoted securities repayable in between two and five years.

For a society to be allowed to invest in assets listed in Part II of the schedule it first had to have 7½ per cent of its funds invested in Part I assets. Similarly, in order to make investments in Part III assets a society first had to have invested a further 7½ per cent of its funds in Part II assets. This effectively ensured that a building society could not invest in long maturity securities unless it had a liquidity ratio of at least 15 per cent as at the end of the previous financial year.

The other regulatory control on building societies in respect of their liquidity arose from the requirements for trustee status, which is a condition of membership of the Building Societies Association. To be eligible to apply for trustee status a society must have assets in excess of £10 million; have liabilities not exceeding twice the amount due to holders of its outstanding shares; and have liquid funds not less than 7½ per cent of assets, reduced by the amount owing by the society in respect of any loans made to it under the House Purchase and Housing Act 1959, and by any amount by which the book value of the society's investments exceeds their market value. However, it must be emphasized that the Chief Registrar was under no obligation to confer trustee status upon a society even if these conditions were met. He could, for example, refuse trustee status if he considered that the society's affairs were not being conducted with appropriate prudence.

Table 4.4
Building Societies' Liquidity Ratio, 1970 to 1985

Year end	%	Year end	%
1970	18.4	1978	18.4
1971	19.1	1979	18.0
1972	16.5	1980	19.4
1973	16.3	1981	19.1
1974	19.2	1982	20.5
1975	21.0	1983	19.9
1976	18.3	1984	18.8
1977	21.6	1985	18.9

Source: *BSA Bulletin*, various issues.

Table 4.4 illustrates the recent trend in the liquidity ratio for building societies. It may be observed that societies in aggregate have maintained liquidity ratios well above the minimum 7½ per cent required for trustee status. The major reasons for this are to maintain the confidence of depositors in the ability of the society to meet demands for withdrawal of funds without delay; to stabilize mortgage lending in the face of variations in building society competitiveness without having to resort to immediate variations in the interest rate structure; and to cover unusually large outflows of funds, for example, in relation to the payment of composite rate taxation.

Table 4.5 shows the composition of building societies' liquid asset holdings for the years 1983 and 1984. The dominance of listed investments in the total values is clear, and the importance of bank deposits and cash balances is also evident. However, in more recent years, not only has the overall liquidity ratio fallen somewhat, but also the composition of liquid asset holding has changed to some extent.

An important factor underlying these trends has been the higher level of competitiveness within the building society sector, and between societies and other retail financial intermediaries. This has tended to push the rate of interest charged on mortgages towards its market clearing level, and hence has made mortgage loans more profitable relative to

Table 4.5
Building Societies' Liquid Assets by Category, 1983 and 1984,
year-end values, percentage distribution

Category	Percentage of Total Liquid Assets		Percentage of Assets	
	1983	1984	1983	1984
Listed investments	58.1	57.0	11.7	10.9
Unlisted investments	18.3	21.2	3.7	4.0
Interest accrued	2.2	2.2	0.5	0.4
Bank deposits	17.1	17.3	3.5	3.3
Current accounts and cash	4.1	2.4	0.8	0.5
Total	100.0	100.0	20.2	19.1

Source: Building Society Fact Book, 1985.

liquid assets. The decision by the Inland Revenue in 1984 to tax societies' profits derived from their holdings of gilt-edged securities has further influenced the observed trends, and there has been a definite shift by societies away from listed investments and towards unlisted investments and mortgage loans. In addition, the increasing use being made by societies of the wholesale money markets is likely to reduce the importance of the cushion of liquid assets held, as it is possible to raise substantial amounts of funds at short notice (and often on fairly attractive terms) from these markets.

Reserve Requirements

An important part of the prudential constraints upon building societies was the requirement that they maintained certain reserve ratios (defined as total reserves divided by total assets). Reserves may be thought of as a measure of societies' net worth, since they represent the difference between total assets and liabilities (including investors' balances), that is, they can be considered as a measure of the solvency margin of societies. These reserves are required in order to meet possible mortgage and investment losses, and to a certain extent they act as the balance sheet counterpart to the purchase of fixed assets and equipment, and hence are important to the longer-term expansion of societies.

Although no statutory requirement existed pertaining to reserve ratios, there was a requirement concerning eligibility for trustee status. The regulations were embodied in the Building Societies (Designation for Trustee Investment) Regulations 1972, and amendments were made in 1977 and 1982 raising the minimum total assets required for trustee status from £1 million to £2.5 million, and from £2.5 million to £10 million respectively. In addition, the 1981 Authorisation Regulations specified that a minimum of £50,000 in reserves and/or deferred shares must be held for trustee status to be granted. The regulations provided a sliding scale for required reserve ratios such that reserves should not be less than:

2.5 per cent of assets not exceeding £100 million;
2.0 per cent of assets exceeding £100 million but not exceeding £500 million;
1.5 per cent of assets exceeding £500 million but not exceeding £1,000 million;
1.25 per cent of assets exceeding £1,000 million.

Societies may add to their reserves by generating an operating surplus (which is basically the difference between normal income and normal expenditure flows), or they may earn exceptional income from realized profits on sales of securities. Table 4.6 illustrates the derivation of the addition to reserves for societies in aggregate during 1984.

Table 4.7 shows a less detailed breakdown of the additions to reserves for the years 1978 to 1984. It may be observed that whilst the additions to reserves as a proportion of mean assets have been on a generally upwards trend during the first half of the 1980s, this was largely due to profits on investments rather than the generation of operating surpluses. Investment profits tend to be highest at times when market rates of interest are declining from historically high levels, since there exists an inverse relationship between interest rates and fixed coupon security prices. The

Table 4.6
The Derivation of Additions to Reserves for UK Building
Societies, 1984

	£m	£ per £100 mean assets
Normal income		
Mortgage interest	8,844	9.38
Investment and bank interest	1,654	1.76
Commission	262	0.28
Rents	22	0.02
Others (net)	13	0.01
Total	10,795	11.45
Normal expenditure		
Management expenses	1,110	1.18
Share deposits and loan interest	6,900	7.32
Income tax on interest	2,240	2.38
Corporation tax	236	0.25
Total	10,486	11.13
Normal income less normal expenditure	309	0.32
Investment profits and other items (net)	313	0.34
Added to general reserves	622	0.66

Source: *BSA Bulletin*, January 1985.

pressure on operating margins in recent years has been due largely to the more intense competition for retail funds, and hence their higher marginal costs.

Indeed, the aggregate management expense ratio for the societies in aggregate has been increasing only slowly in recent years, and in fact actually declined in 1983, which is perhaps a further manifestation of the growing competitive pressure on the sector's activities. Nevertheless, despite these developments, not only did reserves continue to grow in absolute terms, but also the reserve ratio reached its highest value for six years in 1983. However, the decision of the Inland Revenue to subject profits from the sale of gilts to corporation tax had a marked effect on the net investment profit level for 1984. It was undoubtedly this factor which

Table 4.7

Building Society Reserves, 1978 to 1984

| Year | Amount added to reserves | | | | | | Reserves end-year | Reserve ratio end-year |
| | Income less expenditure | | Investment profits | | Total amount added to reserves | | | |
	£m	£ per £100 mean assets	£m	£ per £100 mean assets	£m	£ per £100 mean assets	£m	%
1978	142	0.38	70	0.19	212	0.57	1,477	3.73
1979	127	0.30	38	0.09	164	0.39	1,641	3.58
1980	180	0.36	67	0.13	247	0.49	1,888	3.51
1981	265	0.46	127	0.22	392	0.68	2,280	3.69
1982	214	0.32	310	0.46	524	0.78	2,804	3.84
1983	192	0.24	496	0.63	688	0.87	3,491	4.07
1984	351	0.37	275	0.29	626	0.66	4,117	4.01

Source: Building Society Fact Book, p. 22.

slowed the rate of growth of reserves and consequently caused the reserve ratio to decline during 1984.

There are good reasons for believing that building societies will find it necessary to pay more attention to their 'profitability' in the future. A major factor in this respect relates to the reform of the legislation on building societies which at least some members of the sector have taken advantage of in order to diversify their activities away from their traditional areas of expertise and to engage in more risky operations. In particular, some societies have chosen to offer facilities for unsecured lending to customers, which by necessity will imply a more highly capitalized organization if the level of financial integrity is to be maintained.

Similarly, the setting-up costs for new technology, such as automatic teller machines (ATMs) and home banking facilities may be very substantial, and there is still much uncertainty over their likely effects on overall operating costs. Indeed, it was made quite plain by the Chief Registrar, in his reports for 1983 and 1984, that societies may have to change their priorities from building up market shares to building up reserves if they are to take full advantage of the wider powers available under the new legislation. The increased volatility in their operational environment has merely served to accentuate the potential problems awaiting societies in the future. To give but one example, between 1970 and 1984 the ratio of withdrawals from building society accounts to the average balance in those accounts rose from 21.6 per cent to 64 per cent. This increased propensity for investors to switch funds between societies in search of the best return offers definite implications for both societies' reserves and liquidity positions.

The Taxation Position of Building Societies

The Composite Tax Arrangement

Since 1894 building societies have been subject to a special arrangement through which they discharge the tax liability of their depositors in respect of interest payments received. This is known as the composite tax arrangement, and it was introduced primarily for the administrative convenience of the Inland Revenue. Quite simply, building societies are charged at a rate of tax (the composite rate) on gross interest payments which generates the same amount of tax revenue as would have been raised had the gross interest payments been distributed and then the recipients taxed at their basic rate. So long as some building society investors are below the income tax threshold, the composite rate will always be set below the basic rate of income tax. As a result of this arrangement, basic rate taxpayers receive their building society interest net of composite tax rate but have no further tax liability to discharge. Investors paying higher rate income tax incur a further charge equal to the difference between their marginal rate of tax and the basic rate (not the composite rate). Investors below the income tax threshold are unable to reclaim the composite rate tax paid on their behalf by the building society. This system was consolidated in the Income and Corporation Taxes Act 1970, and initially it applied only to investments with societies up to fixed limits. However, since 6 April 1985 there have been no limits to the amounts which fall within the composite rate system.

Many commentators have argued that the composite rate system, unique to building societies until April 1985, conferred upon them a competitive advantage relative to other retail intermediaries and especially to the banks. For example, in April 1984 the Building Societies Association (BSA) advised net ordinary share rate was 6.25 per cent, which was the equivalent of a gross share rate of 8.93 per cent to basic rate (30 per cent) taxpayers. However, at this time the composite rate was 25.25 per cent, meaning that the interest grossed up at the composite rate was 8.36 per cent. Thus, building societies were able to advertise a gross eqivalent ordinary share rate for basic rate taxpayers of 8.93 per cent whilst incurring a total interest cost of only 8.36 per cent gross. However, it should be recognized that on many occasions building societies' net ordinary share rate has been above the clearing banks' 7-day notice deposit account rate which formerly paid interest gross. Thus, whatever competitive advantage building societies have had *vis-à-vis* banks, it cannot have been wholly attributable to the composite rate system.

The competitive situation of the banks worsened somewhat in the first half of the 1980s with the tendency for an increasing proportion of building society accounts to offer premiums over the ordinary share rate. In 1980, for example, over 80 per cent of all share and deposit balances with societies were in ordinary share accounts. By 1984, however, only 32 per cent were in this type of account, with almost 45 per cent of balances being in short-notice accounts which offered a premium rate of interest in return for some amount of notice of withdrawal. A further 20 per cent of balances were in the form of term accounts, which typically offered a guaranteed premium over the ordinary share rate in return for a fixed term commitment from the investor.

The extent to which the composite arrangement has in fact conferred a fiscal privilege upon building societies has been questioned within the sector itself. The BSA, for example, points out that the composite arrangement does not permit societies to pay interest gross to their depositors, nor does it allow their non-taxpaying customers to claim rebates from the Inland Revenue for tax which had been deducted for them by societies but for which they were not in fact liable. The argument continues that although it is true that the system does allow building societies to pay attractive rates to taxpaying investors, they are in fact being subsidized at the expense of the non-taxpaying investors. Indeed, building societies could be at a competitive disadvantage *vis-à-vis* banks for non-paying customers due to the composite system. For whereas the banks could offer a net return of 6.25 per cent to their non-taxpaying customers at a cost to themselves of 6.25 per cent, for building societies the cost of providing an equivalent net rate would be 8.36 per cent as was shown above. The position has been summarized by the BSA as follows:

Whether or not the arrangement gives building societies a competitive advantage in the savings market depends solely upon the interest sensitivity of taxpayers and non-taxpayers . . . It can only be said that building societies possess a competitive advantage if the additional savings attracted from the taxpayer by virtue of the gross equivalent yield being higher than the cost of funds to societies is not counteracted by reduced receipts of savings from those not liable to tax, whose gross yield is considerably lower than the cost to societies of paying the interest. It is impossible to quantify the relative interest sensitivity of taxpayers and non-taxpayers and so the competitive effects of the composite rate system will probably never be accurately measured.

(*BSA Bulletin*, 'Building societies and taxation')

The Committee of London Clearing Banks in their evidence to the Wilson Committee argued that taxpaying investors were more interest-sensitive than their non-taxpaying counterparts, and hence they concluded that the composite rate arrangement did confer a competitive advantage on the building society movement. Although the BSA do concede that this is probably the case, since non-taxpaying society investors are comprised primarily of children and the elderly, they do argue that banks did in the past gain some advantage from being able to offer interest gross. Investors may, for example, prefer to have their interest paid gross since they may be able to use the interest for up to 12 months before paying tax on it. Furthermore, the BSA argue that the clearing banks possess a considerable fiscal privilege to the extent that many current account holders pay no bank charges, since notional interest paid on current accounts is more than enough to offset the charges incurred. Since this notional interest is not taxable the building societies argue that current account holders are able to purchase banking services out of tax-free income, and that the annual loss of tax revenue to the exchequer is substantial.

In the past the composite rate has been agreed between the Inland Revenue and the Building Societies Association in the May or June of the fiscal year in question. In order that the Inland Revenue may meet its legal obligations to raise as much money through the composite rate system as it would raise if all investors were assessed and taxed separately, it periodically undertakes a sample survey of building society accounts. For example the 1978/79 survey, which was used to calculate the composite rate for 1981/82, sampled 140,000 accounts: 1 in 700 containing less than £1,000; 1 in 75 containing between £1,000 and £15,000; and 1 in 20 containing more than £15,000. As a result of that survey, the Inland Revenue estimated that 85 per cent of the interest paid by building societies went to basic rate taxpayers, and thus the composite rate was set at 85 per cent of the basic income tax rate, that is, at 25.5 per cent. Clearly, as tax allowances alter so too will the proportion of building society investors who do not pay tax. Table 4.8 shows the composite tax rate for the years since 1970, and the implied percentage of building society investors who were not liable to pay basic rate tax.

Table 4.8
Composite Tax Rates and the Implied Percentage of Building Society Deposits Held by Non-Taxpayers 1970/1 to 1985/6

Financial year	Composite rate of tax	Basic rate of income tax	Composite rate as % of basic rate	Implied % of non-taxpayers
1970/71	32.75	41.25	79.4	20.6
1971/72	31.00	38.75	80.0	20.0
1972/73	30.00	38.75	77.4	22.6
1973/74	23.50	30.0	78.3	21.7
1974/75	26.25	33.0	79.5	20.5
1975/76	27.75	35.0	79.3	20.7
1976/77	27.75	35.0	79.3	20.7
1977/78	24.25	34.0	71.3	28.7
1978/79	22.50	33.0	68.2	31.8
1979/80	21.00	30.0	70.0	30.0
1980/81	22.50	30.0	75.0	25.0
1981/82	25.50	30.0	85.0	15.0
1982/83	25.25	30.0	84.2	15.8
1983/84	25.00	30.0	83.3	16.7
1984/85	25.25	30.0	84.2	15.8
1985/86	25.25	30.0	84.2	15.8

Sources: *BSA Bulletin*, 'Building societies and taxation'; *BSA News*, January 1985.

The most noticeable feature since the late 1970s has been the sharp rise in the composite rate as a percentage of basic income tax rate, and the consequent decrease in the implied percentage of building society deposits held by non-taxpayers. This trend obviously tended to diminish any tax advantage which might have accrued to building societies from the operation of the composite rate system.

The fall in the implied share of building society deposits held by non-taxpayers probably reflects both the building societies' success in penetrating the taxpayer market, aided by their supposed fiscal privilege, and also their loss of non-taxpaying investors to competing institutions which have been able to pay interest gross in the past. Also, the effects of inflation on real tax thresholds has tended to push more building society depositors into the tax net since the late 1970s. In addition to this, during the early 1980s nominal interest rates rose to relatively high levels, and this tended to magnify the margin between the net rates being offered by societies and by other institutions. In 1980, for example, the ordinary share rate stood at 10.5 per cent net (and gross to non-taxpayers) which was equivalent to 15.0 per cent gross to basic rate taxpayers. Thus in effect, taxpayers were being offered by societies a gross rate which exceeded that being offered to non-taxpayers by some 4.5 per cent. This was clearly a great incentive for non-taxpayers to overcome their interest-insensitivity and to transfer their funds to competing savings institutions in order to receive a higher gross (and net) return.

There have been calls for the abolition of the composite tax arrangement from bodies such as the National Consumer Council and the Wilson Committee. The latter came to the conclusion that the composite arrangement permitted building societies to offer higher rates of interest to depositors, and to charge lower rates to borrowers, than would otherwise be possible, and hence that societies were endowed with a competitive advantage over other institutions. The committee recommended that a unified system of taxation for interest payments should be introduced which would cover all deposit-taking institutions, and which would allow non-taxpayers to receive interest payments gross.

As mentioned above, a major advantage of the composite rate system is that it is extremely convenient for administrative purposes for the Inland Revenue. Also, by its very nature, it ensures that all tax payments due on building society interest are received by the authorities. No such guarantee exists where interest is paid gross and investors are asked to declare the payments on their annual tax returns. In fact, mainly due to these factors, the composite rate arrangement was ultimately extended to other private sector deposit-taking institutions which had previously been allowed to pay interest gross. But whilst the clearing banks had long been claiming that the arrangement conferred a fiscal privilege on building societies, it had been their hope that the imbalance would be removed by the abolition of the composite rate system. Examination of the relative interest rate structures for banks and building societies in mid-1984, as shown in Table 4.9, should provide the reason for banks' reluctance to take on the composite tax rate.

Using the composite rate which previously applied to building societies, it may be seen that in 1984 the banks were particularly uncompetitive *vis-à-vis* the societies. At the prevailing rates the banks would have had to advertise their 7-day deposit rate of 5.7 per cent gross as 4.29 per cent net, worth 6.13 per cent to the basic rate taxpayer under a composite arrangement, and this would thus have compared very unfavourably with the building society share and 7-day grossed-up rates of 8.93 per cent and 10.36 per cent respectively. It is quite clear that having to publish their rates net, thus allowing direct comparison with societies' net rates of interest, would make the clearers' uncompetitiveness far more transparent. However, despite the objections of the clearing banks, a common composite rate was introduced for both banks and building societies for the 1984/5 tax year, although it is planned to undertake a wider survey of depositors so that a more accurate rate may be calculated for use in the 1988/9 tax year and beyond. The new regulations dictate that the composite rate should be decided by 31 December in the year prior to the fiscal year in question, rather than in the May or June of that year as previously was the case. Furthermore, the composite rate is

Table 4.9

Clearing Banks' and Building Societies' Interest Rates, Pre-Tax and Post-Tax, mid-1984

	Net of tax non-taxpayers (%)	Grossed at 25.25% cost to the institution (%)	Grossed at 30% to basic rate taxpayer (%)
Building societies			
Share account	6.25	8.36	8.93
7-day account	7.25	9.70	10.36
Extra interest account	7.50	10.03	10.71
Banks			
7-day account	4.29	5.75	6.13
Extra interest account	6.54	8.75	9.34
Non-taxpayer account	5.75	7.61	8.29

Source: Lloyds Bank Economic Bulletin, no. 67, July 1984.

to be set so as to reflect changing tax rates, levels of income and personal allowances.

It seems questionable as to whether the extension of the composite rate system to other deposit-taking institutions has in fact achieved fiscal neutrality between such institutions, as advocated by the Wilson Committee. It is now the case that both banks and building societies are at a fiscal disadvantage with respect to the National Savings movement, which can still pay interest gross to investors. It may also be argued that the composite rate does not apply quite so rigorously to the clearing banks as to building societies. For example, the clearing banks are permitted to pay interest gross on deposit accounts and high interest current accounts held in their offshore centres such as the Channel Islands and the Isle of Man, where the composite rate does not apply. This in effect provides a tax loophole for bank customers since they can approach their high street branch and open an account in, say, Jersey, and have the interest paid gross into an onshore account. This loophole is effectively closed to building societies which have no such branches, and have been actively discouraged from opening them. Early in 1984, for example, the UK authorities blocked plans by the Halifax Building Society to set up an offshoot in the Isle of Man in order to take deposits and pay interest gross. The problem was that since existing legislation did not permit building societies to set up or make payments to subsidiaries, it was felt that the Halifax would not be in a position to stand behind its offshoot should it run into difficulties.

The clearing banks are still permitted to pay interest before tax to corporate bodies and on certificates of deposit and time deposits of £50,000 or more, although the latter two provisions have also been extended to building societies in recent years. The ability of societies to pay interest gross on certificates of deposit was essential for them to be able to raise funds in the wholesale money markets in an appreciable way, since interest paid net of tax would not have been acceptable to the markets. Consequently, the first Finance Act of 1983 included a clause permitting societies to pay interest gross on certificates of deposit of £50,000 or more and with a maturity of less than 12 months. The issue of certificates of deposit, however, was restricted to societies with assets in excess of £2,000 million, and hence only the largest building societies are able to issue such certificates. Also, since the autumn of 1983, societies have been able to pay interest gross on wholesale time deposits.

Corporation Tax

It was not until 1932 that building societies were first taxed on their 'trading profits'. Between 1973 and 1984 they were subject to a special rate of 40 per cent on their operating surplus, that is, the excess of normal income over normal expenditure. As the clearing banks, in common with most other companies until April 1984, paid a higher 52 per cent rate of corporation tax, the clearers frequently alleged that building societies were in a privileged position. They have argued that this advantage *vis-à-vis* clearing banks was further compounded by virtue of societies' mutual status which allowed them to amass reserves instead of paying out surpluses to shareholders, and due also to building societies not having to pay capital gains tax on the sale of government securities.

However, the argument that building societies are doubly privileged by virtue of being able to retain their surpluses as well as paying a special rate of corporation tax on those surpluses ignores two important considerations. In the first place it was precisely because of their mutual status that building societies and other mutual organizations were granted a special rate of corporation tax. The special rate was introduced in 1973 with the imputational system of corporation tax. The inability of mutual institutions such as building societies to pay dividends would have meant that they could not benefit from the imputational system's partial relief for distributions, and this would have left them disadvantaged relative to their position prior to 1973, and also relative to other institutions. Secondly, banks have in the past been able to reduce their liability to corporation tax via their leasing activities, an option which was not open to building societies. Although the correctness or otherwise of the 40 per cent special rate for societies may be debatable, evidence has been produced which suggests that it is misleading to focus solely on the nominal rates of corporation tax payable by banks and building societies, since by taking advantage of their leasing operations banks have been able to reduce their real corporation tax rate well below the nominal rate. Table 4.10 shows the actual tax rate paid by the 'big four' banks as the proportion of pre-tax profits paid as corporation tax for the years 1984 and 1985. These proportions are fairly typical of their results, at least since the late 1970s.

It may be observed that for the 'big four' clearing banks the actual rate of corporation tax paid was well below the nominal rate. For 1985, for example, the average actual rate of tax paid was only 26.0 per cent, as compared to the then existing 41.25 per cent nominal rate. It is also interesting to note that the clearing banks appeared to become more adept at reducing their corporation tax liability from the mid-1970s onwards. However, in order to place these figures in perspective they should be compared with the corresponding figures for the building society sector. Table 4.11 shows that, in contrast to the clearing banks, building societies have tended to pay a rate of corporation tax on their operating surpluses which has been very close to the nominal rate of 40 per cent (ruling until April 1984), and which has been fairly stable in recent years.

In addition to their operating surpluses, building societies have often made profits from their investments in gilt-edged securities, and prior to 1984 these were not subject to corporation tax since societies were not deemed to be traders in gilts. However, consideration of the actual corporation tax rate on building societies' total gross surplus (including investment profits) shows that although it has been somewhat below the nominal rate of 40 per cent, at least until 1982 it was still well above the actual rate paid by the clearing banks.

Whatever the previous position of banks and building societies in respect of their liability to corporation tax, it is likely that the balance between the two institutions will

Table 4.10

Major UK Clearing Banks' Profits and Tax Charges, 1984 and 1985

Bank	1984			1985		
	Pre-tax profit £m	Tax charge £m	Tax rate %	Pre-tax profit £m	Tax charge £m	Tax rate %
Barclays	623	165	26.5	854	261	30.6
Lloyds	468	136	29.1	561	124	22.1
Midland	135	55	40.7	351	88	25.1
National Westminster	671	80	11.9	804	195	24.3
Total	1,897	436	23.0	2,570	668	26.0

Source: Annual reports and accounts, 1985.

Table 4.11

UK Building Societies: Gross Surplus and Tax Charges, 1978 to 1985

	Gross operating surplus	Total gross surplus	Corporation tax charged in BS accounts	Corporation tax as % of operating surplus	Corporation tax as % of total surplus
1978	232	302	90	38.8	29.8
1979	208	245	81	38.9	33.1
1980	293	360	113	38.6	31.4
1981	420	544	153	36.4	28.1
1982	331	641	117	35.3	18.3
1983	292	788	100	34.2	12.7
1984	545	858	236	43.3	7.5
1985	1,189	1,281	480	40.4	37.5

Source: Building Society Fact Book, 1985.

improve in the future in this respect. Banks are no longer in such a favourable leasing position since measures were announced in the 1984 budget which led to the phasing out of first year capital allowances by April 1986, and hence to a reduction in the tax advantages of leasing. For building societies, the progressive reduction in the corporation tax rate, again announced in the 1984 budget, to a common lower rate of 35 per cent will eradicate whatever privilege societies previously derived from their special rate of corporation tax.

As mentioned earlier, building societies were formerly not deemed to be dealers in gilt-edged securities, and hence the only tax liability they incurred in respect of gilts was on dividend payments and on capital gains arising from their sale. However, societies were exempt from capital gains tax liability so long as they held their gilts for over one year, and since most of the profits made by societies were on gilts held for more than one year there was, in effect, no tax liability on societies' investment profits. In other respects the tax treatment of societies was very similar to that of individuals and companies. By contrast, the treatment of banks has always been different because they are deemed to be traders in gilts, and hence any profits realized from such trading have been treated as trading income and taxed as such at the banks' corporation tax rate. The banks have for a long time argued that building societies should be taxed in the same way on their gilts' profits, and on 23 February 1984 an announcement was made by the Inland Revenue that from midnight on the same day building societies' profits from gilts transactions would be taxed at the special corporation tax rate of 40 per cent (or 38 per cent for those societies whose corporation tax surplus did not exceed £100,000). It was the stated opinion of the Inland Revenue that societies were no longer holding gilts purely as a long-term investment but were beginning to trade much more actively in gilts, and henceforth would be treated in a fashion comparable with the treatment of banks in this respect.

The decision to alter the tax treatment of building societies' profits from gilts was not only taken very suddenly, but it was also quite unexpected because since the time that societies entered the gilts market on a large scale in the late 1970s many of the gilts purchased by societies had been issued specifically with them in mind. That is, several issues of gilts were made offering only low yields (of 2½ or 3 per cent) which were subject to tax, but which guaranteed a good tax-free capital gain. Furthermore, the gilts were designed so that, for example, dividend payment dates would be such that the tax liability for societies would be minimized. Consequently, societies' share of shorter-dated gilts rose sharply from 10.6 per cent in 1975 to 23.9 per cent in 1983, with the 'big five' societies being the keenest participants. However, in support of the Inland Revenue's decision, it is the case that many societies in the 1980s have been treating the capital gains from gilt sales as normal income in order to compensate for the reduced operating margins which had resulted from the fierce competition for retail funds and from the high interest accounts introduced by many societies in order to attract savings. Traditionally, profits on the sale of gilts have been treated not as normal income but as exceptional income. To the extent that some societies were not following their traditional accounting practice, then the authorities might legitimately argue that if these investments profits were being treated as trading income (which is subject to corporation tax), then they should no longer be exempt from corporation tax on these profits.

Over the longer term it is likely that the change in the taxation of gilts profits for building societies will have significant effects on the mode of their operations. Because it has been the tax-free profits from gilts which have allowed many societies to maintain very slim operating margins in recent years, it seems likely that margins will have to be widened in the future. This means either that borrowers will have to pay more on mortgages or that rates to investors will have to be reduced, and the initial response from societies seemed to indicate that the latter would be the case. However, the competition which societies face on both sides of their balance sheets presents them with a difficult problem in this regard, and societies may be faced with the necessity of increasing mortgage lending not by attracting more savings but by reducing liquidity in order to shift their asset portfolios away from gilts, although this action is obviously limited in its scope. Apart from increasing mortgage assets, the options open to building societies to diversify away from gilts are somewhat narrow given the regulations surrounding the deployment of their liquid assets.

The Recommended Rate System

Between 1939 and 1983 the setting of interest rates in the building society sector was strongly influenced by the Council of the Building Societies Association. The BSA Council met once a month and recommended the rate of interest to be paid on ordinary share accounts. By convention, rates of interest on deposit accounts tended to be set at a margin of 0.25 per cent below the recommended ordinary share rate. Between 1977 and 1981 the BSA Council also recommended maximum rates to be paid on term shares and subscription shares. The maximum margin for term shares, which were introduced in the mid-1970s, ranged from 0.5 per cent over ordinary share rates for a two-year-term share to 2 per cent over a five-year-term share. The margin for subscription shares was typically a maximum of 1¼ per cent above ordinary share rates. In addition, the BSA Council also recommended rates to be set on annuity mortgages, and although no recommendation was made concerning endowment mortgages, the majority of societies tended to charge 0.5 per cent above the annuity rate.[6]

The interest rate decision took place on two levels. First, the BSA Council had to decide upon the absolute level of the basic interest rate structure, and given competition for retail funds this decision could not be made without reference to prevailing market rates of interest if the desired inflow of funds was to be achieved. Secondly, the margin between investment and borrowing rates had to be determined. As mentioned earlier, smaller societies are required to hold higher reserve ratios than larger societies, and since reserves can only be added to from yearly surpluses the BSA had to ensure that the margin of the borrowers' rate over the investors' rate was sufficient to allow the smaller, and perhaps less efficient, societies to generate adequate surpluses in order to maintain their reserve ratios.

Although the BSA's decision regarding the recommended rate structure began with a consideration of the desired level of mortgage lending, it was not the BSA's intention to adjust rates so as to satisfy mortgage demand at every point in time. To quote from a statement by the BSA:

> Building societies generally seek to chart a middle course on interest rates and do not react immediately to every change in competing rates . . . At a time of rising rates societies do not wish to impose additional burdens on . . . borrowers unless it is absolutely necessary.
> (*Studies in Building Society Activity 1980–1981*, BSA, March 1982, p. 24)

Thus, building society interest rates tended to adjust sluggishly relative to market rates as societies charted a 'middle course' over the interest rate cycle. However, since the early 1980s building society interest rates have tended to adjust more quickly, and to move in line with prevailing market rates. In the 1970s the BSA interest rate policy resulted in building society rates being above or below market rates for long periods, as is evidenced in Figure 4.1. When market rates were rising building societies tended to become uncompetitive in the market for funds, and this led to a lack of available mortgage finance. Conversely, when market rates were falling the competitive position of societies improved, as did the availability of mortgage funds. Thus, the interest rate setting strategy of the BSA resulted in the so-called 'feast' or 'famine' characteristic in the UK mortgage market, and this occurred despite the building societies' tendency to use liquid asset holdings as a sort of buffer stock to even out the flow of mortgages over the interest rate cycle.

A major consequence of the recommended rate system was that mortgage lending rates were kept below market clearing levels in most periods, and hence there was often a

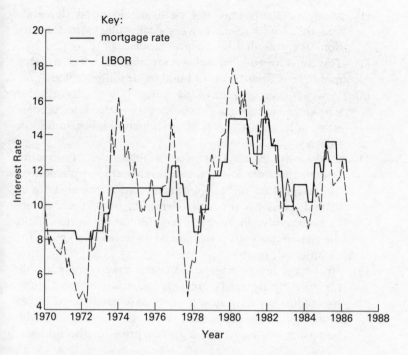

Figure 4.1 Building Society Mortgage Rate and 3-Month LIBOR, Monthly Averages, 1970 to 1986

Source: *BSA Bulletin and Financial Statistics*, various issues.

serious excess demand for mortgage loans. Furthermore, being unable to ration mortgage loans by price, societies had to resort to non-price rationing, and the presence of mortgage queues was commonplace. Indeed, non-price rationing has often been based on loan/income and loan/value ratios, characteristics of the prospective borrower (such as whether he is a first-time borrower or an existing owner-occupier) and length of saving record.[7] However, the inefficiency associated with the non-price forms of allocation is widely recognized. For example, the Stow Report (1979) drew attention to some of the major problems:

117

(1) Mortgage loans may not be available upon demand, and this could result in very costly delays in transactions for potential house purchasers.

(2) The housing construction sector may be affected detrimentally if cash flows to builders are interrupted.

(3) When individuals have to move home urgently for employment reasons, they may be forced to borrow from alternative sources at much higher rates of interest.

(4) Investment in housing may be made very rewarding when artificially low mortgage rates are supplemented by tax relief on mortgage interest and in the absence of capital gains tax on realized profits from house sales. Consequently, individuals have an incentive to obtain the maximum loan possible and to defer repayment for as long as possible.

(5) Artificially low mortgage loan rates may be responsible for exerting upwards pressure on house prices. Thus, the reduction in housing costs associated with lower mortgage rates may well have been offset by the borrower having to pay a higher price for the house.

Aside from the specific problems associated with mortgage rationing there are other costs which may be identified with and attributed to the BSA's recommended rate system. The fact that the BSA set rates to ensure that all societies operated on margins which were sufficient to ensure that adequate surpluses were generated could be said to have led to a lack of incentive to cut costs generally, since the cartel to a certain extent protected inefficiency. This point was emphasized as early as 1966 by the National Board for Prices and Incomes.

With price competition to a large extent precluded by the recommended rate system, it might be expected that the commercial pressures affecting the activities of building societies would lead to the growth of non-price competition, and in fact this is precisely what did occur, particularly in terms of intensified branching activity. In the 1960s, for example, the annual rate of growth in the number of branches varied between 4.4 per cent and 8.7 per cent, whereas in the 1970s it varied between 8.9 per cent and 12.2 per cent. Whereas in 1970 there were 2,016 building society branches, by 1980 the figure had reached 5,684. To the extent that branch proliferation of this magnitude would not have been necessary in an environment of price competition, the recommended rate system may be considered to have been wasteful of resources. Aside from the economic resource costs to the nation of this form of competition, it is also likely that it had cost implications for building societies themselves. The 1966 Report of the National Board for Prices and Incomes concluded that the management expenses of building societies would appear to have risen relative to the work done, mainly because of the rapid expansion of branch offices.

The recommended rate system tended to be defended by the BSA on two main grounds. First, that the cartel was unique in the sense that it kept the price of credit low rather than high as one would expect from a normal cartel situation. Indeed, this is the major reason why the building societies' 'cartel' was exempted from the 1976 restrictive practices legislation. Secondly, that the cartel attempted to balance the interests of both depositors and borrowers. This position was put very strongly by the then chairman of the BSA, Ralph Stow, in 1978:

> Even though building societies are managing to maintain an exceptionally low lending rate and high borrowing rate, there are critics of the industry who suggest that there is a cartel, and this, *per se*, is monopolistic. People think of a cartel as being an undesirable organisation which seeks to keep prices up, yet there is no doubt that the main effect of the system of recommended rates of interest which the BSA practise is to keep rates of interest down.
>
> At the present time the mortgage rate is below the market clearing level and thus if there were a free for all and no recommendations in respect of interest rates societies would be tempted for inter-competition reasons to raise their rates of interest all round knowing that they have little difficulty in lending out the money to house purchasers.

119

> Societies being mutual institutions, which operate without the profit motive have no need of special arrangements to increase their operating margins and the whole purpose of the recommended rates system is to bring about as far as possible the best balance of benefits between existing investing and borrowing members, but on a voluntary basis so far as member societies are concerned.
>
> *(Building Society Affairs*, no. 93, March 1978)

However, despite the absence of an explicit profit motive the BSA can be criticized for having set margins which were wider than necessary for the majority of societies. Although the motive was to protect the smaller, less efficient, societies (which itself tended to propagate inefficiency and raise the industry's costs), the result was that the more efficient societies were able to work with substantial margins. Nevertheless, as the report of the Wilson Committee pointed out, the use of an average for administrative expenses in calculating recommended rates did exert some pressure on inefficient societies to reduce their expenses. But the report also went on to say that

> Only an extremely inefficient society could not compensate for this by charging a modest amount more for mortgages. There is, therefore, little competitive pressure to weed out the more inefficient societies and only limited incentives for the most efficient societies to keep their expenses below average.
>
> (Wilson, 1980, p. 108)

In considering the absolute structure of building society interest rates it is clear that although the BSA were attempting to protect the interests of their borrowing members by keeping rates below market clearing levels, they were actually discriminating against potential borrowers by so doing as they were unable to meet the full demand for loans at the artificially low rates. Moreover, the claims made that the recommended rate system provided for equity between borrowing and investing members of societies has been disputed by several commentators. For example, Gough and Taylor (1979) argue that a necessary consequence of keeping borrowing costs low was that the interest rates paid to investors would also have to be kept at low levels. They pointed out that due to the effects of inflation both investors and borrowers faced negative net real rates of interest for much of the 1953–74 period. The increasingly negative real rates of interest in the 1970s resulted in a substantial transfer of wealth from savers to borrowers. Furthermore, the net savers in building societies tend to be more numerous than net borrowers, and whereas net savers tend to be older people widely distributed across the socioeconomic groups the net borrowers tend to be the younger and relatively well paid members of society. They therefore conclude that the losers from the system substantially outweighed the gainers, and that the cartel arrangement which held down the mortgage rate in favour of the borrower actually worsened the inequity between borrowing and investing members.

The demise of the recommended rate system may be said officially to have taken place in October 1983 when the BSA Council announced that recommended rates were to be replaced by advised rates. The recommended rate system had never been binding on societies, and participation in the recommended rate agreement was not a condition of membership of the BSA. Aside from adhering to the rates recommended by the council, participation in the cartel arrangement also entailed an interest rate undertaking by which societies agreed to notify each other of the interest rates they paid to investors and charged to borrowers, and to give 28 days' notice of changes in the basic rate on all investments. As from October 1983 this second part of the cartel arrangement also lapsed. From that time the previous interest rate undertaking was replaced by an information agreement which merely required prior notification of a change.

Although many of the smaller societies often chose to ignore the rates recommended by the BSA, the larger societies which held the bulk of the industry's assets tended to adhere to the system. In fact, under a Memorandum of

Agreement entered into with the government in 1973, the eighteen largest societies agreed that they would follow the interest rates recommended by the BSA. However, following the BSA's decision to abandon the recommended rate system in October 1983, all societies were set free to decide their own rates for borrowers and lenders. The BSA's decision was, in fact precipitated by the notice of withdrawal from the interest rate undertaking given by the Abbey National Building Society (the UK's second largest society) in September 1983. Without the formal notice of proposed interest rate changes it would be impossible for the BSA to maintain the operation of the cartel. However, the arrangement had been coming under increasing pressure for several years prior to this, and was becoming increasingly irrelevant to building society activities. At the time of its demise ordinary share accounts (the only ones on which the BSA Council formally recommended rates) held less than one-half of societies' aggregate deposits.

The activities of the smaller societies were always a source of frustration to the larger societies who adhered to the recommended rate system. These smaller societies were able to draw deposits away from the larger societies by offering more attractive rates to investors. Due to the excess demand, which was the feature of the mortgage market until recent years, they were able to on-lend these funds to eager borrowers at rates of interest which provided adequate margins to cover management expenses and a provision for surplus. However, it was always external competitive pressures which put the greatest pressure on the cartel and which were the single greatest factor leading to its demise. As financial conditions became more volatile during the early 1970s, societies found that they could not hold their interest rates as stable as they would have liked. Furthermore, in the search for greater inflows of funds societies began to offer an increasingly wide range of deposit facilities the position of which, relative to the recommended rate system, was often uncertain.

It was to be expected, with more retail funds being raised at rates above the recommended ordinary share rate, that more and more mortgage lending would be made at rates above the recommended annuity mortgage rate. This was indeed the case, and from the mid-1970s many societies were charging differential rates on mortgage loans over £15,000. Competitive pressures were further stimulated by the simultaneous upsurge in competition for mortgage loans from the banks, and for retail funds from the National Savings movement, during 1980 and 1981. The competition from National Savings was prompted by the government's desire to finance the public sector borrowing requirement in a non-inflationary way via the non-bank private sector. This entailed offering above-market rates on investments with the National Savings Bank, and attractive rates and terms on index-linked and non-indexed-linked Savings Certificates. In 1981/2, for example, the government targeted £3½ billion to be raised via National Savings.

The re-entry of the banks into the mortgage market at this time raises the obvious question as to why the banks had not entered the mortgage market in a big way previously, given the excess demand in the market. One of the primary reasons why the banks had chosen not to raise their share of the mortgage loan market was that they had been con-strained by official monetary controls throughout much of the 1970s. Nevertheless, at the beginning of the 1970s and prior to the introduction of the supplementary special deposits ('corset') scheme by the Bank of England in December 1973, the banks had accounted for about 10 per cent of mortgage loans. The corset was abandoned in June 1980, and whereas banks accounted for only 10 per cent of new mortgage loans in early 1981, by the end of that year the figure had risen to about 40 per cent of all net advances. The market share of building societies was correspondingly reduced from over 80 per cent in 1980 to just under 50 per cent by late 1981. The banks, however, began to reduce the amounts they earmarked for mortgage lending by late 1982, and by 1983 were taking a lower profile in the mortgage market.

There are a number of reasons why mortgage lending by banks began to slow down from late 1982. First, the period of rapid growth in lending in 1981/2 can be viewed partly as a period of stock adjustments in banks' loan portfolios following a period when they had been inhibited from lending as much as they would have liked in the mortgage market. Thus, it would be expected that there would be some slow-down in the rate of net new lending given that banks had been aiming to achieve a target percentage of their total loan portfolios in the form of mortgage loans. Secondly, the sharp rise in banks' longer-term lending led to concerns over capital ratios. Finally, the mortgage market became less profitable than it had been previously. The slice of the mortgage market originally targeted by the banks was that involved with larger loans, in relation to which building societies were charging size-related differentials. Initially, the banks were able to make substantial headway into this profitable sector of the market by undercutting the building societies' differential rates. However, once the building societies saw that their competitive position was being eroded and that their share of the market was falling rapidly, they began to take retaliatory action in an attempt to restore their former position. To begin with, the Woolwich and then other societies abandoned their differential mortgage rate policy on a temporary basis. As a consequence mortgage lending for the banks was made much less profitable, as they had to match the now lower building society rates. Furthermore, since the banks tended to have higher managerial expenses and operating costs than the building societies, and since they also had to provide costly money transmission services, the profitability of banks' mortgage business was highly dependent upon movements in the general level of interest rates. Nevertheless, the activities of the banks had served as an important catalyst in the erosion of the building societies' interest rate cartel. The competitive forces unleashed by this occurrence continue to have extremely important ramifications for the evolution of the building society sector.

The Performance of Building Societies

Technically, building societies are mutual institutions which are owned by their depositors and borrowers who are given voting rights, usually on a one-member one-vote basis. Consequently, the analysis of the commercial objectives of building societies is somewhat problematic. However, many commentators have argued that the concept of mutuality has become increasingly irrelevant in recent years, especially for the larger societies, and even the building societies legislation has tended to keep to the spirit rather than to the letter of mutuality. The problem is illustrated clearly by the fact that the Halifax Building Society (the UK's largest) had over 7.7 million members in 1983 as compared to the 100,000 shareholders of the UK's largest bank, the National Westminster Bank. The power of an individual ordinary member to influence managerial decisions of the building society is almost negligible. In fact, even for the smaller building societies, where there exists the possibility of members exercising some control, it is generally the case that relatively few turn up at annual general meetings. It is probably correct to assert that the majority of building society shareholders consider themselves as comparable to depositors with banks and are unaware of the full implications of their society membership.

Mutuality raises a difficult problem with regard to viewing profitability as an objective for societies since most of the members have no real interest in the profitability of their society. Furthermore, there is the irony that if a society aimed to maximize its profits this would have to be achieved at the expense of its own members. Thus building societies have traditionally not had profit maximization as an objective, but this is not to say that they do not make 'profits', which are usually described as 'surpluses' in their annual reports and accounts. As mentioned earlier, capital reserves are crucial to the operations and long-term growth of societies, and the only way for these reserves to be amassed is through the generation of surpluses. Thus, rather than being non-profit-making institutions, building societies may be better characterized as being non-profit-distributing institutions. The extent to which societies do strive for profits is still a source of great debate, but recent trends would imply that, in all probability, they will become more profit-oriented in the future.

Analysts have often assumed that building societies attempt to maximize the growth of their assets, and have constructed models of building society behaviour on this basis. However, this objective can never be fully divorced from the consideration of the surpluses which societies generate as these are crucial to the maintenance of minimum reserve ratios. Using a formula derived from the work of the Hardie Committee (which analysed the need for building societies to hold reserves), Parkin and Ghosh (1970) showed that the faster a society grows the larger must be the annual surplus generated. The appropriate formula is

$$S = \frac{G \times R}{0.5G + 100}$$

where S is annual surplus expressed as a percentage of mean assets in that year, G is percentage rate of growth of total assets, and R is reserve ratio at the beginning of the financial year. Table 4.12 shows the surplus needed for various rates of growth given a reserve ratio of 3.58 per cent.

However, the formula stated above does not help to determine what is the commercial objective of building societies. Rather than using the formula to argue that the higher is the annual surplus generated the higher can be the growth of the society, the formula can easily be manipulated

Table 4.12
Relationship between Net Surplus and Growth Rate

Growth rate (%)	Net surplus required (£ per £100 mean asset)
10	0.34
12	0.41
14	0.47
16	0.53
18	0.59
20	0.65

Source: BSA.

to show that the higher is the growth rate the higher can be the surplus generated for a given reserve ratio. This latter interpretation suggests that societies are attempting to maximize the surplus generated subject to a desired reserve ratio.

In general, it would appear that the success of building societies has been measured, by both academics and the societies themselves, by the growth of their assets, although as an objective measure of performance, both for individual societies and for the sector as a whole, this does have a number of drawbacks. An important issue in this respect is the effect of inflation on the real growth rate of assets. Table 4.13 illustrates the significant differences observed in nominal and real asset growth between 1970 and 1985.

Although total assets grew by approximately 1,013 per cent in nominal terms during the period 1970 to 1985, their real growth was only 118 per cent overall. It is also apparent

Table 4.13
The Effect of Inflation on Growth of Assets, 1970 to 1985

Year	Actual assets		Assets revalued at 1970 prices		Retail prices index increase
	£m	% increase	£m	% increase	%
1970	10,819	16.5	10,819	9.6	6.3
1971	12,919	19.4	11,808	9.1	9.4
1972	15,246	18.0	12,993	10.0	7.1
1973	17,545	15.1	13,702	5.5	9.2
1974	20,094	14.5	13,529	−1.3	16.1
1975	24,204	20.5	13,118	−3.0	24.2
1976	28,202	16.5	13,121	0.0	16.5
1977	34,288	21.6	17,766	4.9	15.8
1978	39,538	15.3	14,657	6.5	8.3
1979	45,789	15.8	14,968	2.1	13.4
1980	53,793	17.5	14,905	−0.4	18.0
1981	61,815	14.9	15,304	2.7	11.9
1982	73,033	18.1	16,655	8.8	8.6
1983	85,868	17.6	18,720	12.4	4.6
1984	102,688	19.6	21,313	13.9	5.0
1985	120,363	17.2	23,554	10.5	6.1

Source: *BSA Bulletin*, 'Building Society Performance Indicators'.

that in some years there was an absolute contraction of assets in real terms. For individual societies this growth indicator may be somewhat misleading simply because it is much easier for smaller societies to generate larger percentage growth figures since they are starting from a lower base. Furthermore, in the past, the pressure exerted on the larger societies by the recommended rate system, and by governments wishing to hold down mortgage loan interest rates, had made it easy for the smaller societies to offer attractive rates to investors and to charge correspondingly higher rates to borrowers who were unable to obtain mortgage loans elsewhere. Consequently these smaller societies were able to exhibit very favourable growth rates due simply to the constraints operating on other societies rather than to any superior efficiency on the part of themselves.

Reported growth rates for societies can also be markedly affected by the particular accounting period used by societies. Thus, for example, during the early months of 1983 building societies' deposit rates were relatively uncompetitive, and as a consequence the inflow of funds to societies was quite depressed. Therefore, other things being equal, a society with an accounting period covering the calendar year of 1983 would exhibit a lower annual rate of growth of assets than a society whose accounting period ran from 1 April 1983 to 31 March 1984. Clearly, it is necessary to compare the trends in asset growth over the longer term if meaningful results are to be derived.

The aggregate balance sheet of UK building societies at 30 September 1985 is shown in Table 4.14. This structure is typical of that which has been experienced throughout the past decade. The formal limitations on the non-mortgage loan assets which may be held have largely been responsible for the dominance of British government and government-guaranteed securities and local authority investments in the 19 per cent of the portfolio not accounted for by mortgage loans. However, a substantial amount of cash and bank balances is also held, as would be expected given the importance in the liabilities portfolio of retail deposits and shares with a relatively short average maturity.

Table 4.14

UK Building Societies: Aggregate Balance Sheet,
30 September 1985

	£m	%
Assets		
Cash and bank balances	5,032	4.4
Local authority investments	2,526	2.2
British government securities	10,457	9.1
Other investments	1,847	1.6
Mortgage loans	92,905	81.1
Other assets	1,808	1.6
Total assets	114,575	100.0
Liabilities		
Shares and deposits	100,211	87.5
Accrued interest	2,426	2.1
Other borrowing	4,520	3.9
Other liabilities and reserves	7,418	6.5
Total liabilities	114,575	100.0

Source: *BSA Bulletin*, January 1986.
Notes:

(1) 'Other investments' largely comprise overseas government securities, sterling certificates of deposit, tax instruments and Treasury bills.

(2) 'Other assets' largely comprise land, buildings and equipment.

(3) 'Other borrowing' comprises certificates of deposit, negotiable bonds, bank loans, and time deposits, net of building society certificates of deposit held by other building societies.

Growth and Building Society Branching

Given the constraints on price competition imposed by the recommended rate system prior to 1983, it was to be expected that the desire for faster growth amongst societies would surface in the form of non-price competition. The expansion of branch networks proved to be one of the most important channels for this activity. Davies and Davies (1981) argue that the evidence on building society branching

129

tends to support the view that a firm's share of total turnover in the market in which it operates increases more than proportionately with the size of the firm. In fact it was during the 1970s, when the rate of branching was at its height in the UK, that building societies in aggregate began to raise their share of the growing market in personal sector savings. The Wilson Committee offered further support for this broad view when it addressed the question of whether building societies with larger-than-average branch networks for their asset size were more successful at attracting new deposits. The evidence received by the committee suggested that:

> Societies with larger than average, but static, networks [were] no more successful than the average at attracting new deposits but [had] higher administrative costs. Societies in the process of expanding their branch networks, on the other hand, [did] appear to attract more new business than might otherwise be expected and [had] lower than average administrative costs.
>
> (Wilson, 1980)

Given the domination of the sector's asset holdings by the largest five societies, it is perhaps surprising that they accounted for only 39 per cent of all society branches at the end of 1982. This contrasts with Group B societies which, despite having only 9 per cent of the industry's assets, owned 16 per cent of the industry's branches. However, this may be explained, at least in part, by the fact that the larger societies tend to operate somewhat larger branches than their competitors, as is illustrated in Table 4.15.

It may be observed that the A_1 societies managed the accounts of over 8,600 shareholders per branch – more than twice as many as the A_2 societies. Furthermore, in value terms, the A_1 societies handled £15 million in share and deposit balances per branch in contrast to £8.4 million for the A_2 societies, and only £5.8 million for the B societies. Further evidence on the disparity in the size of branches between different categories of societies can be found by looking at employment statistics. At the end of 1982, for

Table 4.15
Building Society Branching

Group	Branches	Shareholders		Share & deposit balances	
		Total 000s	Per branch	Total £m	Per branch £m
A$_1$	2,554	22,100	8,653	38,418	15.0
A$_2$	2,252	9,067	4,026	18,891	8.4
B	1,043	3,147	3,017	6,021	5.8
C	511	1,704	3,335	3,761	7.4
D	120	574	4,783	1,316	11.0
All	6,480	36,609	5,649	68,423	10.6

Source: *BSA Bulletin*, 'Concentration and Mergers in the Building Society Industry'.

example, the largest societies had around eight full-time staff per branch in comparison to the A$_2$ societies with around four full-time staff and the B societies with three.

The distribution of branches amongst the different size categories has shown remarkable stability during the 1970s and early 1980s. The A$_1$ societies, for example, have maintained their share of total branches between 37 per cent and 39 per cent during this time period, while all societies with assets over £100m have maintained a share of around 88 per cent throughout the period. However, despite the stability in branch concentration there has still been an increasing concentration in terms of sector asset holdings, as the larger societies have tended to open the larger branches and have also benefited from the phenomenon mentioned above whereby market share increases proportionately faster than the number of branches maintained.

The preponderance of building society branches, particularly in the centre of towns, has come in for a great deal of criticism, especially from groups such as the Bow Group, and has been regarded as one of the undesirable but inevitable conseqences of the BSA cartel, which precluded price competition for all but the smaller societies and which led naturally to 'non-price' branch competition and later to competition in savings facilities. The Bow Group in January 1980 argued that

> If you walk down the high streets of any provincial town and compare it with the high streets of ten and twenty years ago the most obvious change is how on so many of the prime sites useful shops have been replaced by building society offices, whose emptiness of customers often seems to be a notable feature. Nor is there any end in sight to this process: although the number of building societies is falling as the smallest societies are swallowed up, there remains a large number of medium sized societies still largely regional in character but with ambitions to operate nationally. Unless some means of promoting rationalisation in the industry is invented . . . this trend is bound to continue.
>
> (Mabey and Tillet, 1980, p. 3)

However, just as the proliferation of society branches, particularly after 1970, was the natural outcome of increasing competition coupled with the BSA's recommended rate system, so the increasingly competitive financial environment combined with the effective demise of the cartel could have been expected to result in a deceleration of branch expansion within the industry. This is, in fact, precisely what happened during the early 1980s, as is shown in Table 4.16. Furthermore, it seems more than likely that this trend will continue into the future. The recent spate of merger announcements involving relatively large societies seems certain to continue as societies attempt to prepare themselves to use the wider powers which have recently been granted to them, and this seems certain to be accompanied by a rationalization of existing branch networks. However, it must also be recognized that there have been a number of aborted merger plans during 1985 and 1986 which perhaps raises questions on the true gains to be obtained by participating societies.

The US experience of major retailers entering the financial services industry by incorporating 'financial service centres' in existing stores at very little incremental cost, seems set to

132

Table 4.16
Growth of Building Society Branches

Year	No. of BS branches	Growth % p.a.
1970	2,016	11.6
1971	2,261	12.2
1972	2,522	11.5
1973	2,808	11.3
1974	3,099	10.4
1975	3,375	8.9
1976	3,696	9.5
1977	4,130	11.7
1978	4,595	11.3
1979	5,147	12.0
1980	5,684	10.4
1981	6,162	8.4
1982	6,480	5.2
1983	6,643	2.5
1984	6,816	2.6
1985	6,926	1.6

Source: *BSA Bulletin*, various issues.

be emulated in the UK with retailers such as British Home Stores and Marks and Spencer already having similar projects in the pipeline. The evidence from the USA suggests that this may well foster the demise of many building society and bank branches. Furthermore it seems likely that the increased use of technology in the form of automatic teller machines (ATMs) and home banking facilities will further reduce the need for large expensive branch networks. The Leicester Building Society (now Alliance and Leicester Building Society) introduced a very popular scheme called Leicestercard which obviates the need for excessive branching since customers can make deposits and withdrawals at their local post office. For those with access to a branch, the Leicestercard provides for instant withdrawals and deposits at an ATM. The Halifax Building Society also has its own ATM network offering a cashcard account which pays interest yet offers instant withdrawal and deposit facilities. The Nottingham Building Society in a collaborative effort with Prestel and the Royal Bank of

Scotland is already pioneering a home banking service in which transactions with the bank and building society can be originated and monitored using the Prestel system on the customer's own television set. Finally, societies such as the Anglia are pioneering electronic funds transfer at the point of sale (EFTPOS), which over the longer term is likely to reduce substantially the amount of cash required for everyday transactions. Again these developments, if they take off, would tend to obviate the need for extensive branch networks.

Although it has been argued that a number of factors suggest a diminished role for extensive branch networks in the future, it is unlikely branch networks will disappear entirely. The reason is that an emerging trend in recent years has been the development of financial institutions willing to offer a much wider range of financial and professional services than has hitherto been felt appropriate. The 'one-stop financial supermarket' described in the more popular press may not yet exist, but there is little doubt that the recent legislative changes in respect of building societies will offer to them the opportunity to participate in such developments should they wish to do so. This would seem to suggest that there will continue to be a role for branch networks in the future, whether it be as a centre for the provision of a wide range of financial services, or rather as part of a rationalized network with certain branches being targeted towards the provision of specific financial services.

Management Expenses as a Measure of Performance and Efficiency

The problems associated with using profitability or asset growth as criteria by which to judge building society performance have led many commentators to turn their attention to management expenses as an indicator of efficiency. Table 4.17 illustrates the composition of management expenses for 1983 and 1984.[8] It may be observed that staff expenses are by far the largest component of management expenses, with office expenses taking second place.

Table 4.17

Composition of Management Expenses, 1983 and 1984

Component	1983		1984		Increase 1984 over 1983, %
	£m	£ per £100 mean assets	£m	£ per £100 mean assets	
Directors' emoluments	8	0.01	8	0.01	–
Staff	475	0.60	523	0.55	10.1
Office expenses	249	0.31	271	0.29	8.8
Advertising	77	0.10	81	0.09	5.2
Commission and agency fees	70	0.09	91	0.10	30.0
Depreciation	80	0.10	99	0.11	23.8
Other expenses	38	0.04	35	0.04	(7.9)
Total	996	1.26	1,108	1.18	11.2

Source: Building Society Fact Book, 1985.
Derived from the Annual Reports of the Chief Registrar of Friendly Societies and BSA estimates.

These items are, of course, heavily affected by the rate of general price inflation, and hence may lead to problems with the interpretation of the data.

Table 4.18 illustrates the very strong correlation between the growth in the retail price index and the growth in the management expense ratio. The increase in the rate of inflation from 9.2 per cent in 1973 to 24.2 per cent in 1975 was accompanied by an increase in management expenses of 65 per cent in the same period. However, the effect of inflation is more problematic than it appears at first sight, since inflation does not affect total assets in the same way as it affects management expenses. A given rate of inflation may well raise the inflow of savings into societies in a proportional fashion given the associated rise in incomes, but it will not lead to a similar rise in the total volume of savings balances unless the building society offers a rate of interest equivalent to the rate of inflation and interest earnings are not withdrawn. Thus, a 10 per cent rate of inflation, for example, may well raise management expenses by 10 per cent but it will not raise total assets by the same proportion. Societies find, therefore, that they experience a sharp rise in the management expenses ratio during inflationary times. Inflation has also had an indirect impact upon the management expense ratio in the past. In inflationary times nominal interest rates tend to be revised upwards as investors demand an interest premium in order to maintain their real returns. Due to the operation of the recommended rate system, however, building society interest rates in the past tended to lag behind market rates and hence render societies relatively uncompetitive in inflationary times. Thus, with management expenses rising in line with inflation but with total assets increasing much more slowly, the management expense ratio would again prove to be a particularly poor indicator of building society performance over time, especially for comparisons with institutions whose interest rates tended to be more competitive.

The BSA has used the above line of reasoning to suggest that the rise in the management expense ratio has been due to the effects of inflation rather than to a deterioration in the performance of building societies. This is not an argument

Table 4.18
Management expenses, 1970 to 1985

Year	Management expenses £m	Management expenses £ per £100 mean assets	Increase %	Increase in RPI %
1970	68	0.68	4.6	6.3
1971	85	0.78	14.7	9.4
1972	102	0.73	−6.4	7.1
1973	119	0.73	0.0	9.2
1974	145	0.77	5.5	16.1
1975	197	0.89	15.6	24.2
1976	237	0.91	2.2	16.5
1977	297	0.95	4.4	15.8
1978	363	0.97	2.1	8.3
1979	449	1.05	8.2	13.4
1980	590	1.18	12.4	18.0
1981	731	1.26	6.8	11.9
1982	875	1.30	3.2	8.6
1983	996	1.25	−3.8	4.6
1984	1,108	1.18	−5.6	5.0
1985				6.1

Source: *Building Society Fact Book*, 1986.

which is accepted by the Bow Group, however. They argue that in inflationary times individuals, rather than saving less, do in fact save a higher proportion of their current income in order to maintain the purchasing power of their savings. The truth of this contention would appear to be supported by the fact that the personal saving ratio rose from around 9 per cent in the early 1970s to almost 15 per cent by 1980, but began to decline again subsequently as inflation subsided. The Bow Group go on to argue that as a consequence the total assets of building societies have in fact been growing faster than inflation. As we have seen, however, building societies are widely presumed to have a growth objective, and we would therefore expect them to exhibit some real growth in total assets, which as we have seen in Table 4.13 has in fact been the case. However, it would be very difficult to disentangle the effect of inflation on total assets from the effects of advertising and general competitiveness. The main point stressed by the BSA is that inflation can be expected to affect the management expense ratios of societies since it acts on management expenses and total assets differently. The BSA argues, therefore, that a major performance indicator is influenced by factors quite outside societies' control.

Although there are problems associated with using the management expense ratio to judge the performance of the building society sector over time – due, for example, to effects of inflation – it can be argued that the same problems are not present when comparing the performances of individual building societies in any given year. Indeed, the management expense ratio has been used in empirical research as a proxy for unit costs in an attempt to test for the presence of economies of scale in the building society sector.

Economies of Scale in the Building Society Sector

In the past the conventional wisdom was that economies of scale were present in the building society sector. In 1966, for example, the National Board for Prices and Incomes argued that the BSA cartel was providing margins sufficient to keep the smallest societies in business, and that the large number of societies was acting as an impediment to efficiency. Thus, there was clearly an implicit belief by the NBPI that economies of scale did exist in the building society industry, or in other words that larger societies were more efficient and had lower unit costs than smaller societies. This is a view which has been echoed at various times by the Chief Registrar of Friendly Societies.

This conventional wisdom was challenged, however, by Gough (1979). The first problem addressed by Gough was how to measure efficiency. The use of profit as a guide to efficiency was ruled out on the grounds that societies have a mutual constitution and hence cannot be considered to be profit maximizers. Gough considered that the managerial costs of handling funds was the best available measure of efficiency, and hence he attempted to assess the size–efficiency relationship by analysing the relationship between the management expense ratio (management expenses divided by total assets) and the size of society (measured by total assets). Gough considered this to be analogous to the investigation of the long-run cost function for the sector where one is regressing average costs against plant size. Since Gough was attempting to investigate the size–efficiency relationship, other things held constant, he used cross-section data and regressed the management expense ratio against total assets for a sample of different-sized societies in the same time period.

Gough's results generated little support for the view that economies of scale did exist in the building society sector. However, statistically, Gough's results were extremely poor, and the methodology has been subject to criticism. Indeed, simple inspection of statistics produced by the Chief Registrar (Table 4.19) show that on average smaller societies are more expensive to run than larger societies.

Clearly this type of aggregative data can only be suggestive as to the nature of the size–efficiency relationship since it is composed of averages of what might be quite disparate observations, and since it amounts to attempting to infer a

Table 4.19
Management Expenses as a Percentage of Total Assets
(pence per £100 of total assets)

Year	Overall	A	B	C	D	E
1975	89	86	93	94	82	121
1976	91	86	97	98	89	111
1977	95	88	105	100	93	125
1978	98	90	109	103	102	126

Society groupings:
A 5 largest societies
B total assets over £100m
C total assets between £25m and £100m
D total assets between £2m and £25m
E total assets under £2m
Source: Chief Registrar of Friendly Societies, *1978 Annual Report*.

relationship from only five observations in any one year. However, this type of data, and earlier reported observations, must raise some questions concerning Gough's conclusions. Nevertheless, Gough used his empirical results to reject the efficiency motive for merger, and therefore he must provide an alternative explanation for this activity. He states:

> An alternative explanation of merger is offered in terms of the motivation of managers, senior staff and directors of various societies. The salary and other rewards of management may well be maximised by pursuing an objective of growth in size, and in this connection merger is one important means of growth.

Further research by Cooper (1980) appeared to suggest that economies of scale do exist, but only for the small societies (that is, those with total earning assets of less than £10 million). For larger societies Cooper found evidence of diseconomies of scale. In order to put these results into perspective it is necessary to look at the size distribution of the building society industry. In 1982 there were 227 societies on the register; of these 79 had assets over £45 million and 16 had assets over £900 million. In the smaller size ranges, 148 societies had assets below £45 million and only 53 had assets of less than £2 million. Thus, it can be seen that according to Cooper's results economies of scale persist only up to relatively small-scale societies. Clearly, there is much controversy in respect of this issue, yet it is one which is at the very heart of the rationale for merger and branching activity which still persists, albeit on a smaller scale than in the past.

Building Societies and the Savings Market

In 1974 just over 90 per cent of all savings balances with building societies were held in ordinary share accounts. However, in response to a situation in 1974 when societies found that their ordinary share rate was particularly uncompetitive relative to market rates, many societies began to offer term accounts. These term share accounts offered a guaranteed premium over the variable ordinary share rate in exchange for a fixed term commitment by the investor. Initially term shares offered only a 2-year maturity, but by 1979 terms of up to 5 years were available. Prior to 1980 no withdrawals were permitted from term shares before they matured, but after this time most societies allowed premature withdrawals after a period of notice and with an interest penalty.

In further response to the increasing competition for retail funds societies began to introduce short-notice accounts in the early 1980s. These accounts offered a variable premium over the ordinary share rate in exchange for which the investor gave 1, 2 or 3 months' notice of withdrawal. Often instant withdrawals were available at the cost of an interest penalty. Currently, competitive pressures have resulted in notice periods being reduced so that for the most part instant access accounts are available offering a premium over ordinary share rates for those willing to maintain minimum balances.

It can be seen from Table 4.20 that by 1978 term shares accounted for almost 10 per cent of all share and deposit balances, with ordinary accounts approaching 80 per cent. From this time on, however, the decline in the importance of ordinary accounts accelerated with the further expansion of term shares in the late 1970s and early 1980s, and the introduction of short-notice accounts in 1981. By the end of 1985 these ordinary accounts constituted only 22.6 per cent of all balances. Term accounts grew in popularity until 1982/3 after which time they declined as the more attractive short-notice accounts were heavily marketed by the building societies. These short-notice accounts increased dramatically from just under 10 per cent of balances in 1981 to just under 60 per cent in 1985, accounting for nearly all of the decline in the share of ordinary accounts in total balances. This illustrates an important problem facing societies in recent years, that of the internal migration of funds. As building societies have introduced new competitive retail products to attract savings balances from other institutions (including

Table 4.20
Share and Deposit Balances by Type of Account

End period	Ordinary accounts	Short-notice accounts	Term accounts	Regular savings	Other
1974	87.2	—	5.6	3.8	3.5
1975	85.7	—	7.3	3.6	3.4
1976	84.6	—	8.5	3.6	3.3
1977	83.2	—	9.4	3.4	3.9
1978	83.1	—	9.9	3.5	3.5
1979	80.5	—	13.0	3.4	3.0
1980	79.0	—	14.7	3.5	2.8
1981	67.3	9.8	17.2	3.2	2.5
1982	54.2	16.9	23.4	2.9	2.6
1983	45.1	26.3	23.4	2.7	2.5
1984	32.3	44.8	19.4	2.1	1.3
1985	22.6	58.4	16.4	1.4	1.2

Source: BSA.

other societies), they have found that their own customers have shifted out of ordinary share accounts in search of the higher-yielding instruments. This trend has increased the cost of retail funds to societies in recent years, and was a major factor behind the fall in societies' aggregate surplus from £688m in 1983 to £626m in 1984.

Table 4.21 gives a more detailed breakdown of the different types of accounts offered by societies in recent years. This table gives a clear indication of the preference of individuals for liquid investments. In April 1985, for example, a typical instant access account was paying 9.75 per cent net of composite rate tax. This same rate was also available on a one-month notice account in the same building society. It is not surprising, therefore, to see that between 1984 Q4 and 1985 Q4 seven-day instant access accounts increased from 19.2 per cent to 26.3 per cent of balances outstanding, whereas one month-notice accounts witnessed a sharp fall from 14.2 per cent to 7.3 per cent. This readily illustrates the increased sophistication of today's savers, and their willingness to overcome inertia and to seek out the best investment in terms of rate, liquidity, or

Table 4.21

Balances Outstanding by Type of Account (% of total)

	1984 Q4	1985 Q1	1985 Q2	1985 Q3	1985 Q4
Ordinary accounts	32.3	29.6	26.9	24.9	22.6
Seven-day and instant access	19.2	21.3	22.8	24.1	26.3
One-month notice	14.2	13.3	11.7	8.9	7.3
Longer notice	11.4	14.3	15.9	20.6	24.8
Term accounts with withdrawals	15.7	14.3	16.4	15.8	13.8
Term accounts without withdrawals	3.7	3.5	3.2	3.0	2.6
Regular saving and SAYE	2.1	1.9	1.7	1.5	1.4
Other	1.3	1.3	1.3	1.5	1.2

Source: BSA.

combinations of the two. In today's savings environment individuals demand to be compensated for any loss of liquidity. For example, although the longer-notice accounts increased from 11.4 per cent to 24.8 per cent over the year, this was achieved only at a cost to societies, such that in April 1985 a typical 90-day notice account was paying 10 per cent, representing ¼ per cent over the instant access rate and 2¼ per cent over the ordinary share account.

So great has been the competitive pressure in the savings market that yet another product innovation was introduced in late 1985, when many societies improved the terms on their instant access accounts by introducing a tiered rates structure paying higher interest rates for larger investments (Table 4.22). Such is the pace of product innovation that many societies found that their own withdrawal-restricted capital accounts were uncompetitive relative to the new 'tiered' instant access accounts, particularly for sums of £5,000 and over.

The period 1980–1 may be regarded as something of a watershed in building society history. As mentioned earlier it was at this time that the banks, freed from credit constraints, entered the mortgage market providing competition in the major market where the societies had enjoyed a virtual monopoly in the past. It was also at this time that societies came under simultaneous pressure on the liabilities side of the balance sheet. This competition in the savings market came primarily from the government. A major component of the Conservative government's Medium Term

Table 4.22
Tiered Interest Rate Structure on a Typical
Instant Access Account as at June 1986

Investment (£)	Interest rate (%)
500–1,999	7.00
2,000–4,999	7.25
5,000–9,999	7.50
10,000 and over	7.75

Source: BSA.

Financial Strategy (MTFS) involved the control of the growth of the money supply in order to reduce the rate of inflation. An important aspect of this policy was for as large a proportion as possible of the public sector borrowing requirement (PSBR) to be covered by issues of gilt-edged securities and through deposits with the National Savings Bank and sales of National Savings instruments. In short, the authorities were attempting to avoid inflationary borrowing through the banking sector (including the Bank of England).

The emphasis on the use of National Savings channels for the financing of the PSBR was of especial relevance to building societies' activities. The growing competitiveness of National Savings was seen as early as 1979 when the index-linked retirement issue of National Savings Certificates was introduced. With an inflation rate of around 18 per cent in 1979/80 these so-called 'Granny Bonds' proved extremely popular, and from 3 December 1979 the government increased the limit applying to the issue from £700 to £12,000 per purchaser. It is estimated that this first retirement issue drained as much as £1 billion of savings from the personal sector, with much of it coming from building societies. Competitive pressure intensified further as the rate of interest on the National Savings Bank Investment Account increased in line with clearing bank rates, as the Bank of England's Minimum Lending Rate (MLR) rose to a high point of 17 per cent in late 1979. As MLR fell back again to 14 per cent in late 1980, however, National Savings Bank Investment Account rates remained at 15 per cent, emphasizing the government's aggressive stance in the savings market. Further competitive initiatives were taken by the Government early in 1981 as the limit on the holdings of the 19th issue National Savings Certificates (which had become very competitive as market rates fell) was increased from £1,500 to £5,000. A far more serious competitive threat to building societies came in the budget of 1981, when the government extended the eligibility of the index-linked retirement issue (which was previously only available to those over 60) to individuals in the 50–60 age-group. The BSA estimated at the time that around 20–5 per cent of building society shares and deposits, equivalent to some £11–14 billion, were held by investors in this particular age-group.

With the unveiling of the MTFS in 1980, the government had announced a target for National Savings funding of the PSBR for the year 1980/1 of £3 billion. This target was not met, however, as National Savings in total contributed only £2,239 million to government funding (although this represented a huge increase on the previous year's total of £968 million). In spite of this, the government increased the target in the 1981 budget from £3 billion to £3.5 billion. That this target would be achieved was never really in question as the government eventually abandoned any age restriction on index-linked issues from September 1981, issued a highly competitive 23rd issue on 9 November 1981 which paid 10.51 per cent tax-free if held for the full 5 years, and raised the National Savings Investment Account interest rate by 2 per cent in the latter months of the year at a time when interest rates generally were falling. The great success of the 23rd issue certificate, for example, can be gauged from the fact that it was so promptly withdrawn from the market – but not before taking £200 million in the single day between the announcement of its withdrawal and its removal from the marketplace.

National Savings provided much less severe competition for building societies after mid-1982 for a number of reasons. First, the budget of 1982 announced a lower £3 billion target for 1982/3 (a target which was to remain the same over the coming years). Secondly, falling rates of inflation severely reduced the competitiveness of the indexed-linked certificate issues. Finally and most significantly, as Table 4.23 illustrates, by 1982/3 accrued interest on outstanding balances was contributing as much to total National Savings as was new funding, and this would clearly be expected to reduce the competitive pressure on societies.

In general banks have not, until recent years, paid as much attention to securing savings deposits in the retail market as they have to wholesale funding. Liability management techniques were perfected through the 1970s in wholesale money markets, and the proportion of clearing

Table 4.23
Contribution of National Savings to Funding PSBR

Financial year	National savings Net receipts £m	Interest accrued £m	Total £m	PSBR £m	Total NS as % of PSBR
1979/80	283	685	968	9,919	9.8
1980/81	1,299	940	2,239	13,187	17.0
1981/82	2,859	1,365	4,224	8,785	48.1
1982/83	1,511	1,525	3,036	9,164	33.1
1983/84	1,453	1,686	3,131	9,753	32.2
1984/85	1,200	1,800	3,000	7,250	41.4

Source: BSA.

banks' branch retail deposits to total sterling deposits declined steadily from 61 per cent to less than 40 per cent between 1975 and 1984, as shown in Table 4.24.

The banks changed the balance of their funding away from the retail market towards wholesale money markets, and in the process they lost the image of being 'savings' institutions, an image largely transferred to building societies. Banks took the view that it was not imperative to compete with building societies for a number of reasons. First, societies and banks were not in competition on the assets side, and hence if the societies gained deposits it would not threaten the lending business of banks. Secondly, building society gains in deposits were not believed to represent losses to the banks as the funds stayed within the banking system. All the building societies seemed to do was to change the ownership of existing bank deposits but not the total. Finally, the banks faced a dilemma with respect to the pricing of their 7-day deposit accounts, since if they attempted to compete with societies on rates they ran the risk of cannibalizing their own interest-free current accounts, which still accounted for over 30 per cent of sterling retail deposits during the late 1970s. Hence, if the banks had competed more vigorously on rates they may have seen the cost of funds rise with little net new money attracted. In

Table 4.24

The Balance between Wholesale and Retail Funding for the London Clearing Banks and Subsidiaries

	1975	1976	1977	1978	1979	1980	1981 Banking sector	1981 Monetary sector	1982	1983	1984
Total sterling deposits	28,291	30,564	34,191	38,687	46,749	52,785	61,735	62,252	78,667	85,811	94,860
Branch retail deposits (£)	17,270	17,872	19,524	21,733	25,781	29,497	31,863	32,072	34,110	35,101	36,430
Branch retail deposits as % of total sterling deposits	61	58.5	57.1	56.17	55.14	55.88	51.6	51.5	43.35	40.79	38.40
Implied % of non-traditional (wholesale) funding	39	41.5	42.9	43.83	44.86	44.12	48.4	48.5	56.65	59.21	61.6

Source: *Abstract of Banking Statistics*, May 1985.

choosing not to compete on deposit rates the banks were aided during the 1970s by the societies' cartel which tended to keep investors' rates below market clearing levels.

Figure 4.2 indicates the extent to which bank deposit rates have been below the basic building society investment rate, for the years 1967 to 1984. It is interesting to note that 1979/80 – the only time when banks were competitive for any length of time – coincides with a marked improvement in their market share from 37.5 per cent to nearly 42 per cent. This was not sustained into the 1980s, however, as bank deposit rates again became uncompetitive relative to building society rates at a time when building societies were becoming much more aggressive in respect of their marketing and more innovative in the variety of savings schemes they offered.

The strategy of banks has changed, however, as they now give a higher priority to securing retail deposits and to reversing the trend in the balance between wholesale and retail funding evident since 1970 (see Table 4.24). There are a number of factors which have induced this change in the targeted balance between wholesale and retail funding by banks: (1) they view the development of retail funding as a

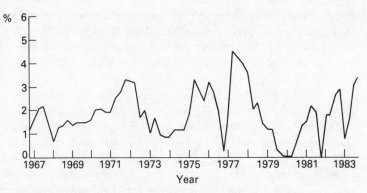

Figure 4.2 Differential Between Building Society Recommended Net Share Rate and Net of Tax 7-day Bank Deposit Rate

Source: 'The demand for liquidity aggregates in the UK personal sector', R.I. Johnston, *Treasury Working Paper No. 36*, June 1985.

mechanism for selling retail financial services and developing stronger customer relationships in the new competitive environment; (2) considerations of portfolio balance suggest that the balance might have shifted excessively towards wholesale funding even though the latter is now frequently cheaper; and (3) the change in the competitive position between banks and building societies has itself been a factor inducing a change in the banks' funding strategy in the sense that since 1981 it has no longer been the case that banks and building societies are not competing on the asset side of the balance sheet.

Although the general factors outlined above were extremely important to the evolution of banking activities, it is generally agreed that it was specific factors which finally prompted the banks to reassert themselves in the market for personal sector savings in late 1984 and early 1985. Primary among these factors was the approach of the 6 April 1985 deadline when banks had to join the building societies in deducting tax from depositors' interest at source at a composite rate of 25.25 per cent. The fact that banks would have to quote rates to customers on a net rather than gross basis was bound to make their already uncompetitive rates even more transparent to investors, and to prompt the banks to take a more competitive stance. Added to this was the fact that 1984 witnessed the first-ever fall in the number of bank current accounts outstanding (which had by this time fallen to 20 per cent of sterling deposits), and the rise in the building societies' share of personal sector liquid assets to over 50 per cent.

In response to these specific pressures the banks began to introduce high interest deposit accounts, and in September 1984 the Midland Bank announced a high interest cheque account. The so-called 'saver-plus account' paid interest on all balances above a £100 minimum, and featured a tiered rate of interest on higher balances. The popularity of this product, and the fact that many building societies were introducing accounts which paid interest and which featured cashcard services and/or cheque-book facilities in conjunction with a bank, prompted the other banks to follow suit in 1985.

Many of the banks openly admit that their biggest mistake in the retail market was to cease Saturday opening. The building societies, with the advantage of largely non-unionized labour, thus had the huge advantage of Saturday morning opening as well as longer weekday hours. Barclays opened selected branches on Saturday in 1982, which despite costing an estimated extra £6 million per year was very successful with customers. Despite its success, how-ever, the move was not followed by the other banks until 1984. In September 1984 with the introduction of composite rate taxation looming, the National Westminster Bank, and eventually the other clearers, followed the early lead of Barclays on Saturday opening.

The banks benefited from the fact that their base lending and investment rates were increased in January 1985 – a move which was not followed immediately by building societies – so that as they began quoting interest rates net of tax, ahead of the deduction of composite rate tax on 6 April 1986, they were unusually competitive. The success of the banks' resurgence as a competitive force in the savings market through their high interest deposit and cheque accounts, and more recently the move to free banking, can be gauged from the fact that during the first three-quarters of 1985 they increased their share of new deposits from 18.9 per cent to 29.4 per cent. The building societies in consequence saw their share fall from 65 per cent to 56.9 per cent.

The banks have recently been offering rates of interest which are highly competitive, both relative to building society rates and to money market rates. Building societies, however, will be in a strong position to regain the initiative in the next few years as they now have ATM networks to challenge the banks, and now the new legislation has reached the statute books they are able to provide money transmission services which have for so long been the preserve of the banks.[9] Thus, it seems likely that the competition between banks and building societies in the retail savings markets will remain fierce in the foreseeable future.

Wholesale Funding

While banks were developing liability management techniques in the wholesale markets during the 1970s, building
societies concentrated on funding solely in the retail market.
Although in the early 1980s some societies had begun to
raise modest amounts via syndicated bank loans and
negotiable bonds traded under Stock Exchange Rule 163,
societies were effectively prohibited from making appreciable use of the wholesale markets by their inability to pay
interest gross on money market instruments (net interest
being unacceptable in the wholesale markets). However, in
the 1983 Finance Act building societies were given the
power to pay interest gross on qualifying certificates of
deposit (CDs), and by the end of August 1983 ten of the
eleven largest societies had issued certificates of deposit. A
building society certificate of deposit is a negotiable bearer
security issued by a society, having a fixed maturity and
usually attracting a fixed interest rate. In order to qualify
under the 1983 Finance Act these certificates of deposit had
to be issued in amounts of £50,000 or more and with a
maturity of less than 12 months.

Originally building societies were empowered, under the
Authorised Investments Order, to hold CDs only if they
were issued by banks authorized to take deposits from
building societies. This prevented building societies from
holding other societies' CDs, and hence hindered the
development of an active secondary market in building
society CDs. Following lobbying by the BSA this point was
conceded by the Chief Registrar and the Treasury, and an
appropriate amendment was made to the Building Societies
Authorised Investment Order which allowed societies to
hold CDs which had been issued by other societies with
assets in excess of £2,000 million. In order to take account of
the fact that purchases of one society's CDs by another
society adds nothing to the aggregate liquidity of all building
societies, the Chief Registrar imposed a limit of 2½ per cent
of total assets which could be held in the form of other
building societies' CDs.

The fact that only the larger building societies would have the standing to raise money in the wholesale markets via the issue of CDs prompted the BSA to press the government to permit societies to pay interest gross on time deposits of more than £50,000 having a maturity of less than 1 year. This, it was argued, would give the smaller societies comparable access to the money markets, and in fact this power was granted from 1 October 1983. This change, coupled with societies' ability to issue CDs, resulted in a dramatic increase in the volume of funds raised from 'non-traditional' sources. Whereas in 1982 only £230 million came from the wholesale markets, by 1983 this figure had risen to £1,584 million.

Building societies were given increased scope to operate in the wholesale markets when the Chancellor of the Exchequer proposed, in the 1985 budget, that societies should be able to pay interest gross to non-resident holders of Eurobonds after 6 April 1986. Societies were quick to seize this new opportunity, and in September 1985 the Halifax became the first UK building society to issue Eurosterling Floating Rate Notes (FRNs) to the value of £150 million. The issue was for 7 years, and in this case the FRNs pay interest quarterly at a rate of ¹⁄₁₆ per cent per annum above LIBOR (London Interbank Offered Rate). The exception to this was the first interest instalment, which because of the timing of the new powers could not be paid until 7 April 1986, and hence the first interest rate period was 6 months rather than the usual 3 months. The Halifax was quickly followed by the third largest building society, the Nationwide, with the largest Eurosterling tranche issue ever made. The Nationwide's issue was for £200 million over 10 years, but with investors' 'put options' (that is, the option to sell back before the redemption date). These initial issues were so successful that many other societies took advantage of the new powers and made Eurobond issues in late 1985; they are summarized in Table 4.25.

The ability to issue Eurobonds has given building societies much greater flexibility in the use they make of wholesale market funding. Whereas CDs are generally fixed rate instruments (although the Abbey National recently raised

Table 4.25
Building Societies and the Eurobond Market, 1985

Month of announcement	Society	Amount (£m)
September	Halifax	150
	Nationwide	200
	Abbey National	150 (+ 200 in April 1986)
	Bristol and West	100
October	Britannia	75
	Alliance and Leicester	150
November	Woolwich Equitable	200
December	Anglia	100

Source: BSA Bulletin, no. 45, January 1986, p. 4.

£50m with the first building society floating rate CD issue), the Eurobond market offers fixed or floating rate money, and most societies have opted for the latter thus matching variable rate assets with variable rate liabilities. The Eurobond market also offers much greater flexibility on the maturity of issues. Rather than being restricted to maturities of up to 1 year as with time deposits and CDs, and hence to a mismatch between long-term lending and short-term funding, Eurobonds can be issued for maturities of between 5 and 15 years. One society, the Abbey National, has already taken advantage of the long maturities available in the Eurosterling market with its 15-year issue in September 1985. Most societies, however, have tended to opt for maturities of 7 years which coincide with the average life of a mortgage loan and hence permit societies to match the maturity of their liabilities more closely to the maturity of their assets. Figure 4.3 illustrates the growth of wholesale funding in recent years both in gross and net terms.

A major advantage for building societies of using whole-sale money market funding is that it is frequently cheaper than raising funds through retail deposits at the margin. Figure 4.4 compares the maximum retail deposit rate of societies with 3-month LIBOR (a representative money market rate), and it is apparent that there has been a

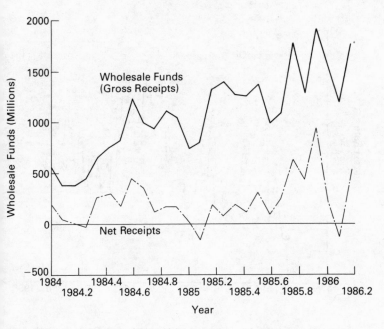

Figure 4.3 Trends in Wholesale Funding by Building Societies, 1984 to 1986

significant change in the relationship with the deposit rate rising substantially relative to LIBOR, and since 1983 it has been invariably higher than the wholesale money market rate.

The recent rise in retail rates relative to wholesale rates is reflected by the selection of retail and wholesale interest rates shown in Table 4.26. (In this context retail rates are calculated at the gross cost to the societies, that is, after composite rate tax.) It may be observed that only the ordinary share rate is below the three wholesale rates. But although the weighted average cost of retail funds was around 10 per cent societies cannot, in the retail market, differentiate between one set of depositors and another. For example, if new funds can only be attracted by the offer of higher interest rates, the higher rates will have to be paid on both new (marginal) funds and on existing deposits. The

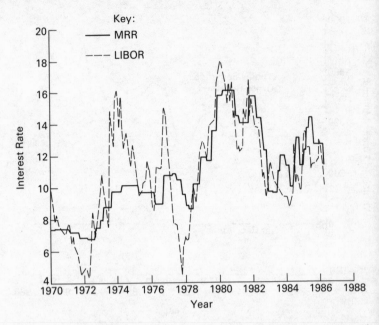

Figure 4.4 Building Societies' Maximum Retail Deposit Rate and the 3-Month LIBOR, Quarterly Data, 1970 to 1986

marginal cost of new funds can therefore be very high. Access to wholesale markets offers a particular advantage to building societies, therefore, because marginal funds can be secured without paying a higher rate on deposits already secured.

A further advantage of using the wholesale markets is that they offer a degree of flexibility (in terms of amount, timing and borrowing conditions) which is often greater than in the retail sector. In this sense societies can secure greater control over the volume and nature of funds taken. This will become an increasingly important consideration as building societies have adopted a more competitive stance in the mortgage market with mortgage loans being made available virtually on demand. Moreover, wholesale funding can be used to lengthen the average maturity of liabilities, which is a particularly relevant consideration given the trend towards

Table 4.26
Selected Building Society and Wholesale Interest Rates,
percentage per annum, October 1985 and April 1986

	October 1985	April 1986
Building society ordinary shares	9.4	8.0
Instant access accounts	12.7	10.6
90-day shares	12.7	11.3
LIBOR	11.4	10.4
Wholesale time deposits	11.5	10.5
Floating rate notes	11.6	10.6

instant access accounts in respect of retail funds. In general, long-term funding in the retail market has always been difficult, partly because of a general inclination of the personal sector to prefer liquidity for its discretionary savings, and partly because there are powerful tax advantages in making contractual savings elsewhere, notably pension funds and (until recently) life assurance. A major advantage of wholesale funding is, therefore, that it can secure long-term funds at variable interest rates in order to bring the liabilities structure closer to that of asset holdings. In short, the markets represent a facility to adjust the maturity profile of liabilities. Finally, wholesale funding is a sensible strategy for building societies wishing to diversify their funding options and structures. In the process this will reduce their dependence on a single market – the retail deposit market – at a time when the competitive pressures in this sector are intensifying. In general, as is shown by portfolio analysis, a more diversified liability structure (especially if the alternative forms have different risk and market characteristics) will tend to reduce exposure to financial risk.

Wholesale funding, because of its flexibility, may replace the strategic use of the liquidity ratio as a means of smoothing the flow of mortgage loans relative to deposits over the interest rate cycle. Figure 4.5 indicates that in the 1970s the liquidity ratio was used in this strategic manner as it was increased when the interest differential moved in

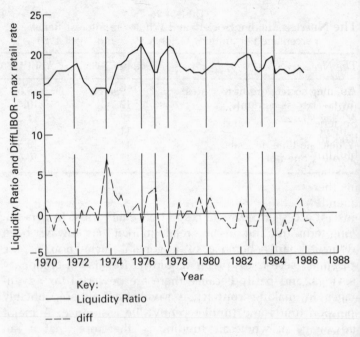

Figure 4.5 Building Society Liquidity Ratio and the Differential between LIBOR and the Maximum Building Society Retail Deposit Rate, Quarterly Data, 1970 to 1986

favour of the societies and vice versa. The pattern is very clear in each phase of the interest rate cycle up to 1980. However, since 1980 the relationship has become more uncertain as both the liquidity ratio and the interest rate differential have been comparatively more stable, and the volatility of the liquidity ratio has declined relative to that of the interest rate differential. Although the pattern re-emerged in 1982 and 1983, the decline in the strategic use of the liquidity ratio is consistent with the use of wholesale funding as an alternative mechanism to smooth the flow of mortgage loans.

The New Building Societies Legislation

The Need for New Legislation

As mentioned earlier, building societies used to operate under legislation which was consolidated by the Building Societies Act 1962, and the basic framework of which dated back to 1874. During the early 1980s it was recognized by the building society movement generally that new legislation was needed if societies were to be able to operate effectively in the new competitive financial environment. Consequently, in June 1981 a working group was formed under the chairmanship of Mr John Spalding to report to the council of the BSA. The working group examined the existing legislation, and ventured various proposals for reform. The Spalding Report[10] was published in January 1983, and its contents formed the focus of the debate, which was to continue for the following three years, on the desired nature and scope of future developments in building societies' activities.

The report emphasized that the legislation under which societies operated was related more closely to the original, small, local organizations than to the large, national, multi-million-member financial institutions into which societies had evolved by the 1980s. The report stressed that the past success of building societies had depended in part upon two factors:

(1) Building societies had been lending to a favoured market – the market for mortgage loans which enjoyed tax privileges.
(2) Government restrictions had prevented the building societies' biggest potential competitors from competing effectively.

By the time of the Spalding group's deliberations, however, the situation had changed markedly. Building societies faced severe competition from National Savings and, later, banks on the liabilities side of the balance sheet, and from banks in the mortgage loans market. It was no longer the case that clear demarcation lines could be drawn between the activities of different retail financial institutions, and the group felt that building societies would be at a competitive disadvantage *vis-à-vis* other financial institutions if they were not permitted to diversify out of their traditional saving and mortgage lending business.

The Spalding Report argued that societies should be permitted to offer a package of services to potential home buyers, and therefore that societies should be able to:

(1) Act as estate agents in respect of property mortgaged or to be mortgaged to the society.
(2) Carry out structural surveys for existing and prospective borrowers.
(3) Undertake conveyancing for current and prospective borrowers.

These new powers advocated by the Spalding Report were argued to be powers involving very little risk. More controversial, however, was the report's recommendations that a building society's powers should be extended to allow it to establish, acquire or invest in either by itself or jointly with one or more other societies:

(1) A bank recognized or capable of being recognized under the Banking Act 1979.
(2) An insurance company.
(3) A body corporate which would be able to acquire and hold land for such purposes as the nature of the body chosen permitted.
(4) A subsidiary limited company under the Companies Acts empowered to make personal loans and to transact hire purchase finance.

The report stressed that building societies needed new legislation in order to enable them to play a wider role in the housing market, where societies had become increasingly involved in housing initiatives since the mid-1970s, and to enable them to respond to competition in the market for financial services and to the increasing needs and demands of their members for a wider range of services.

In the comments generated by the Spalding Report, which was intended as a consultative document, there was strong criticism not of the new powers it advocated but of the suggestion that banking and other 'risky activities' such as personal and hire-purchase lending, insurance, and the acquisition and holding of land, should be undertaken only by a separate 'subsidiary body corporate'. The motivation behind this proposal was the belief that any potential financial problems of the subsidiary would be isolated from the main business of the society in question, thereby minimizing the risk of loss to the investor. Societies were, however, subsequently advised that this would not be the case. Lord Richardson, former governor of the Bank of England warned the BSA annual conference in May 1983 that if societies were to operate as banks via subsidiaries then the Bank of England would require the parent to support the subsidiary in case of difficulty. Building societies were further advised that they would be unable to under-take banking activities through a subsidiary recognized as a bank, not least because societies did not intend to become full-scale bankers providing international and large-scale financial loans which would have been required if the subsidiary was to be recognized as a bank.

After a careful consideration of the responses to the Spalding Report the BSA published its definitive proposals in a report entitled 'New Legislation for Building Societies'.[11] In this report the BSA was careful to stress that it had no wish for member institutions to become full-scale bankers, and in fact the proposal that societies should be able to own subsidiary banks and finance houses was dropped, and was replaced by a suggestion that building societies should be permitted to offer a wide range of financial services directly. Apart from this change the recommendations made by this latter document were broadly similar to those put forward in the Spalding Report.

The BSA's final report emphasized strongly that societies had no desire to depart from their existing functions of being housing finance and savings institutions, and that the additional powers being sought should support, and be incidental to, the development of these primary objectives. Specifically, the report advocated that societies be given the power to extend their existing retail banking services. It was envisaged that this would involve the removal of the restriction on societies of lending on first mortgage, so that they be empowered to have a limited percentage of their assets in unsecured loans, and so that 'modest' overdraft facilities be permitted on certain accounts. This, it was argued, would enable societies to offer cheque-books, credit cards, personal loans, and hire-purchase on the same terms as other financial institutions. Under the existing legislation societies could not provide cheque guarantee cards, for example, unless this was done in conjunction with a bank, since the provision of cheque guarantee cards is tantamount to offering facilities for unsecured lending which under the 1962 Act was *ultra vires*. The BSA's report was able to draw support from a report by the National Consumer Council entitled 'Banking Services and the Consumer' published in December 1983. The latter report confirmed that significant numbers of building society customers wanted their societies to offer payment services, which traditionally had been the exclusive preserve of the banks. The report further argued that the removal of the lending on first mortgage restriction would also enable societies to make modest second mortgage loans when the first mortgagee was unwilling or unable to provide a loan.

In relation to the housing market the BSA's report advocated that building societies be empowered to hold land other than for the purpose of conducting their business to which they were restricted by the 1962 legislation. It was argued that this would enable societies to participate more effectively in shared ownership schemes and index-linked and equity sharing mortgages, as well as holding land for the purpose of housing development, particularly in the areas of assured tenancies, low-cost housing for sale and the development of mixed-use schemes. Furthermore, the BSA advocated that societies should be empowered to offer services relating to house-buying, such as estate agency conveyancing, structural surveying and insurance broking.

This would, it was argued, make house purchase more convenient, as the customer would be required to deal with fewer organizations which would be likely to speed up the process of house purchase.

On matters of constitution, both the Spalding Report and the final BSA document on new legislation advocated that building societies should retain their mutual status in law. The Spalding Report argued that

> The building society concept is one that is well understood, has served the industry and the nation well and these are advantages not lightly to be thrown away. Accordingly, it is recommended that the present special legal nature of a building society (i.e., with investing and borrowing members) should be retained.
>
> (p.8)

The Spalding Report did recognize, however, that even new legislation offering wider powers might be too restrictive for some societies, and it was therefore advocated that there should be a procedure whereby a society could convert itself into another form of body corporate, such as a company under the Companies Acts, an industrial and provident society, or a friendly society.

In July 1984 the government published its Green Paper 'Building Societies – a New Framework'. This paper shared the view expressed by the BSA that societies should retain their mutual status and continue to concentrate on their traditional business. The Green Paper further recognized that societies needed wider powers, and for this purpose introduced the concept of asset categories. Class 1 assets were designated to be loans to owner-occupiers of residential property secured by first mortgage, and the view was expressed that these should account for at least 90 per cent of commercial assets (total assets less liquid assets and fixed assets). Class 2 assets were to consist of other wholly secured lending. Some of this is permitted under the 1962 legislation such as loans to bodies corporate and on non-residential property, and these were catered for under the special advances provision. But some Class 2 lending would be new lending, including loans on second mortgage, equity mortgages, and loans beyond the valuation of the property so long as the advance was secured by a local authority indemnity. It was the Class 3 category of assets, however, which represented the most significant diversification away from societies' traditional business. There were three main types of Class 3 assets outlined in the Green Paper:

(1) Unsecured loans, which were felt to be a logical extension of building society business. It was felt to be prudent to put an upper limit on unsecured loans to any one individual of £5,000 initially, since this type of lending was felt to be inherently more risky than mortgage lending and would need particular expertise on the part of societies which would probably be gained over time.

(2) The ownership of land and property which would enable societies to develop property for sale and to act directly as landlords and to own the rented element of shared-ownership accommodation, thus simplifying shared-ownership schemes immensely. These powers were to be available directly or through a subsidiary.

(3) Equity investment in subsidiaries and associates. The Green Paper stressed that in principle there should be no reason why societies should not own the equity of a company, although it was stressed that this should not be perceived as a way of avoiding prudential constraints. Consequently, it was advocated that societies should invest in subsidiaries only to provide, solely or jointly, services which they could legally provide individually to their members. Furthermore, societies should not set up subsidiaries with potentially heavy contingent liabilities, nor be permitted to undertake further unsecured lending via a consumer credit subsidiary.

The Green Paper stressed that as Class 3 assets were generally more risky than other business they should be covered by proportionally higher reserves. Furthermore, the power to hold most Class 3 assets should be restricted to societies with free reserves (reserves less fixed assets) in excess of £3m, and an upper limit of 5 per cent of commercial assets placed upon Class 3 assets within the 10 per cent of non-Class 1 assets.

In so far as liquid assets were concerned the Green Paper made no firm proposals, stating only that societies should ensure that liquid assets were sufficient for their business, and suggesting that an upper limit of one-third of total assets should be liquid assets. This suggestion of an upper limit on liquid funds was made in order to ensure that societies did not stray too far from their traditional role by, for example, acting like an investment trust holding liquid assets rather than a building society raising funds primarily to lend to owner-occupiers. Similarly, to ensure that societies remained predominantly member-based it was proposed that a minimum of 80 per cent of funds should be raised from individual members. It was also felt that this would provide a safeguard against societies relying too heavily on the wholesale markets since a maximum of 20 per cent of funds would be available from 'non-traditional' sources.

The Green Paper effectively provided for building societies to offer a fuller range of personal banking and money transmission services, since the new unsecured lending powers would enable societies to underwrite payments to third parties. It was further suggested that the Building Societies Bill might explicitly provide for societies to guarantee certain categories of payments so that cheque-books, comparable to those offered by banks, could be offered by building societies, and that they be able to enter into reciprocal payment arrangements with other societies or financial institutions.

The Green Paper did not give full approval for societies to operate an integrated house-buying service. While wishing to see increased competition in this area, the Green Paper stressed that potential conflicts of interest might arise, especially with respect to societies offering estate agency and conveyancing services, although little potential conflict of interest was envisaged with regard to societies being able to undertake structural surveys.

The response by the BSA to the Green Paper was, on the whole, very favourable since the paper conceded most of the new powers for which building societies had been pressing. One area of disappointment for the BSA was the lack of positive commitment to allow societies to operate in other European countries. The Green Paper stressed that:

> The government favours the establishment of a genuine common market, including financial services, but is doubtful about the scope for early progress in this particular field.

However, after receiving comment on the Green Paper proposals the government announced in June 1985 (ahead of the publication of the Building Societies Bill) that it intended to give societies the power to invest in subsidiaries doing business in other countries of the European Community.

The Building Societies Act

The Building Societies Bill was published on 6 December 1985 and was enacted in July 1986 when it replaced the Building Societies Act 1962 and the Building Societies (Northern Ireland) Act 1967 as the primary legislation pertaining to building societies. The Act also replaced two pieces of secondary legislation. First, the Designation (for trustee status) Regulations which were made under the House Purchase and Housing Act 1959, and which provide for minimum liquidity and reserve requirements (although these requirements had been made partially redundant by the Authorisation Regulations). Under the Building Societies Act 1986 all authorized societies are able to accept investments from trustees. Secondly, the Authorisation Regulations themselves, which were introduced in 1981 under the authority of the European Communities Act 1972, are incorporated in primary legislation within the Building Societies Act 1986. Under the new legislation a building society will normally be authorized to raise funds and borrow money provided that:

166

(1)   a society has qualifying capital (deferred shares or reserves) of at least £100,000;

(2)   the chairman of the board, the executive directors, the chief executive, the secretary and any managers be fit and proper persons to hold their respective offices;

(3)   the above-mentioned persons have the capacity to ensure that the society's affairs will be conducted 'prudently' and that the investments of shareholders and depositors will be adequately protected.

The objects clause of the Act, Section 5(1) states that:

A society may be established under this Act if its purpose or *principal* purpose is that of raising, *primarily* by the subscriptions of the members, a stock or fund for making to them advances secured on land for their residential use

(a)   mortgages of freehold or leasehold in England and Wales or Northern Ireland, or

(b)   tenable securities over land in Scotland, being land for their residential use.

(italics added)

The important difference from the objects clause contained in the 1962 legislaton is the use of the words 'principal' and 'primarily'. The use of the word 'principal' provides for societies to lend other than on first mortgage secured on residential property, and the use of the word 'primarily' provides for societies to raise funds other than via retail sources.

Table 4.27 summarizes the categories of commercial assets (total assets less assets held in liquid form, and fixed assets) which building societies are now permitted to hold under the new legislation, and the limits pertaining to these categories.

In the Green Paper it was envisaged that the power to hold most Class 3 assets would be restricted to societies with over £3 million in free reserves. The Building Societies Act, however, changed the criteria. Under the new legislation the power to hold Class 3 assets such as unsecured loans and the ownership of land and property for residential use is

Table 4.27
Categories of Commercial Asset

Category	Section	Broad description	Limit in respect of commercial assets
Class 1	10	Loans secured by first mortgage of an owner-occupied house	At least 90%
Class 2	11–15	Other loans secured on property, e.g. loans to housing associations, loans to housebuilders, loans on non-residential property, 2nd mortgage loans on owner-occupied property	Together with Class 3 assets, not more than 10%
Class 3	16–18	Unsecured loans and secured loans not coming within Class 1 or Class 2 up to £5,000, ownership of land and property for residential use, investments in subsidiaries and associates	Not more than 5%

Source: Building Societies Bill, BSA Commentary, BSA, 1985, p. 17.

restricted to societies with commercial assets over £100 million, the definition of which was felt to be better understood by societies than the concept of free reserves. In practice, this means that societies with commercial assets of less than £100 million are restricted to holding Class 3 assets only in the form of investments in subsidiaries and associates.

Table 4.28 illustrates the minimum/maximum amounts of the various asset categories implied by the Building Societies Act for the end–1984 aggregate of building society assets. It is clear that with the advent of the new legislation, societies as a whole are in a position to commit well over £4 billion in unsecured lending.

There were provisions in the original Building Societies Bill for the percentage of Class 2 and 3 assets to be varied up

Table 4.28
Lending by Category: Amounts Based on
end-1984 figures, £ million

Category	Amount £m
Commercial assets	82,400
Class 1 minimum (90%)	74,200
Class 2 and 3 maximum (10%)	8,200
Class 3 maximum (5%)	4,100

Source: *Building Societies Bill, BSA Commentary*, BSA, 1985, p. 18.

to a maximum of 10 per cent for Class 3 and 20 per cent for Class 2 and 3. Any increase would be made through a statutory instrument made by the Treasury and requiring an affirmative resolution from both Houses of Parliament. Following the Committee stage of the Bill, however, the government announced that it was increasing these maximum limits from 20 per cent to 25 per cent for Class 2 and 3, and from 10 per cent to 15 per cent for Class 3 assets. When announcing this amendment to the original Bill Mr Ian Stewart, Economic Secretary to the Treasury, stressed that he did not foresee the proposed 5 per cent level for Class 3 assets being raised in the foreseeable future given the fact that 5 per cent of all societies' assets constituted around £5 billion.

Section 34 of the Building Societies Act specifically provides for societies to be able to provide, either directly or through a subsidiary, a whole range of new services including[12]:

(1) money transmission services;
(2) foreign exchange services;
(3) making or receiving of payments as agents;
(4) management, as agents, of mortgage investments;
(5) management, as agents, of land;
(6) arranging for the provision of services relating to the acquisition or disposal of investments, either on behalf

169

of an investor or the institution providing the service;

(7) arranging for the provision of credit and providing services in connection with loan agreements;

(8) administration of pension schemes;

(9) arranging for the provision of insurance of any description;

(10) estate agency services;

(11) surveys and valuations of land;

(12) conveyancing services.

There are, however, some restrictions pertaining to these new services. Societies with commercial assets below £100 million are not permitted to undertake land management, although they are free to provide all the other services. The power to provide estate agency services is, under the new legislation, available only to a subsidiary of a building society.

Two areas which were the subject of much debate during the Bill's passage through Parliament related to the provisions on pension schemes and conveyancing. On pension schemes the original wording of the Building Societies Bill would have enabled societies to provide pension schemes themselves, giving them wide investment and possibly limited underwriting facilities. However, after questions were raised in the House of Commons concerning how these activities were to be authorized, an amendment to the Bill in the Committee stage deleted the reference to societies being able to establish pension schemes. Sir George Young, who moved the amendment, argued for the government that:

> We see building societies as having an important role in making personal and portable pension schemes more widely available. But the Government see no question of societies taking on the full role of pension providers. That would involve the direct provision of life and sickness insurance, underwriting pension annuities and providing a long term investment management service.[13]

The amendment would have effectively limited societies to

marketing and adminstering pension funds only as intermediaries, and would have prevented them from taking full
advantage of the personal pension provisions in the Social
Services Bill due to become law in April 1988. Under these
provisions individuals will be free to opt out of their
company schemes or the state earnings-related pension
scheme (SERPS) and make their own money purchase
pension provisions with an approved financial institution.
Estimates suggest that this will be a £1 billion a year market
when the new rules are in force. Following fierce lobbying
by the BSA, the government agreed that building societies
should be given the power to invest in a subsidiary or
associated company established for the sole purpose of
making provision for pensions on a money purchase basis.
But the caveat to this approval was that the subsidiary or
associate would need to operate as a unit trust to be
authorized under the Financial Services Legislation. Nevertheless, this change of heart by the government will bring
building societies into direct competition with the life
insurance companies which hitherto have enjoyed a virtual
monopoly on the provision of personal pensions in the UK.

The Building Societies Act seeks to change the primary
legislation relating to conveyancing so that financial institutions such as building societies are able to provide conveyancing services. However, the Act itself does not enable
building societies to undertake conveyancing. Section 124 of
the Act brings in Schedule 21 which simply empowers the
Lord Chancellor to make rules recognizing building societies
as being suitable to provide conveyancing services. In a
response to a parliamentary question released to coincide
with the publication of the Building Societies Bill, the
Solicitor General made it clear that building societies and
banks would not be able to offer a conveyancing service to
their own members. He stated that:

The Government had concluded that there is no difficulty
in principle in such institutions providing conveyancing to
persons to whom they are not also offering a loan.
However, the Government is not satisfied that lending
institutions could safely be permitted to offer both con-

171

veyancing and a loan in the same transaction. It is therefore proposed to prohibit lending institutions from providing conveyancing either directly or through a subsidiary company in which they hold a majority stake, to those who are also borrowing from them.

In order to protect the interests of the consumer, Section 35 of the Building Societies Act prohibits societies from making primary advances conditional upon other services being provided by the same society. Furthermore, the same clause requires that where services are provided in conjunction with a primary advance they should be priced individually. Both these procedures are unique to building societies since many banks, for example, make it a condition of obtaining a mortgage that the customer has his/her bank account with that bank. The latter provision – that of pricing services separately – does not prohibit societies from offering services free, for example, for promotional purposes, as long as a zero price is quoted for that service. This effectively prevents societies from quoting an all-in-one price for a 'house-buying' package. The measure was introduced, according to the Economic Secretary to the Treasury, to bring cross-subsidization clearly above-board. However, as the BSA has pointed out, the Act does not provide for this as it would require separate costing as well as separate pricing.

In addition to the provisions made in the Act concerning commercial assets, there are also provisions concerning the holding of liquid assets which were largely foreshadowed by the Green Paper. Section 21 requires a society to keep an adequate proportion of its assets in liquid form. The Act does not provide a minimum liquidity ratio such as the $7\frac{1}{2}$ per cent liquidity ratio which societies have had to maintain in the past under the Designation Regulations for Trustee Status. However, the Act states that 'In deciding what is an adequate proportion the building society shall have regard to the range and scale of its business and the composition and character of its assets and liabilities' (Section 21.3).

Whilst not specifying any minimum liquidity ratio Subsection 3 of Section 21 does place an upper limit of 33½ per ⌉ cent on a society's holdings of liquid assets. This upper limit is unique in building society regulation. Under the previous legislation the only thing that prevented societies from holding very large proportions of liquid assets was the objects clause (of the 1962 Act) which required societies to raise funds for the purpose of making mortgage loans.

On the liabilities side of the balance sheet the Act introduces the 20 per cent limit on non-retail funds which was outlined in the Green Paper, and defines non-retail funds and deposits as marketable securities (such as bonds, certificates of deposit and Eurobonds), time deposits and all liabilities to corporate bodies. The previous 1962 legislation had, by default, an upper limit on non-retail funds since that Act required that deposits outstanding did not exceed two-thirds of the amount of a society's mortgage assets. However, the Chief Registrar has in recent years required, for prudential reasons, that any society wishing to have more than 5 per cent of its liabilities from wholesale sources should obtain the permission of the Registry of Friendly Societies. This permission has been granted in a number of cases, and many societies have been operating in recent years with proportions of non-retail funds as high as 10 per cent.

Provisions Concerning Mergers

The major innovation in the new legislation concerning amalgamations (previously unions) and transfer of engagements is that borrowers are given voting rights on proposed mergers. For both amalgamations and transfer of engagements a special resolution must be passed by 75 per cent of eligible voting shareholders as under the 1962 legislation. However, for the proposed amalgamation or transfer of engagements to fulfil the requirements of the new legislation a borrowers' resolution must also be passed by 50 per cent of eligible voting borrowers.

The new legislation makes a special provision for mergers between societies of disproportionate size, that is, where one society is less than one-eighth the size of the other. In a case such as this 20 per cent of the total membership of the smaller society would have to vote in favour of the proposed merger, in addition to the usual requirements mentioned above.

Section 96 of the Building Societies Act provides for the provision of compensation for loss of office of directors and senior executives in a merger, and for the distribution to its membership of part of the 'excess reserves' of a society involved in a merger. This is a provision which has been strongly opposed by the BSA. They argue, for example, that:

> It means that the societies with the highest reserve ratios are those best able to pay out bonuses to their members and this may make them particularly attractive, either to predators from outside the industry or to societies within the industry . . . A society which is prudently managed and has built up its reserve ratio, perhaps in anticipation of high capital spending or in anticipation of new powers, will therefore always be vulnerable to the threat of a takeover . . . This might lead some such societies to run down their reserve ratios which, for other reasons, would be totally inappropriate.
> ('The Building Societies Bill', *BSA Commentary*, December 1986, p. 150)

One of the most controversial parts of the new legislation is the provisions regarding opposed mergers. Under Clause 84(2) and Part II of Schedule 13 of the original Bill a mechanism is provided by which a society can seek to amalgamate with, or induce a transfer of engagements from, another society without the consent of the board of that society. The way in which this would be done is that the appellant (predator) society would inform the directors of the respondent (target) society of its wish to merge. If after 3 months the board had not circulated merger proposals to its own members, the appellant society would seek access to the register of members of the respondent society. If access is granted (which will be at the discretion of the new Building Societies Commission) the appellant society could send to the respondent society a merger statement requesting that the members move a merger resolution at the next AGM. If this merger resolution were to be defeated then the appellant society would be unable to make any further move under Schedule 13 of the legislation for the next 3 years.

The opposed merger proposal was one of the most hotly contested during the Bill's passage through Parliament. Some MPs and building societies expressed concern that access to the membership of a respondent society would be a breach of confidentiality. Further concern over the possibility that the appellant society could offer inducements in the form of distributions to members was expressed both during the debate preceding the second reading of the Bill, and during the Committee stage. One of the problems with this procedure is that ill-thought-out mergers could be approved by the membership simply because of the inducements offered. For example, a society with a very poor reserve ratio could seek a merger with a 'cash-rich' society simply to improve its reserve ratio.

In response to the debate concerning the opposed merger provisions, amendments were introduced following the Committee stage of the Bill. An important new proposal was that an approaching society should be prevented from including bonus payments as part of a proposed merger without the consent of the directors of the receiving society. The amended provisions are based on an obligation on societies' boards to report to the AGM any merger proposals made during the year. Thus, an opposed merger proposal will in effect be a three-stage process. First, members will be informed of the merger approach to see if they wish to acquire further details. If they do not there will be no further action. If they do they can be given details and asked whether they would like negotiations to take place. If they do not, again the matter would not proceed. If they do, however, formal merger documents will be put to them by special resolution and borrowing members' resolutions.

Prudential Supervision under the New Legislation

The Building Societies Act has established a Building Societies Commission which has taken over the regulatory function previously exercised by the Chief Registrar of Friendly Societies. The commission consists of between four and ten members appointed by the Treasury, and the initial Chairman of the Commission, the First Commissioner, is Mr Michael Bridgeman, formerly the Chief Registrar. The role of the commission will be

(1) To promote the protection by building societies of investments held with them.
(2) To promote the financial stability of building societies.
(3) To secure that the principal purpose of building societies remains that of raising, primarily from their members, funds for making advances to members secured on residential land.
(4) To administer the system of regulation of building societies provided under the Act.
(5) To advise and make recommendations to the Treasury or other government departments on any matters relating to building societies.

The new Building Societies Act gives the Commission wide-ranging powers in order to carry out this supervisory role. These include the power to: determine whether a particular activity of a society is within the power of that society, and if it is not, to prohibit the activity; impose conditions on, or revoke authorization; request a society to renew its application for authorization; petition for the winding-up of a society's operations; make an order specifying how liquid assets should be invested; impose limitations on the acceptance of deposits or making of advances; require alteration in the conduct of business (that is, to ensure requirements such as those relating to asset and liability structure are met); control advertising; prevent associations with other bodies; obtain information and documents; appoint persons to investigate the business of any society.

Of particular significance with regard to prudential supervision is Section 45 of the Act which sets out criteria for the prudent management of a society. Subsection (1) of that clause provides that in the event of the criteria not being met then this is to be taken as evidence that the society in question is prejudicing the security of investments with it.

Subsection (3) goes on to set out the criteria for prudent management:

1 Maintenance of adequate reserves and other designated capital resources.
2 Maintenance of a structure of commercial assets which satisfies the requirements of Part III [of the Act].
3 Maintenance of an adequate proportion of total assets in liquid form.
4 Maintenance of the requisite arrangements for assessing the adequacy of securities for advances secured on land.
5 Maintenance of the requisite accounting records and systems of control of business and of inspection and report.
6 Direction and management –
   (a) by a sufficient number of persons who are fit and proper to be directors or, as the case may be, officers.
   (b) conducted by them with prudence and integrity.
7 Conduct of the business with adequate professional skills.

In view of the probable need for more capital as societies enter into new, higher-risk lending, criterion number 1 is very significant. This criterion seems to imply that items other than reserves, for example, subordinated loan capital, could in the future be counted as capital for capital adequacy purposes. Indeed, Subsection (5) specifically provides for the commission to specify descriptions of capital resources by statutory instrument. A discussion paper on capital adequacy for building societies is expected in the near future, and if it does permit subordinated loan stock to count as capital, as is the case for banks, then this will greatly increase the ease with which societies can increase their capital base to cover new lending. \Previously capital could only be raised through annual surpluses. It should be noted that there is no specified minimum reserve ratio in the Act such as the sliding scale in the current Authorisation Regulations, although some minimum figure may well be advocated in the forthcoming capital adequacy paper.

Although the new commission will have wide-ranging powers under the new legislation it could be argued that these powers will be lacking in some important areas. The new commission, for example, will be unable to enforce the winding-up of a society. The Act merely allows the commission to petition to the courts, despite the fact that wider powers in this respect were advocated as early as June 1980 by the Wilson Committee Report:

At present, if investigation reveals a society to be in financial difficulties, either through fraud or incompetence, the Registrar can prevent it from advertising or from accepting further deposits. He cannot, however, force the society to merge with another or wind itself up. While therefore he can protect investors from further investments in an unsound society, he can do little or nothing to help existing investors, who may not have the know-how or the ability to influence the way in which their society is run. He may, moreover be inhibited from using his present powers by the fear that they could be counter-productive. When the circumstances give rise to a near certainty of loss, the Registrar clearly has no alternative but to impose a prohibition on the acceptance of further investments. But the impositions of the prohibition in cases which, though unsatisfactory, fall some way short of this may seriously increase the likelihood of failure through stimulating a 'run' on the society's liquid funds. We *recommend* that the Registrar should be given power to promote mergers or to enforce the winding up of a society for prudential reasons subject to an appropriate right of appeal and without restriction on the amount of assets involved.

(Wilson, 1980, p. 332)

The Wilson Committee Report also stressed that the prudential monitoring of societies was not of an adequate standard, as was evidenced by the examples of the Wakefield Building Society in 1976 and the Grays Building Society in 1978. In both cases fraud and the falsification of accounts had been perpetrated by the general manager, and this had

178

been compounded by inadequate auditing. In the case of the Wakefield the misappropriations amounted to £633,000, while in the case of the Grays Building Society they totalled £7 million (including interest forgone) for a society with assets on paper of only £11½ million. As in the past these cases were dealt with on an *ad hoc* basis by the BSA. The Wakefield Building Society had its engagements transferred to the Halifax, whilst in the case of Grays Building Society the Woolwich Equitable took on the society's operations and the losses to investors were made good through contributions from members of the BSA. The case of the Grays Building Society was so severe, however, that the Chief Registrar urged the BSA to set up an investor protection scheme along the lines of the policyholders' protection scheme for insurance companies and the deposit protection scheme for banks. The Wilson Committee Report also advocated an investor protection scheme to be set up for societies stressing that to be consistent with the treatment of banks and insurance companies it should be set up on a statutory basis. However, it was a voluntary rather than a statutory scheme which was introduced in the spring of 1982. This scheme was sponsored by the BSA (but not confined to its members) and signatories (amounting to 167 societies accounting for 99.9 per cent of the industry's total assets in March 1984) agreed to contribute to the protection fund which effectively guaranteed 90 per cent of the value of shares in contributing societies and 75 per cent in non-contributing societies. Contributions to the fund were limited to 0.3 per cent of total assets for individual societies.

Under the new legislation the investor protection scheme for building societies has been brought into line with the statutory scheme operating for banks under the 1979 Banking Act. Like the banks' scheme the level of protection given will be 75 per cent of amounts of shares and deposits up to a limit of £10,000. However, unlike the banks' scheme which has a standing fund, under the building societies' scheme there is no provision for a fund unless the Building Societies Investor Protection Board deems that one is needed.

Conversion to Company Status

A consultative paper on the 'Conversion of Building Societies to Company Status' was issued by the Treasury to coincide with publication of the Building Societies Bill. Although the Bill contained, in Clause 88, provision to allow societies to convert themselves into public limited companies the government felt it wise, in view of the complexity of issues involved, to seek comments on the proposed mechanics of conversion. After reviewing the comments it was the government's intention to introduce substantive provisions into the Bill during its passage through Parliament.

The primary reason for permitting building societies to change to company status was the recognition by the government that the Bill was restrictive in allowing only limited diversification and ensuring that societies continued to play their traditional savings and mortgage lending role in the financial sector. The government felt, therefore that

> Some [societies] may in due course find that the logic of their further commercial development is no longer consistent with the constraints appropriate for building societies generally. The option of becoming a company, no longer subject to building society legislation, would be an important one in such cases.[14]

If a building society does choose to convert to company status in the future then it will no longer be covered by building society legislation and would not be permitted to use the words 'building society' in the company title. Instead it would be registered under the Companies Acts and would be required to apply for a deposit-taking licence under the Banking Act 1979. Furthermore, the newly formed company would find itself under the prudential supervision of the Bank of England rather than the new Building Societies Commission.

In proposing the mechanics of the conversion procedure the government was guided by two major principles. First, that any conversion should be in the best long-term interest of the society rather than in the short-term financial interest of the members of the society. Secondly, that the procedure ensured that the rights of members were fully protected.

The main procedural proposals advocated in the consultative paper were:

(1) That a proposal for conversion would require the approval, by at least 75 per cent of investing members voting, of a special resolution of the society, and that those members expressing their approval for the conversion should constitute not less than 20 per cent of the total number of investors eligible to vote. Furthermore, conversion would also be subject to a 'borrower member resolution' requiring the support of 50 per cent of borrowers voting.

(2) That no person, or connected group of persons, may hold 15 per cent or more of shares issued for the first five years of the new company's life. This provision is intended to ensure that the former society preserves its independence during the first five years of its existence as a company, and that the new company should not be vulnerable to take-over bids simply because the business and investment community had not had sufficient time to assess its prospects. There is a provision, however, that a take-over could proceed after the first two years if the holders of at least 75 per cent of share capital voted in favour. A much more stringent proviso is made for the possibility of an immediate take-over by an outside institution. In that case a society would be allowed to transfer its engagements to an existing company, rather than a new company set up by the society, only if 50 per cent of eligible investors voted in favour and these investors constituted 90 per cent of the share capital.

(3) That investing members of the society would have statutory priority subscription rights in the public offer of shares for sale. Those members subscribing to the issue would receive a bonus scrip issue after one year recognizing their interest in the reserves of the society before conversion. After two years other investors who had not subscribed to the issue but had retained their deposits would be offered either special shares in the company (that is, these shares may not confer dividends or be fully marketable but simply continue the voting rights of former members) or a limited cash bonus (not exceeding 1 per cent).

181

These latter measures are intended to ensure that former members retain an interest in the society and do not simply cash in their shares immediately. In order to minimize the possibility of speculative flows of investment funds occurring between societies due to 'conversion rumours' the consultative document also advocates that the further benefits outlined in (3) should be confined to members of some standing with the society in question.

The government had originally intended to introduce amendments to the clauses of the Bill dealing with conversion at the Committee stage. However, by the time of the Committee stage the government had not considered all the responses to the consultative paper and hence no amendments were made. The Economic Secretary to the Treasury did point out during the debate at the Committee stage, however, that the Act would simply set out the basic criteria which all conversion schemes should meet, and that the individual societies would be free to decide upon the detailed mechanism suitable for their particular circumstances. The government finally incorporated the detailed proposals on conversion into the Bill at the Report stage, and these showed little change from the proposals outlined in the consultative paper.

At the time of writing few societies had expressed a desire to abandon their mutual status and convert to a public limited company. It seems likely, however, that the decision, if it is taken, will be one of necessity rather than choice. As we have seen, the profitability of societies has been under increasing pressure in recent years and societies have done well to increase their aggregate reserve ratio since 1980. In 1984, however, the reserve ratio fell from 4.06 to 4.00 due primarily to the change in the tax provisions relating to societies' gilts profits in February 1984. Although societies, due to their mutual status, have not operated on large reserve ratios in the past, recent evidence on official thinking suggests that they will be under pressure in the future to build up capital adequacy. Recent statements from the First Commissioner and the government suggest that official thinking on reserves focuses on three main areas:

(1)   the use of free reserves (gross reserves less fixed assets) as the best indication of capital adequacy;
(2)   the need for reserves to reflect the circumstances of a particular society;
(3)   the need for adequate capital backing for additional types of business following the new legislation.

Societies will clearly find it difficult to increase their free reserve ratios from the 2½–3 per cent level of recent years in the face of increasing competitive pressure on their annual surpluses, and it is this particular capital constraint which is likely to be the catalyst (particularly for the larger societies wishing to diversify into new business) compelling societies to undertake conversion. Many societies, however, feel that they may, in practice, be unable to convert due to the highly restrictive requirement that they ensure that 20 per cent of their membership vote on any conversion proposal. The Abbey National Building Society, which was among the first to declare an interest in conversion, has pointed out that these stringent procedures will require approximately 1.6 million of the Abbey's 7–8 million members voting on a conversion proposal when typically only 1,500 vote at AGMs. Thus, societies could find themselves in the unenviable position of having new powers at their disposal but being unable to take full advantage of them because of an unavoidable capital constraint.

Notes

1 See Price (1958).
2 Upon merging a building society was created which held approximately 18.2 per cent of the sector's total assets.
3 Mortgage interest relief at source (MIRAS) places a much greater administrative burden on building societies in respect of the calculation of tax relief available to borrowers on interest payments.
4 The issues surrounding the size–efficiency relationship for building societies are discussed on pp. 138–40.
5 See *Building Societies Act*, published 5 December 1986.
6 With an endowment mortgage the borrower pays the interest

on the loan and also pays a regular premium on an endowment insurance policy. The capital sum from the matured policy should be more than sufficient to repay the original loan, and the borrower receives the surplus funds. The normal annuity mortgage simply involves the borrower in regular repayment of principal with interest.

7   For a technical analysis of the issues surrounding non-price allocation of building society loans, see Nellis and Thom (1983).

8   It should be noted that there is some dispute over the inclusion of elements such as depreciation in management expenses for purposes of analysing building society efficiency. On this issue see Gilchrist and Rothwell (1980).

9   The Halifax has its own cashcard network consisting of over 350 machines. Link is a shared network introduced in January 1985 and includes the Abbey National and Nationwide societies. Matrix is a national network of shared ATMs set up by Electronic Funds Transfer (EFT). Seven of the top eleven societies are founder members and the network was launched in February 1985.

10 *The Future Constitution and Powers of Building Societies*, published by the BSA.

11 BSA, February 1984.

12 The new powers available under the 1986 legislation are not automatically conferred on building societies. Rather, each society must have a memorandum of powers which details the adoptable powers and any restrictions it has assumed, and which must be agreed by a special resolution put before the membership.

13 Reported in *Building Societies Gazette*, March 1986, p. 26.

14 *Building Societies Bill. Conversion of Building Societies to Company Status, A Consultative Paper*, HM Treasury, December 1985, p. 1.

CHAPTER FIVE

Finance Houses

Introduction

Finance houses comprise a rather heterogeneous group of financial institutions. A high proportion of the value of transactions undertaken by this sector are performed by members of the Finance Houses Association (FHA). The membership of this organization currently stands at 44 institutions, and includes subsidiaries of UK banks, companies owned by major overseas financial institutions (often based in North America) and several independent companies. A major function of UK finance houses is to provide instalment credit facilities both to industry and to consumers in the UK.[1] In relation to corporate customers they provide a wide range of facilities to assist with the acquisition of all types of assets, ranging from office equipment through to aircraft, ships and oil refineries. In respect of consumers, finance is provided for the purchase of consumer durable goods such as cars and electrical goods, as well as housing finance and personal loans for home improvements, and for other purposes. These latter facilities are often provided either through branch offices or at the point of sale through retailers and wholesalers acting as agents for finance houses. In addition, some of these institutions offer revolving credit card facilities. On the liabilities side of their balance sheets they may carry both time and sight accounts for deposits, as well as claims arising through the issue of various forms of marketable instruments.

In 1985, new advances by member companies of the FHA

185

had a value of £11.7 billion, which was approximately 19 per cent above the figure for the previous year. Outstanding credit increased by 18 per cent, exceeding £20 billion for the first time at the end of 1985. Correspondingly, finance houses' aggregate liabilities have increased substantially in recent years, and in 1985 were some 80 per cent higher in real terms than they were in 1980. Tables 5.1 and 5.2 show respectively the total amounts of outstanding credit and the new credit extended for the years 1980 to 1985. It may be observed that whilst there has been a steady increase in the amounts owed by both personal consumers and by business customers, there has been a slight shift of emphasis towards the consumer.

Table 5.3 shows the composition of new credit extended for the major categories of borrowers for 1984 and 1985. For both consumer and business sectors by far the largest use of funds has been to purchase new and used cars. In respect of consumers, funds related to personal loans and revolving credit cards have grown substantially in recent years. The provision of funds for the purchase or lease of industrial plant and equipment has been an extremely important element of activities in respect of business customers. It is also clear that the finance houses provide funds for a wide array of different purchases, and this reflects the increasing diversification of operations which has taken place during the past decade. In common with most retail financial intermediaries, the finance houses have felt the effects of increasingly severe competition from other domestic and overseas institutions offering similar forms of services. In general, the finance houses have reacted with vigour and imagination, and have continued to prosper despite the pressures experienced.

The Evolution of the Finance Houses

It is possible to trace the history of credit provision through finance houses back more than 150 years to the development of the 'hire and purchase system'.[2] From the outset it was clear that the type of assets suitable for purchase through

186

Table 5.1

UK Finance Houses: Outstanding Credit, end-year values, 1980 to 1985

	1980 £m	%	1981 £m	%	1982 £m	%	1983 £m	%	1984 £m	%	1985 £m	%
Outstanding to consumers	2,515	30.8	3,008	29.7	3,598	29.6	4,706	32.8	5,881	33.7	7,243	35.1
Outstanding to business customers (excluding leasing)	2,667	32.6	2,947	29.1	3,482	28.7	4,116	28.7	4,893	28.1	5,467	26.5
Leasing (written down value of leased assets)	2,989	36.6	4,164	41.2	5,064	41.7	5,529	38.5	6,655	38.2	7,912	38.4
Total	8,171	100.0	10,119	100.0	12,144	100.0	14,351	100.0	17,429	100.0	20,622	100.0

Source: Finance Houses Association.
Note: These figures include all outstanding amounts whether or not payable by instalment.

Table 5.2

UK Finance Houses: New Credit Extended, 1980 to 1985

| | 1980 | | 1981 | | 1982 | | 1983 | | 1984 | | 1985 | |
	£m	%	£m	%	£m	%	£m	%	£m	%	£m	%
To consumers	1,924	36.8	2,372	39.0	2,909	40.2	3,804	47.0	4,427	45.0	5,034	43.1
To business customers (excluding leasing)	1,749	33.5	1,743	28.7	2,206	30.8	2,459	30.3	2,698	27.4	3,137	26.8
Leasing (original cost of assets purchased for lease)	1,551	29.7	1,963	32.3	2,092	29.0	1,838	22.7	2,710	27.6	3,524	30.1
Total	5,224	100.0	6,078	100.0	7,207	100.0	8,101	100.0	9,835	100.0	11,695	100.0

Source: Finance Houses Association.

Table 5.3

UK Finance Houses: Analysis of New Credit by Class of Goods and by Class of Borrower, 1984 and 1985, £ million

	Consumer		Business (excl. leasing)		Leasing	
	1984	1985	1984	1985	1984	1985
New cars	897	987	721	869	} 395	} 649
Used cars	924	1,011	239	349		
Retail credit	499	609	—	—	—	—
Home improvements	616	596	—	—	—	—
Property	303	404	206	285	—	—
Personal loans	563	714	—	—	—	—
Revolving credit and credit cards	334	482	—	—	—	—
Commercial vehicles	—	—	442	476	321	418
Farm equipment	—	—	81	85	165	215
Computer and office equipment	—	—	132	136	454	589
Industrial plant	—	—	419	462	907	879
Ships and aircraft	—	—	—	—	267	584
Oil exploration and extraction equipment	—	—	—	—	100	70
Other	291	231	458	475	101	120
Total	4,427	5,034	2,698	3,137	2,710	3,524

Source: Finance Houses Association, *Annual Report*, 1986.

instalment credit would be those with a long life offering security if customers should default on repayments. From the creditors' viewpoint the supply of credit to the more affluent members of society, where the credit risk is relatively low, is preferential, and also, where possible, the real assets involved should generate income in order to enable the debt to be serviced. However, it is evident that the possibility for assets involved in hire-purchase transactions to generate an income rests exclusively with business assets. In this respect, one of the earliest uses of hire-purchase finance was by the 'wagon companies', some of which were formed in the 1860s, in order to finance the sale of special purpose trucks to the then thriving collieries. The original objectives of many of these companies were to construct railway wagons, engines and machinery for railways or agriculture, and to sell, let or hire such equipment. These wagon finance companies played an important role in the early development of hire-purchase and in the provision of commercial industrial finance.

After the First World War finance houses benefited from the rapid growth of the UK motor industry, and hire-purchase finance developed quickly. Its convenience as a means of financing the sale of mass-produced goods, in conjunction with the absence of official regulation of activities, obviously contributed to its successful evolution. Indeed, it was not until 1938 that the government took direct steps to counter the occasional malpractice perceived in the industry with the passing of the Hire Purchase Act. This was the first of a series of related legislation culminating in the comprehensive Consumer Credit Act 1974 (which is described below).

The early history of the finance house sector is summed up concisely by Drury (1982). He states that the development of the sector

is essentially about the emergence of hire-purchase as a form of instalment credit. There were to develop many hundreds of small hire-purchase companies which either supported the selling effort of their manufacturing or retailing parents or were the vehicle by which entrepreneurs were able to generate profits from the process of making finance available at the point of sale.

The outbreak of the Second World War brought to an end a period of expansion for the finance house sector, and for almost two decades after the end of the war finance houses were subject to checks on their growth as the government sought to influence economic activity for the purposes of controlling inflation and dealing with balance-of-payments problems. The Borrowing (Control and Guarantee) Act 1946 gave powers to the Treasury to control companies' borrowing and raising of capital by the issuing of shares. However, this resulted in the establishment of a number of new hire-purchase finance companies, which in itself tended to undermine the opportunities for growth for the existing members of the sector. The second element of official control came in the form of guidance letters issued by the Governor of the Bank of England. Qualitative control was exercised as the authorities indicated to commercial banks where their priorities should lie in respect of their on-lending. As these banks were large providers of funds to the finance houses, there were clear implications for the future expansion of the latter's business. The powers to restrict the availability of capital and borrowed funds were supplemented on numerous occasions by 'terms controls' imposed by the government. These took various forms, but were directed towards holding down the growth of instalment credit. The initial deposit that the customer had to put down for the purchase of an asset was stipulated, together with a limit on the length of the repayment period. Nevertheless, there is some controversy over the ultimate effect of these official controls on the finance house sector. As Greaves (1959) states:

> It is doubtful whether the financial controls on hire-purchase have had much effect on the volume of hire-purchase business. The finance companies soon made good their restricted bank overdrafts from other sources and the general shortage of credit created a great demand for an expansion in hire-purchase finance. The financial controls did, however, have two important consequences:

they gave rise to the formation of a great number of small hire-purchase companies and they weakened the long-standing relationship between the older companies and their bankers.

At the beginning of July 1958 the Chancellor of the Exchequer announced the cancellation of directives to the banks on their lending and stated that restrictions on the raising of capital would be relaxed. In particular, favourable consideration would be given to applications from finance houses seeking to raise fresh capital if this would improve the stability of the hire-purchase financial system. There followed a spate of investments by banks in finance houses, and the capital bases of these institutions were strengthened considerably. Consequently, during the late 1950s and early 1960s the finance house sector prospered in the relatively buoyant financial environment of the time. However, this position was to change markedly during the second half of the 1960s, as the finance houses entered a period of almost continual restriction.

In May 1965 the finance houses faced, for the first time, quantitative lending controls. The Governor of the Bank of England wrote to the members of the Finance Houses Association asking them to exercise the same measure of restraint as had been requested of the joint stock banks. Thus it was desired that the level of advances (both instalment credit and loans) should increase by no more than 5 per cent during the year to March 1966, which clearly limited the scope for the further development of activities. But by the end of the 1960s, although terms controls remained, the climate of intellectual, political and banking opinion in the UK became much more favourable to the encouragement of free competition in banking, and much more hostile both to the interest rate cartel operated by the clearing banks and also to such counter-competitive techniques of monetary policy as restrictive lending ceilings applied to banks and finance houses individually. Consequently, a new monetary control framework was introduced by the Bank of England in the autumn of 1971 under the broad heading of the Competition and Credit Control regulations. A major aim of these regulations was to establish a more uniform system of credit control for banks and finance houses. As part of the control mechanism all banking institutions were required to maintain a minimum of 12½ per cent of their eligible liabilities (which largely comprised sterling deposits with less than two years to maturity) in the form of eligible reserve assets (which were high-quality liquid assets drawn from a prescribed list issued by the Bank of England). This reserve requirement also applied, with minor variations, to finance houses, although some of the major companies applied for and were granted the status of authorized banks and hence came within the standard 12½ per cent reserve requirement.

A second objective of the 1971 measures was to achieve control of credit creation through variations in interest rates rather than through direct regulatory controls. Thus the demand for (instalment) credit would be dampened by manipulation of its price, rather than through non-market rationing. However, in practice, the growing use of liability management techniques by banks, which drew upon funds from the wholesale money markets, supported the surge in bank lending that followed the removal of the direct restrictions, and the actual degree of control established over credit creation was the subject of considerable controversy. Nevertheless, for the finance houses the early 1970s were once again a period of buoyant activity and optimism similar to that which had been experienced a decade earlier. But on this occasion the relative prosperity was to be only short-lived since a major secondary banking crisis developed rapidly which was to have considerable repercussions for the operations and structure of the finance houses sector.

Following the deregulations of 1969–71, prudential standards of loan assessment and liability management outside the primary banking sector were undermined both by competitive pressures and also by demands for credit from borrowers, particularly in the field of commercial property. New lending institutions grew up in the secondary banking sector, and for a time these flourished free from controls on the expansion of their assets and in a position to tap the wholesale markets in order to fuel their growth. In the winter of 1973–4, the end of the boom in commercial property caused their prosperity to vanish and deposits to be withdrawn. A crisis then ensued as these institutions found themselves in severe liquidity difficulties. In general the finance houses came through the crisis with little long-term damage, although the position of United Dominions Trust (UDT) was in doubt for several years and, despite re-establishing its financial stability, it was ultimately absorbed by the Trustee Savings Bank Group in 1981. Indeed, it was probably the adverse effect on confidence in the financial system resulting from the secondary banking crisis which ultimately led to the absorption of many of the remaining major independent finance houses by banking groups.

Since the abolition of reserve requirements and direct monetary controls on banking activities in 1981, not only has there been more competition within the banking sector, but finance houses as a whole would also appear to have entered a new phase in their development. In 1982 the government abolished terms controls which undoubtedly benefited the finance houses. It is argued by some commentators that the record number of new car registrations in 1983, and the high level subsequently sustained, were almost entirely due to the higher volume of new cars financed on credit provided by finance houses. During 1984 approximately one-third of all new cars registered in the UK were financed by funds obtained from finance houses. However, as illustrated in Table 5.3, the provision of funds for motor car purchase has recently accounted for well below 50 per cent of total new lending to consumers, thereby demonstrating the importance of finance house activities for the health of the UK economy in general. Furthermore, it must be remembered that the emphasis of many finance houses has been on the provision of business credit, and in particular, in recent years, on factoring and leasing activities. The limitation on the opportunities to provide funds to the personal sector has generated pressures for innovative credit facilities for business customers, and the finance houses have been at the forefront of these activities.

The Structure and Operations of UK Finance Houses

There are 44 members of the Finance Houses Association, and the bulk of finance house transactions are carried out by the UK bank-owned companies within this group. Table 5.4 lists the UK finance houses with capital bases in excess of £1 billion. It is interesting to note that each of these five institutions is owned by a major UK retail banking group.

These finance houses are currently facing strong competition from the more recently established subsidiaries of US financial institutions, which have tended to take an aggressive approach to marketing their services and have shown substantial innovative style. These institutions include Citibank Trust Ltd. (with Citicorp as its parent company), HFC Trust and Savings Ltd. (Household International) and Boston Trust and Savings (First National Boston Corporation). It must be emphasized that some finance houses are owned by non-banking companies; for example, the Ford Motor Credit Co. Ltd. is owned by the Ford Motor Co. There are also a number of independent finance houses such as the London Scottish Finance Corporation, although these are becoming fewer in number as the competitive pressures within the broader financial environment take their toll. Indeed, until recently one of the few surviving independent companies was the Wagon Finance Corporation which was founded just after the turn of the century. This continued to

Table 5.4
UK Finance Houses: Five Largest Institutions by Capital Base, end 1985 accounting year

Finance House	Capital (£ million)	Parent Company
Mercantile Credit	3,548	Barclays Bank
Lombard North Central	2,990	National Westminster Bank
Lloyds Bowmaker	2,184	Lloyds Bank
Forward Trust	2,142	Midland Bank
United Dominions Trust	1,118	Trustee Savings Bank Group

Source: *The Banker*, April 1986.

operate as a separate entity until being subject to an agreed take-over bid by MAI plc in February 1986.

Facilities Offered by UK Finance Houses

The broad nature of the facilities provided by UK finance houses has already been outlined above, and the distribution of credit made available in recent years has been clearly shown in Table 5.3. However, it is useful to consider the major types of facilities offered by finance houses in a little more detail. These facilities may be divided into the forms of instalment credit offered to consumers and the forms of credit offered to industrial and commercial customers.

There are seven major types of instalment credit available to personal consumers:

(1) *Hire-purchase* This is perhaps the best-known facility offered by finance houses. Under a hire-purchase agreement the customer hires goods for an agreed period and may purchase them at the end of the period for a very small sum. It is only when all the instalments and the option fee have been paid that the customer legally owns the goods.

(2) *Conditional sale* In this case the price of the goods is payable over an agreed period of time, but the goods remain the property of the seller for some stated period (usually until the last payment has been made).

(3) *Credit sale* Under this type of agreement the customer purchases the goods but there is a condition that the customer is allowed to pay for them by instalments. In other words, the customer obtains title to the goods at once, but is allowed to make deferred payments.

Under each of the above facilities, the finance house provides finance for the transaction, and the purchaser of the goods will usually repay the cash price of the goods plus a percentage interest payment. The amount by which the credit price exceeds the cash price of the goods depends upon the extent to which the vendor of the goods is willing to absorb the finance house charges. As a marketing ploy, a vendor of goods may absorb all the finance charges and so advertise 'interest-free' credit to purchasers of his goods.

(4) *Personal loans* These are straightforward loans of money which are repayable with interest over a fixed period of time, and usually by equal instalments. Normally, loans are unsecured, and the decision whether or not to lend is based upon a 'credit-scoring' system. This technique takes an objective approach using data about the prospective borrower and applying statistical probability methods in order to establish the likelihood that the funds will be repaid. Consequently, there is no requirement that the funds be borrowed for the purpose of purchasing specific assets.

(5) *Secured personal loans* When advancing larger sums of money over longer periods of time the risks involved for the finance house are clearly greater than for modest shorter-term loans. Thus, it is far more likely that in such circumstances security will be sought from the prospective borrower. For example, money advanced to pay for home improvements or a house extension may be secured by a first or second mortgage of the property concerned. Alternatively, an assignment over a life insurance policy or a charge on stocks and shares may be taken as an alternative security.

(6) *Revolving loans* These allow the customer to borrow up to a multiple of an agreed monthly payment to the finance house. For example, the customer may agree to pay £75 per month to the finance house, in return for which he may be allowed a credit limit of 20 times this amount (£1,500). The customer may use the funds for any purpose desired, so long as the agreed payment is made each month. A proportion of this payment is used to pay off the monthly interest charged to the account, whilst the remainder is used to pay off the capital borrowed. The customer also has the right to top up his borrowing continually to the originally agreed limit.

(7) *Even spread repayment loans* These loans allow the customer to make fixed monthly repayments whilst at

the same time having the interest payments linked to prevailing market rates. The fixed repayments are calculated on the basis of the lender's view as to the likely interest rates over the term of the loan. At the end of the agreement period, or at agreed intervals of time, the actual interest payments due (which are usually based on the Finance House Base Rate)[3] are calculated and the customer pays any undercharged interest or is repaid any overcharged interest.

The facilities made available to industrial and commercial customers may be divided into five groups:

(1) *Industrial hire-purchase* The nature of hire-purchase finance for business customers is exactly the same as that for personal customers, although the real goods subject to the underlying transactions may take on a much broader variety. It is common for this form of finance to be used for the purchase of items ranging from photocopiers to combine harvesters to fleets of motor vehicles. There are clear benefits to the company using hire-purchase finance: assets may be obtained without excessive short-term cash flow implications; an immediate VAT credit may be claimed from Customs and Excise which may be set off against the next quarterly VAT payment by the company; and the borrower may claim the available capital allowances as offsets to corporate tax, since the underlying real asset eventually becomes the property of the borrower. (This does not occur with leasing, as the lessor is the legal owner of the underlying real asset and hence has the right to claim the capital allowance.) If fixed rate hire-purchase is arranged, accurate budgeting of costs and cash may be carried out, although many hire-purchase contracts for businesses are priced at floating rates, perhaps making an even-spread loan (as explained in point (7) above) more attractive in this context.

(2) *Leasing* This is an extremely important form of business financing and is dealt with separately below.

(3) *Block discounting* This relates to the purchase of debts

198

from a trader at a discount to the full value of the debts. The trader benefits by removing a block of debtors from his books whilst simultaneously receiving a large proportion of their value in cash. The underlying debts may be of a hire-purchase form, but in any event the finance house takes on the risk of default in return for the discounting fee.

(4) *Stocking loans* These are loans made to traders to allow them to hold sufficient stocks of goods in order to maximize sales potential. These types of facilities are quite popular in the motor trade, where the funds advanced may be secured against the stock of new cars held for sale. However, funds may be made available in this context on an unsecured basis, or perhaps against the personal guarantee of the trader.

(5) *Commercial loans* These include both secured and unsecured facilities, with funds repayable by instalment. These loans are increasingly being custom-made to meet the precise financing needs of the customer, and they may be made for a wide variety of purposes including the improvement of a business's working capital position. As with all industrial and commercial lending, the finance house will be concerned to ensure that risks of default are minimized, and will determine the nature of the facilities to be made available on the basis of the prospective borrower's track record, the skill of the directors, the audited accounts, and so on. In many instances a long-standing direct relationship between the finance house and the prospective borrower exists, and this, of course, makes evaluation of creditworthiness much simpler.

The Marketing of Finance House Facilities

Finance houses may make contact with their customers either directly or indirectly by way of introduction by a third party. Direct contact may be established through the branch networks operated by many of the finance houses. In addition to these institutions having longer opening hours than banks, they are often perceived as being less formal and bureaucratic than banks whilst offering a range of near-banking services (often including the provision of current accounts which pay interest and allow guaranteed overdraft facilities). Branch offices form a point of contact for both personal and corporate customers. In addition, direct mailing of both previous and potential new customers is being used increasingly for marketing purposes. This is particularly so where there is a link between the finance house and some other organization whose members or clients form an attractive pool of prospective customers for financial services. For example, for more than twenty years Lombard North Central has been providing Royal Automobile Club members with specially formulated 'Members' Finance Plans', offering them the opportunity to apply for unsecured personal loans at preferential rates. Representatives of finance houses also maintain regular direct contact with commercial and industrial customers, so that transactions may be negotiated on the basis of ongoing established relationships which allow the finance house to obtain detailed insight into their customers' business activities.

Despite the importance of direct provision of financial services by finance houses, it has been their ability to offer instalment credit through traders (especially to the consumer sector) which has been at the heart of their success. Indeed, the existence of point-of-sale outlets has been one of the main reasons for banks buying into finance house businesses. In such circumstances banks have tended to maintain the original names of the finance houses, believing them to be a useful characteristic for marketing purposes. Barclays, for example, which normally prefers to use its own house name on group products, has maintained the name of Mercantile Credit for its finance house subsidiary. However, as pointed out by Blanden (1986), indirect approaches are not wholly satisfactory for finance houses:

> The drawback of point-of-sale finance . . . is that it does not encourage any kind of loyalty by the borrower to a particular lender. The customer is interested mainly in how much it will be necessary to pay each month, not in which company is providing the finance. As a result it has

not been easy for finance houses to capture repeat business or to cross-sell other types of services.

Furthermore, as direct mailing becomes increasingly accepted, and as market segmentation becomes more complex as new technology permits ever more accurate identification of target groups of customers, the drawbacks of indirect selling of services are likely to become more apparent from the marketing viewpoint.

The Raising of Funds by Finance Houses

Usually finance houses support the growth of their asset portfolios through a mix of sources of funds, but both the bank-owned finance houses and the independent institutions tend to make extensive use of wholesale money market sources, either through their parent organizations or directly as appropriate. Of the major finance houses, only Lombard North Central aims to maintain a significant proportion of its inflows of funds from retail deposits, with approximately one-half of its resources coming through this channel. In respect of raising funds, the finance houses are obviously affected by the ongoing developments in the monetary environment and by the Bank of England's broad monetary controls. Also, changes in the maturity and structure of finance houses' assets will have a strong influence on the desired nature of their liabilities' portfolios. Indeed, the importance of managing the liabilities side of the balance sheet in the face of changes in asset holdings cannot be overemphasized. Whilst maturity transformation of funds is at the very heart of financial intermediation activity, excessive mismatching of assets and liabilities by any individual organization may threaten its longer-term financial stability.

In recent years there would appear to have been a general lengthening in the maturity of finance house assets, with an increased proportion of funds being on-lent to the corporate sector. Moreover, it is believed that approximately 40 per cent of the funds provided to the corporate sector are lent on a fixed interest rate basis, along with the bulk of funds lent to the personal sector. The major risk for finance houses arising from the mismatching of assets and liabilities relates to interest rate movements. That is, market interest rates may move adversely and force finance houses to fund their on-lending within the maturity of fixed rate loans at rates of interest which make the loans non-viable commercially. Protection from this eventuality may be sought either by setting initially wide margins between borrowing and lending rates (but this may make loans appear expensive to the potential borrower) or by pricing loans on a floating rate basis (which may not always be acceptable to the borrower). For these reasons it is advisable for finance houses to increase the average maturity of their liabilities in response to an increase in the maturity of their assets.

Table 5.5 shows the broad structure of funds for the finance house sector during the early 1980s. Given the reliance on funds borrowed from commercial banks and through money market channels, variations in market interest rates may seriously interfere with the underlying pricing strategy of finance house agreements. There is little doubt that in an environment of relatively volatile interest rate movements, the pressure will increase for finance houses to arrange an even larger proportion of their on-lending at floating (market-related) rates.

Table 5.6 shows the aggregate balance sheet, at the end of 1984, of the UK finance houses which are pure non-bank

Table 5.5

Finance House Sector: Distribution of Sources of Funds, average for early 1980s

Source	%
Share capital and reserves	14
Borrowing from commercial banks	32
Borrowing from money markets	24
Deposits from the general public	10
Deferred taxation	17
Other funds	3

Source: Finance Houses Association, *Credit Quarterly*, February 1983.

Table 5.6
Non-Monetary Sector Finance Houses: Aggregate
Balance Sheet, 31 December 1985

	£m	£m	%
Assets			
Cash and bank deposits		58	1.3
Certificates of deposit		7	0.2
Other current assets		146	3.1
Loans and advances:		3,859	83.0
Block discounts	3		
Industrial and commercial	1,041		
Personal customers	2,815		
Other assets		578	12.4
Total assets		4,648	100.0
Liabilities			
Commercial bills		772	16.6
Funds from monetary sector		2,603	56.0
Short-term	1,346		
Long-term	1,257		
Other financial institutions		33	0.7
Other UK suppliers		70	1.5
Overseas		26	0.6
Other current liabilities		252	5.4
Capital and reserves		892	19.2
Total liabilities		4,648	100.0

Source: *Financial Statistics*, June 1986.

intermediaries (that is, companies which are not recognized as banking institutions within the provisions of the Banking Act 1979). It may be observed that approximately 70 per cent of funds (excluding capital and reserves) came from the monetary (banking) sector and other financial institutions, with issues of commercial bills accounting for a large proportion of the remainder. Contrary to the norm for finance houses as a whole, these pure non-bank institutions emphasize the provision of credit for personal customers, although funds provided to the company sector still form a significant element of their assets portfolios.

Leasing

The major finance houses pioneered the development of leasing in the UK, and today many of the leasing companies are finance houses. Leases are contracts where one party, the lessee, hires capital equipment from another party, the lessor. The lessor is the legal owner of the equipment and is thus able to claim any available capital allowances for tax purposes, whilst the lessee is the user of the equipment. There are two broad categories of leases: financial and operating. With financial leases the rentals are fixed such that the lessor is assured of recovering the full cost of the equipment leased together with a suitable return on capital (assuming, of course, that the lessee does not default on his commitment). An operating lease has a shorter life than the asset itself, and it is the lessor's hope that profits may be made through successive leasing transactions for the same asset. In 1984, some 15 per cent of all investment in new plant and machinery in the UK (both public and private sector and including service sectors) was financed by leasing. This widespread use of the facility has led to a large number of variants on the basic forms of contract mentioned above.

Leasing first became a major area of financial activity in the UK in the 1970s, with the total new assets acquired for leasing rising from just £130 million in 1972 to £1.2 billion in 1978. By 1985 the annual purchase of new assets for leasing stood at approximately £5 billion. Virtually all types of plant and machinery are handled through leasing, with the biggest category being industrial plant which may vary from individual items of office equipment through to entire factories with contents. More than one-half of all UK equipment leasing business is accounted for by the finance house subsidiaries of the major clearing bank groups. The merchant banks are also an important direct force in leasing activities.

A major factor stimulating the growth of leasing as a flexible low-cost means of financing capital expenditures was the tax regime in the UK between 1971 and 1984.

204

During this period, companies were allowed for corporation tax purposes to write off in the year of acquisition the full cost of plant and machinery acquired for use in the business. However, many industrial and commercial companies were unable to make full use of their allowances owing to inadequate profit levels, and this produced an ideal opening for leasing activities. Quite simply, leasing companies were able to purchase plant and equipment (for use by customers unable to take advantage of the tax allowances) and claim the associated tax allowances themselves. The gains to the leasing companies through tax savings were then distributed between themselves and the lessees through the leasing charges negotiated. Effectively, many finance houses provided tax shelters for their parent banks through this mechanism, whilst at the same time providing favourable financing terms to corporate customers wishing to make use of capital equipment.

With the new rules for capital allowances introduced in the 1984 budget, the leasing industry is facing a period of change. The 100 per cent first year allowance for capital expenditures was phased out, by April 1986, to be replaced by a 25 per cent annual writing-down allowance on a diminishing balance basis. This adjustment was accompanied by a phased reduction in the level of corporation tax from the 52 per cent rate down to 35 per cent by the 1986/7 tax year. In the short term these measures had the effect of giving leasing activity a substantial boost as companies rushed to take advantage of the higher allowances remaining. The future is somewhat more uncertain, although it must be recognized that leasing exists in other European countries and in Japan where generous tax concessions have not been available to boost the activity.

It has been suggested that for some industrial companies benefits may still flow from leasing equipment depending upon their tax position. The 25 per cent writing-down allowance should still allow leasing to offer a cost advantage of between 1 and 2 per cent relative to normal bank borrowing for the company unable to claim the tax allowance directly. In addition, it is expected that innovations in leasing services will continue, and there is likely to be a growth in 'sales aid' leasing. The latter involves the distributor or manufacturer of capital goods offering leasing finance to a prospective client on the behalf of a third party leasing company as part of a sales package. A further example of the more specialist leasing operations is that of the 'big ticket transactions' developed by Lombard North Central in the late 1970s. These transactions usually relate to major items of capital expenditure such as aircraft, ships and large petro-chemical plant. One finance company takes the lead and co-ordinates finance with a number of other institutions. The partners in the venture are able to share expertise and also spread the financial risks related to projects which would otherwise probably be inaccessible to individual companies.

Factoring

The difficult trading conditions experienced by many businesses in recent years has helped to focus attention on the need for efficient management of working capital. With an average debtor collection period in UK industry currently of between 50 and 70 days, and with debtors seeking to extend their credit periods in the face of their own cash flow problems, the potential financial difficulties for suppliers of goods are all too clear. Partly as a result of these developments the use of factoring has increased dramatically since 1980, and finance houses have been at the forefront of the provision of factoring services.

The factoring company may assist the creditor company in three main ways:

(1) Administration of the client's invoicing, sales accounting and debt collection may be undertaken by the factoring company. Many of these institutions have invested heavily in computer systems which allow for the efficient processing of large volumes of client transactions. The client is able to allow the level of sales to increase without the need to employ extra clerical staff. The fee for this service depends upon the size of

the turnover involved and the factor's assessment of the risk in the debtor portfolio, but typically it is in the range of ¾ to 2 per cent of the book value of the debts.

(2) Credit protection is offered whereby the factor takes over the risk of loss from bad debts and so effectively insures the client against such loss. The factoring company may provide 100 per cent cover on all sales which it has approved. Indeed, it is common for factors to allow their clients to sell goods to the majority of their customers without continually having to seek credit approval on an item-by-item basis.

(3) The factoring company often makes payment to the client in advance of collecting the debts. It is common for factors to make payments on account of up to 80 per cent of the value of sales at the time of invoicing, which leads to an immediate improvement in the cash flow position of the creditor company. The cost of this service includes interest on the effective advances made to creditor companies (which is usually charged at a rate in excess of that charged on bank overdrafts) and a factoring fee of between 1 and 2 per cent of turnover.

Therefore, the gains to be obtained through the use of a factoring company include savings in accounting and the administration of debt collection; the elimination of risk from bad debts; the improvement of cash flows; and the freeing of management time for more constructive purposes. It may be assumed that these gains to the client company outweigh the costs of using the factoring service.

Institutions involved in the provision of factoring services are represented by the Association of British Factors, whose members include finance houses, other subsidiaries of clearing banks, merchant banks, and other major financial institutions. However, it must be emphasized that finance houses have played an especially important role in the development of factoring, although other financial institutions were quick to recognize the business potential, often setting up separate organizations to promote its provision.

The Regulatory Framework

The Consumer Credit Act 1974

As stated above, the first piece of legislation directed explicitly at the major activities of the finance houses was the Hire Purchase Act 1938. This Act set out the broad roles of the individual or company providing the borrowing facilities (and referred to as the 'owner' of the asset underlying the transaction) and of the hirer of the asset. Under the terms of the Act, owners were required to provide a written statement of the cash price of the goods before the agreement was signed in order to enable the hirer to know the extent of the finance charges. The hirer was also to be informed of his right to terminate the agreement at any time before the final payment fell due; and of the statutory restrictions on the owner's right to recover the goods. This latter issue referred to the owner's claim to repossess the goods, which was considerably restricted once the hirer had paid one-third of the hire-purchase price. After this cut-off point a Court Order was required before legal possession could commence.

Subsequent Hire Purchase Acts enlarged or strengthened the hirer's protection until the Crowther Committee was appointed in 1968 to enquire into the ruling law and practice governing the provision of credit to individuals for financing the purchase of goods and services for personal consumption. The committee reported in 1971 and the main thrust of its proposals was ultimately embodied in the Consumer Credit Act 1974, although certain provisions of this Act did not come into force until over ten years later. The 1974 Act established a system of licensing covering all individuals and institutions involved in the provision of consumer credit and hire-purchase facilities. Responsibility for overseeing the implementation of the provisions of the Act is vested in the Director General of Fair Trading, and those provisions regulate any agreement to grant credit of up to £15,000 whether by way of hire-purchase, conditional sale, credit sale, or the taking out of a personal loan. However, it should be noted that certain types of lending facilities to consumers, and in particular bank overdrafts, are explicitly exempt from the statutory requirements of the Act. The Act regulates the form, content and enforcement of consumer credit and hiring agreements, and imposes rather onerous conditions on the lender in relation to documentation (as a means of protecting the borrower from exploitation by the lender). It also regulates the form and content of advertisements and to some extent protects the individual from unsolicited 'cold calling' by agents of financial institutions.

The Consumer Credit Act 1974 has brought into being an extensive and complex set of rules and regulations which have provoked a wide range of comments, not all of which have been favourable. For example, in 1983 the chairman of the Finance Houses Association stated[4] that 'What I have seen arising with the passage of time (as the provisions of the Act were implemented) are some injustices, too many complexities and the need for clarity. Too often the comprehensive cannot be reconciled with the comprehensible.' Nevertheless, it is widely accepted that the problems presented by the Consumer Credit Act for finance houses are not insurmountable provided that all lenders are treated equitably and that free competition is allowed. Particular reference has been made to the building societies sector in this respect in the light of the wider powers offered to them by the new Building Societies Act. The major concern of the Finance Houses Association is that building societies may not be controlled as rigorously as the finance houses themselves, and hence they may be given an unfair competitive advantage in respect of the provision of consumer credit.

Terms Controls

During the postwar period terms controls were often used as an instrument of the government's macroeconomic policy, aimed primarily at limiting the volume of consumer credit made available to the personal sector. However, in July 1982 the Conservative government announced that all hire-purchase controls relating to consumer goods would be abolished by an order taking immediate effect. The aim of this deregulation was to provide free competition amongst lenders, to remove economic distortions and, indirectly, to provide a boost to the UK motor industry. It is generally agreed that the action did lead to a fairly rapid stimulation of the demand for used cars, and ultimately, in 1983, for new cars. Since that time the business of finance houses in this area has remained fairly buoyant. However, despite fears to the contrary, it would appear that the abolition of terms controls did not lead to imprudent granting of credit by finance houses. Indeed, the members of the Finance Houses Association were congratulated by the Governor of the Bank of England for their measured response to the removal of terms controls.[5] Nevertheless, the governor stressed the need for institutions to plan for the future on the basis of more restrained growth rates after the initial surge of lending, thus implying that an explosion of credit facilities as a result of the newly found freedom would not be welcome to the authorities.

Supervision of Finance Houses

The dilemma for all regulatory authorities, whether statutory or non-statutory, is to devise effective methods of regulation which do not stifle competition within the sector for which they are responsible. In the UK, central bank supervision of the banking sector had traditionally been informal and largely unpublicized, in contrast to the general pattern in other developed countries where supervisory responsibilities were exercised under force of law. However, the nature and scale of the 1973 Secondary Banking Crisis provided clear evidence that, in the more competitive climate fostered by the Competition and Credit Control regime of deregulation, the banking system as a whole had become potentially less stable than it had been prior to 1971. Consequently, the Banking Act 1979 came into force with the specific objective of formalizing the regulatory framework for banking institutions, including those finance houses falling within the requirements of the Act. The basic theme of the Act was that institutions not explicitly covered by other pieces of legislation would be required to obtain specific authorization from the Bank of England should they wish to take deposits from the general public. Also, the legislation drew a distinction between those institutions providing a wide range of banking services which would be classified as full (or recognized) banks, and other banking institutions which would be classified as licensed deposit-takers (LDTs).

The 1979 Act contained certain broadly drawn prudential criteria against which the Bank of England would evaluate applications for full-bank or LDT status. These criteria related to the integrity of management, the adequacy of capital and liquidity bases, and the prudence with which operations were to be undertaken. Many finance houses chose to apply for LDT status under the Act, but some elected to be classified as full banks.

The most recent developments in relation to the supervision of banking and related financial institutions have arisen as a result of the crisis surrounding Johnson Matthey Bankers (JMB) in October 1984. The collapse of JMB and its subsequent rescue by the Bank of England, in concert with a number of other financially robust institutions, raised important questions as to the effectiveness of the existing supervisory framework. The consequent government White Paper on this matter, published in December 1985, took into account the recommendations of a review committee set up by the Governor of the Bank of England in the light of the JMB affair, and it is intended that the Banking Act 1979 will be amended accordingly. It is proposed that the distinction between recognized banks and LDTs will be abolished, and will be replaced by a single category of banking institutions to be authorized against a unified set of criteria. This unified authorization will mean that all finance houses will be placed on an equal footing in respect of the broad supervisory framework. In addition, the new supervisory requirements will be based upon those currently applicable to LDTs, and will relate to such matters as capital adequacy, liquid reserves, provisions for bad debts, and management expertise. All institutions will be expected to operate adequate internal management control systems and maintain specified accounting records. Institutions will need minimum net assets of £1 million to operate as banks, and issued capital must be at least £5 million if they desire to include the word 'bank' in their name. In general these proposals have been welcomed by representatives of the finance house sector as a means of bringing some degree of consistency to the regulatory framework within which they must operate.

The Future Development of Finance Houses

UK finance houses have shown considerable confidence in the face of substantially increased competition in recent years. This competition is likely to intensify following the recent liberalization of the legislative framework surrounding the activities of building societies. Finance houses have always operated in a competitive environment, and so it may be expected that they have amassed the necessary management and marketing skills to allow for their continued prosperity. Nevertheless, with the ongoing changes taking place in th UK's financial services sector, the finance houses are likely to experience increasing pressure on their lending activities, especially in respect of personal sector business. The specific threats faced by the finance houses include the following:

(1) The growth in the use of credit cards in recent years is extremely significant, particularly in the light of the rather aggressive marketing of the prestige 'gold' cards offered by banks. The holders of such cards are effectively guaranteed substantial overdraft facilities which might be used to purchase, for example, a new car without recourse to finance house credit.

(2) Developments may also take place in the use of credit cards in conjunction with electronic funds transfer at the point of sale (EFTPOS). The latter facility is a rather sophisticated money transmission/payments service whereby a customer's bank account is automatically debited at the time of purchase of goods. In itself this

212

poses little real threat to the finance houses, given their emphasis on the credit function. However, if a national network of EFTPOS terminals were to be established, the potential for providing direct credit to customers in an efficient cost-effective manner through a credit card link might easily undermine finance houses' point of sale business.

(3) Personal sector financial liabilities have grown rapidly in recent years, having doubled in the first five years of the 1980s alone. The continued strength of consumer borrowing, coupled with a slower growth in savings, may involve future difficulties for some individuals in servicing their debt, especially as the overall ratio of debt to liquid assets of the personal sector has also been rising. The situation has not been helped by the high levels of redundancies and short-time working and the rising incidence of divorce, which all contribute to the occurrence of arrears in debt repayments. Indeed, concern has been expressed by the Finance Houses Association over the implications of recent trends, and it has argued strongly in favour of the establishment of a national credit register, the purpose of which is to provide complete and accurate creditworthiness information on personal customers, as an aid to responsible granting of credit.

(4) The market for business credit in both leasing and non-leasing areas is also likely to undergo a period of change in the near future. As explained above, leasing business has recently experienced a boom period in response to the phasing out of exceptionally generous tax allowances on capital expenditures by companies. In future the growth of leasing commitments is likely to be much more restrained, and contraction of activity is quite feasible. However, it is probable that the non-leasing activities of finance houses will gain from the readjustment of financing modes following the alterations of tax concessions. Of course, much will depend upon how the finance houses react to the changed financial environment. According to Blanden (1986), as finance houses plan for the 1990s

there is likely to be a marked change in the pattern of their operations. They will be involved in further substantial spending on technology which has already enabled the finance houses to undertake a good deal of centralisation of credit records and scoring techniques for assessing potential borrowers. The functions of corporate and consumer lending are likely to become increasingly separate with specific branches dealing with the corporate borrower and aiming to design packaged lending (both leasing and non-leasing).

Notes

1   Instalment credit may take several different forms, but at the basic level it involves the purchase of goods through the payment of a deposit (some minimum proportion of the selling price of the goods) and the subsequent payment of the residual, usually in equal regular amounts over a specified period of time. The provider of the credit takes on the risk that the purchaser of the goods will default. An interest charge is usually levied on the credit extended, and is always levied when it is extended by an institution such as a finance house which is a third party to the underlying real transaction. Clearly, a large retail store chain may provide interest-free credit to its customers as a means of stimulating sales.

2   One of the earliest recorded references to hire-purchase finance in England relates to the activities of a Bishopgate piano maker, Henry Moore, who, in 1846, claimed to have invented the system. A detailed account of the history and development of finance houses is given by Drury (1982).

3   Finance House Base Rate is published monthly and is widely used as the basis for floating interest rate charges in the finance house sector. It is calculated as the average of the three-month London inter-bank offered rate (LIBOR) in the eight-week period prior to its publication.

4   Reproduced in *Credit Quarterly*, Finance Houses Association, June 1983, p. 6.

5   In a speech to the Finance Houses Association in March 1985, reproduced in *Credit Quarterly*, FHA, July 1985.

CHAPTER SIX

The National Savings Movement

Introduction

The term National Savings embraces those facilities provided by the State or which are under strict State
supervision and control and which are designed for,
though not confined solely to, the small or unsophisticated saver. The sums deposited or invested in these
media are mainly for the use of the Central Government
and wholly for the public sector.

(*Report of the Committee to Review National Savings*,
June 1973, Cmnd 5273, p. 1, para. 5)

This succinct definition of National Savings activity, as
proposed by the Page Committee, focuses clearly on its key
characteristics, which are the tapping of the flow of savings
from relatively small or unsophisticated savers, for the
ultimate purpose of contributing towards the financing of
public sector borrowing. However, the methods by which
this operation has been undertaken, and the vigour with
which the objectives of the National Savings movement
have been pursued, have varied markedly over time,
depending upon the perceived needs of government sector
financing, and the ongoing development of the financial
environment.

It must be emphasized that the original activating force
behind the establishment of the National Savings movement
was not the financing of public sector expenditure *per se*, but
rather was a combination of concern for the condition of the

poor (especially the industrial working classes); dissatisfaction with the available facilities for providing aid to the poor; and a fundamental belief in the moral virtue of thrift and self-reliance. Nevertheless, the overriding desire of the originators of the National Savings movement to provide the relatively poor members of society not only with a means through which they might build up savings, but also one which would earn for them a reasonable rate of return with the minimum of risk attached, almost inevitably constrained the ultimate repository of funds to government-backed debt instruments. The legislative framework which evolved around the early National Savings movement merely served to consolidate its role as a *de facto* channel for government sector financing.

The roots of the National Savings movement may be traced back to the year 1810, with the establishment of the Ruthwell Bank in Scotland. This organization was formed within the legal confines of the Friendly Societies Act of 1793, and involved a certain level of democratic management by depositors. There followed a fairly rapid growth of such savings banks in Scotland, which initially redeposited their funds with local joint stock banks, paying the interest earned, less expenses incurred, to their depositors. The absence of interest payments on deposits with English joint stock banks, or at very best the payment of only modest interest rates, effectively suppressed the establishment of comparable savings institutions in England. It was not until after the enactment of the Savings Bank Act of 1817 that the more widespread growth of savings banks occurred within Britain. The Act provided that the funds of savings banks in England and Wales[1] were to be invested in an account at the Bank of England (to be referred to as the 'Fund for the Banks for Savings'), which would be managed by the National Debt Commissioners. The latter would pay a fixed rate of interest on the savings banks' deposits, which would be set at a higher level than the yield on British Government Consols. This move was intended to provide assistance to the relatively poor members of society who were willing to help themselves through the accumulation of personal savings. However, in order to restrict the exploitation of the interest rate advantage by the wealthy, the Act also limited individual depositors with savings banks to a maximum deposit of £100 in the first year, and of £50 per annum thereafter. In addition, the voluntary nature of the savings organization was consolidated by the requirement that no treasurer, trustee or manager should derive any financial benefit from his office.

By 1819 there were 465 separate privately controlled savings banks in Britain. Between 1820 and 1860 several Savings Banks Acts were passed, which concentrated mainly on the nature of the interest to be paid to depositors, and the legal responsibilities of the unpaid trustees. But it was the Trustee Savings Bank Act of 1863 which finally consolidated the position of these savings institutions in the British financial system. It is therefore somewhat ironic that these trustee savings banks, which provided the initial driving force in the National Savings movement, are today no longer regarded as being a part of that movement. Despite a number of legal obstacles, relating primarily to the ownership of the trustee savings banks, the TSB Group was floated as a public limited company in October 1986. Since the TSB Act of 1976, the TSBs have been drawing away from their role as an arm of the National Savings movements, and their functions today are qualitatively indiscernible from those performed by the long-established UK clearing banks. It is for this reason that the development of their activities will be pursued no further as a separate topic in this book.

The remainder of this chapter is devoted to an examination of the nature and significance of the elements of the National Savings movement which have always been controlled directly by the state. These elements, which would appear to have shown a resurgence in their relative importance in the UK financial system in recent years, may be divided into the operations of the National Savings Bank, and the issue of National Savings Treasury Securities.

The National Savings Bank

In 1861, two years prior to the consolidating legislation for the trustee savings banks, the Post Office Saving Bank was formed. Its broad functions were to be largely the same as those of the trustee savings banks, but it was envisaged that the greater accessibility to post offices for the general public,[2] and the widespread confidence in their organizational structure, would enhance the attractiveness of accumulating funds for the small saver, and hence would facilitate the objectives of the National Savings movement.

Initially, for each individual, deposits with the Post Office Savings Bank were to be limited to no more than £30 in any one year, with a maximum accumulation of £150 (plus accrued interest of up to £50). All funds would be handed over to the National Debt Commissioners for investment in government securities. Thus, there was to be a great similarity with the operations of the trustee savings banks, although the rate of interest to be paid on deposits with the Post Office Savings Bank would only be 2½ per cent per annum, which was somewhat lower than the rate obtainable on trustee savings bank deposits. However, despite this lower return, and notwithstanding the government's expressed intention that the Post Office Savings Bank was not established deliberately to compete with the trustee savings banks, it was in 1861 that their number began to decline for the first time. By 1871 over 1.3 million accounts were held at the Post Office Savings Bank, which was only marginally less than the number held with the combined trustee savings banks. Clearly, the government's view on the importance of ease of access to savings facilities had been correct, but it must never be forgotten that funds deposited with the Post Office Savings Bank were backed directly by the Treasury, whilst no such absolute assurance was attached to deposits with trustee savings banks. Nevertheless, it must also be recognized that the average level of balances held with trustee savings banks has always remained substantially higher than the average of balances held with the Post Office Savings Bank, which may offer at least some indication of the income level of the average account holder at the latter; alternatively, of course, it might simply demonstrate the desire of wealth holders to keep only small amounts of funds readily available in a convenient interest-bearing repository.

Whilst various changes were made to the limits on allowable balances, and to the forms in which deposits would be accepted (crossed postal orders, cheques and dividend warrants ultimately being permitted), and whilst (in 1930) a periodic payments service for account holders was introduced, the basic operations of the Post Office Savings Bank remained largely unaltered until the mid-1960s. Indeed, it was not until 1966 that the simple ordinary account facility, which had continued to pay 2½ per cent per annum interest, was joined by an investment account facility. In 1969, the Post Office became a public corporation and ceased to be a department of government. However, the Post Office Savings Department remained within civil service control, being directly responsible to the Chancellor of the Exchequer, and it also changed its name to the Department for National Savings. At the same time the Post Office Savings Bank was also renamed as the National Savings Bank (NSB). The constitutional structure of the NSB means that supervisory responsibility over its activities is vested in Parliament. The NSB Act of 1971 requires that the NSB must provide to Parliament each year the full set of accounts relating to the services that it provides.

Today, the NSB offers its facilities through Britain's 21,000 Crown post offices and sub-post offices, and there is also a 'save-by-post' option available to investment account holders. An interesting feature of the NSB is the very large number of accounts maintained, but many of which contain relatively small balances. It is estimated that there are currently in excess of 20 million active accounts with the NSB (the vast majority being ordinary accounts).

Ordinary Accounts

These accounts may be opened by individuals at most post offices, and they are also available to clubs, societies and formally constituted trusts upon direct application to NSB headquarters in Glasgow. Currently, a two-tier fixed interest rate (depending upon the level of balance held) is guaranteed in advance for the calendar year, with exemption from taxation for the first £70 of interest per annum. The maximum deposit limit for individuals is £10,000, but under certain circumstances this sum may be exceeded. There is relatively easy access to funds, with cash withdrawals up to £100 on demand, and certain banking facilities are offered such as standing orders and direct payment of certain bills at the post office counter.

Investment Accounts

These accounts are available to individuals through most post offices, and may also be opened by clubs, societies, formally constituted trusts and commercial organizations upon application to the NSB headquarters in Glasgow. The accounts, which have a maximum deposit limit of £10,000 pay a competitive interest rate, and funds may be withdrawn upon one month's notice. Furthermore, interest is paid gross, but is taxable at the recipient's marginal rate of income tax.

All the funds collected by the NSB are invested on its behalf by the National Investment and Loans Office. The funds are ultimately backed by Treasury guarantee in order to meet any deficiency if the claims of depositors should exceed the value of investments held by the NSB. Ordinary account funds are invested in government and government-guaranteed securities. Any surplus income from these investments, once interest has been paid to depositors and various running costs have been covered, is paid over to the Treasury. Since the early 1980s, the moneys received through investment accounts have been paid directly to the Treasury's National Loans Fund, from which interest is paid to depositors. In respect of all NSB work, sub-postmasters are paid a fixed fee per transaction, and the Post Office receives remuneration for the time spent by Crown office staff on NSB business.

National Savings Treasury Securities

The Department for National Savings also administers a range of other savings instruments, which generate funds to be channelled directly to the Treasury. Once again, the Post Office is the major outlet for the marketing of these instruments, although some are available through banks or via mail order. National Savings Treasury securities, as these instruments are known collectively, were first introduced in 1916 in the form of War Savings Certificates, expressly intended for purchasers with relatively low income levels. Since that time an array of related instruments has been issued, and these may be summarized under the following heads.

National Savings Certificates

These instruments are the direct descendants of the original War Savings Certificates, and are currently in their 32nd issue.[3] In addition to the normal certificates, which provide a fixed, guaranteed initial return on a lump sum investment, there are also index-linked certificates, which earn interest on top of the repayment of principal, linked to the retail price index. National Savings Certificates may also be purchased by means of a 'Yearly Plan', involving the payment of a regular sum over the period of a year, at the end of which certificates are issued to the value of the payments plus interest accrued. The certificates subsequently earn a higher rate of interest.

An attractive attribute of National Savings Certificates is that they guarantee a fixed interest rate for 5 years from the date of purchase (in the case of index-linked certificates, this is a guaranteed rate over and above the inflation adjustment), and there is a variable rate payable on certificates held beyond 5 years. All returns on these certificates are free of UK income tax and capital gains tax, which is especially useful for higher marginal rate income tax payers. Only 8 working days' notice has to be given for withdrawal of funds (or 14 days' in the case of Yearly Plans), and interest accrues until the date of repayment. National Savings Certificates are available to individuals, trusts, charities, registered friendly societies and approved voluntary bodies. There are maximum permitted holdings for each issue of certificates taken separately; for example, the 32nd issue is limited to £5,000 per person.

National Savings Stamps and Gift Tokens

As long ago as 1880 the government allowed postage stamps to be attached to an official form with the purpose of accumulating the minimum deposit required for the Post Office Savings Bank. National Savings stamps proper were first introduced in 1917, but they did not become redeemable for cash until 1930. These low-denomination bearer securities were withdrawn from sale in 1976, following strong criticism of their cost-effectiveness. The turnover of National Savings stamps, as a proportion of the total value outstanding, was often almost 100 per cent per annum. Also, the absence of any return offered to their often young or relatively poor holders led to the argument that they were, to some extent, being exploited by the National Savings movement. The major justification for their existence was, perhaps, social, in the sense of providing some encouragement to save to people who would not otherwise do so.

National Savings Gift Tokens, first introduced in 1940, are still available today, and are seen largely as a marketing ploy by the Department for National Savings. They provide a very short-term repository for funds, between their purchase by the 'donor' and their use by the recipient to purchase National Savings Certificates or Premium Bonds, or to make deposits into an NSB account.

National Savings Bonds

Today, there are three forms of National Savings Bonds available: these are Income Bonds, Indexed-Income Bonds, and Deposit Bonds. These instruments superseded British Savings Bonds, which were withdrawn from sale in 1979. All bonds may be held by individuals, trusts, charities, voluntary bodies, registered companies and other corporate bodies. The three types of bonds necessitate minimum holdings of £2,000, £5,000 and £100 respectively, and so clearly they are not specifically aimed at those individuals who might usually be thought of as small savers. The Indexed-Income Bond offers a guaranteed monthly income for 10 years, which is raised in line with the rate of inflation over the preceding year. The other two instruments offer a variable interest payment, with 6 weeks' notice to be given by the Department for National Savings in the event of proposed alterations in the rate, although holders of all bonds must give a full 3 months' notice of withdrawal of funds. In addition to the competitive interest rates paid on these instruments, a notable feature is that all interest payments are made gross with tax payable by the recipient at his marginal income tax rate.

Premium Savings Bonds

These instruments were first introduced in 1956, in order to attract funds from individuals who wished to participate in a regular prize draw, without risking the loss of their capital funds. The notional interest paid on the outstanding Premium Bond fund is divided into prizes ranging from £250,000 down to £50, which are distributed by weekly and monthly computerized draws to winning bond holders. All prizes are free of UK taxation. The minimum holding of these bonds is currently £10, and the maximum holding is £10,000 per person.

Other Services from the Department for National Savings

Between April 1969 and May 1984, Save-As-You-Earn (SAYE) contracts could be taken out with the Department for National Savings. These were intended to secure a regular commitment to saving from individuals, with an agreed deduction direct from pay. An index-linked SAYE 'issue' was introduced in 1975. The Yearly Plan, mentioned above, has effectively superseded the basic SAYE contract, although there is a recently introduced share option issue of SAYE for individuals entitled to purchase shares under a share option scheme approved by the Inland Revenue.

Finally, it should be noted that individuals and corporate bodies are able to purchase a wide range of marketable government stocks through the National Savings Stock Register. Currently, up to £10,000 may be invested in any particular stock on any one day, and there is no limit to the amount of stocks which may be held. Transactions for the purchase or sale of stocks on the register are made by post through the Department of National Savings' Bonds and Stock Office at Blackpool. Commission charges on transactions usually prove to be relatively attractive for small- to medium-sized lots of stocks.

The Structure and Growth of National Savings Debt

It is clear from our earlier discussion that the Department for National Savings employs a wide range of instruments in order to effect its basic financial intermediation role. Furthermore, there is little doubt that the department's objectives go well beyond the mere provision of a repository for the savings of the poorer members of society. These objectives will be considered below, but for the moment it should be recognized that in recent years there have been important changes in the underlying structure of the outstanding National Savings debt. The positions in 1975, 1980 and 1985 are summarized in Table 6.1.

Following their introduction in 1975, index-linked National Savings Certificates rapidly gained in popularity despite the fact that initially they offered a zero real return, providing merely a guarantee that the principal invested would be index-linked. However, this was still an attractive proposition following the significant negative real rates of return which had been obtained, for several years, on most easily accessible retail savings media. Purchases of index-linked certificates reached their peak in the early 1980s, and in 1981 these instruments made the largest single contribution to National Savings inflows. It is, perhaps, not coincidental that 1981 was the year in which these certificates were made available to all investors, having been limited, until that time, to higher age-groups. Nevertheless, it would appear that as the rate of inflation subsided in the UK, and fixed nominal rates of interest on non-indexed assets remained relatively high, the index-linked certificates lost much of their appeal. The subsequent payment of supple-

National Savings Instruments: Absolute Amounts Outstanding and Percentage Distribution, end 1975, 1980 and 1985

	£m	1975 £m	%	£m	1980 £m	%	£m	1985 £m	%
National savings certificates:									
Index-linked:		212	3.0		2,634	18.9		4,304	14.1
Principal	212			2,110			2,930		
Index-linking/bonus	—			524			1,374		
Fixed interest:		2,418	34.8		5,255	37.6		12,822	41.9
Principal	1,878			4,092			9,115		
Accrued interest	540			1,163			3,707		
British savings bonds		791	11.4		474	3.4		3	—
Income bonds		—			—			3,464	11.3
Deposit bonds		—			—			347	1.1
Premium savings bonds		1,110	16.0		1,448	10.4		1,808	5.9
National savings stamps/gift tokens		46	0.7		1	—		1	—
Yearly plan/SAYE:									
Index-linked:		13	0.2		519	3.7		493	1.6
Principal	13			425			368		
Accrued interest/bonus	—			94			125		
Fixed interest:		208	3.0		30	0.2		187	0.6
Principal	187			24			176		
Accrued interest	21			6			11		
National Savings Bank									
Ordinary accounts		1,525	22.0		1,740	12.4		1,711	5.6
Investment accounts		616	8.9		1,871	13.4		5,496	17.9
Total		6,939	100.0		13,972	100.0		30,636	100.0

Source: Financial Statistics, various issues.

mentary bonuses on the certificates, endowing them with a guaranteed positive real return, has not been sufficient to stem the net redemptions which have taken place since 1983, as is illustrated in Table 6.2. A similar pattern of purchases and redemptions was also seen in relation to index-linked Yearly Plan Certificates and SAYE.

Whilst the period since 1975 has seen the rise and fall of the index-linked certificates, the value of outstanding fixed rate certificates has continued on a steady upwards path. Only during 1980 and 1981 were the contributions made by fixed rate certificates overtaken by those of their index-linked counterparts. Their obvious popularity in recent years has been underpinned by the very competitive rates of interest which they attract, the guarantee attached to the interest rate, and the tax-free status of the interest payments.

Since their introduction, Deposit Bonds and Income Bonds have proved to be successful instruments for attracting funds, and have more than compensated for the rundown of the outstanding stock of British Savings Bonds.

Table 6.2
Net Transactions in National Savings Instruments,
1981 to 1985, £ million

	1981	1982	1983	1984	1985
National Savings Certificates:					
Fixed interest	1,354	1,604	1,511	1,916	1,182
Index-linked	1,912	548	−243	−271	−275
Income Bonds	—	643	942	961	917
Deposit Bonds	—	—	53	159	134
Premium Bonds	46	57	95	97	66
SAYE/Yearly Plan	86	13	8	4	19
British Savings Bonds	−158	−103	−86	−75	−49
National Savings Bank:					
Ordinary accounts	−48	−16	71	−7	−29
Investment accounts	1,000	899	641	544	540
Total	4,192	3,645	2,992	3,328	2,505

Source: Financial Statistics, March 1986.

226

Premium Savings Bonds have also continued to make a modest but significant positive contribution in recent years.

In respect of NSB activities, the relative fortunes of ordinary account and investment account balances could hardly have been more dissimilar. Between 1980 and 1985 there was little net change in the volume of outstanding ordinary account deposits, and consequently these declined markedly as a proportion of the rapidly growing total value of National Savings debt. The relatively uncompetitive nature of the ordinary account interest rate must surely take much of the blame for this occurrence. However, during the same period, the investment account deposits grew strongly, with their end-1985 value being some three times the level of the end-1980 value. Today, these deposits represent the second largest component of the National Savings portfolio.

The Taxation of National Savings Interest Payments

Throughout its history the National Savings movement has always been able to depend upon the availability of fiscal incentives to add to the attractiveness of its 'products'. The initial intention of the Government, namely to provide small savers with returns matching those available to wealthy investors, may perhaps still be one underlying factor in the often generous tax treatment of interest payments on National Savings instruments. But today it is more probably the Government's desire to cover a minimum proportion of its borrowing through the issue of National Savings instruments which motivates their continued special treatment for tax purposes.

It is inherently logical for the Government to allow interest to be paid tax-free on certain National Savings instruments, rather than pay a necessarily higher gross rate only to claw back a proportion of the payments through the income tax system. Nevertheless, despite these points, the special (and differential) tax treatment for National Savings instruments can only serve to make it more difficult for the saver to compare the returns on these assets with those available on alternative, privately supplied instruments. This issue is a particularly disturbing aspect of the marketing of National Savings instruments, given that the major intended target groups of holders for most instruments are lower level income earners, many of whom would not pay income tax in any event. Thus an important social implication of the tax-free interest payments is that they provide the least benefit to the most needy. From the social welfare viewpoint, a higher, but taxable gross interest rate may be a preferred option.

In recent years, the major criticism of the tax regime in respect of interest earnings on retail financial assets has not been directed so much to the privileged position of National Savings in relation to tax-free interest payments, but rather to the ability of the Department for National Savings to make taxable interest payments without deduction of tax at source. As was mentioned in Chapter 4, since April 1985 the composite tax regime has been applicable to interest payments on retail deposits with UK banks as well as to comparable deposits with building societies. As this tax is deducted at source, and cannot be reclaimed by non-taxpayers, then other things being equal the National Savings movement is endowed with a competitive advantage in relation to potential savers who fall outside the income tax net.

The position of the National Savings movement in respect of taxation was clearly summarized by the Wilson Committee:

> The concessions given to Department for National Savings schemes are justified largely on the grounds of administrative convenience, both to the Government and to the relatively unsophisticated small-scale savers for whom the Department provides a service. But similar arguments of administrative convenience could also apply to other deposit-taking institutions. Moreover, it is not always obvious that it is the unsophisticated savers who benefit most from the concessions. Non-taxpayers by definition receive no benefit, although this may not always be clear to them. The benefit to depositors who do pay tax rises

proportionately with their marginal rates of tax . . . We recommend that the tax arrangements for Government borrowing should generally be brought into line with those which apply to other borrowers, and that if special arrangements for small savers are needed, the same opportunities should be allowed to other borrowers.

(*Report of the Committee to Review the Functioning of Financial Institutions*, June 1980, Cmnd 7937, pp. 204–5)

As implied above, the recommendation of the Wilson Committee, which echoed the earlier conclusion of the Page Committee,[4] was not taken up by the authorities. Indeed, it is probably correct to suggest that the degree of inequity in respect of taxation of interest payments has increased since 1980.

The Commercial Position of the National Savings Movement

It is difficult to evaluate absolutely the competitive position of the National Savings movement *vis-à-vis* other retail financial intermediaries. National Savings instruments are unique in that they are ultimately backed by Treasury guarantee, which, for all practical purposes, removes the risk of default. Also, as explained above, interest payments on these assets benefit from significant fiscal privileges. But perhaps a more fundamental issue is that the Department for National Savings is unlike private sector financial inter- mediaries in that it does not have to hold a portfolio of assets to back its liabilities, and hence does not have to comply with official liquidity and solvency requirements. Thus, its activities are not constrained in the normal sense by the evolution of the broad monetary and financial environment. Nevertheless, it is possible to consider the relative returns on, and conditions attached to, National Savings instruments, and hence to identify changes in what are essentially the bench-marks for competition within the retail savings markets.

The ability of the Department for National Savings to

operate almost independently of commercial factors is illustrated clearly by the following quote from the Wilson Committee Report.

> Since 1977 [the National Savings Bank] has been pursuing a more market-orientated interest rate policy which, coupled with more aggressive marketing, has begun to reverse its previous decline. The combination of this with an unchanged investment policy has, however, created a technical insolvency. The high rate of interest paid on the investment account in recent years would not have been feasible for a commercial organisation following the same investment policy without the backing of a government guarantee.
>
> (Wilson, 1980, p. 365, para. 1381)

During the early 1980s the officially proclaimed importance of National Savings as a source of finance for the public sector borrowing requirement, raised the profile of the National Savings movement as a competitive force in the retail financial intermediaries sector. One reason for this growing emphasis on National Savings was official concern about the possible effects on the corporate sector of excessive public sector borrowing in the long-term capital markets. Further to this, the ability to finance public sector borrowing in a non-inflationary manner[5] has proved to be most attractive to the Conservative government, and targets have been specified by the Chancellor of the Exchequer for the contribution of National Savings to the financing of public sector borrowing. This targeting of saving volumes has naturally led to some criticism from private sector financial intermediaries, for it implies that the government is willing to underwrite the activities of the Department for National Savings with little immediate concern for the private commercial implication of retail interest rates being bid upwards. Clearly, the greater is the intensity of competition generated the more that normal market relationships will be distorted, especially in respect of the activities of the building societies and the clearing banks. However, it must be acknowledged that the Department for National Savings has introduced a number of new innovative versions of savings devices in an attempt to meet the needs of the smaller saver, and has not simply relied upon bidding up interest rates to attract funds. Irrespective of the broader implications of National Savings activities, it is evident that the targets set for net inflows of funds have been met comfortably in recent years, as is illustrated in Table 6.3.

National Savings within the British Financial System

As was shown in Chapter 3, claims on the Department for National Savings form a significant element of UK personal sector liquid asset holdings, amounting to over 15 per cent of the total at the end of 1985. Furthermore, in recent years, according to the most widely accepted definitions, these claims have basically maintained their relative importance within the financial system, despite the increasingly competitive environment within retail savings markets. However, it would be incorrect to measure the economic significance of National Savings merely in terms of the absolute volume of funds outstanding. As mentioned above, the special characteristics of National Savings instruments, and particularly their risk-free property, endows them with a bench-mark status. Even modest changes in the rates of interest paid on National Savings instruments, or in the conditions attached to their holding, must always raise serious questions for the financial decisions of other retail financial intermediaries.

There is little disagreement that the National Savings movement possesses a great deal of potential for future development, not least because of the large number of outlets at its disposal (the post office network accounting for a larger number of branches than all UK retail banking institutions taken in aggregate). Moreover, it may be presumed that the government would introduce any changes to the legislative and fiscal frameworks thought to be necessary to facilitate the desired evolution of National Savings activities. Nevertheless, it is important to recognize that just as other financial intermediaries are ultimately

231

Table 6.3

National Savings and the Central Government Borrowing Requirement (CGBR)

Financial year	Target net inflow £bn	Actual net inflow £bn	Excess of actual inflow over target £bn	Proportion of CGBR covered by National Savings inflows %
1980/1	2.0	2.27	0.27	17.9
1981/2	3.5	4.25	0.75	55.9
1982/3	3.0	3.04	0.04	23.9
1983/4	3.0	3.28	0.28	26.7
1984/5	3.0	3.01	0.01	29.8

Source: Department for National Savings.

constrained by the requirements of ultimate borrowers, so too the activities of the Department for National Savings are constrained by the government's requirements for borrowed funds. Therefore, in the light of the present government's desire to reduce public sector borrowing, and accepting the longer-term desirability in maintaining a viable gilt-edged securities market, there must be some doubt as to the likelihood of any significant expansion of National Savings operations in the foreseeable future. Indeed, given the present government's benign stance in respect of the private provision of services through the market mechanism, it is hard to believe that a broader role for the National Savings movement would ever be sanctioned officially. A change of government could, of course, alter this perspective entirely. A shift towards more interventionist macroeconomic policies, perhaps involving a state-controlled channelling of savings to domestic business investment projects, could quite easily draw the Department for National Savings into an even more central position in the British financial system.

Notes

1   The provisions of the Act were extended to Ireland in the same year, but it was not until 1835 that they became effective in Scotland.
2   In 1861 there were about 3,000 money order post offices in Britain, as compared to only around 600 trustee savings banks.
3   In fact only 30 issues have actually been made, as the 17th and 22nd issues were planned but were not put on sale.
4   Page Committee, op. cit., p. 270, pt (iv).
5   To the extent that total public sector expenditure exceeds taxation revenue and public sector income from other sources, the government must borrow funds. Borrowing from the Bank of England leads to the creation of high-powered money, and hence inflates the potential reserve base for bank credit creation; borrowing from the commercial banks also adds to the money supply as banks create credit (deposits) to purchase debt instruments from the government. Borrowing from the non-bank private sector, through the issue of National Savings instruments or the taking of deposits with the NSB, has no direct implication for money supply growth.

CHAPTER SEVEN

Insurance Companies

Introduction

The proverbial 'man in the street' commonly underestimates
the true significance of the insurance companies as a
component of the UK financial system. Some idea of their
significance can, however, be gained by reference to their
premium income for business written in the UK of £18,438
million in 1984; to the cash value of their net acquisitions of
assets in the same year of £6,932 million; and to their
outstanding investments with a market value of £114,630
million at 31 December 1984. In order to understand how
insurance companies have achieved their position of
strength within the UK financial system, it is first necessary
to examine briefly the origins and history of the insurance
industry.[1]

Insurance, in the context of trade and commerce, can be
traced back over 2,000 years, and there is evidence that it
was well established among the major European trading
nations in the Middle Ages. In this respect, the UK was a
comparative latecomer, since there is no widespread evidence of insurance before the sixteenth century. This
insurance was concentrated in the area of marine risks, and
it is notable that trade and commerce were the major
markets for insurance in these early phases. The continued
increases in the volume of trade, and the massive increase in
the output of manufactured products associated with the
Industrial Revolution, ensured that not only did the demand
for insurance continue to rise, but also that it was associated

with a commensurate increase in risks to be insured against. Only in more recent times has there been a substantial demand for insurance from private individuals, arising primarily from the accumulation of sufficient assets to be worth insuring, as well as the introduction of compulsory insurance in some areas (for example, in relation to the running of motor vehicles). Table 7.1 provides some detail on the dates from which various types of insurance were available in the UK, from which it is clear that many are comparatively recent.

The principal division of insurance business is into *general* business and *long-term* business. Designated by the EEC, and embodied into the 1982 Insurance Companies Act, are seventeen classes of general insurance business and seven classes of long-term business. Details of these are given in Table 7.2, together with the number of companies authorized to conduct business in each class as at 31 December 1984. It will be apparent that the seventeen classes of general insurance business relate more properly to forms of risk rather than to types of insurance business, and accordingly eight types of general insurance business are usually identified, as set out in Table 7.3.

Table 7.1
Approximate Commencement Dates of Various
Types of Insurance Business

Type of insurance	Approximate date started
Marine	1550
Life	1590
Fire	1680
Personal accident	1850
Industrial life	1850
Employers' liability	1860
Sickness	1860
Theft	1887
Permanent health	1870
Motor	1890
Credit	1890
Contractors' all-risks	1920

Table 7.2

Insurance Companies in the UK: Classes of Business and
Authorised Companies, at 31 December 1984

Classes of general insurance business	Number of companies authorized
1 Accident	578
2 Sickness	462
3 Land vehicles	327
4 Railway rolling stock	443
5 Aircraft	442
6 Ships	445
7 Goods in transit	542
8 Fire and natural forces	450
9 Damage to property	452
10 Motor vehicle liability	322
11 Aircraft liability	441
12 Liability for ships	449
13 General liability	404
14 Credit	422
15 Suretyship	527
16 Miscellaneous financial loss	476
17 Legal expenses	446

Classses of long-term insurance businesses	Number of companies authorized
I Life and annuity	287
II Marriage and birth	276
III Linked long-term	284
IV Permanent health	278
V Tontines	0
VI Capital redemption	276
VII Pension fund management	280

Source: *Insurance Annual Report 1984*.
Notes:

(1) The *total* number of authorised insurance companies at 31 December 1984 was 847 (848 on 31 December 1983). Of these 847, 218 companies were authorised for long-term business only, 557 for general business only, and 72 were composites. The figures above do not take account of the special situation of Lloyd's. Included amongst the long-term insurance groups were 12 industrial insurance companies.

(2) Tontines refers to an extinct class of business where a group of individuals would contribute a sum to a pool and thereby receive an annuity with the income of those dying being redistributed among the surviving members.

Table 7.3
Insurance Companies in the UK: Types of Insurance Business

Designation	Composition
1 Accident and health	Classes 1,2
2 Motor	Classes 3,7,10, part of 1
3 Marine and transport	Classes 4,6,7,12, part of 1
4 Aviation	Classes 5,7,11, part of 1
5 Fire and other damage to property	Classes 8,9
6 Liability	Classes 10,11,12,13
7 Credit and suretyship	Classes 14,15
8 General	All classes

Given the wide range of different types of insurance, and given the widely ranging commencement dates of those different types of insurance, it follows that most companies in the insurance industry have tended to specialize to some degree. The majority of companies are wholly involved in *either* general *or* long-term business (as the figures in Table 7.2 indicate), although many of the major names in the industry are, not surprisingly, 'composite' insurance companies with a significant presence in both the general and long-term areas of business. Since, as noted earlier, many areas of business have only developed comparatively recently, the composite insurance companies have tended to establish themselves in many of their areas of business by means of acquisition and merger rather than by internal development, though it should be noted that many of the larger companies which restrict themselves either to long-term or to general business have also achieved their position of influence within the industry or sector by means of acquisition.

A subgroup of the companies operating in the long-term sector of the industry deal with industrial assurance. This was defined in the Industrial Assurance Act of 1923 as being the business of effecting insurance upon human life, premiums in respect of which are payable at intervals of less than 2 months and are received by means of collectors who make house-to-house visits for the purpose. The term 'industrial' therefore stems not from the type of business written but from the urban, industrialized areas from which the majority of the business was generated; the business was to provide small insurance policies for the ordinary working man (in the early years, often taken out simply to pay for funeral expenses). The Pearl Assurance plc and the Prudential Assurance Co. Ltd. started as 'industrial life' companies, and other companies with a substantial industrial life business include the Co-operative Insurance Society Ltd., Britannia Assurance plc, United Friendly Insurance plc and Refuge Assurance plc. Not surprisingly, this element of their business has been declining for some years.

The extent of foreign competition within the industry is relatively slight. Indeed, the UK insurance industry has an international reputation which leads to substantial invisible exports. Within the industry, there are a sizeable number of foreign companies operating, particularly in the area of general insurance business, but the market share of these foreign companies is low. Very often, they specialize in particular niches of the insurance market. The insurance industry – and others outside the industry – became particularly concerned about the extent of foreign competition when Allianz of West Germany make a take-over bid for Eagle Star, a composite UK insurance company. Although Eagle Star eventually went to BAT, the bid raised the possibility of other household names in the industry subsequently falling into foreign ownership. Table 7.4 provides some information on the number of UK and foreign-owned authorised insurers.

Table 7.4
Authorised Insurance Companies Operating in the UK

	UK	Foreign	Total
Life business only	193	25	218
General business only	428	129	557
Life and general business	63	9	72
Total	684	163	847

Source: Insurance Annual Report 1984.

As regards the ownership of the UK insurance companies, the major composite insurance companies, such as Commercial Union, Royal Insurance and Norwich Union, are independent. Some of the smaller insurance companies, such as Barclays Life and Hambro Life, are subsidiaries of other, larger financial institutions, but in general the changes in the UK financial system have not as yet influenced the ownership of insurance companies in any major way.

Lloyd's

Lloyd's is a unique organization within the insurance industry, with its uniqueness stemming from the fact that it is a collection of individuals rather than a company. The basis of Lloyd's operation is that an *individual* (referred to as a 'name'), rather than a company, undertakes to insure a particular risk. In doing so, the name accepts unlimited liability, and is therefore liable for all his personal wealth in the event of a claim. In practice, no Lloyd's name offers insurance on his own, but will do so as part of a syndicate. Plainly, where the risk is very large, the number of names in the syndicate will be commensurately large. As of 31 December 1984, there were 23,346 names grouped into a total of 380 syndicates. It is usual for the names to take no part in the business itself (to that extent, membership of Lloyd's can be regarded as a personal investment similar to any other). Each syndicate appoints an underwriting agent who conducts business on their behalf. Often, a syndicate will only insure a proportion (say 5 per cent) of the risk, and in such circumstances a number of syndicates will provide cover for the entire risk.

Although the membership of Lloyd's and its premium income have been increasing steadily in recent years, it is also true that the organization's market share has been falling; from more than 23 per cent of the London insurance market in the 1960s (excluding long-term business), it now accounts for less than 15 per cent. Against this background of falling market share, the mix of its business is also changing progressively into a pure reinsurance market.[2] Around two-thirds of Lloyd's business is now reinsurance, although it still maintains a substantial presence in the marine insurance market, and has a reputation for insuring the more exotic risks. The reasons advanced for the declining market share and changing mix include increasing numbers of insurers operating in the market and foreign markets becoming more protective about their own insurance. Also, for large multinational companies it may be economically worthwhile not to take out insurance against specific risks, and simply to absorb any ensuing uninsured losses within the business. Effectively, such large organizations form 'captive insurance companies', and these obviously limit their requirement for normal insurance facilities.

Types of Insurance Policy

In order to understand the nature of insurance companies' business operations, it is necessary to appreciate the types of policy that the companies sell. For general insurance business there is no particular difficulty, as the insurance company simply insures the policyholder for an identified risk for the duration of a specified period. Naturally, the insurance risks will take an enormously wide variety of forms, and the period over which the risk is insured will also vary. The nature of the contract remains, however, essentially the same. For many, but by no means all, contracts the period will be for one year. It is important to note, however, that claims under an insurance contract might not be made for some considerable time after the contract has ended (because, for example, the loss or damage may not be identified until after some time has elapsed), and insurance companies will have to make provision for this.

For long-term insurance business, the picture is more complicated. In the first place, although the terms 'long-term' and 'life' are often used interchangeably, a substantial proportion of long-term insurance contracts do not provide life insurance cover; that is, there may be no payment on the death of the policyholder. Indeed, in the case of pension contracts, payments by the insurance company will often *cease* on the death of the policyholder.[3] Given that, one may identify four main types of long-term insurance contract:

(1) *Term policy*: the insurance company will pay a benefit – usually fixed – only if the death of the policyholder occurs within a specified period.
(2) *Whole-of-life policy*: the insurance company will pay a capital sum – often variable – on the death of the person, irrespective of when death occurs.
(3) *Annuity policy*: the insurance company provides the policyholder with a regular income for a specified period, usually until the policyholder's death. An annuity may be paid for either by a lump sum (single premium policy) or by continuing payments until a certain time is reached (for example, pension contracts).
(4) *Endowment policy*: the insurance company pays a capital sum – not usually known precisely in advance – at some agreed date in the future, or when the policy-holder dies if earlier. Endowment and whole-of-life policies are written in one of three main forms:

    (a) 'Without profit': This is the 'base'-type policy, where an insurance company undertakes to pay an absolute sum at some point in the future, and it invests the premiums it receives in order to achieve that. If the insurance company, by means of careful investment of the premiums, achieves more than the guaranteed sum, the surplus will constitute profit to the company; if it fails to achieve the guaranteed sum, as a result either of poor investment returns or the early death of the policyholder, the deficit will constitute a loss.
    (b) 'With profits': This is the more common type of policy, where the company guarantees a minimum sum which is augmented by 'bonuses' declared by the company, which in turn depend upon the profits achieved by the company. The bonuses that

241

are declared by a company can be either 'reversionary', which means that the bonuses are declared periodically (usually annually), with interest subsequently being earned on those bonuses, or 'terminal', where a bonus is declared as an increment to the final payment.

(c) 'Unit-linked': Where an insurance company writes unit-linked policies it maintains an underlying fund which is divided, for accounting purposes, into 'units'. The company will then pay out, on the maturity of the policy, either the guaranteed sum or the value of those units allocated to the policy if this is greater. Although under such schemes the insurance companies have been represented as running their own unit trust, this is not, in practice, the case. The investments made under a unit-linked policy will not generally be in the units of a unit trust. They may occasionally be in only a narrow range of assets – of which unit trust units might form a part – with some companies operating different funds and allowing the policyholder to switch between the funds. More usually, however, the investments will be in a broad spread of assets, in order to combine the advantages of high yields and the spreading of risk. As an extension to these policies, some companies allow partial withdrawals.

An Overview of Current Activities

The importance of insurance companies as financial intermediaries stems from the fact that they hold very large sums from which to meet future claims and liabilities. In the case of general insurance business, where the contract is invariably of a short-term nature (one year or less), the 'pool' of funds arising from premium payments, and from which claims are met, is in principle only available for investment purposes for a relatively short period. In the case of long-term insurance business the premiums are available for investment for a much longer period – in respect of pensions business, for example, conceivably for forty years or more.

As insurance companies undertake their financial inter-mediation role as a *by-product* of their primary activities of providing cover for risks, little emphasis is normally placed on the sources of their funds. In practice, insurance companies acquire their funds from two major sources; namely, the premiums on the contracts they write and the investment income from the funds they hold to meet future claims and liabilities. The importance of investment income to the UK insurance industry is illustrated by the fact that in 1984 the net premiums received for worldwide general insurance amounted to £14,315 million, whilst the invest-ment income arising from the general insurance funds amounted to £2,142 million, representing almost 15 per cent of the value of net premiums.[4] Indeed, it has become normal in recent years both for individual insurance companies and for the general insurance industry as a whole to make an underwriting loss (that is, for claims on policies to exceed premium income), but for this loss to be covered by the investment income of the general insurance fund, thus resulting in an overall trading profit. For life insurance business, where many of the contracts written have a substantial savings element, the importance of investment income is correspondingly greater. The net premium income (UK and overseas) amounted to £14,212 million in 1984, whereas investment income amounted to £7,877 million, and other income (including currency adjustments for overseas business, realized net gains from investment, and so on) amounted to £6,173 million.

As implied above, insurance companies acquire their premium income from a wide diversity of different types of insurance business, with the industry's products displaying little homogeneity. It is also true, however, that a high proportion of that premium income emanates directly from the general public, and to that extent the companies involved can be viewed as being essentially retail organiza-tions. For the most part, the companies deal on an individual basis with the general public, albeit often via an insurance broker. Bulk sales of insurance are uncommon, with the two most significant exceptions being in pension provision (where an insurance company may sell a block of pension policies to a company) and in permanent health insurance schemes (again, frequently sold in blocks to companies).

Of the total 1984 net premium income for general insurance business of £14,315 million, some £7,807 million

Table 7.5
Sources of Premiums for Insurance Business Written
in the UK, 1984

General insurance business	Premiums, £m	
Marine, aviation and transport		
Aircraft	160	
Ships	392	
Goods in transit	234	
		786
Direct motor, fire and accident		
UK risks		
Accident & health	512	
Motor	1,943	
Property damage	2,204	
General liability	521	
Pecuniary loss	529	
		5,439
Other business written in the UK		240
Total		6,465

Long-term insurance business	Premiums, £m
Ordinary individual life insurance	4,380
Ordinary individual linked life insurance	1,050
Individual annuities	6
Industrial life insurance	1,210
Personal pensions	887
Permanent health insurance	112
Pension and life insurance schemes (exc. personal pensions)	4,000
Total	11,639

Source: Association of British Insurers.

(54 per cent) was generated in business written overseas. This high proportion reflected the strength of the UK industry in the international general insurance market, and it is notable that this proportion has been increasing in recent years. However, of the total premium income for long-term business of £14,212 million, only £2,282 million (16 per cent) was generated from business written overseas, reflecting the more important domestic base for this element of the insurance industry. A further breakdown of the sources of premiums for business written in the UK is given in Table 7.5.

Since the premiums received for long-term insurance business during a given period of time derive from contracts entered into over many years, the spread of premiums attributable to the different elements of long-term business offer a good insight into the history of the industry. However, in order to discover the nature of the long-term insurance business currently being entered into, it is appropriate to consider the premiums for *new* individual business in a particular year. Table 7.6 identifies separately the new yearly premiums payable to the insurance companies as a result of contracts agreed during 1984, and the payments received in 1984 in respect of single premium contracts for which the insurance companies will have obligations stretch-

Table 7.6
UK Insurance Companies: New Long-Term Individual Insurance Business, 1984

	Yearly premiums, £m	Single premiums, £m
New ordinary individual life insurance	997	2,080
New individual annuities	1	481
New industrial life insurances	229	—
New personal pensions	296	433
Totals	1,523	2,994

Source: Association of British Insurers.
Note: New ordinary individual life insurance includes unit-linked policies.

ing into the future (for example, for immediate and deferred annuities).

UK Insurance Companies: Assets Portfolios

All portfolio choice is influenced by two considerations, namely return and risk, where the risk relates not only to the assets held but also to the position of the holder of the portfolio. The return and risk characteristics of the *assets* in insurance company investment portfolios will be examined later. First, the risks to which the insurance companies are exposed will be examined, along with the effects of these risks on the companies' asset portfolio selection.

Long-Term Funds

When writing long-term insurance contracts, companies are exposed to four major risks, namely that

(1) mortality experience proves worse than forecast by actuarial calculations;
(2) management expenses turn out worse than expected;
(3) there is a higher rate of early surrender of policies than expected;
(4) a smaller yield on the portfolio than expected arises due to changes in interest rates, etc.

The first two risks, while important in themselves, do not carry strong implications for the portfolio chosen by a long-term insurance company. However, the third and the fourth risks involve similar and very significant considerations for portfolio composition. The fundamental issue here relates to what may be termed the *yield risk*; that is, the risk that the yield on the portfolio will prove to be smaller than expected. This yield risk has two aspects:

(1) The capital value risk: this arises from the possibility that an insurance company may be forced to realize marketable assets at a time when their prices are depressed and thereby incur a loss.

(2) The income risk: this relates to the possibility that the interest and dividends earned by the insurance company may fall below the levels expected when the contract was written.

This risk stems from the unique nature of most long-term insurance contracts: a minimum return is guaranteed or assumed when the policy is sold, but the premiums (to be used to purchase the necessary investments) are received after – often very much after – the contract is written. Thus assets may have to be purchased by the insurance company when market prices are high and/or interest rates low.

Not surprisingly, the principles by which these risks can be minimized have been subject to much discussion. The earliest, widely used principles date from 1862, are known as Bailey's five canons, and may be summarized as follows:

(1) The major consideration should be given to the security of the capital.
(2) Given the first, overriding, principle, the highest rate of interest should be achieved.
(3) A small proportion of funds should be held in liquid securities to meet current claims.
(4) The proportion remaining from that held to meet current claims should be invested in securities that are not readily convertible, since these would command a higher interest rate.
(5) The capital should be employed to aid the life insurance business.

These principles went largely unchallenged until the 1930s. It is debatable, however, to what extent the principles were actually adhered to. For example, following the first two principles would have required companies to invest the whole of the fund in Treasury Bills (short-term British government securities), which would have quickly led them into insolvency due to the relatively poor yields such securities offer. Nevertheless, much attention was paid to the capital-certainty and marketability of the assets held, presumably because long-term insurance companies were perceived as requiring liquidity in order to meet obligations as they arose; to meet early surrenders of policies; and, to a lesser extent, to meet the rights of some policyholders for loans from the company. In more recent years this need for liquidity has been adequately met by the inflow of premiums consequent on a rising volume of business. Furthermore, and particularly in the case of a company which has been expanding rapidly, obligations can usually be met for some time into the future from incoming premiums even if the company has ceased to write any new policies, due to the flow of premiums guaranteed by contracts written in the past.

One implication of this approach to portfolio management is that long-term insurance companies will usually have a ready supply of cash for investment. Economic theory suggests that expectations are an important influence on what companies do with this cash: for example, if interest rates are expected to rise, one might expect to see fund managers purchasing fairly liquid assets, and holding these until such time as the interest rate rises and longer-term investments can be acquired more cheaply. As an extension of this view, one might expect fund managers to *borrow* money at different times in order to take advantage of market developments. However, in practice, this behaviour is not observed for two possible reasons. First, insurance companies are price-makers in many asset markets. If they stay away from a particular market for a period, they may simply find that the price moves against them as soon as they re-enter, thus defeating the object of staying away from the market in the first place. It is for this reason also that insurance companies are active in the new issue market, in buying blocks of shares privately, and in being long-term holders of many securities. Secondly, there is a tradition that *savings* institutions should not borrow, especially for speculative purposes. In addition, of course, borrowing funds for speculative purposes exposes the company to an additional risk.

Given the nature of the 'income risk' identified above, where future changes in earnings from assets could prevent a company from achieving the return implicit in its contracts, attention was focused on ways in which a long-term insurance company could protect itself from this risk. The question was posed as to whether a long-term insurance company could set up its portfolio to insulate itself from future changes in earnings. The answer that emerged was that it could, *given* a range of restrictions about the types and quantity of policies which it was selling, and more particularly about the assets which it held. In general, it would involve the company in selecting only a very narrow range of assets (in particular, gilt-edged securities), which would immediately conflict with the other factors normally influencing composition.

As a consequence of the fairly unsatisfactory result of that debate, there was some attempt to redefine the objectives of a life fund and to move away from Bailey's canons. It became increasingly apparent that the attainment of the maximum yield on assets was an appropriate expression of the objective, with 'yield' to include here all aspects of the return on assets, and thereby all possible income and capital payments. In this way the 'security of the capital' and the earning of a high rate of return became compatible, the view being taken that a false distinction had been created initially by not concentrating on the total yield.

If the objective of maximum yield is accepted, the next problem to be addressed is how that maximum yield is to be achieved. While the maximum yield may be attained on a very narrow range of assets, the risk in so doing has to be recognized. A diversified portfolio then becomes appropriate, and in particular one with a mix of assets with a low risk covariance (that is, where the value of different assets would not be expected to be moving in the same direction at any one point in time). Naturally, such an answer to the problem merely raises the question of the relative weight to be given to the objectives of achieving maximum yields and avoiding risk by portfolio diversification. In general terms, the industry seems to have been content to leave the answer to this question to the individual fund managers.

There is a further reason for asserting that long-term insurance companies will be more interested in maximizing the total yield rather than the simple interest return, which is that many of their policies are of the 'with-profit' type, and hence the minimum rate of interest that they have to achieve in order to maintain solvency is actually very low. In the longer term, however, their ability to compete and survive in the market-place will be dependent on the yield on their with-profits policies, so that maximization of overall yield is the more appropriate objective.

Two other constraints on the investment portfolio of long-term insurance companies are worth noting at this stage. First, there are considerations relating to policies written in a foreign currency, where the writing of such policies will involve a currency risk, unless the related liabilities are covered by assets of the same amount denominated in the same foreign currency. Given the inflow of premiums over the duration of the non-single premium policies, currency matching of assets and liabilities becomes problematic. Secondly, there are taxation considerations which will be examined in greater detail later on. For the present, it should be noted that the particular incidence of taxation – especially the relative treatment of income and capital gains – will influence the portfolio composition.

General Funds

As explained above, the purpose of a general insurance fund is very different from that for a long-term insurance fund. The primary function of a general insurance fund is to provide a 'pool' from which to meet an uncertain stream of claims. Given that the size of claims fluctuates quite considerably from year to year for many types of business, and given the need for reserves to cover outstanding claims and unexpired risks, adequate holdings of funds are obviously of the greatest importance. At the end of 1984, general insurance funds amounted to £26,653 million, representing approximately one-and-a-half times the value of premium income for that year.

The repeated, and substantial, underwriting losses of general insurance companies in recent years has made it especially important that the general funds should yield a satisfactory return. Also, of course, payments out of general funds have had to be made in order to meet such losses, and whilst a proportion of these payments has constituted investment income, a proportion has been covered by asset realizations. Taken in conjunction with the fluctuations in the volume of claims, it could be expected that a significant element of any general insurance fund will be held as cash, agents' balances and as short-term assets in order to meet claims on the company's policies.

Given the need to offset any underwriting losses and to remain profitable, it may be taken for granted that general insurance companies will be concerned with maximizing the yield on their assets. On the face of it, such companies would want to hold relatively liquid assets, since the majority of their policies are of a short-term nature. However, two other considerations enter here. First, although the majority of their business is short-term, very few general insurance companies would expect their premium income to fall dramatically from one year to the next. This being so, they would not expect their general insurance funds to fall dramatically from one year to the next either, and on that basis they would be prepared to invest a proportion of their funds in higher-yielding, longer-term assets. Indeed, if a company anticipated a stable position where incoming claims could be paid from incoming premiums, after allocating some part of its fund to short-term assets for unforeseen contingencies, a high proportion of the fund could be allocated to longer-term assets. Secondly, holding short-term assets carries the consequence of repeated reinvestment, which involves costly administration and the evaluation of alternative assets. Holding longer-term assets is a way of reducing these costs. In practice, the general insurance companies have tended to concentrate on holding *readily marketable* assets, in the hope of being able to avoid excessive capital loss should their realization prove necessary. Provided the company does not have to sell the assets repeatedly, by purchasing longer-term assets it can benefit from higher yields.

Tables 7.7 and 7.8 summarize UK insurance companies' aggregate asset holdings at the end of each of the years 1982–4 inclusive.[5] Table 7.7 covers general insurance funds

Table 7.7

UK Insurance Companies: Aggregate Assets of General Funds, 1982 to 1984, end of year, £ million (market values)

	1982	1983	1984
Short-term assets			
UK			
Cash and balances with monetary sector	1,056	1,342	1,713
Certificates of deposit	72	130	101
Other financial institutions	55	64	61
Local authority bills and temporary money	51	46	42
Other short-term assets	414	475	729
Overseas short-term assets	79	139	81
Borrowing	(202)	(351)	(915)
Total net short-term assets	1,525	1,845	1,812
British government securities			
Index-linked	88	124	142
Up to 5 years	1,428	1,617	1,736
Over 5 and up to 15 years	2,370	2,844	2,616
Over 15 years and undated	383	324	273
Total British government securities	4,269	4,909	4,767

Local authority securities	80	76	119
UK company securities			
Ordinary shares	4,447	3,713	3,074
Other	799	692	630
Overseas securities			
Company securities			
Ordinary shares	977	795	600
Other	777	531	549
Government securities	1,651	1,001	843
Loans and mortgages, UK			
House purchase loans	236	224	210
Other	142	236	165
UK land, property and ground rents	1,657	1,640	1,568
Agents' balances, etc.	2,423	2,978	2,575
Other assets	218	142	166
Total net assets	20,019	18,782	16,293

Source: Financial Statistics, January 1986.

Table 7.8

UK Insurance Companies: Aggregate Assets of Long-term Funds, 1982 to 1984, end of year, £ million (market values)

	1982	1983	1984
Short-term assets			
UK			
Cash and balances with monetary sector	1,777	2,050	3,460
Certificates of deposit	90	96	163
Other financial institutions	212	297	401
Local authority bills and temporary money	169	212	308
Other short-term assets	736	812	314
Overseas short-term assets	117	68	211
Borrowing	(552)	(778)	(1,656)
Total net short-term assets	2,549	2,757	3,201
British government securities			
Index-linked	993	1,448	1,822
Up to 5 years	1,106	1,634	1,766
Over 5 and up to 15 years	8,433	10,663	14,079
Over 15 years and undated	12,250	12,049	9,992
Total British government securities	22,782	25,794	27,659

Local authority securities	658	691	793
UK company securities			
Ordinary shares	22,234	27,985	35,865
Other	2,565	3,312	3,932
Overseas securities			
Company securities			
Ordinary shares	4,788	7,326	9,335
Other	263	385	530
Government securities	738	1,148	1,773
Unit trust units	2,328	3,829	5,405
Loans and mortgages, UK			
House purchase loans	1,987	2,096	2,334
Loans on companies' policies	316	356	663
Other	1,354	1,482	981
UK land, property and ground rents	15,993	17,169	18,749
Agents' balances etc.	768	909	893
Other assets	435	529	738
Total net assets	79,759	95,768	112,851

Source: *Financial Statistics*, January 1986.

and Table 7.8 covers long-term insurance funds. Figure 7.1 also illustrates the allocation of assets both for general and for long-term funds, at the end of 1984. Although, as noted earlier, the total premiums in respect of general and long-term insurance were broadly similar, the total value of assets held in long-term funds is plainly very different. The total value of assets held in long-term funds is more than five times that held in general funds, reflecting the longer-term investment characteristic of the contracts written.

It was suggested above that insurance companies would not, in general, be expected to hold significant volumes of short-term assets. The data in Figure 7.1 bear this out, with less than 3 per cent of long-term funds and 10 per cent of general funds being held as short-term assets at the end of 1984. It is also notable that almost 79 per cent of the assets of the general funds were classified outside the 'short-term assets' and 'agents' balances' groups. For in addition to the meeting of unpredictable levels of claims, some assets will necessarily be held in a short-term form prior to being used for the purchase of longer-term assets. This aspect will not only comprise incoming premiums but also investment income and the proceeds of the sale or redemption of longer-term assets. Holding short-term assets might also be a conscious investment strategy. If the securities market is particularly volatile and uncertain, fund managers might see the holding of short-term assets as a means of reducing risk without forgoing all investment return until greater stability returns to the market.

Comparison of the figures for 1982, 1983 and 1984 in Tables 7.7 and 7.8 indicates that the portfolio of assets held in both general and long-term funds were subject to considerable change over time. Some of the more notable changes in portfolio composition illustrated by those tables relate to the more substantial holdings, such as UK ordinary shares, overseas securities and British government securities. For general funds, total net assets at the end of 1984 were 6.6 per cent greater than at the end of 1983, compared to which holdings of UK ordinary shares rose by 20.6 per cent, and holdings of overseas securities rose by 31.4 per cent, whereas the value of British government securities held fell

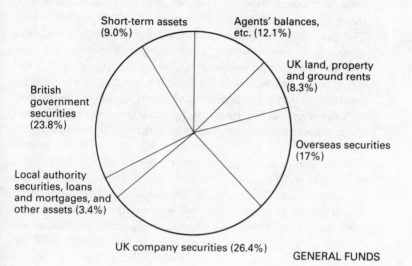

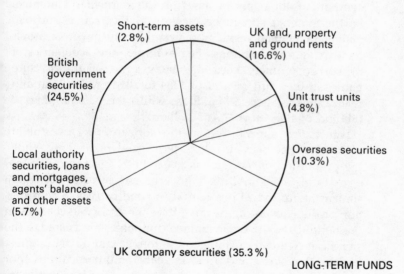

Figure 7.1 UK Insurance Companies: Distribution of Assets by Grouping, at 31 December 1984

Source: Financial Statistics, Central Statistical Office, January 1986.

by 2.9 per cent. For long-term insurance company funds, total net assets rose by 17.8 per cent, compared to which there were increases in holdings of UK ordinary shares by 28.2 per cent, overseas securities by 31.4 per cent, and British government securities by 7.2 per cent.

It must be emphasized that the figures in Table 7.7 and 7.8 refer to *market valuations*, which implies that a strong performance in a particular asset group could, of itself, lead to an increase in the proportion of the portfolio held in that group. In addition, the passing of time will also, of itself, cause a change in the structure of the portfolio unless positive action is taken to maintain the distribution. Various securities will mature, or in the case of British government securities, will change classification (for example, an 'over 5 and up to 15 years' security will eventually become an 'up to 5 years' asset) before finally maturing. But despite these considerations, many of the changes in the portfolios shown are nevertheless substantial, with the changes in the various components of overseas assets being particularly notable. Furthermore, it should be recognized that active portfolio management may result in a very high turnover of assets relative to total holdings. For example, the acquisition of British government securities by general insurance companies in the third quarter of 1984 totalled £888 million and realizations totalled £990 million, whilst the total holding, at the end of 1984, was £4,767 million.[6]

Figure 7.1 shows clearly the longer-term investment perspective taken by the long-term fund managers. While the proportion of the total assets of both general and long-term funds held in British government securities is very similar (at around 24 per cent at the end of 1984), examination of the relevant figures in Tables 7.7 and 7.8 reveals that the holdings of the life insurance companies are geared, to a significantly greater extent, to the longer end of the market (that is, the 'over 5 and up to 15 years' and, particularly, the 'over 15 years and undated' classifications). Also, holdings of UK company securities (particularly ordinary shares), and investments in land and property both constitute a greater proportion of the total for life funds than for general insurance funds. In so far as these classifications represent longer-term investments, the conclusion that life insurance companies take a longer-term investment perspective is strengthened.

Finally, it must be stressed that the figures in Tables 7.7 and 7.8 relate to the whole general and long-term insurance industries (respectively) and not to any particular company. Differences in the nature of a company's liabilities especially, and differences in the strategies adopted by fund managers, may lead to portfolio compositions very different from those discussed above.

Attributes of Assets Held in Insurance Company Investment Portfolios

It is sometimes argued that long-term insurance companies will attempt to match the liabilities inherent in their contracts with the investments which they make, so that investments will mature at the same time as their policies, thereby enabling the payments to policyholders to be made. However, in practice, and especially in relation to larger companies, this is unlikely to be a significant influence on portfolio selection, as the fund generated by new business may often adequately cover the payments that fall due. To the extent that this occurs, the funds of the life companies can be described as 'open' funds. Additionally, the possibility of early surrender of long-term policies makes exact matching impossible.[7] Therefore, it is much more likely that insurance companies hold assets for their inherent attributes, rather than for matching purposes.

The attributes of British government securities are that they are default-free, that they give security of income over their life, that they are readily marketable, even in large blocks, and that they are available in a range of maturity dates and coupons. In addition, at the time of writing, any capital gains consequent on dealing in government stocks are free of tax. Given these attributes, it is not surprising that insurance companies, both general and long-term, hold a substantial portion of their funds in government securities. However, commensurate with their advantages, they suffer from two major disadvantages; they offer no prospect of capital growth at maturity (indeed, with the exception of the index-linked gilts, their real capital value is eroded by inflation), and their market value is subject to variation. Prior to maturity, although real capital gains can be secured at a time of falling interest rates, capital losses are suffered when interest rates rise.[8]

The principal attribute of ordinary shares is that, under normal circumstances, real capital growth is possible. In addition to the income return in the form of dividends, an increase in the market value of a shareholding is normally expected, although it is necessary to take a long-term view. (The dramatic fall in the value of ordinary shares in 1974/5 underlined the riskiness of ordinary shares.) Naturally, shares in some companies will prove to yield a better overall return than shares in others, and insurance companies will have to devote resources to evaluating the prospects of those companies in which they might wish to invest. The costs of monitoring shareholdings are not inconsequential, and since there are likely to be economies of scale in such activity a substantial element of ordinary shares in the portfolio becomes worthwhile. An alternative strategy is to 'buy in' portfolio management expertise from an outside stockbroker, though it has then to be recognized that this may prove to be expensive, and also that such expertise may not be exclusive to one insurance company.

Investment in overseas securities has seen a marked growth in recent years, particularly since the ending of all foreign exchange controls in 1979. Prior to that time, insurance companies were constrained in the extent to which they could undertake overseas investment, and since then they have taken the opportunity of restructuring their portfolios. Insurance companies may wish to invest overseas in order to take advantage of higher expected returns, as well as to spread portfolio risk more widely. Also, of course, it may allow them to match more closely their assets and liabilities. If an insurance company, for example, writes a number of policies in a foreign currency, it is exposing itself to the risk of currency exchange rate movements, and to purchase assets equivalent to its liabilities in that foreign currency would negate this risk.[9] The ending of foreign exchange controls has, therefore, enabled the insurance companies to compete more effectively in foreign markets. They are now undoubtedly willing to write policies denominated in foreign currencies despite the higher degree of exchange rate volatility.

Investment in land and property has the major attribute for insurance companies of being an excellent hedge against inflation. It must necessarily be viewed very much as a long-term investment, since the secondary market in land and property is quite imperfect. Although investment in land and property will yield income in the form of rents, due to various legal and institutional interferences (for example, rent controls or the periodicity of commercial rent revaluations), the more important part of the return on such investment is seen as being its increasing capital value over time. In recent years, insurance companies have become active property developers, often in conjunction with local authorities, or other commercial institutions. The types of property involved have been diverse, but they have tended to be mainly commercial properties, especially offices and retail premises. Also in recent years, insurance companies have become major landowners, especially of farming land.

As Tables 7.7 and 7.8 show, fixed interest securities other than government debt represent only a fairly small proportion of insurance companies' portfolios. To a certain extent, this reflects the availability of such assets in the UK. In recent years the tax system has militated against the use by companies of fixed interest securities as a means of raising finance, and the issue of local authority securities has also been restricted. Also, the volatility of both the inflation rate and interest rates since the mid-1970s has rendered fixed interest company securities unattractive to both borrowers and lenders. To an insurance company, such assets have similar attributes to government securities, except that with corporate securities there is a significant risk of default, and the secondary market in such securities is often thin (implying that the price of such assets may not be independent of the dealings of insurance companies in them). Furthermore, the availability of corporate securities of this type is naturally variable, depending on the profitability of the issuing companies concerned, and hence their needs for external funding. Nevertheless, non-government fixed interest securities do have an important asset-matching attribute. Given the combination of their (usually) relatively short maturity and fixed interest, they may provide a good match for expected annuity payments related to certain classes of policies.

A major attribute of mortgages and of loans secured against industrial and commercial property is that they offer a very high level of security. As a consequence, mortgages constituted a major part of insurance companies' portfolios in earlier years, especially when many security markets were underdeveloped. However, their major defect is their lack of liquidity in the sense that there is (virtually) no secondary market in them,[10] and they offer no protection from inflation. In addition, they can be expensive to set up, often with significant time lags involved in finalizing arrangements. In recent years it has usually been the case that insurance companies have used mortgages as a means of obtaining new business in other product lines, rather than compete actively in the mortgage market.

Insurance companies, in common with many other financial intermediaries, have been subjected to criticism on the basis that they are very conservative lenders. From industry's point of view, they have been reluctant to invest money in the more speculative, higher-risk projects or to participate in what has become termed the provision of venture capital. Despite the fact that smaller firms often generate higher returns than larger firms, insurance companies have tended to concentrate their shareholdings in the larger, well-established 'blue chip' companies with correspondingly less interest in smaller companies. The comment originating from many quarters is that this has helped to contribute to the UK's poor record of economic growth. As should be clear from the foregoing discussion of the attributes of various forms of investment, a major consideration in an insurance company's investment strategy is the marketability of the asset, and investments in smaller companies do not, in general, meet this requirement. Whilst investments in unquoted companies may offer high returns, they often possess a low level of marketability, and furthermore may be expensive to set up. Investment in the shares of companies quoted on the Unlisted Securities Market and on the Over-the-Counter Market offer a better secondary market, but even here trading in such shares is frequently very thin, with a few institutions holding a high proportion of the total shares. Naturally, such investments offer a higher anticipated return, albeit at a higher risk, but given the spread of investments in the rest of the company's portfolio this is not, however, a serious drawback. In view of the inadequacy of the secondary market in such assets it would be surprising to find insurance companies being particularly actively involved. However, it is important to note that they do maintain a worthwhile presence. Some insurance companies have made very positive moves into the area of providing venture capital, of which one of the best known is Prutec, a subsidiary of Prudential Assurance that specializes in the provision of venture capital for high-technology projects.

UK Insurance Companies: Profitability and Efficiency

Due to the nature of their business, insurance companies face certain difficulties in assessing their profitability that are additional to those faced by other companies. For general insurance business, an important problem relates to the necessity for companies to make provisions for claims that may arise some time after the period of insurance ends. Different estimates of, and different conventions of, how to deal with these provisions will influence the perceived profitability of the company. Although the various pieces of legislation impinging upon insurance companies lay down certain minimum criteria, freedom of action for any insurance company to go beyond this remains.

Further difficulties arise because a major portion of the income of any company engaging in general insurance derives from investments. Once again, differences in accounting conventions in respect of this income make the assessment of profitability difficult.[11] The 'income' from a general insurance fund has two parts: the receipt of interest, dividends, rents and so on, and the capital appreciation of the fund over time. While the former is uncontentious, the latter is rather less so, since a distinction is normally made between realized and unrealized gains. Tradition established that while realized gains were to be regarded as income, unrealized gains were not. One implication of this was that, in the short term, those insurers with a high turnover of their portfolio would be recording higher profits than those with a low turnover. However, Eagle Star (a major composite insurer) broke with tradition in 1985 by including unrealized gains on its general investment portfolio (albeit by reference to a 5-year moving average to introduce an element of conservatism), which resulted in a boost to profits of some £95 million.

These two areas of difficulty in assessing profitability are by no means the only such areas, although they are significant ones. Other peculiarities of general insurance business (for example, the 3-year accounting basis usually employed for marine, aviation and transport business), and the relatively lax and flexible disclosure requirements for insurance companies which allow variations in accounting methods, serve to make assessment and comparison unreliable. Nevertheless, it is undeniably true that the profitability of general insurance has not been good in recent years. As Table 7.9 demonstrates, the industry as a whole has made a repeated underwriting loss, and within these aggregated figures the majority of individual general insurers have also made losses. However, the industry's underwriting losses have usually been more than covered by its investment income, although overall trading profits have remained low. When expressed as a percentage of premiums received in order to obtain some measure of a rate of return (see Table 7.9, bottom line), this low profitability and its declining trend in recent years is emphasized.

For long-term insurance business the difficulty of assessing profitability is substantially greater than with general insurance. Whereas the latter business requires companies to make some provision for claims after the expiration of

Table 7.9

UK Insurance Companies: Overall Trading Profit, Worldwide General Insurance 1980 to 1984, £ million

	1980	1981	1982	1983	1984
Net premiums written	8,147	9,654	11,053	12,199	14,315
Underwriting profit/loss for 1 year account basis (motor and fire & accident)	−302	−565	−992	−1,041	−1,784
Transfer to profit and loss account for other business:					
Marine, aviation and transport	−38	−46	−83	−83	−76
Other	n/a	n/a	−171	−240	−331
Total underwriting profit/loss	−340	−611	−1,246	−1,364	−2,191
Total investment income	1,131	1,436	1,734	1,913	2,142
Overall trading profit/loss	791	825	488	549	−49
Profit as a percentage of premiums	9.7	8.5	4.4	4.5	−0.3

Source: Association of British Insurers.

policies, long-term insurance business requires that virtually all provision for claims and liabilities takes place in the future. As a consequence, profits from any long-term insurance business can only be assessed on the basis of actuarial valuations of the fund involved – for which, naturally enough, conventions will vary.[12] Also, it is common for life insurance companies to be operated, at least in part, on a 'mutual' basis, where the distinction between 'owners' and 'customers' becomes blurred. In many companies this takes the form of 'with-profits' policies, where the holders of such policies are entitled to a high proportion (often as high as 90 per cent) of the distributed profits of the company (or fund), with the shareholders receiving the balance. Plainly, the impact of this mutuality is to render the measurement of profit difficult, since the distinction between profit and returns to policyholders becomes problematic. While any individual life insurance company is able to identify profits attributable to its shareholders, aggregation of such statistics, given the disparity of product portfolios between different companies and the changing nature of the portfolios over time, would be largely meaningless. Nevertheless, it is undoubtedly true that since the mid-1970s long-term insurance business has been consistently profitable, and in this respect stands in marked contrast to general insurance business.

Given the inadequacy of profit figures as a measure of efficiency, attention has switched, particularly for life insurance business, to using expense ratios for the purpose. In principle, the proportion of premiums which goes towards commission and to management and other expenses should provide a measure of efficiency for the industry, and for comparing firms within the industry. In addition, this data should be of use to potential purchasers of a life insurance policy since, other things being equal, the more money that is absorbed in expenses the less there is available to pay to policyholders. As with all summary measures, however, expense ratios for insurance companies conceal as much as they reveal.

In the context of life insurance business there are two main areas of deficiency. First, the type of business which the company writes will play a significant part in determining the expense ratio. At one extreme, a company heavily involved in industrial life insurance would incur heavy expenses, while at the other extreme a company writing a high level of group schemes, where the premiums would be large, would incur low expenses. Similarly, specializing in term insurance would result in comparatively small individual premiums, with associated high costs, while specializing in pensions business would result in larger premiums and correspondingly lower costs. To this extent, therefore, differences in expense ratios are liable to reflect differences in the types of business written by companies rather than in their relative efficiency. Secondly, a life company's rate of growth will have an impact on the expense ratio. The greater part of a company's expenses is incurred when a new policy is written, while maintaining that policy incurs relatively little cost. Consequently, a high rate of growth will force the expense ratio up. At the same time, however, it is worth noting that inflation will lead to many of a company's older policies becoming expensive to maintain, as inflation erodes the real value of fixed premiums. In seeking to contain expenses, a life company will therefore need to look at both its growth rate and the inflation rate, and seek to balance their effects. It remains true, however, that when comparing the expense ratios of different life insurance companies, their relative growth rates have to be taken into account.

A further complication, at least from the viewpoint of a potential policyholder, is that there is little correlation between the expense ratio of a company and the returns achieved on a policy. A recent study[13] demonstrated that life insurance companies which produced the best results in respect of two different types of with-profit policy had widely differing expense ratios (expressed as expenses divided by total premium income), both at the time of the policy's inception and at its maturity. From the point of view of a life insurance company, however, the problem is conceptually simple. Thus, if the company is able to reduce the costs of attracting and maintaining business, then it will be able to furnish better returns on its with-profit policies

267

and to offer improved terms on its non-profit policies. Clearly, whilst a life company can utilize its investment expertise and the tax privileges available to its longer-term policies to offer a high rate of return on premiums received, these advantages will be lost unless it is able to contain its expenses. Consequently, unduly high expenses will undermine the industry's ability to attract business, as potential policyholders start to perceive that equally attractive returns are available from alternative investment media, perhaps in conjunction with greater flexibility.

This problem facing the life insurance companies has been made worse by the widespread, and persistent, rise in expense ratios in recent years. To some extent, the companies have been the victims of their own success. High growth rates of the life insurance business, coupled with the high inflation rates of the 1970s, caused expense ratios to rise dramatically in many cases. Very few companies were able to reduce their expense ratios during the 1970s, and of the few that did succeed a significant proportion had high expense ratios at the outset. Although expense ratios are subject to marked differences between companies, during the early 1980s a ratio of expenses to total premium income of less than 10 per cent was very rare, and a figure in the region of 20–30 per cent was quite common. For some of the smaller companies and societies engaged mainly or exclusively in industrial insurance, the expense ratio was substantially above 50 per cent. Their ratios of expenses to total income (including investment income) were, of course, commensurately lower.[14]

The life companies have placed great emphasis on the control of expenses in recent years, recognizing that in the changed, and vastly more competitive, savings market of the 1980s, their ability to compete will depend crucially on achieving a low expense ratio. Also for general insurers, facing consistent losses on their underwriting account, improvements in efficiency in order to reduce expenses are increasingly seen as the way to return to profitability. This is especially so given the increased willingness on the part of the public to make claims for losses due to theft, motor accidents and so on. In addition the growing competition for business has created some resistance to higher premium rates.

Developments in technology, particularly in computer systems, have been implemented at a rapid rate by the insurance companies. Computerization of many tasks has rendered many clerical jobs obsolete, and many insurers have been able to reduce staff numbers substantially. By means of direct contact between insurance brokers and a company's computer, a broker is able to obtain an instantaneous quote for a customer, providing details on such matters as the premium payable, and the projected sum at maturity. If the details of the policy are not satisfactory to the customer in some respect, additional quotes can be obtained until a satisfactory policy is found. This process avoids the repeated completion of proposal forms and preparation of quotations, as well as delays resulting from the use of the postal system. Consequently costs are likely to be reduced substantially for both insurance companies and customers, with the result that the number of policies sold is likely to increase. New technology is being increasingly viewed both as a means of cutting costs and also of increasing business.

Other cost-saving strategies that insurance companies are following include the relocation of head offices and rationalization of branch networks. Insurance companies have found that they do not need large numbers of people at head offices in the City of London, since the bulk of the administrative services can be carried out where operating costs, especially rents, are lower. This is illustrated by Commercial Union, a major composite insurer with a prestige office block in the City, which found that the opportunity cost of occupying all the space itself was too high, and accordingly relocated a substantial part of its head office activities to sites outside central London. At the same time, Commercial Union reduced its number of branches by one-third, a policy followed by a number of other composite insurers.

Regulation and Supervision

The early attempts by government to regulate the activities of insurance companies were designed to ensure that they had adequate solvency, particularly with respect to life insurance activities involving longer-term commitments. The Life Assurance Companies Act of 1870 required life assurance companies to hold a bank deposit of £20,000 before they could commence business, and to submit detailed accounts and actuarial returns to the Board of Trade in order that their solvency could be monitored. Later legislation (Assurance Companies Acts of 1909 and 1946) was more extensive in its scope, covering general insurance, and the 1946 Act also changed the means of ensuring solvency from a deposit system to one based upon a margin. Thus, companies were required to have assets exceeding liabilities by at least 10 per cent of the premium income of the previous year, subject to a minimum of £50,000. In addition, a minimum paid-up share capital of £50,000 was required. For general insurance business these solvency margins were increased under the 1967 Companies Act, with the increases impinging particularly on the smaller, and more recently established companies.

The bulk of the legislation relating to insurance companies is now embodied in the Insurance Companies Act 1982, which both consolidated and extended the pre-existing legislation, and took into account EEC Directives on insurance business. The failure of some insurance companies, notably the Vehicle and General Insurance Co. in 1971, had demonstrated the inadequacy of the earlier legislation. The 1982 Act is a complex piece of legislation, although it may be viewed as having two primary objectives: first to protect the policyholder from the failure of an insurance company, and secondly to protect the individual from being sold insurance policies unsuited to his needs. The objective of protecting the policyholder from the failure of an insurance company is intended to be achieved through four powers conferred upon the Department of Trade and Industry by the Act, relating to authorization of companies to conduct business;

stipulation of solvency margins; monitoring of the business of insurance companies; and the authority to intervene in the running of an insurance company.

The 1982 Act makes it an offence for an individual or company to conduct insurance business in the UK without prior authorization. For this purpose, the Act defines various classes of insurance, specified in Tables 7.2 and 7.3, and companies are thereby authorized to write particular classes of insurance although they are not given a blanket authorization for all classes. Authorization is granted if the applicant is deemed to be 'fit and proper' to conduct the insurance business applied for, where the basis of the 'fit and proper' test is the replies to a detailed questionnaire about financial forecasts, how the business would be run, types of policies offered, and so on. It should also be recognized that the secretary of state is empowered to withdraw authorizations where, for example, a company has failed to comply with any obligation under the Act or grounds exist for the refusal of authorization (Section 11), or where the insurer has ceased to carry on the class of business concerned (Section 13). Withdrawal of authorization under Section 11 for one or more classes of business was applied to eighteen companies in 1984.[5]

All insurance companies are monitored by the Department of Trade and Industry for circumstances where authorization might be withdrawn. Each year, all insurance companies are required to lodge with the Department detailed information on premiums and claims, and a detailed set of accounts. For life assurance business, an actuary is required to declare whether or not, in his opinion, the recorded liabilities of the company's long-term business represents an accurate assessment of the true liabilities, and every three years to present a full report on the company's financial position in respect of its long-term business.

Inadequate solvency margins are one possible reason for the withdrawal of authorization, or the refusal to grant authorization. In order to ensure equality in the evaluation of solvency margins throughout the EEC, those margins are expressed in terms of European Currency Units (ECUs), and a minimum of the higher of two alternative methods of calculation (respectively the 'premium basis', similar to that under the 1946 Act, and the 'claims basis') is required. Slightly different minimum solvency margins apply according to whether the company is a UK company, an EEC company with head office outside the UK, or a non-EEC company. It is generally agreed that these requirements have comparatively little impact on the larger, well-established companies within the industry. However, they are likely to have a greater impact upon the smaller insurance companies, particularly those that are growing rapidly. A small insurance company that in any one year writes a lot of new long-term business is likely to find itself running close to the statutory minimum solvency requirements comparatively easily.

The secretary of state is empowered by the 1982 Act to intervene in the running of insurance companies. He may force them to stop issuing or renewing policies; to modify investment strategy; to liquidate or repatriate assets; or to provide information if the protection of policyholders is thought to require such immediate action. These powers of intervention were used on over a hundred occasions in 1984, although in addition companies voluntarily provided information or took remedial action when asked. However, should a company get into difficulties, the Policyholders Protection Act of 1975 provides for a guarantee scheme to protect private policyholders. Basically, they will be reimbursed to the extent of 90 per cent of the failed insurance company's liabilities, and this charge will be met from a levy on other insurance companies.

The protection of the individual from being sold unsuitable policies is provided by a number of requirements in the 1982 Act relating to advertisements, relationships between an insurance company and an intermediary, 'cooling-off' periods for long-term contracts, and so on. This area of protection was considered as part of a much wider review of investor protection undertaken during 1985, following the report of an investigation into this issue made by Professor Gower in 1984 (Cmnd 9125) and the publication of a White Paper (Cmnd 9432) in January 1985. Insurance companies have become involved in this debate due to the number of policies written which emphasize the investment element and which offer virtually no insurance cover in the conventional sense, but which are not subject to the controls imposed on other investment media. There are two related areas of concern, namely the marketing of life insurance contracts and the payment of commission to salesmen and intermediaries. To varying degrees, many salesmen and intermediaries are connected with particular insurance companies, and hence the question has been raised as to whether there is a conflict of interest that may cause policyholders to be misled and to be provided with inadequate advice. Furthermore, there is concern that the level of training given to many salesmen is inadequate, with the consequence that they are not capable of identifying which policies would be most appropriate for any particular individual even if they were prepared to sell such policies. Despite efforts on self-regulation in this area, the outcome has been largely ineffective, and it was proposed in the White Paper on investor protection that a new Marketing of Investments Board would lay down rules and codes of conduct for the sale of life insurance policies, while also allowing it to recognize self-regulatory initiatives in the field.

The payment of commissions by insurance companies to intermediaries has proved to be a more intractable problem, with the industry failing to reach any degree of unity on this issue. One problem with commissions is not that free competition is liable to lead to very *low* commissions, but rather the reverse, since if a company wishes to obtain more business then one way of doing so is to pay higher commissions to the intermediary in the hope that the intermediary will pass more business to it. Not only does this enhance the conflict of interest discussed above, and thereby creates a reduced prospect of impartial advice by intermediaries, but it also leads to higher prices for, and hence lower returns on, policies sold by the companies. Attempts by the industry to obtain agreement on maximum commissions have failed, though it is hoped that such agreement will eventually emerge. The other aspect of commissions given attention in the White Paper relates to their disclosure. Traditionally, they have never been disclosed to purchasers of policies. The view of the present government is not only that disclosure of commissions is necessary for adequate comparison between investments to be made, but also that it will help to prevent commissions from rising. Not surprisingly, the insurance companies are not enthusiastic about having to disclose commissions, since they fear that if individuals discovered how much of their premiums was absorbed in this way a great many sales would be lost. They argue further that the commissions are high at present because for every completed contract there are nine unsuccessful calls, the costs of which must be covered. Against this, however, it can be argued that a system which results in only one sale for every ten attempts is extremely inefficient, and the disclosures of commissions would force the industry to develop more efficient sales techniques and, perhaps, to develop more standardized products.

The proposed strengthening of the framework for investor protection is likely to have a widespread impact on the activities of life insurance companies. They will find it necessary, under the new legislation, to control the activities of their salesmen more effectively, a factor which, combined with the proposal to force the disclosure of commissions, is likely to make it more difficult for life insurance companies to compete with other forms of saving.

It should be recognized that not all long-term insurance is sold by insurance companies. Industrial life insurance, where policies are sold in people's homes and the premiums normally collected fortnightly or monthly, is also sold by friendly societies. Although the bulk of industrial insurance business is sold by life insurance companies, there remains a worthwhile element that is provided by some 400 friendly societies and some 20 'Orders'. These organizations are not subject to the Insurance Companies Act of 1982, but rather are subject to the Friendly Societies Act of 1974 and to the Industrial Assurance Acts 1923 to 1968. Also, they are supervised by the Chief Registrar of Friendly Societies, and are therefore operated within a separate regulatory system. The great majority of these friendly societies exist primarily for their social and charitable activities, and the straightforward life insurance policies they offer are seen as an extension of these activities. There are, however, a number of much more commercially minded friendly societies which market a range of sophisticated policies and bonds that render them indistinguishable from the mutual life insurance companies. In order to ensure compliance with the EEC Life Assurance Directive these societies have now been brought within a regulatory framework similar to that for insurance companies.

Within the context of the Financial Services Act 1986 it is the intention of the authorities that insurance companies and insurance intermediaries which sell or give advice on endowment and unit-linked policies will have to obtain authorization to conduct their business. However, the Act does not disturb the existing supervisory regime flowing from the Insurance Companies Act 1982, and insurance companies will be able to take a special route to authorization which recognizes the role of the Department of Trade and Industry in respect of the requirements of the 1982 Act. Nevertheless, insurance companies are now subject to any rules made within the confines of the Financial Services Act relating to the marketing of investments (for example, involving advertising, cold calling and cooling-off periods). Furthermore, friendly societies which also carry on insurance business are subject to a similar regime. It is also proposed that brokers and consultants acting as life assurance intermediaries must be authorized, and they must operate subject to the regulations of a recognized agency or self-regulatory organization. Therefore, it would appear that the supervisory regime, as it relates to insurance activity, has been broadened and has been brought more into line with the supervision of other investment businesses; however, the core of technical regulations will remain firmly entrenched in the Insurance Companies Act 1982.

Finally, it is appropriate also to consider areas of activity over which legislation and regulation does *not* apply. As demonstrated above, the insurance companies are responsible for controlling massive investment funds, but it is notable that, apart from prudential requirements, there is no control over the direction of these funds. Subject to the guidelines laid down by the company itself, the fund managers have very substantial freedom as to how and where to invest; indeed, with the abolition of exchange controls in 1979 their freedom was increased. This absence of control is not common to insurance companies in other countries, nor in the light of the proposals from the Labour Party to introduce legislation which would effect control over insurance companies' investment, will it necessarily remain so in the UK.

Taxation

The growth of life insurance policies as an investment medium for individuals has probably been facilitated by the fact that the regular payment of a moderate sum to an insurance company is a relatively painless method of accumulating savings, and that there are taxation benefits from saving in this way. The taxation benefits related to life insurance contracts arise at both the level of the company and in respect of the taxation position of the policyholder himself.

As regards the taxation of the life insurance companies, concessionary rates apply to a life company's investment income after deduction of management expenses. At the time of writing the tax rate on unfranked income (that is, earnings on fixed interest securities, income from properties, and so on) is 35 per cent. The rate on franked income (mainly dividend payments) allocated to policyholders' funds is set equal to the basic personal tax rate (27 per cent), since the income is received net of the tax credit which cannot be reclaimed by the insurance company. Chargeable capital gains attributable to life fund policyholders are currently taxed at 30 per cent, but given that life insurance companies are able to hold assets for a long period of time, these realized gains are usually fairly small. In consequence, the effective rate of capital gains tax that applies to the policyholder is kept low. Furthermore, the taxation of capital gains on gilt-edged securities has been preferential in recent years, which accounts for part of the attractiveness of such assets to the insurance companies. However, lest the impression be given that insurance companies escape with paying little tax, it should be noted that in 1984 UK taxation paid by life insurance companies amounted to £454 million, which represented over 3 per cent of premium income for that year.

With respect to the taxation of the policyholder, there is an essential distinction between 'qualifying' and 'non-qualifying' policies. A qualifying policy has to be certified as being so by the Inland Revenue, with the major requirement being that the period over which premiums are payable must be 10 years or more.[16] The proceeds of a qualifying endowment policy (that is, a contract where there is a substantial investment component) will be free of income tax and capital gains tax provided the policy has been maintained for at least three-quarters of its term or 10 years (whichever is the greater), and has not been made paid-up within that period. For a whole-of-life policy the minimum period is 10 years. In addition, the premiums for a qualifying policy issued before 14 March 1984 continue to be eligible for Life Assurance Premium Relief (LAPR) at the rate of 15 per cent. Where this applies, the premiums are paid net of tax relief with the companies obtaining 15 per cent of the value of the premiums from the Inland Revenue.[17] LAPR furnished the life insurance companies with a substantial advantage over other investment media, since, in simple terms, it meant that a policyholder was obtaining a 15 per cent discount. An alternative way of perceiving the advantage is to observe that the insurance companies could incur substantial management expenses yet still remain competitive. However, LAPR was withdrawn in the budget of March 1984, with the result that policies issued after 13 March 1984 are not eligible for premium relief. For non-qualifying policies LAPR was not allowed. Currently, termination of a non-qualifying policy only gives rise to an income tax charge if the policyholder is liable to income tax in a higher-rate band. There is no liability for income tax at the basic rate.[18] It is clear, therefore, that the advantages of qualifying policies have been much reduced with the abolition of LAPR. The continued promotion of qualifying policies, and their acceptance by the public, is probably due to the difficulty of estimating one's liability to higher-rate income tax at some point in the future.

The abolition of LAPR was widely regarded as causing a considerable change in the conditions under which life insurance companies operated, since a major advantage which they had enjoyed for over 130 years was removed without official notice, although rumours abounded. Some commentators, however, maintained that in effect little had changed, and that in particular there was no reason to believe that the underlying demand from the general public for life insurance and for long-term savings media had altered. Therefore, given the reduction in the cost advantages possessed by insurance companies as an investment medium, two things could reasonably be expected to happen: first, that insurance companies would shift towards providing and marketing a greater range of policies offering pure life insurance protection with no savings element, and secondly that they would undertake a careful examination of expenses with the view to reducing costs and thereby maintaining competitiveness with other investment media.

Even after the increase in its cost as a result of the 1984 budget measures, straightforward protective life insurance remains very cheap, since the risk borne by the insurance company is comparatively low. However, the consumer has very often been unaware of this since insurance salesmen have, naturally enough, been more concerned with selling investment-type policies that give rise to larger premiums and larger commissions. If companies do start to market pure life assurance more actively, then competition in this area will increase, premiums will tend to fall, and discounts, such as those to non-smokers or members of sports clubs, will become more widespread. Paradoxically, a shift towards basic insurance and away from the investment-type policies could be beneficial to the insurance companies themselves. With pure life insurance, cover is sold to policyholders for a fixed amount over a fixed term, and there is no distribution of the company's profits as in the case of with-profits investment policies. For existing with-profits policyholders of the companies this would also be beneficial, since they will receive a higher proportion of the investment profits, thus boosting their returns. But what is good news for the companies and for existing policyholders is likely to be less so for the salesmen, since low premiums on pure life insurance produce low commissions. A higher quantity of smaller premiums will also put pressure on the insurance companies to improve their administrative structures in order to contain their costs.

The introduction of Mortgage Interest Relief At Source (MIRAS) in late 1982 saw a short-term boom in the provision of endowment mortgages. With this type of mortgage a home buyer would borrow a sum of money from a building society or some other source for the full term of the mortgage (invariably 25 years), and would pay interest on that sum, with no repayment of capital until the end of the term. Simultaneously, the home buyer would take out a policy with an insurance company which, in addition to providing life cover, would normally be expected to be worth at least the original sum borrowed by the end of the term. The advantage of this scheme was that the home buyer received tax relief on the mortgage interest payments *and* on the life insurance premiums, which reduced the cost of the mortgage over its full term. The disadvantage was that it raised the cost of the total provision in the early years of the mortgage. The particular way in which MIRAS is operated, however, improved the attractiveness of the endowment mortgage schemes by making the cost in the early years very close to that of a straightforward repayment mortgage. Thus, from late 1982 until the removal of LAPR in the 1984 budget, the life insurance industry saw a substantial increase in the number of policies sold for endowment mortgage purposes. However, it should be noted that much of the impetus for these sales did not come from the insurance companies themselves but rather from the building societies, since it was the building societies that set up the endowment mortgages and received the commission. The removal of LAPR reduced the attractiveness of endowment mortgages once again, by raising the cost of the insurance policy element.

It is clear that changes in the taxation system have caused

marked changes in the market appeal of the different types of policies offered by the life insurance industry, and it is to the credit of the insurance companies that they have been able to respond effectively to these changing conditions. At the same time, however, it should be noted that life insurance companies derive much of their stability from policies sold in previous years, since many of these policies generate premiums for long periods of time. A change in the type of product sold does not have the impact on an insurance company that it would have, say, on a manufacturing company. Also, given the 'equivalency principle' underlying the abolition of LAPR (that is, that different forms of saving should be treated in an equal fashion for taxation purposes), future taxation changes might be expected to be relatively small, and this can only enhance insurance companies' operational planning.

The Importance of Insurance Companies within the UK Financial System

The comparatively low profile of life insurance companies tends to conceal their importance within the UK savings market. Nevertheless, as a consequence of the various attributes of life insurance policies as savings media, they now constitute a major element in the portfolio of personal sector saving. For 1983, total personal sector saving in the UK was estimated at £23,235 million, whilst in the same year the net acquisitions of long-term insurance funds amounted to £6,837 million, constituting almost 30 per cent.[19] The significantly higher-profile building societies achieved an almost identical figure, with a net inflow in 1983 of £6,839 million.

The range of policies offered by the life insurance companies has ensured that no significant part of the available market has been left untapped. The combination of a comparatively painless way of saving (by means of regular monthly payments) and the provision of life insurance protection within the same contract, together (usually) with a guaranteed minimum return and a known track record, has caused endowment policies to be included in the savings pattern of many individuals. The particular needs of those with low incomes have been met by the companies specializing in industrial assurance and by the friendly societies. However, given the inherent inflexibility of this type of life insurance policy, which arises as a consequence of its long-term nature (exemplified by the very low surrender values in early years), the achievement of such a significant portion of the total savings market is all the more notable.

Although the range of endowment policies offered by the insurance companies is extensive, it should be remembered that such policies are essentially designed for those individuals with an income who are desirous of accumulating a capital sum. The reverse position, representing those individuals with a capital sum but limited income (typically retired persons), has been accommodated by the industry through the provision of a range of annuities which, as was shown above, represent a smaller, but nevertheless significant, element of their business, and which fulfil an important function in the savings market. Furthermore, an increasingly important element of insurance companies' business has been the provision of pensions, itself a reflection of the increased amount of savings devoted to this purpose. The growth of the pensions business, together with other aspects of the importance of insurance companies in the savings market and within the financial system, will be examined jointly with pension funds in Chapter 8.

Competition: Policies on Marketing of Products/Services

The insurance industry as a whole, but the life insurance element in particular, offers a vast range of products. Consequently, the companies tend to compete on the basis of product differentiation rather than on price. This in turn makes direct comparison of any two life insurance policies rather awkward, as particular benefits and conditions may be applicable to one but not to the other. In general, the

281

intention of the majority of the life insurance companies would appear to have been to compete on the basis of offering the client a policy suited exactly to his needs, rather than to offer the cheapest, standardized, product that approximately fills his needs. The evolution of this approach has led a number of life companies to offer very flexible policies (sometimes known as 'universal life' policies), which provide a core of life cover with any number of 'extras' such as income protection or unit-linked savings plans. It is the hope of the insurance company that the policyholder will use his existing policy when he wishes to modify his insurance cover or longer-term investment portfolio.

It is widely accepted that the level of competition within the life insurance industry is likely to increase. The possible requirement for disclosure of commissions, and the increasing number of participants in the industry, will undoubtedly raise the level of competition both within the industry and between insurance companies and alternative savings media. It is also generally agreed that the selling of life insurance policies is currently a very inefficient business, with substantial effort going into 'lost' sales. There are basically two alternative views on this situation. The first is that the industry will be forced into producing a cheaper product, which will necessarily be more standardized, and that as a consequence competition within the industry, and between insurance companies and the providers of other savings media, will become based much more on price. The second view is that the industry will be forced into reducing its costs, making extensive use of new information technology and gearing its products even more closely to the needs of the potential policyholder. This latter view implies that competition on the basis of price will actually be lessened.

Finally, it should be remembered that competition within the insurance industry is limited by the extent to which the individual companies embrace different specialisms. This is particularly true of the general insurance sector of the industry, where companies specialize in different areas of insurance (and in many cases are only authorized to write certain classes of insurance business) or in different geographical areas (notably UK/overseas). In the life insurance sector the industrial/ordinary life insurance split is the most obvious.

The Future of the UK Insurance Industry

Important developments for UK insurance companies are likely to emanate from the ongoing reform of the social security system initiated by the present Conservative government. As part of this reform it is proposed that the role of the State Earnings-Related Pension Scheme (SERPS) should be significantly downgraded, and that at the same time there should be a boost to incentives for occupational pension schemes and to the freedom of individuals to initiate their own personal pension scheme if they so wish. Given that the insurance companies are heavily involved in the provision of pensions within the UK, it was to be expected that the companies would welcome these developments since they promised an increased volume of business. In practice, however, they were less than enthusiastic in their response to the original proposals which included the total abolition of SERPS.

The reasons for the lack of enthusiasm were essentially threefold. First, the insurance companies were concerned that, due to the precise nature of the government's proposals, the size of the premium for many of the new personal pensions would be very small, and would thus add significantly to costs given that the majority of the companies are not geared up to dealing with a large volume of small premiums. Secondly, the time scale originally proposed by the government for this large-scale shift in the provision of pensions was regarded as too short. In the revised proposals published in December 1985, both these concerns were to some extent allayed. Nevertheless, the proposals were still not viewed as ideal by the insurance companies because they also involved a broadening of the groups of financial institutions which would be allowed to provide pensions to include amongst others, building societies and unit trust companies. The degree to which this proposal represents a threat to the life insurance companies does not solely depend on the ability with which these other intermediaries will be able to compete with the established insurance companies. It also depends on the extent to which they are *interested* in providing personal pensions, in which respect it should be noted that several major institutions have so far expressed an interest.

The third reason for the insurance companies' lack of enthusiasm about the replacement of SERPS is that the proposals effectively ended the political consensus that had ruled up to that time. To take advantage of the phasing-out of SERPS the life companies need to invest substantial sums in modifying their products and their marketing and administration systems. But this might ultimately prove to be a waste of resources should a Labour government be returned to power and SERPS be restored to its previous importance.

With the large-scale changes taking place within the UK financial system, particularly following the 'Big Bang' (the ending of the fixed commissions for Stock Exchange dealings) in October 1986, it would be surprising were the insurance companies to be unaffected by them and not themselves to be seeking to take advantage of them. In this respect, the impact of the changes in the UK financial system impinge more directly upon the long-term insurance business than upon the general insurance sector. As has been noted above, the long-term insurance sector has a more direct involvement with the business of financial intermediation. As a consequence, it is this end of the insurance industry which has been attracting most attention.

It was noted previously that insurance companies are responsible for a significant proportion of Stock Exchange business. Thus, a natural response of several of the larger life and composite insurance companies has been to seek to bring more of the expertise involved in such activities 'in house' by taking a stake in a Stock Exchange firm. However, these moves are only a part of a more widespread response, which involves a diversification of their whole field of activity and a movement towards the creation of financial conglomerates. Indeed, many life insurance companies are putting their available expertise to use in other areas, such as the management of unit trusts. One of the attractions of a major insurance conpany moving into the latter area is that the unit trusts will immediately have a big name behind them, which is of importance when marketing trusts where no track record exists. In a similar vein, some insurance companies are moving more aggressively into the marketing of mortgages, with the intention of competing actively with the building societies.

While there is clear evidence of life and composite insurance companies wishing to extend their spheres of influence into other areas, there is equally clear evidence of other participants within the financial system being attracted into life insurance activities. To give but one example, at the time of writing the Trustee Savings Bank (TSB), which already has a substantial element of life insurance business, is known to be interested in acquiring the life insurance business of another company, and probably one that specializes in the industrial assurance field. The heavy involvement by some life companies in the provision of industrial assurance, traditionally viewed as a burden to such companies, is increasingly being viewed as an area of considerable potential. The specialists in industrial assurance have a large *number* of individuals on their books relative to other insurers, and this is being seen as an advantage to those companies wishing to broaden their fields of activity. It is argued that considerable potential exists for the marketing of other products, especially non-life insurance products, amongst the clientele of the industrial insurance companies.

A final area where there are likely to be changes in the future is in the marketing of life insurance contracts. At the time of writing the marketing of life insurance contracts covers many activities, ranging from the (sometimes unpaid) agents for friendly societies selling simple industrial policies through to sophisticated financial and tax planning consultants providing investment advice in which life insurance policies frequently play an important role. There is no overall official supervision of this marketing system, although registered insurance brokers are controlled by the

Insurance Brokers (Registration) Act of 1977. This is likely to change as all salesmen will come under some degree of supervision, though to what extent, especially with respect to salesmen operating on behalf of friendly societies, remains uncertain. What is certain, however, is that the standards of training required of salesmen of life insurance policies will increase, as will control of their activities. An important objective here will be the increased provision to the general public of impartial advice.

Notes

1   It is the intention here to give only a minimal account of the development of the industry. For more detail see, for example, Franklin and Woodhead (1980).
2   Reinsurance refers to the process whereby insurance companies transfer some of their liability for a particular risk to another insurance company or, in the case of Lloyd's, to a syndicate. An insurance company would wish to do this when a particular risk is larger than it wishes to carry complete liability for, but would stand to lose the whole of the contract if it was not initially prepared to write the contract itself. Use of Lloyd's for this reinsurance purpose prevents any one insurance company becoming dependent on another for the facility.
3   Depending on the contract and the personal circumstances of the policyholder, payments to a surviving spouse or to dependants may continue after the death of the policyholder.
4   These figures are for those companies in the industry that are members of the Association of British Insurers, which transacts some 90 per cent of the worldwide business of the British insurance company market.
5   Legislation requires that the division of insurance business into 'general' and 'long-term' is carried over to insurance companies' investment, and that the funds that arise from general insurance business be held separately from the funds arising from long-term business in the case of composite insurance companies. Thus, for example, it is not possible for a composite insurance company to subsidize its general business from its long-term business, except by means of declared profits.
6   Sources of statistics for turnover in British government securities; *Business Monitor* MQ5.
7   Evidence suggests that a significant proportion of policies are surrendered. One study estimated that, for new industrial

policies, 16 per cent were forfeited within a short period, and that most were eventually surrendered or forfeited. For policies issued by ordinary life companies, an early study by Patrick and Scobbie (1969) found that rates of forfeit and surrender were 6 per cent in the first year, 23 per cent in the first five years and 33 per cent in the first ten. Aggregate data would suggest that surrenders have increased substantially in recent years, and furthermore have been subject to considerable variation from one year to the next.

8   This is, of course, due to the inverse relation between the price of a fixed interest security, and the market interest rate. Where C is the fixed coupon payment on an undated government stock, and r is the market interest rate (as a proportion of 1), the market price of the stock, P, is given by $P = C/r$.

9   Use of foreign exchange options represents another, albeit limited and expensive, alternative.

10 This is changing to some extent, with the creation of (for example) the National Home Loan Corporation, which has the objective of buying blocks of mortgages, in particular from insurance companies and local authorities.

11 'Insurance company accounts . . . are the domain only of the enlightened and the informed, posing a potential health hazard for the great unwashed unfamiliar with the workings of an investment fluctuation account', Ian Griffiths, writing in *The Times*, 26 June 1985.

12 Many life insurance companies, for example, only carry out valuations on a triennual basis.

13 *Planned Savings*, November 1981, pp. 57–65.

14 Additional detail on life companies' expense ratios can be obtained from the *Annual Reports of the Chief Registrar of Friendly Societies*, HMSO, London.

15 *Insurance Annual Report*, 1984, HMSO.

16 Other requirements are that: (1) the premiums payable in any 12-month period are no more than one-eighth of the total premiums payable over 10 years; (2) in the case of a whole-of-life policy, the sum assured must be at least 75 per cent of the premiums payable until the policyholder reaches 75; (3) in the case of an endowment policy, the sum assured must be at least 75 per cent of premiums payable during the term of the policy, with the 75 per cent minimum falling by 2 per cent for each year by which the age of the life assured exceeds 55.

17 Conditions of LAPR included that total gross premiums paid by the policyholder should not exceed the lesser of £1,500 or one-sixth of his taxable income after deducting charges on income but before deducting personal allowances.

18 The formulae for calculating liability to a higher tax rate when the policyholder terminates a non-qualifying policy are compli-

cated, but in principle the profit (excess of surrender value over premiums paid) is divided by the number of years for which premiums were paid to arrive at a sum which is added to the individual's other income for that year to assess his liability for higher-rate tax.

19 It is recognized that these figures are not directly comparable; they do, however, provide some indication of orders of magnitude.

CHAPTER EIGHT

Pension Funds

Introduction

The total market valuation of the investments held by UK
occupational pension funds at the end of 1984 amounted to
£130,291 million. Pension fund assets are broadly comparable in size to those of insurance companies, though their
growth has been somewhat faster in recent years, and the
proposed changes in pension provision in the UK are likely
to cause this trend to continue. It is important to recognize,
however, that the global total disguises the fundamental
division within the arrangements for pension provision
between the *state* schemes on the one hand and the
occupational schemes on the other. It is the latter schemes
which give rise to financial intermediation activity, and it is
these which are the focus of the discussion in this chapter.
Nevertheless, as will be explained subsequently, developments within the state provision of pensions have important
implications for the occupational schemes.

The British government initiated the provision of state
pensions on a means-tested basis during the interwar
period. In the postwar period means-testing was removed
from the (notionally) contributory scheme, and in 1959 there
was introduced the Graduated Pension Scheme which had
the purpose of providing a graduated supplement to the
flat-rate National Insurance pension, based on earnings.
However, employers were given the option to 'contract out'
of the state graduated system, provided that the benefits to
their employees of their own occupational pension scheme

were equal to at least the *maximum* supplement payable under the state scheme. Many employers did in fact take up that option, which provided an important stimulus to the growth of occupational pension schemes.

The Graduated Pension Scheme came to an end with the Social Security Act of 1973. The present State Earnings-Related Pension Scheme (SERPS) was introduced in 1978 under the terms of the Social Security Pension Act of 1975. Once again, employers were given the option of contracting out of the scheme, provided that certain minimum conditions were met, of which the principal one was that a pension should be provided to the employee of at least one-eightieth of his final pensionable pay for each year of service. Employers were given an incentive to contract out of the state scheme as the cost to them of providing an occupational pension to meet the minimum conditions was often less than the cost of remaining within the state scheme.

The practice of employers providing pensions for their retired employees has a long history, but only began to be commonplace after the early 1950s. At that time the benefits payable were rather modest, and were invariably based on the average salary that an employee had earned in his service with the company, with the schemes being restricted to 'staff' as distinct from 'works' employees. However, the combination of rising interest rates and increasing awareness of inflation gave rise to a greater willingness by employers to pay for, and employees to demand, pensions based on some calculation of final salary. The vast majority of pension schemes are now final salary schemes, where the pension is expressed as a fraction (often one-sixtieth or one-eightieth) of the employee's final salary at pensionable age, multiplied by the number of years of 'pensionable service'.[1] The definition of 'final salary' naturally varies. It may be true final salary; the best of the last three (or whatever) years; the average of the last three years; or it may be based on *earnings* rather than salary. Plainly, in time of inflation, it is important to use the final salary as the base of pension calculations, though nothing is implied about inflation adjustment once the pension starts being paid.

290

In 1979, just over half the total number of employees in the UK were members of occupational pension schemes, a proportion which is not thought to have changed materially since that time.[2] The total membership of these schemes in 1979 totalled 11.8 million workers, of whom some 5.6 million were in public sector schemes and 6.2 million in private sector schemes. The total membership of occupational pension schemes has been at about the same level since the early 1960s, and there has been no significant movement away from either the state graduated or earnings-related schemes and towards contracted-out occupational schemes since that time. Currently, there are about 90,000 separate occupational pension schemes, which embrace a wide disparity of scheme sizes as measured by both membership and asset holdings. Furthermore, whilst the total membership of occupational pension schemes has not shown any significant increase in recent years, the same is certainly not true for the volume of assets held. The substantial increase in asset holdings of pension funds has been partly due to the fact that many of them are not 'mature', which is to say, the payments into the schemes by the employers (and sometimes employees) are not yet equal to the payments out to pensioners. In addition, not only have earnings and hence contributions to schemes increased significantly, but also the rates of return achieved by many schemes on their investments have been historically high. Figure 8.1 illustrates the growth of pension fund assets since 1976, and shows clearly the acceleration in the rate of their growth during the early 1980s. Table 8.1 also shows that private occupational pension schemes dominated in the UK at the end of 1984, although substantial amounts of funds were invested in public sector schemes.

Characteristics of Pension Fund Schemes

In the UK there are two alternative methods by which pension schemes are financed, respectively the 'externally funded' system (universal in the private sector), and the 'pay-as-you-go' system (PAYG – common in the public

291

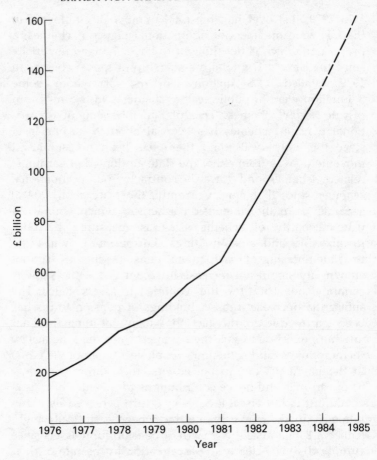

Figure 8.1 UK Pension Funds: Aggregate Assets, Market Valuation end-year values

Source: *Financial Statistics* (various issues).

sector). In pension schemes operated under an externally funded system, the employer hands over a sum of money each period (based on the number of employees and their earnings in that period) to an external agency from which pension payments will, in due course, be made. The employer thereby pays the pension costs in advance, so that the ability to pay pensions at some point in the future is not

Table 8.1
UK Pension Funds: Total Net Assets,
31 December 1984

	£ million	%
Private sector	77,162	59.2
Local authorities	17,649	13.6
Other public sector	35,480	27.2
Total assets	130,291	100.0

Source: Financial Statistics, November 1985.

dependent upon the solvency of the company at that time. Furthermore, by having the money paid to an *external* agency, additional security is afforded the pensioner through a total separation of the pension fund from the employer's business. Thus, a company may go out of business whilst leaving the pension fund to fulfil its commitments. This externally funded system is universal in the UK private sector, not only because of the safeguards to pensioners' rights which it generates, but also because it is able to take advantage of the taxation benefits that favour such schemes.

The externally funded system is not, however, standard practice in other countries. *Internal* (or 'book reserve') funding is the standard mechanism in Sweden, Finland, Germany and Austria, where a book-keeping debt is accumulated which is backed by the employer's assets. In effect, the employer retains the contributions to the pension fund in his own business, but part of that business is then 'allocated' to the pension fund. In addition, the employer must also credit interest to the accumulated fund. However, since such a system is vulnerable to the insolvency of the employer, it is usually accompanied by an insurance cover, sometimes organized by the state. The problems created by the need for insurance are lessened in many of these countries by the fact that the state scheme provides a much higher proportion of total pensions than in the UK. Internally funded schemes carry the substantial advantage to the employer that the funds are retained within the business, and hence that the employer has less need for recourse to external capital markets. Globally, however, this may be seen as a disadvantage, since it could cause capital to be allocated in an inefficient manner. Funds may be tied up internally in barely profitable projects when they could be allocated to more profitable projects by means of an impartial, and larger, capital market that would result from externally funded schemes. Of course, the question then arises as to whether capital markets are able to identify the more profitable projects, and thereby to allocate funds efficiently.

The majority of public sector schemes are *not* funded, either internally or externally, but are operated on the 'pay-as-you-go' system, which simply means that the costs of providing pension payments is met as they arise. All the state pensions are, naturally, provided on a pay-as-you-go basis, and are therefore paid for out of general taxation. This system also applies to the occupational pension schemes for the Civil Service, the NHS, the armed forces, police, fire service and teachers, although notional funds are maintained for the NHS and for teachers. Given that the ability to pay pensions to members of these schemes is ultimately dependent upon a government's power to raise taxation, members of these schemes do not suffer any loss of security by not having their pensions funded. For historical reasons the local authority pension funds represent something of an anomaly, since they maintain funds out of which to provide pensions but rely on money from the rates to pay for any increases in pensions. The schemes of the nationalized industries are externally funded, however, and their assets are correspondingly often very substantial (for example, the British Rail and British Coal pension funds). Given that these industries are owned by the state, there has been some discussion about whether it is either necessary or appropriate that they should be externally funded, with some discussants arguing in favour of the pay-as-you-go system. Indeed, because a number of schemes are inflation-proofed they have become progressively underfunded, and will at some point in the future have to make use of state assistance. In some instances the privatization of public corporations has involved a 'topping-up' of their pensions schemes, and concern has often been expressed by employees in nationalized industries concerning their pension rights following privatization.

Two implications of the pay-as-you-go system of financing pensions are worth noting. First, since no account is taken of prospective liabilities, and since no worthwhile fund is built up, all pension payments are made out of current income. As a consequence, each generation is not providing for its own pensions in the future, but is paying now for those of the previous generation. The expectation, naturally, is that the following generation will pay the pensions for the generation currently in work, and hence there will be transfers of wealth between generations, dependent on such matters as rates of population growth and economic growth. Second, the employer will usually find that the costs of pensions will be relatively low when the scheme is in its early stages, but that they will rise significantly when it becomes mature. A pay-as-you-go scheme also reduces administrative requirements and simplifies the whole pension finance system.

A final division within the pension industry which should be recognized is that between 'self-administered' and 'insured' schemes, although this division is now of much less importance than it was in the past. The essence of self-administered pension schemes is that they are legal entities separate from the employer's business, and are constituted as a trust. This form of scheme became popular largely due to the taxation benefits which accompany it, and these will be examined in more detail later on. However, setting up separate trusts to administer pension schemes is neither easy nor cheap, and so the use of such schemes has remained confined to large employers, whilst smaller companies have tended to make use of insured schemes. Several life assurance companies had begun to market pension (or 'retirement benefit') schemes in the inter-war period, with the cost advantages associated with their setting up ensuring their popularity in spite of the absence of tax relief on investment income for those schemes until 1956.

Insured schemes also benefited from the fact that it was

not until 1970 that self-administered schemes set up as irrevocable trusts could provide lump-sum benefits without forgoing some of their tax concessions. However, since 1970 all schemes have been able to provide tax-free lump sums whether their assets have been invested directly or in insurance contracts, and furthermore since April 1980 schemes have had to be constituted as irrevocable trusts in order to obtain those benefits. As a consequence, the great majority of insurance schemes have been converted into trust funds, which invariably leave the financial arrangements unchanged so that insurance companies have continued to control the investments.

As self-administered and insured schemes now have a common legal structure, the only major difference between them lies in the way their funds are invested. But even here, the distinction is fading as the insurance companies expand their range of financial services, offering facilities which may be attractive to self-administered pension funds. Nevertheless, in practice, insurance companies no longer guarantee benefits in return for a specified level of contributions, not least because the movement towards final salary schemes has rendered such guarantees impractical. The great majority of life insurance companies now offer an investment return which is expected to meet the pension scheme's expected commitments. As a result, far from being an 'insured' scheme, where benefits are guaranteed, such schemes are now simply administered (to varying degrees) by insurance companies.

UK Pension Funds: Assets and Liabilities Portfolios

For many individuals in employment in the UK, membership of the appropriate occupational pension scheme is one of the conditions of employment (necessitated by the contracting-out requirements), with the consequence that the pension fund has a captive market. At the same time, the benefits of the pension fund are normally underwritten by the employer rather than by the pension fund itself, with the pension fund left merely to manage the funds allocated to it by the employer and also by the employees if it is a contributory scheme. Competition within the industry, therefore, is not with respect to the funds themselves but to the management of the investments, with the yields that any particular management group achieves forming the basis of comparison.

Thus, the source of the funds of the pension fund industry is straightforward; it constitutes the required contributions from the employers and employees. Furthermore, the purpose of pension funds, and the legal structure under which the majority are constituted, ensures that they have no discretion over the use of their funds; they are exclusively for the provision of pensions. Therefore, attention paid to the activities of pension funds is concentrated on their assets and liabilities, although even here matters are relatively simple due to the nature of the liabilities. The single, standardized, product of the pension funds (that is, the provision of retirement pensions) ensures that the liabilities of any pension fund may be summarized as an actuarial statement.[3] Each pension fund will have a different liabilities composition reflecting the near-infinite combinations of members in receipt of pensions from the fund relative to those paying in, the age distribution of those receiving pensions and those paying into the fund, the number of years paid into the scheme and therefore the benefit entitlements of the employees, and so forth. Given the range of possibilities, no useful generalizations can be made, though clearly any individual fund will be seeking to allocate its investments in such a way as best to meet its liabilities as expressed in its actuarial statement. The common product of the pension funds nevertheless ensures that the considerations that determine their asset portfolios will differ in degree rather than in substance. For this reason, it is appropriate to begin by considering the distribution of the combined assets of the occupational pension schemes in the UK, before turning subsequently to consider the relative merits and demerits of the individual assets for the purposes of a pension fund.

The aggregate assets portfolio of the occupational pension schemes in the UK at the end of the three years 1982, 1983 and 1984 is given in Table 8.2. Figure 8.2 illustrates the proportionate distribution of the various asset groups at the end of 1984. An interesting characteristic of the portfolio is the concentration of funds in only four assets. First and foremost are UK company securities, which comprised over 48 per cent of the total portfolio at the end of 1984, of which ordinary shares constituted the greater part. The second largest group is British government securities, which represented just over 18 per cent of the 1984 total. Notable in this group is the predominance of longer-dated and undated securities, and significant holdings of index-linked stocks. Holdings of short-dated British government securities (that is with a residual maturity of less than 5 years) constituted just 4 per cent of total holdings of British government securities. The third largest category is that of overseas securities, which was dominated by ordinary shares and

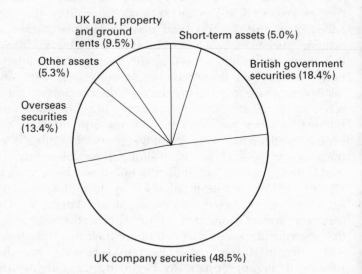

Figure 8.2 UK Pension Funds: Distribution of Aggregate Assets by Grouping, 31 December 1984, Market Valuation

Source: Financial Statistics, January 1986.

Notes: Other assets include unit trust units, property unit trust units, loans and mortgages, UK local authority securities, Local Authorities Mutual Investment Trust and other investments, less short-term liabilities and long-term borrowing.

accounted for 13.4 per cent of the total portfolio. At the end of 1984, the combined total holding of ordinary shares in UK and overseas companies amounted to some £77,894 million, representing very nearly 60 per cent of pension funds' total assets. Furthermore, it may be observed that holdings of ordinary shares in both UK and overseas companies have risen substantially in recent years. The fourth major category of assets is UK land, property and ground rents, comprising 9½ per cent of the 1984 total. Of the remaining assets approximately half were in the form of short-term assets, dominated by cash and balances with the banks.

Attributes of Assets Held in Pension Fund Portfolios

The selection of assets by pension funds is obviously influenced by the nature of their liabilities. In this respect it is important to recognize that most pension fund schemes are committed to making payments based on their members' final pay, and thus the liabilities of the funds are directly related to increases in pay levels. However, the financial implications of this form of commitment are to some extent offset by the ability of pension funds to adjust ongoing contributions in so far as it is felt to be necessary. When calculating the contributions required to meet the commitments of a pension fund, an actuary will usually assume that in the long term the fund will achieve a positive real rate of return on assets of 1 or 2 per cent per annum. If it fails to achieve this result then the contribution rates will require amendment. This element of flexibility clearly lowers the risks related to operations, and it is a facility which is not available to many life insurance companies. Furthermore, in general, the liabilities of pension funds are much longer term than those of insurance companies, and the possibility of early claimants with pension funds is relatively low as there is usually a minimum age below which pensions will not be paid to contributors. Also, transfers between pension schemes are by no means automatic, and very often pensions are 'frozen' so that, although no further contribu-

Table 8.2

UK Pension Funds: Aggregate Assets Portfolio, 1982 to 1984, end-year values, Market Valuation, £ million

	1982	1983	1984
Short-term assets			
UK			
Cash and balances with banks	1,446	2,511	3,894
Certificates of deposit	130	97	232
Other financial institutions	183	217	377
Treasury bills	—	49	34
Local authority bills and temporary money	332	431	514
Other	800	1,217	1,098
Overseas short-term assets	163	218	354
Short-term liabilities	(433)	(874)	(844)
Long-term borrowing	(380)	(417)	(567)
British government securities			
Index linked	2,255	2,970	3,665
Up to 5 years	340	792	1,000
Over 5 years and up to 10 years	6,638	8,966	10,183
Over 15 years and undated	9,016	9,021	9,101
UK local authority securities	152	147	132
UK company securities			
Ordinary shares	36,021	46,620	61,604
Other	1,164	1,323	1,567

Overseas securities			
Company securities			
Ordinary shares	9,540	14,731	16,290
Other	326	440	481
Government securities	429	496	699
Unit trust units	474	709	853
Local Authority Mutual Investment Trust	79	89	138
Property unit trust	1,970	2,202	2,322
Loans and mortgages			
UK			
To parent organization	1	1	1
Other	176	175	193
Overseas	140	150	151
UK land, property and ground rents	10,533	11,062	12,337
Other investments	2,702	3,816	4,482
Total net assets	84,198	107,159	130,291

Source: Financial Statistics, January 1986.

tions are to be made, no pensions will be payable for some years to come. The liquidity position of most pension schemes is helped further by their immaturity, in the sense that the inflow of contributions is expected to exceed the outflow of payments for the foreseeable future.

The UK taxation regime has traditionally been lenient in its treatment of pension funds. The exemption from capital gains tax, and from income tax in respect of their investments, has meant that there have been no tax-induced distortions to portfolio selection. As a consequence, there has been no particular need or incentive for pension funds to concentrate on holding assets which generate longer-term capital gains, as opposed to short-term high incomes. In addition, switching between investments, irrespective of its frequency, has carried no implication for taxation, although, of course, the standard transactions costs would normally tend to constrain this activity.

It should be recognized that pension funds, in common with insurance companies, possess a great deal of freedom with respect to how to structure their asset portfolios. There are virtually no statutory controls on portfolio choice. Nevertheless, given the nature of their liabilities, equities are often regarded as a 'natural' form of investment for pension funds. An increase in asset value in line with inflation (and the salaries of contributors) is clearly desirable, and, in theory, as equities represent a stake in the economy their value should increase broadly in line with inflation. However, there is always some risk involved, for experience of recent years has demonstrated that in the short term there may be substantial movements in share prices away from their long-term trend.

The equities to be found in pension fund portfolios have generally been distributed among the leading UK companies, although since the ending of exchange controls in October 1979 substantial overseas investment in equities has also taken place, with the result that at the end of 1984 over 13 per cent of the total portfolio was held in overseas assets as against only 5 per cent in 1979. Given the inherent exchange risk of investing in overseas equities (since all the liabilities are denominated in sterling, and the matching of assets and liabilities on the basis of currencies does not apply), the extent of the overseas investment is perhaps surprising, and perhaps reflects the long-term investment perspective of pension fund portfolio managers.

Nevertheless, a continuing source of concern for pension fund managers is the possibility of the re-imposition of exchange controls, and the threat of taxation being introduced on overseas asset holdings by a future Labour government. The Labour Party has proposed that tax concessions available currently to pension funds would be dependent on the repatriation of a substantial element of their overseas assets, with the resultant funds being invested in a National Investment Bank. The pension funds would then receive UK government securities in return. The impact of these proposals, if they were to be implemented, would be very far-reaching. For the pension funds themselves, there is the concern that they would have to liquidate investments at less than their true value. This would tend to occur in those markets in which they had a substantial exposure, such as the Hong Kong and Scandinavian stock markets. The impact would be particularly severe on those funds which have chosen to specialize in various types of overseas securities and assets.

Although much of the investment by pension funds in UK companies has been concentrated in the ordinary shares of major listed companies, many of the large pension funds have attempted to broaden the scope of their portfolios. Pressure for such diversification was evident in the late 1970s, when rising cash flows into pension funds coincided with only the limited demands for new funds from the equity market and with the collapse of the property market. Further stimulus was given by the increasing realization that both the less common forms of investment in companies, and investment in smaller companies, offered higher potential returns. Consequently, some pension funds have acquired strategic stakes in small quoted or unquoted companies, whilst others have become involved with the provision of project finance or development capital. The strategic stakes in the smaller quoted companies have been built up in a number of ways, including through the market for the company's shares, through the underwriting of rights issues and through vendors' placings. The development of the Unlisted Securities Market (USM) and, to a lesser extent, the Over-the-Counter (OTC) Market has made an important contribution to the movement of pension funds in this direction. However, it should also be noted that whilst such investments may offer high rates of return, they may suffer from low marketability. Thus the pension fund manager must be prepared to incur capital losses should he wish to offload this type of asset quickly. This possibility has also encouraged pension funds to insist on having representation on the boards of directors of specific companies in which they invest, not merely to safeguard their immediate interests but also to provide additional management expertise to the companies, and hence hopefully to improve their longer-term prospects.

Many of the larger pension funds have set up subsidiaries to provide venture capital to companies. On occasions this activity has been undertaken in conjunction with other pension funds, or with insurance companies, in order to take advantage of economies of scale. For example, 'Prelude' is the venture capital group set up jointly in 1985 by the pension funds of British Gas, British Rail, the Water Authorities' Superannuation Fund and Equity Capital for Industry, the last-named institution being a venture capital fund with subscriptions from 350 investment institutions. Furthermore some of these venture capital operations have tended to specialize in particular industries. An example here is 'CIN Industrial Investments', the unquoted equity arm of British Coal's pension fund, which specializes in small information technology companies.

As was noted in Chapter 7, the quantity of fixed interest company securities has been in short supply in recent years as a consequence both of the unwillingness of borrowers to commit themselves to long-term obligations at high interest rates, and of the reluctance of lenders to be exposed to the threat of negative real returns. But despite a revival in the market for these instruments during the early 1980s, holdings by pension funds have remained low, as is shown by Table 8.1. This is hardly surprising given the nature of

pension funds' liabilities. Nevertheless, fixed interest securities issued by the British government have proved to be
somewhat more attractive to pension funds on account of
their particular attributes. The marketability and relatively
low costs associated with trading in British government
stocks have enabled fund managers to make profits, particularly at times of fluctuating interest rates, by means of active
dealing. This is, of course, on top of the high coupons which
have been offered on many government securities in recent
years.

The third largest group of investments identified in
Figure 8.2 comprises overseas securities, a large proportion
of which are in the form of ordinary shares in overseas
companies. The rationale for holding these shares is basically the same as that for investment in the ordinary shares of
UK companies, but there are two additional attributes. First,
investment in overseas companies may enable higher yields
to be obtained than are available from UK shares; and
secondly, it allows the degree of portfolio diversification to
be increased without sacrificing the benefits associated with
the holding of ordinary shares, although it must be recognized that additional risk (in respect of exchange rate
movements) is taken on board.

The fourth major group of assets is real property. The
property market represents something of a paradox for
pension funds. On the one hand, it is a very volatile, high
risk area, as the experience of the early 1970s demonstrated.
On the other hand, investment in property has proved to be
one of the best hedges against inflation over the longer
term. In particular, by means of leases that allow for
periodic rent reviews, both income and capital values may
be protected from inflation. A high proportion of the
investment in property has been in retail shops, offices,
industrial and warehousing accommodation and agricultural
property. In recent years pension funds have increasingly
taken the initiative in building property rather than in
acquiring it in the secondary market. Partnerships with
property developers have resulted in the construction of
many shopping arcades, office premises and industrial
estates. To obtain a satisfactory yield on property invest-

ment good judgement is essential, and the larger pension funds accordingly make extensive use of outside advisers. A particularly long view is required for investment in property, and a pension fund must be prepared to accept very low yields in the short term in order to secure adequate returns in the longer term.

The need to make use of external advisers, and the size of investment required, meant that the property market was largely closed to the smaller pension funds until the arrival of property unit trusts in 1966. Being exempt from capital gains tax, and being able to reclaim income tax, these have become a useful means by which smaller pension funds have been able to invest indirectly in property, and hence to diversify their asset portfolios. Investment via a unit trust frees the pension fund from the administrative cost and effort associated with managing property, and also that associated with buying and selling property which is only really worthwhile on a comparatively large scale. Specialized unit trusts have also enabled pension funds of all sizes to invest in property overseas, which in the past only the very largest funds had undertaken.

The large-scale investment in agricultural land by the pension funds gave rise to considerable concern that it would lead to a fundamental change in the nature of agriculture in the UK. In fact this has not occurred since the farms that are owned by pension funds (and by other institutions) are generally leased to private farmers, rather than operated by managers appointed by the fund. Furthermore, the resources fed into farms by the pension funds have enabled substantially greater investment in agriculture to take place than would probably otherwise have occurred.

In addition to the four major types of assets discussed above, it should also be noted that at the end of 1984 some 5 per cent of total assets were classed as being short-term, and comprised largely cash and bank deposits. As the majority of pension funds are still not mature, these short-term assets are held largely as a result of active trading in investments, and in readiness for purchasing new longer-term investments. In many respects they form the working balances of the pension funds, and are rarely held as investments proper in themselves. With real estate in particular, investments have to be made when the property comes on the market and not when funds are available for the purpose. In such cases funds are often required at comparatively short notice, and consequently the holding of non-cash short-term assets becomes desirable. However, some pension funds may be able (and willing) to obtain loans from the employer for whom the scheme is operated in order to finance such investments, and thereby to reduce their short-term asset requirements.

The catch-all classification of 'other investments' shown in Figure 8.1 comprises items such as works of art, share options, commodities and financial futures. It is rare for individual pension funds to invest more than a small part of their funds in such assets. The media coverage given to the more exotic investments, for example, the purchase of paintings by the British Rail pension fund, has had the effect of overstating their importance. This type of asset does not, of course, produce any income, and all returns are in the form of capital gains. However, given that pension funds are not taxed on their investment income, the concentration on capital gains does not constitute an advantage for tax purposes. Indeed, there is some doubt over whether the Inland Revenue regards purchases of such assets as 'trading' rather than 'investment', and it is the proceeds only of the latter which are exempt from taxation. There is also the wider social issue as to whether pension funds should be investing in 'unproductive' assets.

It must be emphasized that the data in Table 8.2 and in Figure 8.2 relate only to the assets of the self-administered pension schemes, and do not include those of pension schemes that are operated through special insurance contracts. The assets that accumulate in respect of the latter schemes are included in the portfolios of the insurance companies, and as a consequence the size of the pension fund industry may tend to be underestimated, and the size of the insurance industry to be correspondingly over-estimated. If a pension fund is not self-administered, then naturally the choice of asset composition is delegated to an outside body, although it is most probable that the latter will take the above described considerations into account when constructing the asset portfolio. For the pension fund that chooses not to be self-administered there is now a spectrum of different administration systems available. The pension fund may simply buy deferred annuity policies from an insurance company, or buy 'Deposit Administration' policies where the insurance company offers a relatively undemanding guarantee as to the yield on the fund which it manages.

However, such schemes have to a large extent lost ground to the 'managed fund' policies operated by the insurance companies as a special contract. Many of these managed pension funds were introduced as a defensive measure by insurance companies when a number of pension funds surrendered their deferred annuity policies in order to initiate investment on their own behalf. The essence of the 'managed fund' approach is that a number of different pension funds can pool their assets into a single portfolio of investments, where each pension fund would own a specified share in the total portfolio. In order to facilitate the division of investments and assist marketability these managed funds are 'unitized', which is to say that each fund is divided into a number of units, with the value of each unit determined by dividing the total market value of investments held by the number of units issued. By restricting the ownership of the units to approved pension funds, the managed funds are able to obtain the tax concessions available to self-administered pension funds, that is, exemption from capital gains and income taxes. The contracts are entirely investment-linked, and no investment guarantees are given. Any individual pension fund could reduce its risk by investing in a number of managed funds operated by different insurance companies. Indeed, some insurance companies have responded to this possibility by marketing a range of managed funds specializing in different investment areas, with many companies permitting pension funds to switch between the different managed funds at low cost.

The form of administration of a pension fund will be strongly influenced by the volume of assets for which it is responsible. For a small fund a range of insurance company policies is often appropriate, whilst for a larger fund the use of managed fund policies may be more attractive. As the pension fund becomes larger, it may find that a more direct control over a proportion of its assets, with the remainder in managed fund policies, is the optimal solution, while for the largest funds direct control over virtually all its assets is normal. When a pension fund moves away from managed fund policies towards a more direct control of its assets, it is very often the case that a bank, a stockbroker or a firm of specialist fund managers is appointed to manage the relevant funds on its behalf. Only the largest pension funds will find that it will be worthwhile to employ their own team of investment managers, and even here outside specialists will be brought in to advise on certain areas of investment. Clearly, pension funds may exercise widely differing degrees of control over their investments. However, concern has been expressed in some quarters that the outside management and control of the pension funds' assets, principally by banks, is very much more concentrated than the range of pension funds would indicate. This has obvious implications for the efficiency of asset management, as well as for the market trading power given to those who ultimately undertake the investment decisions.

Regulation and Supervision

In contrast to the regulation and supervision exacted over insurance companies and building societies, which is very extensive, that applied to pension funds *per se* is relatively minimal. There are two main reasons for this phenomenon. First, since the great majority of pension funds are set up as trusts, they are required to fulfil the requirements of the trust deed, and are subject to the legislation relating to trusts. Consequently, as any scheme member may resort to legal proceedings to enforce compliance with the trust's requirements, the pension fund is automatically subject to some degree of broad supervision. Secondly, although pension funds are usually completely separated from the relevant employers, the latter are still required to fulfil the obligations of their pension schemes, regardless of the performance of the investments held. Therefore, any employer, as well as any scheme member, has the incentive to ensure that their scheme is properly managed, not only with regard to investment performance, but also in respect of its efficient administration.

The specific regulation and supervision of pension funds that does exist relates primarily to taxation considerations. In order to obtain exemption from taxation, a pension fund must gain the approval of the Superannuation Funds Office, which is a branch of the Inland Revenue. Approval is conditional upon the pension fund being constituted as an irrevocable trust, with other conditions relating primarily to contribution rates and benefit entitlement, rather than upon how the pension fund is managed. The Superannuation Funds Office can withdraw its approval at any time if it considers that its requirements are not being met. Although some supervision is implicit here, it should be recognized that the requirements for approval are not primarily geared towards the protection of the members of the scheme.

The Occupational Pensions Board (OPB), set up in 1975 (and housed in the same office as the Superannuation Funds Office) does not have any regulatory or supervisory powers. Its two major functions are to consider and to report on matters of public interest relating to pensions that are referred to it by the Secretary of State, and to issue contracting-out certificates to those schemes wishing to contract out of SERPS. Furthermore, there is currently no self-regulation body for the pension funds sector. The National Association of Pension Funds (NAPF) acts as the voice for the pension industry in both the public and private sectors. Although its membership is wide, and includes the majority of the larger self-administered schemes, its function is essentially to make representations to government and to other relevant bodies. However, it should be noted that it is the government's intention that the trustees of pensions schemes will require authorization under the requirements of the Financial Services Act 1986, unless the management of the scheme's assets is conducted through an authorized individual or firm.

In recent years, a number of commentators have

expressed concern over the lack of structured regulation and supervision of pension funds. As a result of this, proposals have been put forward for increased control, including the suggestion that there should be a Pension Schemes Act. It is argued that the Act could lay down the conditions under which pension schemes would operate, and would thereby remove their activities from the legislative area relating to trusts, not least because that legislation was never intended for use in the area of pension schemes. It is also proposed that there be regulation over the disclosure of information to scheme members, that the degree of investment allowed in the employer's company be limited, that a proportion of the membership of the pension trust's governing body should constitute members of the scheme rather than managers of the company, and that a registrar of pension schemes should be created. The rationale for these proposals is that they would afford the members of pension schemes additional protection from poor management of their investments, and would bolster the existing framework of controls.

Finally, it should be recognized that the duties and power of pension fund trustees have been the subject of controversy in recent years. One specific area of disagreement has related to the selection of investments for pension funds, and a notable dispute on this issue took place amongst the trustees of the National Coal Board pension fund, ultimately resulting in a High Court hearing in 1984. The trustees representing the National Union of Mineworkers took the view that the pension fund should refrain from any overseas investment, should not invest in any directly competing energy industries, and should pursue a policy of divestment of any assets in these two areas. The trustees appointed by the National Coal Board opposed this view, and considered that the fund should invest its assets in the best interests of the scheme's members, which broadly meant maximizing the return. This view was upheld by the High Court. More generally, there has been a substantial increase in the level of interest shown by trade unions in the control of pension funds. Demands for greater representation on the boards of trustees have stemmed from a realization that such funds

311

control very large sums, and that by increasing the proportion of union nominees on the boards of trustees of pension funds the unions can increase their control over these funds. While their power to influence investment strategies is not as extensive as that hoped for by the NUM, it is nevertheless substantial, and with increased representation many unions believe that they are better able to protect the interests of their members.

Taxation

The taxation aspects of pension funds are very straightforward in the sense that they are almost entirely exempt from all taxation. The three areas where taxation might apply are the contributions to, the investment returns achieved by, and the benefits paid to pensioners from a pension fund. The contributions to a pension fund, by either the employer or the employee, are exempt from tax provided that no more than 17½ per cent of the earnings of a self-employed individual, or 15 per cent of the earnings of an employee, are paid into pension funds. While contributions of more than these rates are permissible, they do not carry income tax relief. The investment returns achieved by a fund are exempt from taxation provided the investment is within a broad range of prescribed assets. The major exception is where the pension fund invests in an exempt unit trust, and here the excess of unfranked investment income over management expenses is subject to corporation tax. The benefits payable by a pension fund are subject to the pensioner's rate of income tax, except for the tax-free lump sum.[4]

At the time of writing, an area of uncertainty with regard to taxation concerns profits from the use of financial futures. The issue centres upon whether such profits should be regarded as resulting from 'investment' or from 'trading'. In the case of trading activity, contracts in financial futures would not be regarded as exempt assets for taxation purposes. Despite successive legislative attempts to clarify the tax position of transactions in futures contracts, the situation remains unclear, and this affects not only pension funds but also any institutions for which capital gains are taxed differently from trading profits. In addition, the distinction between 'trading' and 'investment' activities gives rise to a degree of uncertainty with respect to other assets, as was explained earlier in respect of works of art.

The Importance of Pension Funds and Insurance Companies within the UK Financial System

There are three major reasons as to why it is appropriate to consider pension funds and insurance companies together in respect of their importance for the UK financial system. First, saving via a life assurance policy and saving via a pension scheme both represent contractual forms of saving involving a regular commitment. This may be contrasted with the various forms of saving which might be described as being 'discretionary' and which include banks and building society deposits, purchases of National Savings instruments and securities of various descriptions, and so on. Secondly, both life assurance policies and pension schemes represent long-term savings media. Individuals enter into life insurance contracts (and included here would be both the regular premium policies and the single premium policies, with the latter being correctly regarded as discretionary savings) because they view them expressly in this light. While individuals do not, in general, have the option as to whether or not to save with pension funds, they clearly represent long-term savings media since pre-retirement encashment of embodied savings is not possible. The final reason for taking life insurance and pension fund saving together is that this reflects the production of the official statistics, and separating out their relative contributions is not possible in all circumstances.

Figure 8.3 illustrates the time path of net savings through life insurance and pension schemes during the decade to 1984. It is clear from the diagram that this saving represented a substantial part of total personal sector saving throughout that period. Indeed, the minimum proportion of

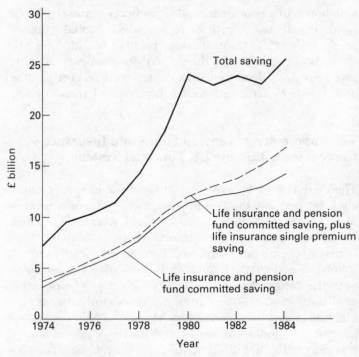

Figure 8.3 UK Life Insurance and Pension Fund Saving Relative to Total UK Personal Sector Saving, 1974 to 1984

Source: Financial Statistics, various issues.

total personal sector saving accounted for by life insurance and pension schemes was in 1975 when the value fell to 46.6 per cent.[5] Although the proportion is subject to quite extensive variation, the diagram demonstrates that it is the saving that takes place through media *other than* life insurance policies and pension schemes that is volatile, whereas the saving that has taken place via pension and life insurance funds has tended to grow comparatively steadily throughout the period. Furthermore, as single premium life insurance policies have never accounted for more than 16 per cent of the combined savings through pension and insurance funds (and have usually accounted for around only 10 per cent of that total), it is clear that the contractual saving which has taken place through these funds has been

Table 8.3

Proportion of Total UK Personal Sector Saving Accounted for by Contractual Saving through Life Insurance and Superannuation Schemes, 1974 to 1984

1974	1975	1976	1977	1978	1979	1980	1981	1982	1983	1984
43.1	44.8	51.8	57.1	53.9	53.5	47.9	52.7	51.8	56.0	55.3

Source: Financial Statistics, December 1985.

a most significant proportion of total UK personal sector saving. Table 8.3 illustrates this point.

Given that neither insurance companies nor pension funds engage in lending to the personal sector to any marked extent, the major contribution of these institutions to the operation of the financial sector has been in their channelling of funds from the personal sector, which in recent years has run a substantial financial surplus, to those sectors which run financial deficits. The latter have traditionally included the public sector and the UK industrial and commercial sector, and also in more recent years the overseas sector. A substantial proportion of this channelling of funds takes place without further intermediation, in particular via the direct purchase of public sector debt and by the purchase of company securities. However, given the occurrence of the financial surplus of the UK industrial and commercial sector in recent years, the acquisition of UK company securities on a large scale by insurance and pension funds has plainly required further intermediation. The importance of the activities of these institutions for the successful operation of the Stock Exchange cannot be overemphasized. According to a 1981 survey,[6] pension funds and insurance companies held approximately 27 per cent and 21 per cent respectively of the total UK listed company shares, and in the light of recent events it is quite probable that these proportions have risen still further of late.

The net inflow of funds to life insurance companies and pension schemes amounted to £17 billion in 1984, whereas the personal sector surplus amounted to just short of £11 billion.[7] Thus, even before account is taken of the net receipts of other financial intermediaries, there existed a deficit which has had to be filled by the personal sector exchanging assets for life insurance policies and pension contributions. Clearly, insurance companies and pension funds played a significant financial intermediation role *within* the personal sector, as well as *between* sectors as outlined above. A major component of this intermediation in 1984 will have involved the sale of UK company securities by the personal sector to the tune of £4.5 billion. However, the particular role of insurance companies in channelling funds away from the personal sector may be emphasized by comparison with the position of building societies, since in their case virtually the entire £13 billion deposited with them in 1984 was used to finance loans for personal sector house purchase,[8] making almost the whole of their financial intermediation take place *within* the personal sector.

Personal Pensions

Important changes in the pensions industry may materialize as a consequence of a number of recent government initiatives. In addition to the proposals for the reform of the State Earnings-Related Pension Scheme (SERPS) (considered, particularly in the light of their impact on life insurance companies, in Chapter 7), the government has advanced the view that individuals should be provided with a greater degree of choice in respect of their pension arrangements, and that there should be a greater degree of competition in the provision of pension contracts. The views with respect to greater individual choice are embodied in the notion of personal pensions. As its title suggests, a personal pension scheme is one which is unique to the individual concerned, who would not, therefore, be a member of an occupational pension scheme. The government has proposed that personal pensions should be available, as of right, to all employees, and that each individual would be free to take his contributions, plus some part of his employer's contributions, from an occupational pension scheme in order to set up his personal pension.

If personal pensions were to become widespread, then life insurance companies, as the hitherto sole providers of such pension schemes, would expect to see a large increase in the volume of their business, especially if the move to personal pensions was away from reliance on the state scheme. However, the government is proposing a significantly greater degree of competition in the provision of pensions, and would appear willing to encourage institutions such as banks, building societies and unit trusts to provide pension contracts. Unsurprisingly, these other institutions have welcomed the proposals while the life insurance companies have been rather less enthusiastic. The position of the life companies is that they are not against competition, provided it is fair, and they argue that these other institutions should be subject to the same solvency requirements as they themselves are in respect of pension business. In addition, concern has been expressed in a number of quarters about the possible administrative costs which would accompany substantial numbers of individuals taking out personal pensions. In response to this, the government has proposed the setting up of some sort of clearing house, financed by the institutions, for this purpose. Nevertheless, some building societies have been gearing up to provide personal pensions in advance of any change in the legislation, and a number are already involved in pension business via Additional Voluntary Contribution (AVC) schemes. Indeed, at least one building society has joined forces with a life insurance company to offer pension savings plans.

Pension Fund Surpluses

In the five years to 1984, the average annual return on assets held by self-administered pension funds was 22.2 per cent for the private sector and 23.3 per cent for the public sector. Over the same period, the average annual growth of earnings was 10 per cent, and that of prices 8.4 per cent. These figures not only demonstrate the very high returns that pension funds have achieved on their investments in recent years, but they also imply that their assets have been growing at a considerably faster rate than their liabilities. This has been particularly true in respect of the pension funds for companies with declining workforces, since many of the members of these schemes will have become eligible for deferred pensions on becoming redundant, in relation to which there is no obligation to increase the value of the pension either in line with earnings or even in line with prices. Consequently, pension funds have accrued large surpluses,[9] and the issue has naturally arisen as to how these should be dealt with. There are three possible courses of action open to the pension funds. First, the company may take a pensions 'holiday'; that is, cease to make any contributions to the scheme for a fixed period. The second possibility is for the company to receive a refund from the pension fund. Thirdly, the benefits to be paid by the pension fund may be increased.

The last possibility, that of increasing benefits, has not occurred to any great extent, except in so far as there has been a greater degree of index-linking than previously. The first possibility, that of the company taking a pensions 'holiday' is, however, becoming increasingly popular, and has been pursued by companies such as Lucas, Mirror Group Newspapers, Spear & Jackson, DCL, Massey-Ferguson, Dunlop Renold, Rockware and P & O, plus a host of minor companies. In general, with contributory schemes, the 'holidays' have been restricted to the employers, meaning that the employees have continued to pay contributions, although the pension 'holiday' arranged by Massey-Ferguson includes employees. On occasions, pension 'holidays' have been initiated by companies as part of their defence against take-over bids, since the absence of pension contributions from a company's accounts causes a significant improvement to its reported profitability.

The second possible way of dealing with a pension fund surplus, that of a refund of contributions, has been used only rarely, not least because it requires approval from the Superannuation Funds Office (SFO) of the Inland Revenue due to the tax implications that may ensue. Although the SFO has refused a number of applications, some companies have managed to obtain refunds, notably James Neill (£2 million) and Redfearn National Glass (£1.7 million). The absence of any guidelines for pension fund refunds, and the apparent inconsistency in the treatment of applications for refunds, has led to a certain degree of dissatisfaction in this area. Many commentators are of the opinion that refunds should not be allowed, and base their view on the argument that there is no evidence to show that the long-term real rate of return on investments of 1 or 2 per cent has altered. If this is so, then surpluses being created currently should be used to offset the poor yields in the 1970s or to offset poor returns that may be achieved in the future.

There are additional consequences that may arise from a company adopting a pensions 'holiday' or a refund of contributions. Consider, for example, the case of Lucas which, by suspending contributions, would save £20 million per year. These moneys could be used to finance additional projects within the business, to reduce borrowings, or to increase dividend payments to shareholders. Whichever course of action is taken, it would have the impact of boosting the Lucas share price. This, in turn, would improve the performance of the Lucas pension fund, which owns 13 per cent of Lucas shares (although this only represents 4 per cent of the total pension fund portfolio), and increase the need to reduce the surplus. Naturally, the performance of any other pension funds holding Lucas shares will also be enhanced, which may then give rise to additional pressure to seek contributions 'holidays'. Some commentators have observed that this process will give rise to long-term instability in stock market prices, since it is pension fund surpluses that are driving the stock prices upwards. While there is adequate scope for disagreement as to the size of this effect, the process does emphasize the importance, to the stock market, of the pension funds.

The trends outlined above are likely to be further encouraged by the 1986 Budget which introduced measures to limit pension fund surpluses. It was proposed that surpluses should be no greater than 5 per cent of asset values, although, in practice, the methods of valuation used by actuaries will probably mean that the real limit is closer to 15 per cent. Nevertheless, with pension funds surpluses estimated to be in the order of £50 billion early in 1986,[10] the possible implications for stock market activity are likely to be substantial.

Inflation-proofing of Pensions

An area of considerable dissatisfaction for many pensioners in recent years has been the extent to which their pensions have kept up with inflation. For civil servants and many others in the public sector, full index-linked pensions have been provided since the enactment of the 1971 Pension (Increases) Act. It was the intention of the government at that time that the private sector would follow this lead, although this only occurred to a very limited extent. The reaction of many of those responsible for the running of pension funds was to guarantee increases of no more than the minimum 3 per cent per annum required. Consequently, many pension schemes did little to protect real pension entitlements during the 1970s when inflation rates averaged almost 13 per cent per annum. The rationale for this was that guaranteed increases of any greater magnitude could impose substantial open-ended commitments for which employers would ultimately be responsible. Accordingly, many schemes set a target for pension increases (often a high proportion or a complete indexation with the Retail Price Index – RPI), but no guarantee.

With the reduction in inflation and the strong investment performance over the last few years, many pension funds have been able to give full index-linking. A number have gone further, and increased pensions by amounts substantially greater than inflation, in an attempt to catch up and repair the effects of inflation in the 1970s. In general, such attitudes have only applied to pensions in payment, and very few funds have made any effort to increase the value of deferred pensions, regardless of the inflation rate. The Social Security Act of 1985 goes some way to remedying this deficiency by requiring pension funds to revalue deferred pensions each year in line with the RPI or 5 per cent, whichever is the lower. In the light of past experience, it seems unlikely that many funds will do more than this minimum. Nevertheless, one company pension scheme has recently offered the option of full index-linking to its retiring staff, but at the cost to the pensioner of a reduction in the initial value of his pension of some 14½ per cent. In order to be able to cover their liabilities for this option, the fund intends to purchase index-linked gilts, but will withdraw the option if their supply dries up. For the individuals about to retire, a difficult decision is in prospect, since whether or not they take the index-linked option will depend not only on their life expectancy and their expectations of inflation over the rest of their lives, but also on the extent to which they expect the fund to raise pensions paid to those not taking the index-linked option. Furthermore, the index-linked option may well reduce the moral pressure to make increases above the statutory minimum for those not taking that option.

Pension Fund Management

The basis of pension fund management fees has tended to vary, with some institutions charging an annual fee that is a proportion of the assets under their control, some (particularly stockbrokers) acquiring their income from the commissions on their securities dealing on the behalf of the fund, and the remainder a combination of the two. With the ending of minimum fixed commissions on Stock Exchange transactions in October 1986, an important element of the costs involved in running pension funds became negotiable. It has yet to be seen how this will affect fund management activities, but there is little doubt that the charges made by pension fund managers will be placed under much greater scrutiny as time passes, and it is likely that changes in the structure of the industry will ensue.

The developments in the UK capital markets have merely tended to intensify the already growing levels of competition within the fund management industry. An important factor in this respect has been the increasing tendency of companies to take contributions 'holidays', as mentioned earlier. Traditionally, the fund management industry has been dominated by the merchant banks, although competition from stockbrokers, insurance companies, specialist investment houses and even US investment banks has become more prevalent recently. Much greater attention is also now being paid to the performance of the fund managers. Whereas in earlier years a pension fund manager would run a fund for a long period of time, the publication of comparative performance statistics, and an increased awareness amongst employers of the cost of pension contributions, has led to a sharply increased dismissal rate. However, this move towards switching fund managers on the basis of a fractional difference in performance may not be wholly desirable. The reason for this is that it encourages fund managers to concentrate on achieving high short-run returns, at least partly at the expense of the long-term prospects for the fund. Consequently, the extremely significant influence of the occupational pension funds on the UK equity market is likely to encourage industry itself to concentrate on high short-term returns at the expense of greater long-term returns.

Pension fund managers may take some comfort from the fact that there has been some tendency in recent years for the employment of external fund managers by the trustees of a pension fund to increase. Along with the realization by employers of the high cost of contributions to a pension scheme has come awareness of the importance of a strong asset performance. Even the very largest pension funds now employ fund managers, if only for specialist areas of investment where it would be more expensive to acquire their own expertise. A related development is the tendency for some pension funds to split the asset management between two or more fund managers. If this division takes place, as it often does, on the basis of a proportion of the total assets in the fund rather than by particular asset groupings, it will naturally ease the problem faced by the trustees of comparing the performance of competing fund management groups as well as allowing some 'hedging'. It may also have the impact of limiting the dominance of the pension fund management industry by a restricted number of management groups.

Notes

1 For example, an individual retiring after 40 years of service in a one-eightieth scheme would receive a pension of one-half of his final salary.
2 *Occupational Pension Schemes 1979 – Sixth Survey by the Govern-*

ment Actuary, HMSO, 1981. No subsequent surveys have been published.

3 This is not to infer that the production of an actuarial statement constitutes an easy task. Indeed, it requires considerable expertise and judgement. The issue is that the absence of any diversified range of products, and therefore of liabilities, ensures that there is no requirement to match assets to the liabilities which would otherwise arise if different products were marketed.

4 There is an upper limit to the size of the tax-free lump sum, set at 1½ times final annual salary after 40 years of service and *pro rata* for fewer years of service.

5 It is generally agreed that a high level of discretionary saving took place in 1975, with the objective of restoring the real value of personal sector assets that was eroded by high inflation in that year.

6 *1981 Stock Exchange Survey of Share Ownership*. It is interesting to note that in 1963 pension funds and insurance companies held only 6.4 and 10 per cent respectively of total UK listed company shares.

7 *Financial Statistics*, Table 1.10, September 1985.

8 The balance largely constituted purchases of British government securities.

9 In this context, a surplus implies that the value of assets held plus the expected future inflows of funds exceed the expected future liabilities of the pension scheme. Clearly, there must always be a degree of uncertainty surrounding the calculation of this 'surplus'.

10 London Business School, reported in *The Economist*, 26 April 1986.

CHAPTER NINE

Unit Trusts

Introduction

A unit trust is a fund to which individuals and companies may contribute in order to obtain a share in the income and capital gains generated by the trust's assets. The moneys contributed are invested by the fund managers in an array of financial assets including bank deposits, UK and overseas company shares and loan stock, government securities, and local authority debt. The investor in the unit trust purchases 'units' at a price which reflects the aggregate value of the trust's net asset holdings divided by the number of units outstanding. Unit trusts are 'open-ended' funds in the sense that they may expand or contract according to customer demand for units. Thus, when investors put more money into a trust, new units are issued; conversely, when existing holders of units decide to withdraw their funds, their units are cancelled as the cash value of those units is returned to the investor. Clearly, during a given accounting period, if new investments exceed redemptions, the trust managers will have additional cash to invest, but if there is a net outflow of funds it may be necessary for the managers to liquidate asset holdings in order to meet these net redemptions of units.

There is no secondary market in units, which must be purchased directly from, and sold back to, the trust managers, possibly through the agency of an intermediary such as a bank, stockbroker, solicitor or accountant. In general, the minimum lump sum investment in a unit trust is in the range of £250 to £1,000, although much smaller amounts are often accepted within the context of regular (usually monthly) savings schemes. When investors purchase units they receive a contract note as evidence of the transaction, and subsequently a unit trust certificate is issued. Units can be sold back at any time to the trust managers who are obliged to repurchase them at the ruling price. The investor merely signs the form of renunciation on the back of the certificate and sends it to the managers. The sale proceeds are normally paid over within 2 weeks. Thus, unit trusts provide a convenient means for individuals to obtain a share in a much larger and more diversified portfolio of assets than they would be able to hold directly. An important development in recent years is that approximately one-third of outstanding funds of UK unit trusts have been associated with the purchase of units through unit-linked insurance policies. In addition, it should be noted that unit trusts are not allowed to issue preference or prior charge capital, except in respect of foreign currency loans. This means that a unit trust's capital cannot be 'geared', unlike investment trusts' capital (which will be discussed in Chapter 10).

The price at which units are sold by the trust (the offer price), and the price at which they are repurchased (the bid price), are set on a daily basis, and both reflect the market value of the trust's net asset holdings, with the difference between these prices being accounted for by brokerage charges, contract stamp, trustees' fees, and the profit of the management company. The Department of Trade and Industry (DTI) currently lays down rules for the calculation of bid and offer prices relative to the net asset value of unit trust units. The maximum permitted spread between bid and offer prices under DTI rules is 15 per cent of net asset value. Thus, for example, if the net asset value of a trust amounted to £10m, and there were 5 million units outstanding, then the net asset value of one unit would be 200p, and a maximum permitted offer price of 215p might be combined with a minimum permitted bid price of 185p. In practice, competition between unit trust managers ensures that the spread is usually in the range 6–7 per cent.[1]

Trusts which invest in gilts have a smaller spread, and trusts which invest in overseas shares a larger spread, in order to allow for different dealing costs. When a fund is expanding the managers tend to price on an offer basis, which means that in relation to the above example the expected offer price might be 214p and the bid price 200p. However, if the fund is contracting because of net redemptions, the managers could decide to switch to pricing on a bid basis. In this situation, bid and offer prices of 185p and 200p respectively might be expected. It is most unlikely that unit trust managers would switch from an offer to a bid pricing basis overnight, and the usual practice is to smooth the transition over a few weeks. Nevertheless, a sudden market collapse might precipitate such a switch, and at the extreme a unit holder who had purchased units on the previous day could find that their resale value had fallen overnight by the full 15 per cent.[2]

The Growth of Unit Trusts

The first unit trust was established in the UK in 1931, and by 1939 there were 15 management companies operating between them a total of 89 trusts, and holding assets with an aggregate value of around £80 million. During the following twenty years, the growth of UK unit trusts was relatively modest, with total asset holdings amounting to little over £200 million by 1960. Indeed, by this date the number of trusts had fallen to 51. However, by 1970 the situation had been transformed, for during the 1960s, the number of trusts increased fivefold, with assets held growing sevenfold. The growth of unit trust activity in the UK since 1970 is illustrated by Table 9.1.

It is clear that during the last decade assets held by UK unit trusts have grown continuously, as has the total number of authorised trusts. Nevertheless, not only has the growth in unit trust activity been erratic, but it has also only been since 1981 that the number of accounts held with unit trust companies has been on an upward trend. Even before the stock market collapse of 1973/4, which undoubtedly

Table 9.1

UK Authorised Unit Trusts: Value of Funds Held, Number of
Accounts and Number of Trusts, 1970 to 1985
(end-year values)

| Year | Value of funds | | Accounts | | Authorized |
	£m	% change over previous year	million	% change over previous year	unit trusts
1970	1,398	−1.0	2.40	0.4	240
1971	1,991	42.4	2.32	−3.3	269
1972	2,648	33.0	2.29	−1.3	295
1973	2,060	−22.2	2.24	−2.2	338
1974	1,311	−36.4	2.20	−1.8	360
1975	2,512	91.6	2.20	0	353
1976	2,543	1.2	2.12	−3.6	352
1977	3,461	36.1	1.99	−6.1	393
1978	3,873	11.9	1.95	−2.0	421
1879	3,937	1.7	1.82	−6.7	459
1980	4,968	26.2	1.72	−5.5	493
1981	5,902	18.8	1.79	4.1	529
1982	7,768	31.6	1.80	0.6	553
1983	11,689	50.5	2.04	13.3	630
1984	15,099	29.2	2.20	7.8	687
1985	20,308	34.5	2.55	15.9	806

Source: Unit Trust Association, London, January 1986.

undermined investors' confidence in all equity-based investments in the UK, there was a discernible downward trend in
the number of accounts held. This trend accelerated during
the second half of the 1970s, despite the substantial increase
in the value of unit trust funds, which was as much due to
the recovery of stock market prices as to inflows of new
investment funds. The years since 1981 have proved to be
record-breaking years with respect to all aspects of unit trust
activity. At February 1986 total funds managed amounted to
£22,940 million, together with approximately 2.64 million
active accounts. During 1985 the net inflow of new funds
amounted to £2,537 million, with both sales and repurchases
of units reaching record levels. An important factor underlying these trends must surely be the unusually drawn-out
bull market for equity shares in the UK in recent years;
indeed, with minor exceptions, all major stock markets

throughout the Western world have experienced substantial increases in share prices. The inherent capital risk involved with investment in shares, albeit indirect investment through a unit trust, would appear to have been more heavily discounted by investors in the face of buoyant expectations of future share price gains. In addition, in the UK, the Conservative government's privatization policy and its desire to encourage the evolution of a 'share-owning democracy' have probably also helped to encourage the growth of interest in unit trusts.

Constitutional Structure

There are always two independent companies involved with the operation of each unit trust. The *management company* (which may be a member of a banking or insurance group, or a specialist independent unit trust company) is responsible for the investment decisions (to be made in accordance with the stated objectives of the trust) and for the administration of the sale and repurchasing of units. The *trustee company*, which is often a subsidiary of a bank or of an insurance company, acts as the guardian of the trust's assets and income on behalf of the unit holders. The terms and conditions governing the management of the unit trust's funds are specified in the trust deed under which it operates. Indeed, the broad investment policy of any unit trust is limited to some extent by the legislation relating to authorization of unit trusts (as will be explained below).

The individual fund managers will often be members of a management group which controls a number of different trusts. Usually, there will be an overall group philosophy regarding liquidity levels, the spread of investments, the size of companies in whose shares the trust should invest, and the forcefulness with which the funds should be managed. This philosophy will be influenced by the group's view of the prospects of both the UK economy and of overseas economies, as well as by its expectations as to likely future developments in specific industrial or commercial sectors. Whilst individual fund managers need not subscribe fully to the group's overall view, they are usually discouraged from making any investment which contradicts the general guidelines laid down for the group.[3] This is, perhaps, an important reason why the performance of an individual trust may tend to reflect the performances of the other trusts under the same management group.

By the end of 1985 there were 146 separate management groups forming the UK unit trust industry. However, these companies were extremely disparate in size, as measured by the volume of funds under management. Table 9.2 shows the top ten management companies at the end of 1985; and these accounted for approximately 54 per cent of the total funds managed by unit trusts. In addition, individual trusts also varied markedly in size, as measured by the volume of funds invested. At the end of June 1986, over fifty trusts each held assets in excess of £100 million (the largest being £366 million), while in excess of 350 trusts each held assets worth less than £10 million.

At the end of 1985 there were just eleven trustee companies responsible for UK authorised unit trusts, and of these eight were either UK banks or companies forming part of UK banking groups. The top three trustees, as measured by the number of trusts under their trusteeship, had responsibility for almost 64 per cent of the sector; in terms of the volume of funds under trusteeship, the top three companies were responsible for approximately 60 per cent of the sector. Clearly, the level of concentration of trusteeship is much higher than the concentration of management of funds, which is probably to be expected given the constitutional structure and nature of activities within the UK unit trust sector.

Formerly, the Prevention of Fraud (Investments) Act 1958 laid down strict regulations regarding the status and the capitalization of trustee companies. These requirements have now been superseded by the provisions of the Financial Services Act 1986. Nevertheless, unit trust trustees are mainly respected financial institutions, the integrity of which cannot be questioned. The specific functions of the trustees are to ensure that the trust is managed within the terms of the trust deed; to ensure that advertisements for

Table 9.2

UK Authorised Unit Trusts: Management Groups (top 10 by funds under management), end of 1985

Name of group	Funds under management (£m)	Percentage share of industry
M & G (quoted company, 41% owned by Kleinwort Benson)	2,036	9.97
Save & Prosper (58.5% owned by Robert Fleming)	1,654	8.10
Allied Dunbar (owned by Hambro Life)	1,533	7.51
Henderson (quoted company)	1,148	5.62
Barclays Unicorn (owned by Barclays Bank)	1,143	5.60
TSB Unit Trusts (part of TSB Group)	863	4.22
Schroder (owned by Schroder Wagg)	854	4.18
Standard	661	3.24
Britannia (part of Britannia Arrow Group)	624	3.06
Mercury (subsidiary of Mercury Securities plc)	559	2.74

Source: Unit Trust Year Book, 1986.

Table 9.3

UK Authorised Unit Trusts: Trustees, Number of Trusts for which Responsible and Funds under Trusteeship, end 1985

Trustee	Number of trusts	Value of funds (£m)
Allied Assurance Co.	11	278.4
Bank of Scotland	80	2,144.5
Barclays Bank Trust Co.	56	1,459.7
Clydesdale Bank	36	568.9
Coutts & Co.	19	463.2
General Accident	24	1,034.5
Lloyds Bank Trust Co.	117	3,057.9
Midland Bank Trust Co.	200	3,758.7
Nat West Bank Trust Co.	64	821.6
Royal Bank of Scotland	263	5,316.8
Royal Exchange Assurance	44	1,482.1

Source: Unit Trust Year Book 1986.

the trust contain no misleading information, and state unambiguously that unit prices may fall as well as rise; to collect the dividend income of the trust and to distribute this dividend to the unit holders; to issue certificates to purchasers of units and to ensure that the relevant certificate is cancelled before sale proceeds from the disposal of units are paid to the unit holder; to act as the registrar for unit holders; and to safeguard the assets of the unit holders (all cash and securities in the fund are held in the name of the trustees in order to prevent any possible misappropriation by the trust managers). However, it should be recognized that it is often very difficult for trustees to know when to intervene in the investments which fund managers wish to make, since all investment decisions are to some extent subjective. Some trustees are prepared to veto any investment which they feel may be contrary to the interests of the unit holders, whilst other trustees take a more relaxed view and will only veto investments which specifically contravene the trust deed. In consideration of their work, the trustees receive a fee negotiated between themselves and the trust managers. A typical fee might be in the region of 1/20 per cent per annum on the net asset value of a fund of £10 million.

Supervision of Unit Trust Management Companies

As explained above, the trustees of a unit trust have a wide responsibility for the oversight of the running of the trust, and technically they have the power to remove an unsatisfactory manager from office. However, whilst the ultimate supervisory role in respect of unit trusts is now performed by the Securities and Investments Board (SIB), at the spring of 1987 the supervisory framework is still largely as specified by the now repealed Prevention of Fraud (Investment) Act 1958. Thus, only unit trusts which are 'authorized' are allowed to advertise to the general public, and in order to obtain that authorization, the trust deed of the unit trust must be approved by the Department of Trade and Industry (DTI). The minimum conditions which must be embodied in an approved trust deed are as follows:

(1) The trust must not hold more than 10 per cent of the share capital of any single company.

(2) The proportion of the trust's portfolio which is invested in a single company must not exceed 5 per cent at the time the investment is made. If the shares rise in value after the purchase the 5 per cent maximum can, however, be breached, and the trustees will not normally intervene in such a situation as long as the value of the shares does not rise to exceed 7½ per cent of the portfolio.

(3) No investments in property or commodities are permitted.[4]

(4) A minimum 75 per cent of the value of the portfolio must be invested in securities which are quoted on a recognized stock exchange. A maximum of 25 per cent can be invested in shares which are quoted on the Unlisted Securities Market. A maximum of 5 per cent of the portfolio may be invested in unquoted shares.

These conditions are partly motivated by the official desire to ensure that managers will always be able to obtain cash for the purpose of meeting net redemptions of units. The liquidity of assets held, as reflected in their general marketability, is thought to be of great importance.

A more informal form of supervision over unit trust activities is undertaken by the Unit Trust Association (UTA). This organization was originally formed in 1959 under the title of the Association of Unit Trust Managers. Its basic rationale is very much in keeping with the widespread desire within the City of London for the maintenance of professional standards and business ethics through a process of self-regulation. The specific objectives of the UTA may be summarized as being: to uphold the standards of unit trust practice, and to maintain the good name of the unit trust industry; to provide, on behalf of its members, an agreed channel of communication and representation to government departments, to the EEC and to other relevant institutions on matters relating to unit trusts; and to act, in co-operation with other organizations, on matters connected with investor protection.

Membership of the UTA is open to any management company of a unit trust which is authorized by the DTI. The work of the UTA is financed by contributions from members, based on the volume of funds managed, and much of that work is carried out behind the scenes in order to ensure that members adhere to the desired standards of unit trust practice. Matters covered by these standards relate to the important issues of advertising, the conduct of selling agents, and the payment of commission to intermediaries. In addition, the UTA is willing to investigate formally the activities of any member about whom a specific complaint is lodged, once it is clear that a direct approach to the unit trust managers by the complainant has not produced a satisfactory result. However, if the complainant is dissatisfied with the response of the UTA, he is still quite free to take his complaint to the trustees of the trust, or, as a last resort, to the SIB and hence the DTI.

The UTA plays an important role as the public relations arm of the unit trust industry. It collects and publishes a wide range of statistics relating to the activities of trusts managed by member companies. The UTA will also answer specific enquiries from the general public on unit trusts, although it does not advise on the relative merits of individual trusts.

UK Authorised Unit Trusts: Assets Portfolios

The assets of UK authorised unit trusts are predominantly in the form of ordinary shares in companies. Indeed, as illustrated by Figure 9.1, approximately 90 per cent of assets by market value comprised company securities at the end of 1984, although this represented a small reduction compared to 1981.

Also, in recent years, there has been a noticeable shift towards overseas company securities, largely at the expense of the proportion of funds going into UK company securities. For example, as shown in Table 9.4, 73.1 per cent of assets were in the form of UK company securities in 1978 and 15.6 per cent in overseas company securities, whereas by the end of 1984, the percentages were 55.5 per cent and 34.2 per cent respectively. It is generally believed that the removal of exchange controls in the UK in October 1979 paved the way for this significant portfolio adjustment by unit trust managers. However, the great interest shown in

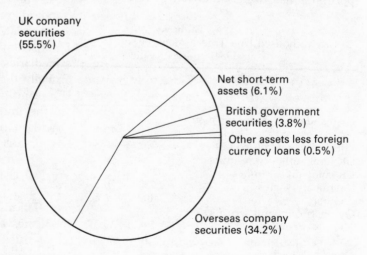

Figure 9.1   UK Authorised Unit Trusts: Distribution of Assets by Grouping, December 1984

Source: Financial Statistics, April 1986.

335

overseas securities was not merely the result of the increased freedom to pursue portfolio diversification (and hence risk spreading). The favourable performance of a number of major overseas economies, and hence stock markets, simultaneously created many attractive investment opportunities. The changing asset portfolio structure in recent years has clearly reflected the growth of trusts investing specifically in equities issued overseas relative to those devoted exclusively to UK-based investments. Whilst trusts investing in UK equities and securities still represent the most dominant sectors of the unit trust industry, there has been a marked shift towards European, North American and Japanese funds, as well as towards the more broadly based international funds. A good indication of the relative trends in the geographical emphasis of available unit trusts, falling within the UTA's standard classification, is implicit in the data reproduced in Tables 9.6 and 9.7.

Table 9.5 provides a more detailed breakdown of changes in the asset structure between 1982 and 1984. It would appear that the proportion of short-term assets held in portfolios has risen somewhat in recent years, although it

Table 9.4

UK Authorised Unit Trusts: Major Asset Groups, 1978 and 1984, end-year values

	1978		1984	
	£m	%	£m	%
Cash and other short-term assets (net)	400	10.3	908	6.1
British government securities	32	0.8	567	3.8
UK local authority securities	2	0.1	3	—
UK company securities				
Ordinary shares	2,732	70.5	7,925	53.6
Other	102	2.6	277	1.9
Overseas company securities				
Ordinary shares	594	15.3	4,943	33.4
Other	10	0.3	120	0.8
Other net assets	2	0.1	54	0.4
Total net assets	3,874	100.0	14,797	100.0

Source: Financial Statistics, April 1986.

336

has yet to re-achieve the levels reached during the late 1970s. One possible explanation of this phenomenon may be the increasingly competitive interest rates offered on short-term assets, which have allowed portfolio managers to maintain a higher level of liquidity (which is desirable in volatile market conditions) without sacrificing the opportunity to earn a respectable return on assets. Furthermore, the recovery in business activity in the UK since 1981 has tended to encourage firms to increase their share issues, and when taken in conjunction with the Conservative government's privatization programme (involving the floatation of huge blocks of shares in potentially desirable enterprises), it was to be expected that portfolio managers would wish to hold a larger proportion of their funds in fairly liquid form, in readiness for new asset purchases.

It may also be observed from Tables 9.4 and 9.5 that, whilst the shift towards overseas company securities continued at least until the end of 1984, the pace of that particular form of portfolio diversification slowed down markedly through 1983 and 1984. Indeed, during 1984 the value of holdings of ordinary shares in UK companies grew much more rapidly than the value of overseas ordinary shares, and whilst this obviously reflected the relative performances of the major stock markets throughout the world, there must have been at least a willingness on the part of portfolio managers to acquiesce in this occurrence.

Taxation and Unit Trusts

Capital Gains Tax (CGT)

Currently, unit trusts themselves are totally exempt from capital gains tax, but when a unit holder disposes of his units he will be liable to CGT in exactly the same way as if he had sold shares which he had owned directly. However, when an individual's total capital gains within the fiscal year fall below a prescribed figure (which was set at £6,300 for the 1986/7 fiscal year), no CGT is payable. As the effect of

Table 9.5

UK Authorised Unit Trusts: Assets and Liabilities, 1982 to 1984, end of year, market values

£ million

	1982	1983	1984
Short-term assets			
UK			
Cash and balances with monetary sector	189	475	615
Local authority temporary debt	27	34	43
Other short-term assets	110	72	74
Overseas short-term assets	67	99	275
Short-term liabilities	(45)	(111)	(99)
Total net short-term assets	348	569	908
Foreign currency loans	(58)	(123)	(118)
British government securities			
Up to 5 years	54	58	106
Over 5 and up to 15 years	166	251	379
Over 15 years and undated	102	106	82
Total British government securities	322	415	567
Local authority securities	1	1	3

UK company securities			
Ordinary shares	4,457	5,954	7,925
Other	154	225	277
Other UK investments	68	73	71
Overseas company securities			
Ordinary shares	2,229	4,091	4,943
Other	49	58	120
Other overseas investments	29	26	101
Total net assets	7,599	11,289	14,797

Source: *Financial Statistics*, April 1986.

inflation can be allowed before calculating taxable gains, many unit trust investors do not pay CGT as their total adjusted gains are too small.[5]

Corporation Tax

Unit trust companies themselves are liable to corporation tax on their total net unfranked income (that is, on receipts such as interest, rents or overseas dividends, less expenses), but not on dividends received on shares owned in UK-resident companies. The latter receipts are referred to as 'franked investment income', and the companies paying the dividends are liable to the related corporation tax on these sums. For the 1986/7 fiscal year, the rate of corporation tax was set at 35 per cent, with a reduced rate of 30 per cent for profits below £100,000, and marginal relief for companies earning between £100,000 and £500,000. There are special rules for unit trusts whose trust deeds confine them to investing in UK fixed interest securities. The interest in this case is subject to the basic rate of income tax, which is currently 27 per cent.

Income Tax

With the exception of the fixed interest unit trusts mentioned above, income tax is payable only by the unit holder, and it is levied on dividends received from unit trusts. The tax position is exactly the same as if the dividend had been received from shares owned directly by an investor. Each dividend is paid net of basic rate income tax, and the recipient is also given a 'tax credit' representing the amount of tax paid on his behalf. For example, if a unit trust paid a dividend of £7.30 net of basic rate income tax to a unit holder, his position in respect of taxation would be as follows:

Tax status of unit holder	Amount paid to unit holder	Tax liability
Non-taxpayer	£7.30	£2.70 (tax credit) can be reclaimed from the Inland Revenue
Basic rate, 27%	£7.30	No further tax liability
50% marginal rate	£7.30	A further £2.30 will be payable to the Inland Revenue (that is, 50% tax on the gross dividend of £10, less £2.70 tax credit)

Unit Trust Savings Schemes and the Structure of Charges

Many unit trusts offer schemes whereby an investor makes regular monthly payments to the managers, who then allocate units at the ruling offer price. The minimum amounts vary from £10 to £50 per month, and payment is usually made by banker's order. There is no contractual obligation to continue the payments, and the banker's order can be cancelled at any time without any tax or other consequences. On cancellation the unit holder may either retain the accumulated units, or sell them back to the managers at the ruling bid price. Taxation liabilities are exactly the same as for lump sum investment.

One of the benefits of buying units by means of a regular savings scheme (as opposed to purchasing units through a single lump sum investment), is that the average cost of the units will never be above their average price during any given period. This phenomenon is known as *pound cost averaging*, and it occurs because a fixed sum of money buys more units the lower are their price. Thus, for example, if an investor makes a monthly payment of £10 for 3 months, the following result may occur:

	Offer Price	Number of Units Bought
Month One	200p	5
Month Two	250p	4
Month Three	333p	3

Average Offer Price = 261p

Average cost = (£30 ÷ 12) = 250p

The practical effect of this statistical phenomenon is that an investor will never commit all of his investment in unit trust units when the offer price is at its peak, although he will lose the opportunity to invest his funds in the form of a lump sum when the offer price is at a relatively low level. The net result of pound cost averaging is to remove the uncertainty which would otherwise surround the timing decision for investment in a unit trust.

Early in 1985 the Unit Trust Association ruled that managers could take up to 20 per cent of the first year's payments as commission on regular savings plans. If this maximum rate were to be levied, the net effect would be that all the first two months' instalments, and 40 per cent of the third month's instalments would be taken by the managers. In other words, if an investor cancelled his banker's order of £10 per month after 3 months, only £6 would have been invested in units, with the remaining £24 being charged as commission. However, such penal charges are not common, and, at the time of writing, the majority of unit trust companies charged only the normal fees implicit in the offer to bid spread. Nevertheless, it is usually better for investors to arrange savings plans directly with the managers, rather than going via intermediaries which often levy charges of their own for the service provided.

There is no formal dealing charge levied on lump sum investments in unit trust units, but the spread between bid and offer prices can be considered as a substitute for commission charges. As mentioned above, average spreads are 6–7 per cent, with less on trusts investing primarily in the UK, and more on trusts investing overseas. Part of the spread covers the managers' front-end loading charge which, with a few exceptions, averages about 5–5½ per cent of the net asset value of the units.[6] There is also an annual management fee of normally between ¾ and 1 per cent of the net asset value.[7] This fee is usually deducted from the dividend paid to the unit holder.

If the investor buys units through an intermediary such as a bank or stockbroker, the managers may pay up to 3 per cent of the amount invested as commission to that intermediary, this limit being set by a UTA guideline. This commission is not charged to the purchaser of the units, but is paid by the managers out of their funds. However, if a unit holder wishes to sell back his units, it may be advisable for him to deal directly with the manager as the latter will never reward an intermediary in this situation, and so there is the possibility that the intermediary will levy his own charge on the unit holder.

The Performance of Unit Trusts

At the end of March 1986, there were 847 authorised unit trusts operated by 125 management companies in the UK, and so clearly there is a very wide choice for a potential unit holder. However, to assist investors with their evaluation of the competing trusts, the UTA now categorizes authorised unit trusts according to their stated aims and investment policies. Every quarter the UTA publishes statistics on the performance of the 'median' trust in each of fifteen specific categories (although a significant minority of trusts do not fall into any of these groups). Thus the unit holder is able to compare the performance of his own trust against the median for the relevant category, and he is also in a position to compare it against returns on bank deposits, building society deposits, and so on.

Tables 9.6 and 9.7 illustrate the form of information published quarterly by the UTA. The statistics quoted show clearly why investors may prefer to put funds into unit trusts, rather than into building society or bank deposits which pay regular interest and carry negligible risk of capital losses. Quite simply, and especially in the longer term, the

Table 9.6

UK Authorised Unit Trusts: Median Fund Performance by Category over 5, 10 and 15 years, as at 1 April 1986, for a Lump Sum Investment

Sector	UK general			UK growth			UK equity income			Mixed income		
Invested . . . years ago	5	10	15	5	10	15	5	10	15	5	10	15
Median fund	2,884	5,982	8,948	2,575	5,853	8,013	2,981	5,737	9,827	2,775	4,488	7,755
No. of funds in sector	68	60	47	69	51	30	65	51	28	10	10	4

Sector	Gilt & fixed interest income			Gilt & fixed interest growth			International			North America		
Invested . . . years ago	5	10	15	5	10	15	5	10	15	5	10	15
Median fund	1,688	2,923	4,936	2,123	*	*	2,290	4,083	6,078	2,228	3,701	5,207
No. of funds in sector	27	4	2	2	*	*	51	37	17	38	17	6

Sector	Europe			Australia			Japan			Far East		
Invested . . . years ago	5	10	15	5	10	15	5	10	15	5	10	15

Median fund	3,661	3,885	6,413	818	1,871	2,947	3,253	5,884	13,093	1,915	4,711	*
No. of funds in sector	8	5	2	4	3	1	11	5	3	14	6	*

Sector	Commodity & energy			Investment trust units			Financial & property		
Invested . . . years ago	5	10	15	5	10	15	5	10	15
Median fund	984	3,114	4,600	2,599	6,244	7,062	2,534	5,777	6,946
No. of funds in sector	17	11	9	5	4	3	12	11	9

Indices	Years ago		
	5	10	15
FT Ind. Ord. Index	3,127	5,089	7,024
FT All Share Index	3,116	7,156	9,728

Sector			
Invested . . . years ago	5	10	15
Bank deposit accounts	1,333	1,880	2,227
Building societies	1,456	2,147	2,932
National Savings Certificates	1,635	2,419	3,264

* Funds are too recent to generate this information.

Source: UTA, *Quarterly Investment Statistics*, April 1986.

Notes:

(1) All figures show the realization value (in £s) of £1,000 invested 5, 10 or 15 years ago, with net income reinvested.

(2) The unit trust performance data are calculated on an offer to bid basis.

Table 9.7

UK Authorised Unit Trusts: Median Fund Performance by Category over, 5, 10 and 15 years, as at 1 April 1986, for Regular Monthly Investment

Sector	UK general			UK growth			UK equity income			Mixed income		
Invested . . . years ago	5	10	15	5	10	15	5	10	15	5	10	15
Median fund	2,334	7,769	16,311	2,156	7,180	14,850	2,416	7,668	16,900	2,286	6,774	13,968
No. of funds in sector	68	60	47	69	51	30	65	51	28	10	10	4

Sector	Gilt & fixed interest income			Gilt & fixed interest growth			International			North America		
Invested . . . years ago	5	10	15	5	10	15	5	10	15	5	10	15
Median fund	1,604	4,538	8,844	1,791	*	*	1,918	6,134	11,935	1,829	6,178	11,021
No. of funds in sector	27	4	2	2	*	*	51	37	17	38	17	6

Sector	Europe			Australia			Japan			Far East		
Invested . . . years ago	5	10	15	5	10	15	5	10	15	5	10	15

... fund	2,839	7,204	13,187	1,201	3,217	6,016	2,408	8,901	16,994	1,779	6,172	*
No. of funds in sector	8	5	2	4	3	1	11	5	3	14	6	*

Sector	Commodity & energy			Investment trust units			Financial & property		
Invested . . . years ago	5	10	15	5	10	15	5	10	15
Median fund	1,169	3,760	7,529	2,203	7,888	15,318	2,279	7,665	14,576
No. of funds in sector	17	11	9	5	4	3	12	11	9

Sector	Invested . . . years ago		
	5	10	15
Bank deposit accounts	1,385	3,134	5,760
Building societies	1,484	3,818	7,199

Indices

	Years ago		
	5	10	15
FT Ind. Ord. Index	2,585	7,656	15,414
FT All Share Index	2,491	8,704	19,180

* Funds are too recent to generate this information.

Source: UTA, *Quarterly Investment Statistics,* April 1986.

Notes:

(1) All figures quoted show the realization value (in £s) of £20 invested monthly for 5, 10 or 15 years, with net income reinvested.

(2) The unit trust performance data are calculated on an offer to bid basis.

average unit trust in each sector has tended to outperform the more conventional investment media used by small savers. It may be observed that it is only in rare instances that the basic fixed capital investments have performed better than unit trusts over 5-, 10- or 15-year periods, and where this has occurred, it has only been in relation to 'specialist' funds. The more broadly based general funds have consistently performed better than fixed capital investments. However, it should also be noted that the median funds in the majority of sectors have consistently under-performed the Financial Times All Share Index, and most median funds have fared worse than the Financial Times Industrial Ordinary Share Index. This implies that the managers of the average unit trust fund have been unable to 'beat the market' consistently,[8] which would suggest that a useful strategy for trust managers might be to hold a portfolio reflecting the composition of the stock market index! Indeed, once a portfolio has been constructed which reflects the full diversity of the market, further investment research costs are minimal, and only occasional minor adjustments to investments are required in order to avoid the portfolio drifting away from the market index.[9] Unfortunately, this strategy is anathema to most unit trust managers, for it runs contrary to the fundamental tenet of investment management, which holds that selective and active portfolio management can lead to the achievement of above-average results. By definition, an index fund can do no better than the market as a whole, and most managers would argue that to hold the index portfolio is to admit defeat from the outset.

Nevertheless, and somewhat ironically, it is probably the case that some of the larger management groups hold aggregate portfolios (taking all their trusts together) which approach the composition of an index fund. The laws of statistics would suggest that at least one of these individual funds will perform better than the index fund, which is extremely useful for marketing purposes, although other individual funds will almost certainly perform worse and, taking the group as a whole, it is likely that their performance will come close to that of the index portfolio in the longer term. It might be argued that whilst fixed capital investments might be alternative repositories for investors' funds, the virtual absence of risk of capital loss means that they are not really suitable as a basis for comparison of the performance of unit trusts. However, a risk ratio concept has been developed by economists at the University of Exeter which basically measures the performance of unit trusts over their life, on a quarter-to-quarter basis, against the Halifax Building Society's 90 Day Account. A ratio of 0.2, for example, means that the Halifax account has generated a better return than the relevant unit trust for only 20 per cent of the time. Utilizing the ratio, it is possible to establish the relative consistency of a unit trust's performance against a fixed capital base, as well as to consider the relative risk attached to specific unit trusts. As might be expected, it is the more specialist trusts which generate the highest risk ratios. In a list of 117 unit trusts with risk ratios of 0.48 and above (published in May 1986), there was not a single general fund recorded.

Unfortunately, the rather heterogeneous nature of the closer substitutes to the holding of unit trust units means that a simple, quantitative comparison of performances is not feasible. Nevertheless, it is useful to consider some of the closer alternatives to unit trusts investment, in order to draw attention to the relative merits of the latter from the point of view of the potential investor.

Single Premium Insurance Bonds

The nature of single premium insurance bonds was discussed earlier, in Chapter 7. It will be recalled that the investor's lump sum payment is split between a small amount of life insurance cover and investments in equities, gilt-edged securities, property and commodities. In general, it would appear that the performance of unit trusts has been better than that of these bonds in recent years, other than for those individuals paying income tax at the highest marginal rate. Table 9.8 gives examples of the performance of equity bonds and unit trusts run by the same insurance

Table 9.8

Comparison of the Performance of Single Premium Insurance
Bonds and Unit Trusts, over 1, 3 and 5 years, as at
1 April 1985

| | | Value of £1000 invested over | | |
		5 years (£)	3 years (£)	1 year (£)
Equity & Law	equity bond	2,131	1,659	1,236
	general unit trust	2,433	1,865	1,342
Legal & General	equity bond	2,485	1,790	1,348
	equity unit trust	2,892	1,923	1,456
Norwich Union	equity bond	2,126	1,795	1,302
	unit trust	2,420	1,945	1,356

Source: *Sunday Telegraph*, 21 April 1985.

companies. In each case the unit trust produced a better
result than the equity bond.

At first sight it may appear to be somewhat strange that a
unit trust can outperform a bond even when the underlying
investments are supervised by the same managers. The
explanation of this occurrence is to be found in the different
taxation treatment of insurance and unit trust activities. As
explained above, unit trust funds are not subject to capital
gains tax through the management company, although if the
investor sells his units he must pay tax himself on the
taxable gain. However, if total taxable capital gains for the
investor during the fiscal year are below £6,300 (1986/7) then
there is no capital gains tax liability. In contrast, insurance
bond funds are liable to capital gains tax, and although
investors do not have to pay the full 30 per cent rate it is
normal for a provision of around 20 per cent to be charged
to the insurance company. Therefore, not only must a
deduction for capital gains tax be made from the surrender
proceeds of insurance bonds, but insurance companies are
also likely to be inhibited from selling investments which
have generated capital gains and reinvesting funds elsewhere. The end result of this situation is that even where a
bond and a unit trust have the same portfolios, the bond

investor is likely to be at least 20 per cent worse off. A recent direct comparison for a number of specialist funds is shown in Table 9.9.

Nevertheless, despite the recently inferior performance of insurance bonds relative to unit trusts, there are certain advantages accruing to their holders. In particular, where active investment is desired, switching between bond funds (managed by the same company) may take place for just a nominal fee, or often without any charge being incurred. This is not so with unit trusts, where the cost of switching between funds may be 3 per cent of the investment value (within one company). However, around two-thirds of bond holders choose to place their investment in managed funds,[10] which effectively delegates decisions over switching the underlying assets to the bond managers. Therefore, it may be the often claimed additional security and stability related to bonds which makes them attractive to holders. Certainly, it must be recognized that there is currently no unit trust (not even the relatively new 'fund of funds' variety)[11] which offers the same degree of flexibility in asset holdings as the managed bonds. The very fact that insurance companies are able to invest directly in property and commodities, and have greater freedom to hold cash balances than do unit trust companies, means that they are able to hold highly diviersified asset portfolios which are more likely to weather the storms of a stock market downturn. Indeed, it is widely accepted by insurance company portfolio managers that whilst the performance of their bonds may be inferior to unit trusts during periods of steadily rising share prices, they can offer a greater certainty of substantial long-term capital growth, even in the face of relatively poor stock market conditions. Finally, it is also sometimes argued that a major reason why many people are advised to buy insurance bonds as opposed to unit trust units is that intermediaries often earn 7 or 8 per cent commission on the sale of bonds, whereas the usual commission for unit trust sales is only about 3 per cent.[12]

Table 9.9

Performance over One Year to 1 April 1986 of Selected Insurance Bonds and Unit Trusts in Specialist Funds

Bond	% gain	Unit Trust	% gain
Lloyds Life/Gartmore Japan	39.0	Gartmore Japan	60.4
Lloyds Life/Britannia Japan	22.5	Britannia Japan	44.1
Gresham/Framlington Income	24.1	Framlington Income	32.9
Friends Provident Stewardship	20.0	Friends Provident Stewardship	25.0
M & G Life European	42.9	M & G European	61.1

Source: Planned Savings (offer to bid price basis) reported in *The Observer*, 20 April 1986.

Discretionary Management of an Individual's Portfolio by an Intermediary

It is difficult to assess the performance of intermediaries (such as banks or stockbrokers) in respect of discretionary management of clients' assets portfolios. As the discretionary management service is 'tailor-made' to suit the client's needs, and the nature of the activity is somewhat confidential, reliable statistics on investment performance are scarce. However, it has been suggested by some commentators that unit trusts are likely to provide better results even for relatively large investments.[13] This is despite the fact that fees for discretionary asset management usually compare favourably to corresponding management charges levied by unit trust companies. It should, of course, also be recognized that intermediaries will often take into consideration the complete financial package which the customer requires in the light of his financial objectives and of his tax position.

Direct Purchase of Gilt-Edged Securities

A unit trust which is limited by its trust deed to investments in fixed interest stocks and gilts, pays only 27 per cent tax on the interest earned. This concession was introduced by the 1980 budget, with the objective of encouraging the formation of unit trusts which would invest in gilts. However, most investors are likely to be better off purchasing gilts directly from the authorities,[14] given the absence of default risk on such assets and the wide array of issues available which makes it possible for the investor to choose the coupon and maturity date most appropriate to his financial and tax position. Nevertheless, as noted above, unit trusts investing primarily in gilts (and other fixed interest assets) have often performed better than fixed capital investments, and so they may still be attractive, especially to the relatively inexperienced investor.

Direct Purchase of Equities

The success of direct equity investment depends upon both the skill and the luck of the individual investor, and obviously there are no statistics available to assess the general performance of such portfolios. But with respect to transactions costs, the spread of 6-7 per cent between unit trust offer and bid prices is rather more than the usual 5 per cent commission charged on the purchase or sale of an equity portfolio. However, the professional management expertise, implicitly purchased by the unit trust investor, is probably well worth the small additional charge. Indeed, various commentators have argued the merits of unit trust investment, as opposed to direct equity investment, for a wide array of potential investors.[15]

The Choice of Unit Trust for the Investor

With the number of unit trusts exceeding 840 at March 1986, and with their ranks growing almost monthly, the choice of trusts into which funds should be placed may be bewildering for the average unsophisticated investor. This fact alone may undermine the attractiveness of unit trusts as an investment medium, despite the fact that they provide a simple means of access to the stock market and professional investment management. Furthermore, although significant short-term gains may accrue to the unit trust investor, unit trusts are usually regarded as being more suited to longer-term investment, with a time horizon ideally being in excess of 5 years. The recognition that bid prices for units may fall (perhaps quite significantly) in the short term, is probably an important reason why unit trusts are not more popular amongst relatively small savers. The possibility that the investor may be forced to sell his units when the market is temporarily depressed, leads most financial advisers to recommend that unit trust investment should only really be contemplated once the potential investor has built up holdings of funds where his capital is safer, such as building society shares or National Savings deposits.[16]

Once the broad decision to invest in a unit trust has been taken, the investor must obviously select a specific management company, and a particular trust under its management, with the view to obtaining an investment which contributes to his overall financial objectives. A vast array of information on unit trust performance is made available both by the individual management companies themselves and by the UTA. Furthermore, comparative analyses of unit trust performance have become a regular feature of the financial press. Clearly, whilst a good performance record does not guarantee good results in the future, it does demonstrate something about the level of expertise and experience available to the unit trust company, although maintaining a good performance will tend naturally to be influenced by the continuity of management. Frequent changes in investment management may bedevil overall group performance because of the consequent changes in investment policy.

A new trust has the initial advantage of possessing a pool of cash which may be invested in accordance with current market conditions, on the basis of the latest research intelligence on investment opportunities. Existing trusts are, to some extent, committed to their past investment decisions, since it may be inexpedient to liquidate a large holding of shares which has already fallen in value, given that this would convert a 'paper loss', which could possibly be recovered, into a 'cash loss', which would be irrecoverable. From the point of view of the investor, the purchase of units in a new trust may also be advantageous, as front-end charges are often reduced or waived in order to attract new investors.

In theory, a small fund should be able to respond more quickly than a large one to changing market conditions, but in practice there is little evidence to support this contention. However, the available evidence does tend to suggest that very large funds only rarely appear at the top end or at the bottom end of performance leagues, and usually tend to perform around the average for all trusts in their relevant category.[17] The implication here, of course, is that an investor who does not wish to take an above-average risk should invest in a large fund as opposed to a small fund. It should also be noted that some large management groups, operating many trusts, may use one of their smaller funds as a 'flagship' for the group in order to improve their market image. Quite simply, the managers will concentrate a high proportion of their expected high performance investments into this flagship fund, so that their other trusts, which are likely to be less successful, can be sold on the basis of the track record of the flagship fund.[18]

The importance of unit trusts in allowing the small saver to have access to a diversified equities/securities portfolio cannot be overemphasized. It has been estimated that for an investor to be able to avoid the damaging effects of unsystematic risk (that is, the risk of selecting specific equities which perform badly)[19] it is necessary for him to purchase at least fifteen different equities from different sectors of the market. As the minimum cost-effective investment in a single share may be as high as £2,000 (due to brokers' fees and other expenses), there is the implication that the minimum cost-effective total investment, in order to obtain a diversified equities portfolio, may be around £30,000. Many unit trusts invest in between fifty and a hundred different shares, and, as mentioned above, an indirect stake in such a highly diversified portfolio may be purchased for as little as £250 (and for much less, through a regular savings scheme). In addition to this obvious investment gain, the purchaser of unit trust units also implicitly avoids the costs related to the detailed paperwork of buying/selling equities, and the decision problems surrounding bonus issues, rights issues, and take-overs which might arise where shares are held directly. In effect, the investor delegates total responsibility for portfolio management to the unit trust managers, but of course in doing this he loses the right to attend and vote at the general meetings of the companies in which he (indirectly) owns shares, and hence may lose some of the satisfaction which is normally associated with share ownership. Finally, bearing in mind that the minimum lump sum invested in a unit trust may be as low as £250, it may be sensible for the investor to hold units in a number of markedly different trusts operating under different managements, in order to obtain an even higher level of asset portfolio diversification.

Unauthorized Unit Trusts

In the UK, a number of unit trusts are 'unauthorized'. This does not mean that their activities are illegal, but rather that the trusts have been precluded from seeking authorization from the DTI, due to the nature of their investments. The legal basis for this class of 'restricted' unit trusts was the 1958 Prevention of Fraud (Investments) Act, which also effectively barred these trusts from advertising for subscribers from the general public. However, these trusts may distribute circulars inviting subscriptions for units, but only to a narrow group of potential investors and with the express permission of the DTI.

The major groups of unauthorized trusts in the UK are the property unit trusts. These institutions invest mainly in real property and sell their units exclusively to tax-exempt bodies such as pension funds and charities, and thus are themselves exempt from all income and capital gains taxes. At the end of 1984, UK property unit trusts held net assets valued at £1.9 billion and holdings of property accounted for about 70 per cent of their asset portfolio value as shown in Table 9.10. Relative to authorized unit trusts property trusts have grown very little in recent years; for example, at the end of 1981 their aggregate assets amounted to £1.7 billion, and these grew in total by only 11.8 per cent over the following three years. Indeed, during 1985 there was a net outflow of cash (amounting to £19 million) from these trusts.

'House funds' are another form of unauthorized trust. These funds are run along the lines of normal unit trusts, by brokers or merchant banks, but they are made available exclusively to their own organizations' clients. Thus, since no general advertising is required, there is no need for the trusts to obtain DTI authorization. There are also 'offshore' unit trusts, which are based outside of the jurisdiction of the British authorities. These funds may be managed by subsidiaries of UK banking institutions, perhaps in the Channel

Table 9.10
UK Property Unit Trusts: Aggregate Assets,
31 December 1984

	£m	£m	%
Cash, bank balances and other current net assets		147	7.5
Property		1,364	70.0
UK	1,213		
Overseas	151		
Other assets		439	22.5
Total assets		1,950	100.0

Source: *Financial Statistics*, April 1986.
Note: At the end of 1984, these trusts had £81m of medium- and long-term borrowing outstanding, giving them a total net value for assets of £1,869m.

Islands or Isle of Man, and hence are generally considered to be completely reputable. However, given the absence of formal British supervision, other offshore unit trusts offering units within the UK should be regarded with some caution, unless, of course, their managers are well known to the City establishment. Offshore funds may appeal to non-resident or expatriate investors because of their tax benefits. However, there are no tax gains for UK resident investors, and, indeed, if the trust distributes less than 15 per cent of its annual income a UK-based investor will be charged income tax on any capital gain arising from the sale of units.

In certain circumstances, the trustees of unauthorized trusts may have only very limited powers to protect the interests of the investor. For example, in 1983, Westgrove Property Unit Trust collapsed, and the trustees, the National Westminster Bank, were powerless to intervene because of the nature of the trust deed. Furthermore, the promotional literature of these trusts is supervised by neither the DTI nor the UTA, and hence the advertising standards cannot be as dependable as those which apply to authorized unit trusts.

The Significance of Unit Trusts within the UK Financial System

Whilst there is no disagreement that unit trust managers have control over substantial amounts of listed shares, their power to influence the activities of the companies issuing these shares would appear to be relatively modest, unless exercised in conjunction with the power held by other institutional shareholders such as pension funds and insurance companies. This position arises largely because authorized unit trusts are not allowed to hold more than 10 per cent of the share capital of any individual company; and, in addition, the aggregate value of unit trusts' holdings of listed equities amounts to only a relatively small proportion of their total quoted value.[20] However, it would seem reasonable to suggest that, if a unit trust did hold the maximum 10 per cent of the share capital of a single company, the decision of the unit trust managers in a contested take-over bid could have a crucial effect on the outcome.

The major significance of unit trusts in the UK financial system is probably in respect of their provision of a convenient and relatively cost-effective channel to equity investment for the small saver. In recent years unit trusts have become an increasingly popular repository for investors' funds, and, as mentioned earlier, following a decade of decline there has been a substantial growth in the number of unit trust accounts held since 1981. Nevertheless, to place this trend into its proper perspective, the 2.55 million accounts held with unit trust companies (at March 1986) should be compared to the number of savings accounts held with building societies which now exceeds 40 million. Furthermore, just as individual savers may hold more than one building society account, so too there is some double-counting in respect of unit trust accounts. The actual number of individuals investing with UK unit trust companies is estimated to be only round 800,000, which is somewhat less than the total which existed prior to the 1973/4 stock market slump. However, in addition to these individuals investing directly in unit trusts, some 3.74 million unit-trust-linked insurance policies were held at the end of 1985; and these accounted for approximately one-third of the total value of funds held with unit trust companies.

It would appear that despite the substantial asset growth and generally good performance of unit trusts in recent years, trust managers still have a long way to go in convincing the general public of the merits of unit trusts as a savings medium. A recent survey found that about 60 per cent of adults in the UK did not understand what a unit trust was or how it could be used towards satisfying their savings requirements. It has also been estimated that unit trust holdings account for only about 1.4 per cent of total personal sector assets in the UK.[21]

The Future Development of Unit Trusts

It is difficult to predict the likely future course of unit trust growth. An extremely important factor is the nature of trading conditions on the world's major stock markets, and on the London Stock Exchange in particular. A major downturn in stock market prices would not only tend to diminish the market value of equities and securities held by unit trust companies (and hence the offer and bid prices for units), but would also tend to undermine the confidence of potential unit holders, and, at least in the early stages of a downturn, may lead to substantial redemptions of units as investors seek to take their past capitalized profits before they disappear. A further important factor is the continuation of the tax advantage of unit trusts in respect of capital gains tax. As illustrated in Table 9.9, this particular concession may make a substantial difference to the relative net returns earned on investments held by small savers.

The policy position of the present Conservative government in relation to financial matters is likely to have mixed implications for the operations of unit trusts. The government's drive for wider share ownership may stimulate interest in investments involving equities, and thus may encourage the holding of unit trust units; conversely, increased interest in equity investments may push more investors into direct investment in equities. The forms of offer made for the recent Stock Exchange floatations of various public sector enterprises would appear to reflect a preference within the government for direct share ownership by small savers. Indeed, the initial proposal for Personal Equity Plans (which are effectively tax shelters for small savers wishing to invest in listed equity shares), put forward in the 1986 Budget, explicitly excluded investments through unit trusts, limiting the benefits only to those individuals wishing to invest directly in equities. However, in the light of the argument that small savers would be dangerously exposed to capital loss with only minimal portfolio diversification, the authorities relented somewhat, and when the detailed proposals were published by the Inland Revenue in May 1986, limited investments in both unit trusts and investment trusts were included within the Personal Equity Plan mechanism.[22]

Whilst there is little doubt that the government's policy of encouraging and facilitating the deregulation of the UK financial sector will have far-reaching effects on the operations of unit trusts, as yet the ultimate form of the aggregate influence remains unclear. The long-term effects of the October 1986 'Big Bang' on the London Stock Exchange, which effectively outlawed minimum fixed commissions for transactions, may give unit trust managers a greater clout in negotiations over the trading of equities and securities, and hence may allow them to raise their competitiveness relative to other savings media. However, it is also quite possible that an increased competitiveness in equity trading will attract more investors into direct investment in equities. Furthermore, the same underlying forces for free competition within the financial services industry are likely to cause institutions not currently involved in the provision of pure equity-based investments for savers to shift in that direction. Several major insurance companies have already established unit trust subsidiaries, perhaps in recognition of the advantages to savers of unit trust investments relative to their traditional insurance-based products.

It is the intention of the government that both the managers and the trustees of unit trusts will have to be authorized within the requirements of the Financial Services Act 1986, and that the nature of their activities will have to comply with the broad provisions of the Act. This legislation is likely to have important implications for the environment within which unit trusts operate, and of especial significance is the creation of a self-regulatory organization known as the 'Life Assurance and Unit Trust Regulatory Organisation', which is to be responsible for the supervision and regulation of the management and selling of unit trusts within the framework of the Act. Although it is thought likely that this organization will delegate its major functions relating to unit trusts to the UTA, intense debate has occurred over the extent to which the limits of activities should be standardized between unit trust and insurance companies. In particular, it has been proposed that the 'cold calling' technique of marketing services (that is, unsolicited calls made to members of the general public by agents of the financial intermediary), should be extended to unit trusts, it already being a standard weapon in the insurance companies' sales armoury. This proposal has itself met with a great deal of resistance from established unit trust groups, as might be expected given their vested interest in the status quo in respect of marketing techniques. But it is the rider that unit holders should be allowed a 14-day 'cooling-off period', within which they may back out of agreements to purchase units, which has caused the most bitter debate. This would certainly bring sales of units in unit trusts into line with the marketing of insurance savings policies, but it would also probably require fundamental changes in the treatment of new moneys from investors and the pricing of units during the cooling-off period. However, it would appear to be unlikely that the proposal will be implemented within the foreseeable future, at least in its original uncompromising form.[23]

The nature of competition within the unit trust sector is also likely to be affected by the clause within the Financial Services Act giving the managers of authorized UK unit trusts the freedom to market their units throughout the

EEC, and giving the managers of unit trusts authorized by other EEC countries the freedom to market their units in the UK. It will also be mandatory for trust managers to disclose the amount of commission paid to intermediaries. However, despite the moves towards easing the restrictions within the UK financial sector, it is intended that the distinction will be maintained between authorized and unauthorized trusts, with the limitations remaining on the types of assets which may be held by the former, and the nature of advertising permitted for the latter.

Notes

1 *Investors Chronicle*, 3 January 1986, p. 82.
2 Advertisements for unit trusts may be somewhat misleading if performance is quoted on an 'offer-to-offer' basis, as this ignores the fact that if an investor wishes to realize his units it is the bid price which is of relevance. The 'offer-to-bid' statement of performance has become increasingly common in recent years, although some major management companies persist with the former presentation.
3 Unit Trust Association, *Unit Trust Year Book, 1984*, p. 25.
4 In 1985, an official proposal was put forward that this rule should be relaxed. However, the Unit Trust Association effectively vetoed this move. See, Unit Trust Association, 'Open Letter' to the DTI, dated 6 August 1985.
5 *Investors Chronicle*, 3 January 1986, p. 85.
6 *Investors Chronicle*, 12 July 1985, p. 31.
7 Ibid.
8 This conclusion is quite compatible with the research findings on stock market efficiency. See Keane, 1983.
9 An example of the cost savings of running an index fund, as opposed to a normal managed fund, is given by the managers of the American National Bank's Index Fund, who claim that their trading costs are less than 0.02 per cent, as compared to the 1½ to 3 per cent for a conventional portfolio. See Keane, 1983, p. 107.
10 *The Observer*, 20 April 1986.
11 The 'fund of funds' development relates to a facility whereby unit trust managers can switch the unit holders' investment between any of the group's trusts without any tax consequences. The potential popularity of these devices is illustrated by the experience of the 'Save and Prosper' fund of funds (its 'Master Fund'), which attracted over £10 million of invest-

ments in the month of November 1985. However, these managed trusts are not without their critics, who argue that they are likely to lead to conflicts of interest as the managers of the individual underlying trust funds may attempt to resist large-scale movements out of their particular funds. In addition, other commentators suggest that a well-managed international fund can achieve equally good results, and avoid the possible disruption within the management group. See, for example, *The Observer*, 27 October 1985.

12   *Sunday Telegraph*, 21 April 1985, p. 26.
13   See, for example, *Investors Chronicle*, 19 April 1985, p. 16.
14   This may be done relatively cheaply through the National Savings Stock Register.
15   See, for example, Winfield and Curry, 1985, pp. 219–21.
16   A survey of unit holders, conducted by the UTA in 1984, showed that the majority of units had been purchased by lump sum investments, and in general had been chosen with the objective of achieving longer-term capital growth or a combination of capital growth and income generation. The survey also found that a high proportion of unit holders were male, over 55 years of age, often retired, with children who have left home. Widows and younger males formed significant minority groups of holders. See, Bulletin from the UTA Information Unit, 16 October 1984, pp. 2–3.
17   Unit Trust Association, *Unit Trust Year Book 1984*, p. 39.
18   See *Investors Chronicle*, 5 April 1985, p. 8.
19   See Reynolds, 1984. Systematic risk relates to the possibility of a downturn in the stock market as a whole. Clearly, no amount of portfolio diversification, at least involving only equities and securities, can remove this risk.
20   According to the 1981 Stock Exchange 'Survey of Share Ownership', unit trusts held approximately 3.6 per cent of UK listed equities by total market value. An estimate by the stockbroking firm of Phillips and Drew in 1982 confirmed this general magnitude (at 4 per cent).
21   Mintel Publications (market research analyst), reported in *The Observer*, 23 February 1986.
22   See *Financial Times*, 13 May 1986, p. 1.
23   See 'The UTA's Response to the Board's Draft Unsolicited Calls Regulations and Cancellation Rules', issued by the UTA on 13 May 1986.

CHAPTER TEN

Investment Trust Companies

The Nature of Investment Trusts

Investment trusts are limited companies whose business is investment of funds, primarily in equity shares of other companies. Investment trusts are not trusts proper, and they do not operate within the confines of trust deeds. These institutions are 'closed end funds', and like other limited companies they are able to raise moneys through issues of equity shares, through issues of debentures and warrants,[1] by retaining income and realized capital gains from previous investments, and so on. Therefore, if an investor wishes to obtain shares in an investment trust company, he must normally bid for these on the stock market, and this action has no immediate financial implications for the company itself.[2] It is only in the special circumstances when there is a floatation of new shares by an investment trust company that an investor may provide equity funding directly to the compnay. Nevertheless, investment trusts provide an important vehicle for individuals and companies to purchase a stake in a much larger and more diversified portfolio than they would normally be able to hold directly, and at the same time to obtain implicitly the benefit of a sophisticated portfolio management service.

Each investment trust company is under the control of its board of directors, operating within the conditions of its articles of association, and subject to the formal approval of actions from the shareholders at company meetings. However, it is usual for the board to concentrate on the setting out of the broad objectives for the company, whilst delegating the actual investment management and administration to specialist individuals and companies. Investment trusts often utilize the services of investment departments of accepting houses or other merchant banks in this respect, although in some instances an investment management firm may be wholly or partly owned by the investment trust company that it manages.[3] Indeed, as will be shown below, in the UK there are some fund management groups which are each responsible for the portfolio management of several different investment trusts.

At any given time the price of shares in an investment trust company will reflect their supply and the demand for them on the stock market. In turn, these variables are likely to be strongly influenced by the value of the company's asset holdings, expectations concerning its future profitability and capital growth, and so on. However, investors in an investment trust do not buy the underlying assets held by the trust (unlike unit trust investors), rather they purchase a general claim on the investment trust company. Furthermore, it must be emphasized that there is no official formula which sets limits within which share prices may move; the value of an investment trust share is purely at the mercy of market forces. The actual cost of obtaining shares will, of course, also depend upon the transactions costs involved in their purchase, which are the standard equity trading costs of broker's commission, value-added tax and stamp duty. Currently, brokers' fees are around 1.65 per cent of the value of a bargain up to £7,000, and 0.55 per cent on the next £8,000, with VAT at the standard 15 per cent paid on these fees. Thus, even with the additional ½ per cent stamp duty, these charges are significantly lower than the normal 5 per cent front end charge on the purchase of unit trust units.

As mentioned above, an investment trust company has the freedom to raise funds from an array of sources. Clearly, to the extent that the company takes on liabilities which must be serviced regularly, whether that be in terms of a fixed interest commitment or one linked to market rates, it will incur charges against the earnings from its asset portfolio which must be met before any distribution of dividends to shareholders can be contemplated.[4] In addition, of course, management fees will be deducted from the gross income of the trust. Recently, these annual fees have averaged around 0.4 per cent of the asset value of the investment trust,[5] which is markedly lower than the annual levy charged by unit trusts (that often being in the region of 0.75 to 1 per cent of asset value). The major reason for this significant difference in annual fees is that the unit trust sector has come to depend heavily upon expensive advertising. This is not so with investment trusts, since as limited liability companies they are forbidden by legislation on companies from advertising with the objective of providing direct encouragement to the general public to purchase their issued shares. In general, they may only engage in publicizing themselves to the extent of informing the general public of their past record and their plans or prospects for the future. The only exception to this is, of course, when a new share floatation is undertaken by a company, in which case the normal rules and legal requirements for stock market issues must be followed.

It should be recognized that investment trusts *per se* suffer no official constraints upon the nature of their investments. Thus, whilst the bulk of their assets are in the form of company securities, there are no legal minimum holdings of listed shares, or maximum holdings of unlisted or unquoted shares for any given size of portfolio. However, any investment trust company which seeks a listing on the Stock Exchange must abide by the listing requirements, which limit its investments in any one company to no more than 10 per cent of its total investments, and its holdings of unlisted shares to no more than 15 per cent of total investments. In practice, it is unusual for investment trusts to invest in small unquoted companies, or to provide venture capital, unless there is strong evidence of an established track record of operations. Investment trusts also have considerable scope in relation to foreign currency transactions, being able both to hedge or take exposed positions in the market and to trade in currency futures and options. Indeed, they are quite free to invest directly in real property (which authorized unit trusts may not), although in practice they hold relatively few of such assets. Therefore, it is clear that investment trusts possess a great deal of flexibility to manipulate their asset portfolios in the light of changing market conditions. Their ability to borrow funds (both long- and short-term) means that they may attempt to maximize the gains from this flexibility, and move quickly to take advantage of new investment opportunities, without necessarily having to divest themselves of existing asset holdings.

The Historical Development of Investment Trusts

The earliest recorded investment trust was formed in 1868 when the Foreign and Colonial Government Trust was established. The purpose of this trust was to allow investors to obtain the much higher returns offered on overseas government securities, relative to the returns available on British government securities, whilst at the same time reducing the risks of a complete loss of investment which might otherwise occur should funds be lent directly to an overseas government. Initially, this trust placed the funds pooled by investors into eighteen overseas governments' stocks, yielding an average 8 per cent per annum return. At that time the return on British government consols was 3 per cent per annum, so despite there being some risks attached to the trust's portfolio it appeared to offer a relatively attractive investment option. The success of this first trust is, perhaps, witnessed by the fact that during the following seven years a further sixteen trusts were formed, each with the specific objective of holding a diversified portfolio of securities on the behalf of contributors to an investment fund.

Initially, investment trusts were constituted as trusts proper. However, in 1879, during legal proceedings against one of these trusts arising from a default on interest payments, it was judged that the trusts contravened the 1862 Companies Act, and that their activities were also illegal under the Lotteries Act. Despite this judgment subsequently being overturned in the Court of Appeal, most of the trusts in fact applied for company status. This trend was encouraged by the growing level of defaults on trusts' investments during the recession of the late 1870s and early 1880s, which meant that the promoters of some trusts were ruined financially due to their personal liability for the trusts' investments. Nevertheless, the trend towards incorporated trusts brought with it a steady growth in their number, and by the turn of the century there were around sixty trusts in existence in the UK.

The early investment trusts were intended largely to attract funds from relatively wealthy individuals. Scotland proved to be a particularly fertile breeding ground for these institutions, with wealthy Scottish industrialists providing substantial amounts of funds to be channelled as capital investments into the growing US economy. Indeed, until the outbreak of the First World War, a very high proportion of the investments of these trusts comprised claims on overseas companies and government bodies. The potential profitability of such investments naturally went hand in hand with their inherent riskiness, and so increasingly the managements of the trusts were able to attract investors through offering access to their amassed knowledge of overseas markets. In 1914 approximately 90 per cent of the trusts' investments originated from overseas. However, shortly afterwards, the proportion of overseas assets in their portfolios began to fall. By the mid-1930s they comprised 55 per cent of the portfolios in aggregate, and by the end of the 1940s the proportion reached its all-time low of 21 per cent. More recently, however, there has been an upsurge in the overseas components of portfolios (as will be described below).

As investment trusts expanded, both in terms of the actual number of trusts and their average portfolio size, it is probably true to suggest that increasingly they became thought of as an appropriate means for the smaller saver to obtain a stake in a professionally managed diversified portfolio. But even by the early 1960s the proportion of investment trust shares held by personal investors was only slightly higher than the corresponding proportion for ordinary shares held in UK companies in general.[6] By that time, around 45 per cent of investment trust shares were held by other institutions, with the insurance companies being especially important in this respect.

Since the late 1960s the ownership of investment trust shares has continued to drift towards institutional investors. Indeed, it would appear that some trust managers have deliberately courted the attentions of institutional investors by raising the degree of specialization of at least some of the trusts under their control. The rationale underlying this move is that institutional investors are likely to hold fairly widely diversified portfolios already, and hence they may wish to build up their interests in specific sectors or geographical regions whilst at the same time gaining the benefits of related expert portfolio management. In addition, there has more recently been a modest decline in the number of separate investment trusts operating in the UK. Thus, in 1978 some 206 investment trust companies made regular returns to the Bank of England, and there were about 30 smaller trusts not required to provide information. By early 1986 there were around 170 active trusts. This reduction has been due largely to mergers and take-overs of companies, together with the voluntary liquidation and transformation to unit trust status in a number of cases. However, whilst the number of individual investment trust companies may have declined somewhat, the total value of investments under their control has risen substantially in recent years.

Between 1967 and 1978, despite relatively high rates of inflation, the total value of investment trusts' assets rose by only about 60 per cent, from around £4 billion in value, to £6.7 billion. The relatively poor performance of UK share prices following the 1973/4 stock market collapse, and the recessionary conditions in most Western nations during the mid-1970s were probably to blame for this phenomenon, but dividend and exchange controls in the UK did not help the situation. The removal of these controls in the late 1970s, and the widespread recovery in the world economy during the early 1980s, provided a tremendous stimulus to investment trust activities, which were helped further by the steady appreciation of sterling between 1977 and 1981 (making overseas assets cheaper to purchase in sterling terms), and its subsequent depreciation (giving the ensuing foreign currency earnings a larger sterling value). By the end of 1985, the aggregate value of UK investment trusts' assets was around £17 billion.

The Current Structure of the UK Investment Trust Sector

Whilst all UK investment trusts share a common legal constitution as limited liability companies, their individual asset holdings and management structures vary considerably. In January 1986 the smallest recorded investment trust company was Vantage Securities, managed by Tarbutt & Co. This trust had a net asset value of just £2 million.[7] By contrast, the largest trust was the Globe, managed by the Electra House Group, and holding net assets valued at £827 million. Between the two extremes there was a diverse array of trusts, with some managed as independent organizations and others managed by larger financial institutions or by members of financial groups. Furthermore, some management groups were responsible for several different trusts, thus giving individual management teams effective control over very substantial amounts of funds. The most important management group in January 1986 was Touche, Remnant which managed eleven separate trusts with total net assets of approximately £1.9 billion.

Table 10.1 lists the major investment trust management groups, together with the number of trusts and total net assets under their control. These ten groups currently control approximately 40 per cent of the total trusts, accounting for around 60 per cent of total net assets.

Table 10.2 lists the largest ten UK investment trusts by net asset holdings. In aggregate these companies, which represented only 6 per cent of total UK investment trusts, accounted for approximately 30 per cent of the sector's net asset holdings at January 1986. It may be observed that the

Table 10.1
UK Investment Trust Management Groups: Largest Ten
Members by Total Net Assets Managed,
31 January 1986

Group	Number of trusts managed	Total net assets managed (£m)
Touche, Remnant	11	1,866
Robert Fleming	10	1,270
Electra House	2	1,118
Dunedin Fund Managers	4	921
Ivory and Sime	11	906
Foreign and Colonial	5	887
Baillie Gifford	7	764
John Govett	4	675
Henderson	5	627
Murray Johnstone	6	602

Source: Money Observer, April 1986.

majority of the largest trusts are managed by groups which are amongst the ten listed in Table 10.1, although three of the largest trusts are independently managed. In addition it should be recognized that some of the largest management groups also manage a number of very much smaller trusts.

Tables 10.3 and 10.4 provide a broader picture of the concentration within the investment trust sector. The data relate to those trusts (the majority) which are members of the Association of Investment Trust Companies, and they show clearly that the degree of concentration within the investment trust industry is somewhat less than that found in many other sectors of the UK financial system, despite the recent merger activity noted earlier.

The majority of investment trusts have the normal corporate status, although there also exist a number of 'limited life trusts'. The simplest form of limited life trust arises where the company is founded on the basis that it will be liquidated after a specified period of time unless the shareholders positively elect to continue the company for a further specified period. The articles of association of such companies dictate the maximum period of time which may elapse before shareholders are obliged to vote on the desired

Table 10.2
UK Investment Trusts: Largest Ten Trusts by Total Net
Assets Held, 31 January 1986

Trust	Management group	Total net assets held (£m)
Globe	Electra House	827
Foreign and Colonial	Foreign and Colonial	652
Edinburgh Investment	Dunedin Fund Managers	610
TR Industrial & General	Touche, Remnant	554
Alliance	Self-managed	494
Scottish Mortgage	Baillie Gifford	472
Witan	Henderson	457
Scottish Investment	Self-managed	397
TR Technology	Touche, Remnant	348
British Investment	Self-managed	341

Source: *Money Observer*, April 1986.

Table 10.3
UK Investment Trust Management Groups: Distribution
by Total Assets Managed, 31 December 1985

Total assets managed by group (£m)	Number of groups	Assets managed as percentage of total for all groups
1,000 and above	3	23.7
800 to 999	2	10.2
600 to 799	2	8.0
400 to 599	6	18.3
200 to 399	8	12.9
less than 200	22	26.9

Source: *Association of Investment Trust Companies, Year Book*, 1986/87.

status of the companies.

A more complex form of limited life trust is the 'split capital' trust (sometimes referred to as a 'split level' or 'dual' trust). In this case the ordinary share capital is subdivided into two distinct classes known as income shares and capital shares. During the life of the trust, all or most of its net

373

Table 10.4
UK Investment Trust Companies: Distribution by Total
Assets Managed, 31 December 1985

Total assets managed by company (£m)	Number of companies	Assets managed as percentage of total for all companies
500 and above	4	15.3
400 to 499	3	7.8
300 to 399	5	10.4
200 to 299	11	15.7
100 to 199	29	25.3
50 to 99	32	14.5
less than 50	80	11.0

Source: *Association of Investment Trust Companies, Year Book*, 1986/87.

income is paid out as dividends on the income shares. The holders of the capital shares receive little or no income. At the liquidation date the income shares are redeemed at a predetermined price (which may only be a nominal value), and all the surplus funds remaining are distributed pro rata to the capital shareholders. During the early stages of the trust's life, it is likely that the capital shares will trade at a high discount relative to their underlying net asset value, as their ultimate worth on liquidation of the company can only be speculative. However, as the liquidation date approaches, the market value of these shares will tend towards their net asset value (after allowing for the associated liquidation costs). For the investor who prefers capital gains to income, perhaps due to his personal tax position, capital shares may be an attractive investment medium although there is obvious risk inherent in their purchase, and this is a risk which will grow the longer is the period prior to liquidation of the company. Similarly, for an investor desiring a relatively high and growing income yield, and perhaps willing to accept a capital loss on his investment in the longer term, the income shares of a split capital trust may prove to be attractive.

A relative innovation is the investment trust savings scheme. This was first introduced at the beginning of 1985 by the Foreign and Colonial Investment Trust, acting in conjunction with the Royal Bank of Scotland. Under this particular scheme investors may make regular contributions into a 'Special Drawings Account' at the bank, the minimum monthly commitment being £25 for non-shareholders (at the time of the scheme's inauguration) or £20 for existing shareholders. Depending upon demand, but in any event at least once a month, the bank will purchase a block of Foreign and Colonial shares and debit the Special Drawings Account correspondingly. As the bank makes bulk purchases of shares, and deals through a single broker, it is able to obtain the benefits of greatly reduced unit transactions costs relative to the amounts which would be payable by individual subscribers to the scheme should they wish to purchase shares directly. Investors receive share certificates for their portion of every bulk purchase made by the bank, and any cash surplus in the Special Drawings Account is carried forward for future investment. The benefits of 'pound cost averaging' for the investor apply in exactly the same way as for unit trust savings schemes. Indeed, the investor may elect to have the dividends receivable on his shares paid directly into the Special Drawings Account, thus giving the investor an asset which has clear similarities to unit trust accumulation units.

Supervision and Regulation of Investment Trusts

Investment trust companies are subject to the requirements of the Companies Acts in respect of their constitutional structure, the issue and redemption of shares, the minimum number of shareholders, the form of and substance of financial reports, and so on. Should they wish to become listed companies, they will also be subject to the listing requirements of the Stock Exchange, which, as mentioned earlier, set broad limits to the nature of their investments in company securities. Where listed investment trusts are involved in merger and take-over activities, they are also subject to the Stock Exchange regulations on these matters. In addition investment trusts may only promote their own shares in the context of a new share issue, and only then through a formally constituted prospectus.

The 1970 Income and Corporation Tax Act, as amended by the 1972 Finance Act, lays down the conditions for investment trust companies to gain 'approval' for taxation purposes from the Inland Revenue. In addition to the company being resident in the UK and listed on the Stock Exchange, it is required to derive most of its income from investments in shares and securities. Also, it should not retain more than 15 per cent of that income, nor more than 15 per cent of its assets should relate to investments in any one company (except in another investment trust), and it should not distribute as dividends any capital gains arising from the realization of investments.

The collective voice and publicity machine of the investment trust sector is the Association of Investment Trust Companies (AITC). This organization performs similar functions to the Unit Trust Association, although technically being a trade association it has no regulatory powers over its members, and it may be seen first and foremost as a mechanism for promoting the interests of its members.[8] The AITC was formed in 1932, and membership is open to any company which operates an investment trust and holds a portfolio of marketable securities. It is important to emphasize that the management groups responsible for the asset portfolios are not members of the AITC; it is the trust companies themselves which participate in the organization. The majority of eligible companies (170 at January 1986) are in fact members of the AITC.

In recent years there has not been complete unanimity over the means by which the AITC should execute its role. Some of the larger members have been unhappy about the industry-wide promotion drives, which, they argue, benefit the smaller companies disproportionately, the expenses of the AITC being met by a levy on members set according to their net asset holdings. One issue over which there has been argument is the association's interest in the ongoing controversy on investor protection. In particular, it has been especially keen to press for the mandatory disclosure of agents' commissions in respect of investment facilities offered to the general public. Understandably, the association wishes to highlight the management costs and other expenses of running investment trusts, which are much lower than the corresponding expenses ultimately charged to investors by many other providers of investment facilities.

Taxation and Investment Trusts

Since the 1980 Finance Act, all capital gains of investment trusts 'approved' by the Inland Revenue, under the terms of the 1970 Income and Corporation Taxes Act, have been free of capital gains tax (CGT). The conditions for 'approval' are listed in the previous section.

For the individual shareholder in an investment trust company, CGT will only be paid on realized capital gains accruing upon the sale of shares, and even here the taxpayer's total capital gains must be in excess of a minimum tax-free amount, which was set at £6,300 for the 1986/7 tax year, before CGT is payable. Therefore, the investment trust shareholder has the same advantage in respect of CGT as the unit trust unit holder, relative, for example, to the investor in a single premium insurance bond. Furthermore, the position of the investment trust company in respect of corporation tax, and the position of the shareholder in respect of income tax, are exactly the same as those described for unit trusts and unit holders in Chapter 9.

UK Investment Trusts: Assets Portfolio

As illustrated by the data in Table 10.5, UK investment trusts have experienced a substantial growth in their aggregate assets, net of short-term liabilities, during recent years. However, the rate of growth has been significantly lower than that experienced by unit trusts in respect of their net asset holdings. As suggested earlier, the dominant element of the aggregate assets portfolio has been company

Table 10.5

UK Investment Trusts: Aggregate Assets Net of Short-Term Liabilities, 1982 to 1984, end-year values, £ million

	1982	1983	1984
UK short-term assets			
Cash and bank deposits	186	273	366
Certificates of deposit	14	14	—
Local authority temporary debt	6	16	44
Other	56	85	125
UK short-term liabilities			
Bank borrowing	(121)	(205)	(162)
Other	(52)	(79)	(93)
Net UK short-term assets	89	104	280
Overseas short-term assets	193	129	212
Overseas short-term liabilities	(33)	(79)	(88)
Net overseas short-term assets	160	50	124
Total net short-term assets	249	154	404
Investments: UK			
British government securities	199	310	306
Listed company securities			
Ordinary	4,245	4,904	5,776
Other	72	71	95
Total	4,317	4,975	5,871

Unlisted company securities						
Ordinary	359		402		546	
Other	57		101		41	
Total		416		503		587
Local authority debt		—		—		1
Public corporation securities		1		1		1
Unit trust units		91		131		192
Other financial assets		99		135		137
Property and other real assets		32		39		32
Investments: Overseas						
Government and municipal securities		290		244		429
Company securities						
Ordinary	4,256		6,570		7,259	
Other	344		396		400	
Total		4,600		6,966		7,659
Other		67		67		36
Total assets net of short-term liabilities		10,300		13,525		15,655

Source: Financial Statistics, April 1986.
Notes:
(1) Liabilities and short-term assets are recorded at book value.
(2) Foreign currency items are translated into sterling at middle-market exchange rates.
(3) Real assets and investments are recorded at market value.

securities, with particular emphasis on ordinary shares. In addition, there was a clear shift towards overseas ordinary company shares during the first half of the 1980s, but the relative importance of government securities (both domestic and overseas) has remained fairly modest. By contrast, property and other real assets have tended to diminish in terms of their relative importance within the portfolio. In terms of the geographical distribution of assets, the recent shift into overseas securities has been largely to the benefit of the United States and Japan, although the strength of the dollar and the yen relative to sterling was undoubtedly partly responsible for the observed changes. These trends are illustrated in Table 10.6. It is also interesting to note the relative insignificance of UK investment trusts' holdings of claims on the rest of Europe.

Short-term assets have tended to remain relatively minor elements of the portfolio, as would be expected for investment institutions whose resources have been derived mainly through share issues, retentions of income and realized capital gains from past investment. Unlike unit trust companies, investment trusts have no commitment to redeem shareholders' (or, in the former case, unit holders') claims upon themselves, and hence the main reasons for holding liquid assets are likely to be in order either to repay fixed term loans which are about to mature, or to be able to take advantage of attractive investment opportunities which may arise at relatively short notice. Figure 10.1 shows the overall distribution of assets by grouping at December 1984.

Table 10.7 illustrates the longer-term trends in the distribution of investment trusts' assets for somewhat more aggregated subgroups of assets. The dominance of investments in company securities is unquestionable, although there would appear to have been a small reduction in the proportion of assets held in this form since the late 1970s. Between the mid-1950s and the late 1970s, this proportion was often in the region of 95 per cent of the total. However, a much more marked trend since the late 1950s has been the shift in favour of overseas securities. In 1962 these accounted for less than 30 per cent of the aggregate assets portfolio, whereas by the end of 1984 they formed almost

Table 10.6

UK Investment Trusts: Geographical Distribution of Assets, 1979 to 1985,
end-year percentage values

	1979	1980	1981	1982	1983	1984	1985
UK	65.0	59.8	56.1	49.8	45.1	45.5	49.6
Total overseas	30.9	37.7	40.8	47.2	53.8	51.9	48.0
of which USA	17.7	21.5	22.7	32.0	30.7	29.4	26.7
Canada	2.3	2.8	2.3	2.5	2.1	1.7	1.0
Europe	2.4	1.6	1.2	1.3	1.6	1.9	5.0
Japan	3.2	5.0	7.5	7.2	14.0	14.3	11.3
Australia	1.7	2.4	2.2	1.5	1.8	7.6	1.0
Other	3.6	4.4	4.8	2.6	3.6	3.0	3.0

Source: Association of Investment Trust Companies, Year Book, 1986/87.
Notes:
(1) Net current assets form the residual element of the assets portfolio base used for calculating the percentage values.
(2) The figures for 1985 are estimates.

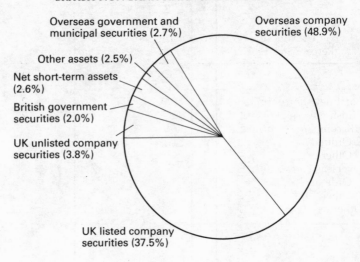

Fig. 10.1 UK Investment Trusts: Distribution of Assets by Grouping, December 1984

Source: Financial Statistics, April 1986.

50 per cent of its value. Over the same period, the proportion of assets held in the form of UK company securities diminished from 60 per cent to just over 41 per cent. Nevertheless, the impression must not be given that the changing structure of the aggregate portfolio has been smooth or without reversals. Indeed, since 1983 UK company securities have regained a little of their lost ground, largely at the expense of overseas securities.

The distribution of investments within the assets portfolio of any individual investment trust company will, of course, depend upon the investment policy of the management team, operating within the broad guidelines laid down by the board of directors of the trust. To the extent that the investment policies of individual companies alter, then over time the structure of the whole sector's aggregate portfolio is likely to change. Whilst a very large number of factors will undoubtedly affect specific investment decisions, in recent years there have been several important events which may be singled out as having had a widespread influence on the investment environment. Of particular significance was the

Table 10.7
UK Investment Trusts: Distribution of Assets by
Percentage, 1962, 1972, 1978 and 1984, end-year values

	1962	1972	1978	1984
Total net short-term assets	0.9	2.5	4.7	2.6
British government securities	2.7	0.7	3.5	2.0
UK company securities				
Ordinary	61.7	56.7	55.9	40.4
Other	4.4	3.6	2.6	0.9
Overseas company securities				
Ordinary	29.1	33.9	31.0	46.4
Other	0.5	1.1	1.3	2.6
Other assets	0.8	1.6	1.1	5.3

Sources: *Financial Statistics*, various issues.

removal of exchange controls on the capital transactions of UK residents in October 1979. However, whilst the greater freedom endowed on investment managers to diversify their portfolios internationally was an obvious contributory factor in the shift towards increased holdings of overseas securities, it is probable that the ongoing deregulation of financial markets, both overseas and domestically, provided an important impetus to this trend. The provision of short-term financing in international markets at increasingly competitive rates, and the growing sophistication of the instruments available to all corporate bodies, can only have further encouraged fund managers to become more flexible in their portfolio selection, and international in their outlook. In the light of this point, and recalling that in recent years the ownership of shares in investment trust companies has become somewhat more concentrated (that is, moving away from the small individual shareholder), it would appear that the operations of at least some of these trusts have reverted towards the emphases noted during the early years of this century.

Finally, it should be recognized that, as with any institution involved in international investment activities, an investment trust's portfolio composition is to some extent at the mercy of market forces, both through exchange rate movements and through changes in the relative strengths of the world's major stock markets. Thus, for example, once an investment decision has been taken, an unexpected appreciation in the exchange value of sterling is likely to reduce the sterling value of assets denominated in foreign currencies. Furthermore, the earning power of these assets, in sterling terms, will also be diminished. However, the portfolio manager may not wish to dispose of the overseas assets, for this could lead to a realized capital loss in sterling terms; and hence he may have little choice but to hold the assets in the hope of favourable exchange rate movements in the future. Similar problems arise when certain major stock markets perform relatively badly. The portfolio manager may feel that he is to some extent limited in his freedom by his past investment decisions. Of course, it could be argued that the astute manager should be able to foresee likely movements in exchange rates, interest rates, and so on, and thus should not find himself wrong-footed by market events. Indeed, the changing trends of expectations probably have a very significant influence on portfolio decisions, and the aggregate effects of these trends are undoubtedly reflected in Table 10.6.

UK Investment Trusts: Medium- and Long-Term Liabilities and Capital

Table 10.8 shows the aggregate values of medium- and long-term liabilities and capital for UK investment trusts for the years 1982 to 1984. By far the largest single item in this context is reserves and provisions. The value of this item reflects the resources which have been generated by investment trust companies through realized capital gains and income from past investments, and which have been retained within the companies. The value for reserves and provisions plus the value for issued shares measures shareholders' equity in investment trusts. In recent years, shareholders' equity has at no time fallen below 92 per cent of the capital funds used by the companies, indicating that the extent to which investment trusts in aggregate have relied upon borrowed funds to finance their investments has been relatively modest. In other words, the gearing ratio within this sector has been fairly low.[9] The borrowed funds which have been employed have been split fairly evenly between loan capital, other UK debt and overseas debt. Also, within the total of borrowed funds, as much as one-half of the value has been denominated in foreign currencies.

The recent growth in reserves and provisions relative to issued share capital is partly explained by the buoyant conditions experienced on most of the world's major stock markets during the early 1980s, together with the general improvement in economic conditions and company profitability. The fact that the proportion of resources generated through loan capital and other borrowing has hardly altered in recent years is perhaps due to the existence of relatively high real interest rates which tend to depress the demand for borrowed funds, counterbalancing the forces which tend to push for higher borrowing when stock market conditions are favourable.

It must be emphasized that the capital structure described above relates to the investment trust sector in aggregate. It may be taken for granted that individual trust companies may have markedly different capital structures, with greater or lesser degrees of gearing and differing proportions of foreign currency borrowing. The precise nature of each investment trust's capital base will, of course, depend upon its management's overall financial objectives, as well as the level of risk they (and their shareholders) are willing to take.

Discounts

As explained above, the price of a share in an investment trust company is determined by market forces of supply and demand. It is usually the case that this price will be somewhat less than the net asset value (NAV) of the share (which is derived simply by dividing the NAV of the trust by the number of issued shares). The difference between

Table 10.8

UK Investment Trusts: Medium- and Long-Term Liabilities and Capital, 1982 to 1984, end-year values, £ million

	1982	1983	1984
Issued shares			
Ordinary and deferred	1,653	1,731	1,879
Preference	138	134	161
Total	1,791	1,865	2,040
Loan capital	296	393	405
Other UK debt			
Sterling bank borrowing	69	73	36
Foreign currency bank borrowing	149	199	271
Other	2	12	27
Total	220	284	334
Other overseas debt			
Foreign currency borrowing	212	339	337
Other	17	15	31
Total	229	354	368
Reserves and provisions	7,705	10,523	12,679
Total	10,241	13,419	15,826

Source: Financial Statistics, April 1986.
Note: The liabilities are recorded at book value.

the share's market price and its NAV is used as the basis for calculating the discount on the share:[10]

$$\text{Discount} = \frac{\text{NAV} - \text{market price of share}}{\text{NAV}} \times 100$$

Several reasons have been suggested for the existence of a discount on most investment trust shares. First, if an investment trust was to be liquidated, not only would liquidation costs have to be met, perhaps including generous compensation paid to the directors or managers, but also the actual amounts of funds realized from the assets' sale might fall short of their current or estimated values, especially if shares were to be placed on the market in large blocks. Secondly, the corporation tax to which investment trust companies are liable may reduce the net income to the investor to below what might have been received had the underlying assets been held directly. Thirdly, the trusts' management expenses must be covered from gross earnings before dividends can be paid to shareholders, thus tending to reduce the value of shares in the company relative to the underlying assets. Finally, the volume of shares traded in investment trust companies may not always be sufficiently large to attract institutional investors, unlike the value of shares traded in the companies in which the trusts themselves invest. Thus the demand for investment trust shares may often be weaker than the demand for shares in the market as a whole. Indeed, the market for shares in the smaller investment trust companies has for many years been relatively narrow, and this has led to quoted prices often being only 'nominal', with the result that the spread between market makers' bid and offer prices has been wider than for shares in general.[11]

Except where a rights issue is planned,[12] the existence of a discount on the shares of an investment trust company may make it awkward for that company to raise new equity capital without harming the financial interests of the existing shareholders. In short, other investors may be able to buy into the company at a price which does not cover the value of net assets underlying the shares, and hence may purchase cheaply the related flow of future earnings. In addition, shares trading at a discount may make the company a tempting target for a take-over bid. A predator may attempt to buy up blocks of shares at a price above the ruling market price, but still at a discount to the NAV, in the hope of obtaining a ready-made portfolio of assets at a bargain price. Without going to the extreme of a full take-over, other financial institutions, such as insurance companies and pension funds, may wish to buy into investment trusts which offer ready-made portfolios with an element of gearing built into the underlying pool of funds.

For the individual investor, the existence of a discount on investment trust shares is only really of concern if there is a desire to sell the shares. In other respects the discount may be advantageous for the investor, in the sense that a given money outlay, even allowing for broker's fees and stamp duty, may effectively purchase shares in a company which has a larger underlying net asset value (and hence larger income-earning potential) than would otherwise be possible. For example, if shares have a market price of 100p, and they stand at a 20 per cent discount, then they would have a net asset value of 125p. Thus, if an investor has £1,000 available, he may be able, after taking account of transactions costs, to purchase £950 worth of shares, but these will have an underlying net asset value of £1,188. It is the latter value of assets which are nominally available to generate his share of the company's income. The shareholder will also find that any capital gain on the company's assets which is attributable to his shares will be larger if the discount falls during the period between the purchase and the sale of the shares. Alternatively, of course, an increased discount would diminish any capital gain which might be realized.

Factors which might lead to an alteration in the discount may operate via market expectations of the trust's future performance. Where an improved performance is expected the discount will tend to diminish. Relevant factors in this context include changes in management or in the investment policy of the trust; a high exposure to an industry sector or geographical region which is expected to produce a very good or bad performance; and the expectation of a possible take-over or unitization of the trust. In addition, general market trends may affect share discounts, with buoyant market conditions tending to reduce the margin. Lower market rates of interest may have a similar effect as equity investments become relatively more attractive. In the short term, the discount on the shares of any particular investment trust company may become larger if substantial holdings of these shares are placed on the market in a single batch. Finally, since it is generally recognized that investing successfully in overseas securities requires somewhat greater management expertise than investing successfully in domestic securities, the service provided by the investment trust company is perhaps more highly valued in this context. Therefore, if a trust company shifts the balance of its portfolio towards foreign securities, then over time it might be expected that the discount would fall so long as this portfolio adjustment is not thought to endanger the longer-term earning power of the company.

Unitization of Investment Trust Companies

Unitization is the term used to describe the process of converting an investment trust into a unit trust. Once the board of directors of the trust has decided in favour of unitization, and the shareholders have been notified of the decision, it is necessary for the company to confirm with the Inland Revenue that the exchange of shares for units will not be considered as a disposal for capital gains tax purposes, and that the company can maintain its investment trust status throughout the conversion period. Without the formal confirmation of the Inland Revenue, the trust itself would be liable for capital gains tax on its own portfolio upon transfer to the unit trust. A liquidator must then be appointed, as well as the trustees for the new unit trust. The Department of Trade and Industry then has to approve the proposed trust deed. At this stage the shareholders are required formally to approve the unitization, whereupon the board hands over the investment trust's assets to the liquidator who proceeds to repay all loan capital (as a unit trust is not allowed to borrow) and to deal with any outstanding warrants issued by the investment trust. Once sufficient assets have been realized in order to cover the redemption of the investment trust's debt and the liquidation costs, the residual assets will be transferred by the liquidator into the name of the new unit trust trustee.

If unitization of an investment trust took place, the shareholders would be transformed into unit holders, with units priced within the limits set by the Department of Trade and Industry formula, and based upon the net asset value of investments held. Thus if shares had been trading at a substantial discount, unitization might appear to be an attractive proposition to the shareholders. However, as implied above, the process is rather complex and costly, and may often take up to a year to complete, during which time market conditions may have altered significantly. Furthermore, the enforced sale of some of the trust's assets in order to cover the repayment of loan stock and to meet other obligations will further reduce the prospect of a profitable outcome from unitization. The advantages of having a fixed capital base which provides stability and continuity to the investment fund, and the ability to gear the fund through borrowing would also be lost. Nevertheless, the availability of unitization may serve as something of a deterrent to inept management of an investment trust's assets.

Gearing

A customary measure of gearing, with respect to investment trust activities, takes the amount of medium- and long-term debt outstanding and divides this by the total of shareholders' equity plus the medium- and long-term debt outstanding. Thus, for example, if a company has £2 million worth of medium- and long-term debt, and its shareholders' equity claims amount to £6 million, then the company's gearing ratio is 25 per cent. As interest payments on borrowed funds, and the ultimate repayment of those funds, must take precedence over the claims of ordinary shareholders, the level of gearing is extremely important to those shareholders. Basically, the gearing ratio will determine the proportionate effect on distributable income of a given percentage change in the net income (before interest) of the company, and the proportionate effect on the net asset value per share of a given percentage change in the total value of the company's asset holdings. Consider the following examples:

Company A: zero gearing.
  Assets portfolio value: £10 million
  Assets attributable to 5 million ordinary shareholders: £10 million
  Net asset value (NAV) per share: £2.
  Now, if stock market prices rise, and the company's portfolio value increases to £20 million, the NAV per share will be £4, thus giving identical percentage increases in both NAV per share and the underlying asset value of the company. The converse effect, with equal percentage changes, occurs when stock market prices fall. Similarly, if the net revenue of the company alters, there will be equal proportionate changes in the income attributable to shareholders.

Company B: 20 per cent gearing.
  Assets portfolio value: £10 million
  Assets attributable to 4 million ordinary shareholders: £8 million
  NAV per share: £2
  Loans outstanding: £2 million.
  In this case, if the value of the company's assets portfolio doubles, the amount attributable to shareholders will rise to £18 million. Thus, through gearing, the shareholders will experience a larger proportionate increase in the NAV of their shares (125 per cent) than the shareholders in Company A (100 per cent). However, the effect of gearing will be detrimental when stock market prices fall. Thus, if the assets portfolio value falls to £5 million (a 50 per cent reduction), the assets attributable to the shareholders will fall to £3 million (a 62.5 per cent reduction). A similar

magnified effect occurs under gearing when the level of the company's net income alters.

Clearly, if an investment trust company is able to borrow funds (and hence raise its gearing ratio) at a time when the stock market is rising, this will always be of benefit to the shareholders in terms of the NAV of their shares. However, from the point of view of income generation, raising the gearing will only be worthwhile if the return expected from utilizing those funds is greater than the interest which has to be paid in order to obtain the funds. The major problem with raising the gearing of the company is that if market conditions are misjudged, not only may the income attributable to shareholders be reduced (even though the company's net income may still be on an upward trend), but any capital losses on the company's portfolio will also affect disproportionately the NAV of the shareholders' claims. Furthermore, borrowed funds entail a commitment to repayment at some future date, and unless the company is able to roll-over its debt, it may find that it is forced to liquidate investments at a time when the stock market is at a low ebb. On the other hand, the holding of a widely diversified assets portfolio by an agile management should give the company some ability to 'degear' without substantial loss. Nevertheless, raising the gearing of the company is a risky strategy, and one which becomes less attractive the higher the market rate of interest and the less certain are future economic prospects. The relatively low levels of gearing within the UK investment trust sector in recent years should, therefore, be of little surprise.

The Performance of Investment Trusts

Given the rather heterogeneous nature of investment trust companies, it is difficult to obtain a general measure of their performance relative to other savings media. The share price of any given investment trust may alter markedly within a very short period of time, and an apparently good return on investment trust shares may quickly degenerate into a poor return. Therefore, it is important that the longer-term trends in performance are considered, although, of course, there is no reason why an astute investor should not make substantial short-term gains through carefully timed purchases and sales of shares. Furthermore, whilst it is usual to consider the average performance of groups of investment trust companies, it must never be forgotten that within any particular group the performance of individual trusts may vary widely, and a reasonable return for the group as a whole may mask a wide array of returns ranging from the excellent to the disastrous. The importance of recognizing the risk inherent in the purchase of marketable equity shares cannot be overemphasized, and ultimately each investment trust must be assessed on its own merits if an informed investment choice is to be made.

Nevertheless, consideration of the aggregate performance of UK investment trusts in recent years is quite informative. The performance statistics reported in Table 10.9 are based on the AITC's standard classification of investment trusts. This involves dividing investment trust companies into twelve categories according to their stated investment objectives. For each category, the average value at 30 April 1986 is calculated of £100 invested in the shares of each trust at various dates prior to that time. It is assumed that the net income attributable to the shares is reinvested in the trust. Thus, for example, £100 invested in the average trust of Group A (which is the most general category of trusts) on 30 April 1984 would have been worth £159.60 on 30 April 1986. For purposes of comparison, Table 10.9 also shows the corresponding values for the Financial Times Actuaries Investment Trust Index and the Financial Times All Share Index. One interesting point which emerges from the data is that for the periods reported, only in respect to a 7-year investment did the investment trust index exceed the FT All Share Index. In other words, investment trusts typically failed to beat the market, and hence the same arguments as outlined in Chapter 9, in respect of the holding of index funds for unit trusts, apply equally here. However, in all fairness, it should be recognized that some groups of investment trusts did perform reasonably well and did

Table 10.9

UK Investment Trusts: Performance by AITC Grouping over 1, 2, 3, 5, 7 and 10 years to 30 April 1986

Group	Broad investment objective	1	2	3	5	7	10
A	Capital and income growth: General	134.5	159.6	211.5	297.6	406.9	687.9
B	UK	144.1	174.3	239.5	320.7	410.4	886.9
C	Capital growth: General	124.4	145.8	181.2	271.1	439.1	679.7
D	International	135.0	156.7	196.2	285.5	391.9	628.7
E	North America	108.8	142.0	145.3	234.6	334.5	549.6
F	Far East	126.8	126.1	200.3	291.8	423.0	744.9
G	Japan	144.8	143.1	232.3	391.8	585.8	877.9
H	Commodity/Energy	83.3	83.1	106.7	119.5	207.6	364.8
I	Technology	111.2	128.3	149.2	237.9	334.0	637.8
J	Income growth	136.3	172.1	214.3	325.1	431.4	703.8
K	Smaller companies	127.8	153.7	192.1	258.0	380.4	736.1
L	Special features	124.6	141.1	186.9	269.1	375.4	635.9
	FT Actuaries Investment Trust Index	132.1	153.8	198.0	279.3	384.7	632.8
	FT All Share Index	135.2	162.5	204.3	292.4	380.7	703.9

Source: AITC, *Performance Statistics to 30 April 1986.*
Note: The figures show the value of £100 invested at the beginning of the period, assuming that all the net dividends received during the period concerned were reinvested in the shares of the trust at the time the shares were declared ex the dividend.

exceed the FT All Share Index in most of the reported periods. The most consistently good performance was returned by Group B, but Groups G and J also generated very good results. At the other extreme, Groups E, H, I and L consistently underperformed the All Share Index. Indeed, investors in the average trust of Group H would have incurred losses over both 1 and 2 years, and even after 3 years the return was a meagre 6.7 per cent in total. This should be compared to the 139.5 and 132.3 per cent returns generated by the average trusts in Groups B and G respectively over the same 3-year period. In recent years, without doubt, the poorest performances have come from the trusts specializing in specific industrial sectors, and particularly those involved with investments in the commodity/energy and technology sectors.

Table 10.10 shows the top ten UK investment trusts by performance over 1 year to 31 January 1986. There is no question that the returns recorded are very good by any standard, but the tremendous difference in returns within the top ten trusts themselves is quite enlightening. Furthermore, there would appear to be little correlation between the value of total net assets managed and performance, or between the broad objectives of the trust and performance. However, during 1985, amongst the non-specialist companies the largest twenty funds as a group produced fairly good results, whilst the largest gains and the largest losses were amongst the medium and smaller funds.[13] This is a similar pattern of results as that achieved by unit trusts categorized according to the amount of assets managed.

Whilst investment trusts may often produce extremely favourable results, it must also be recognized that substantial losses are not uncommon. A recent survey[14] of 154 investment trust companies showed that over the year to 31 January 1986, 9 trusts lost more than 25 per cent of their investment value, and no less than 69 lost some portion of their funds. Furthermore, whilst it must be acknowledged that investment trusts are usually thought of as a long-term investment medium, there were nevertheless 11 companies (from a base of 141) returning losses on investments after 3 years. These figures illustrate clearly the diversity of invest-

Table 10.10
UK Investment Trusts: Top Ten Companies by Performance
over one year to 31 January 1986

Investment trust company	Value of £100 invested	Total net asset value (£m)	AITC category
Lowland	153.1	32	J
Vantage Securities	140.8	2	—
Foreign and Colonial Eurotrust	135.9	24	D
Murray Smaller Markets	125.9	95	D
Jos Holdings	122.9	11	A
Scottish American	122.0	210	K
TR City of London	120.1	137	B
Moorgate	119.0	20	K
General Funds	118.3	66	D
Meldrum	117.8	51	A

Source: Money Observer, April 1986.
Note: Vantage Securities is not a member of the AITC.

ment trust performance, and hence the riskiness of share-holdings in such companies. Of course, in order to minimize this risk, an investor might care to spread his funds between several different trusts, each perhaps operating on the basis of a different investment strategy. Indeed, related to this issue, it should be noted that at May 1986 there were six unit trusts which specialized in the holding of shares in invest-ment trust companies. Whilst all of these unit trusts recorded gains for the year to May 1986, the general level of their performance was below that achieved by the better broader-based unit trusts. Nevertheless, as illustrated by Tables 9.6 and 9.7, the median performance of the unit trusts holding investment trust shares has been quite satisfactory relative to the median performances of the other major categories of unit trusts in recent years.

Investment trusts and unit trusts are often considered as being close substitutes, at least so far as the individual ordinary investor is concerned. Indeed, to the extent that an objective of the investor is to hold an investment which has a value ultimately derived from an underlying diversified portfolio of assets, the two investment media are very similar. However, given the means through which investment trust shares are purchased, and the nature of share price determination, it could be argued that more appropriate bases for comparison of performance are the returns from direct purchases of equities or gilt-edged securities, or the discretionary management of an individual's portfolio by an intermediary. The merits and demerits of the latter forms of investment were examined in Chapter 9. Unfortunately, as was then explained, the form of these alternative investments makes it impossible to derive general conclusions on their performance relative to other forms of investments, including investment trust shares. It can only be reiterated that investment trusts do offer access to a stake in a diversified portfolio of assets, with associated transactions costs being markedly less than would be incurred by the average individual investor wishing to construct a comparable portfolio for himself.

The Future Development of Investment Trust Companies

The data in Table 10.11 show that during the decade 1974 to 1984 the importance of UK investment trust companies, as measured by their stock market valuation, declined somewhat relative to UK listed companies as a whole. However, it is also clear that there was a substantial increase in the stock market valuation of investment trusts during that period which reflected a similar growth in the net asset holdings of those companies. This growth was very much in excess of the rate of price inflation, although it was markedly less than the corresponding growth experienced by UK unit trusts.

It is generally agreed that a significant constraint on the ability of investment trusts to expand their operations has been the restriction on the nature of advertising which they may undertake. Quite simply, a lack of understanding of the operations of investment trusts, and the benefits flowing from the purchase of shares in these companies, probably

Table 10.11
UK Investment Trusts: Market Valuation of Ordinary and
Deferred Shares, 1974 to 1985, end-year values

	Market valuation of ordinary and deferred shares of UK investment trusts (£m)	Total market valuation of UK-registered equity securities (£m)	Investment trusts as a percentage of total
1974	1,510	17,271	8.7
1975	3,445	42,491	8.1
1976	3,175	40,988	7.7
1977	4,201	60,134	7.0
1978	4,084	63,342	6.4
1979	3,873	66,933	5.8
1980	5,782	85,910	6.7
1981	6,123	99,350	6.2
1982	7,322	121,558	6.0
1983	9,670	155,692	6.2
1984	10,991	204,418	5.4
1985	12,265	244,711	5.0

Source: The Stock Exchange, reported in *AITC Year Book, 1986/7*.

depressed the level of demand for shares by ordinary investors relative to what it might otherwise have been. Thus, not only were investment trust companies somewhat disinclined to issue new shares at a heavy discount (which could be seen as harming the interests of the existing shareholders for reasons explained above), but the demand for shares would also probably have been fairly limited in any event. Therefore, the investment trust sector was not as well placed as the unit trust sector to capitalize on the buoyant stock market conditions during the first half of the 1980s. Furthermore, the persistence of relatively high real interest rates can only serve to undermine the future growth prospects of investment trusts, especially following an unusually lengthy upswing in stock market prices. The dangers inherent in raising the gearing of an investment trust company, and in taking on high interest commitments when future stock market trends are uncertain, have already been outlined.

A further reason often suggested for the slower growth of investment trusts relative to unit trusts is that the financial return to investment intermediaries is usually greater if they recommend unit trusts as opposed to advising their clients to purchase shares in investment trust companies. For example, stockbrokers will only earn normal trading commissions on purchases of investment trust shares by clients, whereas most obtain a 3 per cent commission on the sale of unit trust units.[15] The lobbying by the AITC for increased disclosure of the commissions paid to agents of financial intermediaries which took place within the context of the debate on the proposed Financial Services Act is quite understandable, and, indeed, any developments in this respect are likely to be of broad assistance to investment trust companies relative to other providers of investment media. The stability of a closed fund investment, together with the cost-effectiveness of investment trust management operations and their ability to pursue flexible investment options, should underpin the longer-term importance of investment trust companies as a channel for the smaller investor to obtain a stake in a diversified portfolio of assets.[16] Nevertheless, the basic fact remains that an investment in an investment trust company requires the purchase of equity shares, and for many small investors this may still involve the surmounting of psychological barriers.

In relation to government policy on domestic financial matters, the drive for wider direct share ownership by individuals should have been of greater assistance to investment trusts than to unit trusts. This is notwithstanding the initially proposed exclusion from the Personal Equity Plan scheme of investment trusts as well as unit trusts, implying that the authorities viewed these two investment media in a similar light as failing to provide the direct form of share ownership thought to be most desirable. In addition, the Financial Services Act now impinges upon the operations of investment trust companies to the extent that the managers of the funds are obliged to comply with the requirements of the Act and hold membership of an authorized self-regulatory organization. Similarly, investment advisers and brokers have been brought within the framework of self-regulatory organizations acting under the broad supervision of the Securities and Investments Board. The existence of this more formalized supervisory regime should not adversely affect the operations of the majority of well-run investment trust companies, and it may, in fact, bolster the confidence of ordinary individual investors in the respectability and integrity of the investment trust sector, which can only augur well for its longer-term prospects.

Notes

1. Possession of a warrant usually gives the holder the right to purchase shares on or before a particular date for a fixed price. If the actual share price on the date of expiry of an unused warrant is below the price specified on the warrant, then that instrument is worthless. However, the greater is the excess of the actual share price over the guaranteed warrant price, the greater is the potential gain for the holder should he decide to purchase the shares to which he is entitled. Warrants are often issued as part of a package involving new share issues, but are subsequently traded as separate instruments on the secondary market. It should also be noted that investment trust companies may issue convertible loan stock (debentures), which endow upon the holder the right to convert the stock to ordinary shares at a future date at a price fixed close to the underlying asset value. This device effectively provides the debenture holder with the possibility of adding a bonus to his return, and hence may allow the investment trust company to issue debentures at a somewhat lower coupon than might otherwise be possible.
2. However, the existence of convertible loan stock (as mentioned in Note 1 above) should be recognized. Also, on occasions in the past, investment trust companies have issued 'B shares', which involve their holders in receiving no regular dividends, but rather, in lieu, a scrip issue of shares with an underlying asset value equal to the forgone gross dividend. The advantages to shareholders of this arrangement were mainly in terms of limiting tax liability.
3. Some management groups are also responsible for running unit trusts.
4. The implications of gearing within the trust company are considered in detail on pp. 390–2 above.
5. See *The Times*, 20 January 1986, p. 18.

6 See Revell and Moyle (1966).

7 In respect of an investment trust, net asset value is defined as the market value of the company's gross assets less current liabilities and all preferential and prior claim capital loans.

8 In the words of the current chairman of the AITC, the organization's 'central priority' is 'to promote the wider appreciation of the benefits of investment trusts for private investors'. See *The Times*, 20 January 1986, p. 18.

9 The concept of gearing and its relevance for investment trust activities are discussed on pages 390–2 of this chapter.

10 If the market price of a share should exceed its NAV, then the share is said to be trading at a premium, which may be calculated as follows:

$$\text{premium} = \frac{\text{market price of share} - \text{NAV}}{\text{NAV}} \times 100$$

11 Market makers are the stock market traders who buy and sell shares on their own account and thus make the market in those shares.

12 With a rights issue the existing shareholders of the company are given the opportunity to purchase new shares pro rata to their existing holdings, often at a discount relative to the ruling market price of the shares. If all 'rights' are taken up, then all shareholders maintain their pre-existing percentage stake in the company. Where rights are not taken up, an underwriter will usually purchase the 'unclaimed' shares, for subsequent sale on the open market.

13 Wood MacKenzie, *Investment Trust Review of 1985*.

14 *Money Observer*, April 1986.

15 A 3 per cent commission is currently paid automatically to an intermediary if he is registered with the UTA as a provider of a unit trust advisory service.

16 In a number of developing countries, the formation of investment trust companies has been actively encouraged by central governments as a means of overcoming the severe difficulties facing individual savers wishing to place funds with the industrial and commercial sectors.

CHAPTER ELEVEN

The Evolution of British Financial Intermediaries since 1970

Introduction

Since the early 1970s the UK financial system has been undergoing an exceptionally rapid development, with the more fundamental changes in structure coming since 1980. It has often been argued that financial innovation in any particular country is driven by the broader forces of economic development both within that country and throughout the world as a whole. Clearly, whilst this proposition would appear to be intuitively reasonable, it might also be suggested that the basic trends of economic development are themselves strongly influenced by activities within the financial system. It is evident that the efficient and effective channelling of funds to those individuals and companies able to make the best use of them in respect of productive capital investment undoubtedly helps to shape the pattern of evolution of industrial and commercial activities within the economy. Furthermore, the pace of financial innovation in the UK in recent years cannot be explained simply by the concurrent real economic growth, either domestically or in the Western world as a whole. It is probable that the recent high level of adjustment in the structure of the UK financial system is partly due to the removal of official and unofficial controls and restrictions which had tended to store up pressures for change. It may be argued that, had these controls and restrictions not been

402

operational, the pressures for change might not have been generated which have had such marked effects on the financial system in recent years. Certainly, there is no evident justification for the view that in the absence of the now defunct controls and restrictions the financial system would have arrived at the same destination by a different, less spectacular route.

The recent dvelopments in the UK financial system are complex in nature, and there is much controversy over the precise factors which have determined these developments. However, it is possible to identify the fundamental trends, and there are sufficient areas of agreement to allow the broad set of causal factors to be listed, even though their precise interaction and influence are somewhat uncertain. In this context the most visible development has been the rapid growth in the financial services industry. This is not merely in terms of the turnover of funds and of the asset/liability portfolios of financial institutions (which have, in fact, experienced a growth rate significantly in excess of the rate of inflation), but also in respect of somewhat more tangible economic variables such as the higher level of employment and the increased proportion of national income generated by this industry. In short, the UK financial services industry has become an increasingly important element of the UK economy.

The growth of the industry has tended to reflect the growth of the individual financial institutions, but there has simultaneously been a trend towards a greater degree of concentration within most sectors of the industry. This has occurred as institutions engaged in the same or similar lines of business have either merged or been involved in take-over activity, or alternatively as a result of larger institutions growing at a proportionately faster rate than smaller institutions in the same sector. Such moves have been widely observed in the banking, building society and insurance sectors. However, in most instances this trend does not appear to have held back competition within sectors, for not only have the removal of official controls and the dismantling of restrictive practices tended to stimulate intra-sector competition, but the concurrent trend towards

403

diversification of activities has also led to increasing competition between financial institutions based in different sectors of the financial system. Indeed, the establishment of financial conglomerates offering a wide array of services to their customers, and transcending the traditional boundaries of individual financial institutions, inevitably casts doubt upon the validity and relevance of a strictly defined sectoral division within the financial services industry.

So far the bulk of financial services diversification has taken place within the three distinct areas of activity involving the taking of short-term retail deposits (and the making of retail loans), the provision of longer-term savings facilities, and the provision of capital market services. The signs suggest increasingly that much wider diversification of business interests will occur as time passes, and there have already been important exceptions to the general trends. The pressure for greater competition and diversification has been intensified by the third major characteristic of the recent development of the UK financial system, namely the internationalization of financial activities. This has involved not only the growing use of overseas subsidiaries and associated companies to market financial services to a wider customer base, but also the increased willingness of financial intermediaries to purchase assets deriving from overseas and to raise funds in overseas markets.

As implied above, an important catalyst of recent developments in the activities of UK financial institutions has been changes in their regulatory framework. The term 'deregulation' is often used in this context, but the stated intentions of the authorities in respect of investor protection, and the limitation of opportunities for the pursuit of fraudulent activities, would appear to make the term 're-regulation' more appropriate. A major official objective has been to remove distorting and discriminatory regulations and anti-competitive supervisory requirements, rather than to dismantle controls completely. Equity of treatment of institutions within sectors and within specific markets has been the goal, rather than the initiation of a free-for-all in the financial services industry. The encouragement of effective and properly supervised competition is seen as being one of the best deterrents against possible exploitation of users of fianancial services, and the internationalization of activity merely adds a further dimension to the competitive environment.

In respect of the trend towards the internationalization of financial services, the relaxation of exchange and capital controls in major overseas financial markets since the mid-1970s and, in particular, the removal of exchange controls in the UK in 1979, have undoubtedly been important factors, although their occurrence has perhaps been permissive rather than causative. In other words, simply because specific forms of business activities become feasible does not mean that financial institutions will automatically wish to undertake those activities. Commercial motives provide the ultimate driving force for business operations, and conditions in both domestic and overseas financial markets thus provide the key to developments in international transactions. Consequently, great importance can be attached to the growing financial imbalances between nations during the 1970s, and to the increasing financial sophistication of ultimate users and suppliers of funds which offered the opportunity for profitable international financial intermediation activity. Furthermore, the effects of the revolution in computer technology and electronic data processing on the efficiency of international financial transactions have been just as substantial as those experienced by purely domestic activities. Advances in computer technology, interacting with changes in the official regulatory framework, have had marked effects on both the scope of facilities which may be offered by institutions and upon the structure of associated costs, and this in turn has influenced financial institutions' desired portfolio positions. However, it must never be forgotten that the actual portfolios held depend ultimately upon the demand for the facilities of financial institutions, although this itself will be influenced by the ability of institutions to introduce innovations into their products and subsequently to market them effectively. Thus, the markets for financial services have evolved as the supplies of, and the demands for, those services have altered over time in an interactive manner. Just as high-pressure marketing techniques have undoubtedly been used to raise the demand for particular services, which has then been accommodated by a planned increase in supply, so too the pressure of demand for innovative types of financial services has led to their provision as their profit potential has been recognized by institutions in so far as they fell within the bounds of acceptable risk. These interactive supply and demand factors have been at the very heart of the structural changes in the UK financial system since 1980.

In addition to the considerable increase in the physical volume of funds passing through UK financial intermediaries since the early 1970s, there has also been an exceptionally high rate of financial innovation. New forms of marketable securities have been developed in order to provide both financial institutions and ultimate borrowers and lenders with the opportunity to select asset and liability portfolios more suited to their specific financial requirements. In some instances entirely new financial markets have been established in order to trade in new instruments or to provide new services. In both the long-established and the new markets the operational techniques have altered rapidly, and in some cases the methods used for managing funds flows and for coping with financial risk are now fundamentally different from those used only in the mid-1970s. Floating rate interest commitments on securities and loans, the option to convert to equity (in respect of capital market instruments), zero coupon deep-discounted bonds, and so on, have become increasingly popular. So too have the more sophisticated options and futures facilities for hedging risk. The use of foreign currency denominations for financial transactions involving domestic institutions and private individuals has also become more common. Clearly, this latter development introduces yet another form of risk into business transactions, flowing largely from the possibility of unanticipated exchange rate movements, although the gains which may accrue from favourable movements in rates may more than offset this risk.

Some of the observed financial innovations have undoubtedly arisen as a direct response to the increased volatility of financial conditions experienced both in the UK and throughout the Western world since the early 1970s. The level of uncertainty has risen in respect of interest rate and exchange rate movements. International payments crises, relatively high and volatile inflation rates and two major industrial recessions within the space of a decade have joined with the underlying increase in the general awareness of financial opportunities to cause movements of funds both within and between nations to become rapid, substantial and often unpredictable, and hence to increase the risk associated with financial activities. In many cases financial intermediaries have felt obliged to make available new facilities and instruments merely to protect themselves against adverse business conditions, although others have taken a more positive attitude in harnessing the new opportunities for profit-making activities. Specific demands from customers have often been met by the creation of new products, which have then been marketed aggressively in the changing market environment. Financial intermediaries have offered improved versions of existing facilities as well as completely new facilities to replace ones which have been overtaken by events, and have also sought to identify and fill gaps in the market.

Changes in the regulatory framework within which financial institutions operate have already been identified as being crucial to the recent evolution of the financial system. However, official policy on a number of broader issues has also had important implications for the system. In particular, it is generally agreed that for many years the structure of personal and corporate taxation in the UK has had systematic and significant effects upon the portfolio decisions of the users of financial services, as well as upon those of financial intermediaries themselves. For example, it is widely accepted that the personal sector's shift away from direct holdings of equity shares, and towards indirect holdings through claims on pension funds and life insurance companies, has been heavily influenced by the personal tax regime which has traditionally offered substantial tax relief on pension schemes contributions and (until 1984) on life assurance premiums, whilst often penalizing income generated through direct equity investments. Indeed, the relative

favour shown towards capital gains as opposed to investment income for taxation purposes has often led wealth
holders to seek, and intermediaries to devise, investment
schemes which maximize the capital gains potential at the
expense of income generation. Thus the investment decisions of intermediaries, as well as those of ultimate
borrowers and lenders, have been distorted by the tax
regime. However, it must be emphasized that these distortions have not always been deliberate acts of policy, and
they have sometimes been unavoidable side-effects of
policies designed to achieve some other, perhaps socially
commendable, objective. The Conservative government's
commitment to home ownership, and its consequent support
of tax relief for interest payments on mortgage loans, is an
obvious example. The growth of building societies in recent
years can only have been stimulated by this tax concession,
but it may also be argued that the increased competition for
retail deposits generated as a consequence was one of the
factors tending to push up real interest rates in the UK
during the early 1980s, much to the displeasure of the
private business community (whose activities were also
supposedly being encouraged by the government).

A further relevant government policy has been its drive
for wider equity share ownership. In particular, through its
privatization programme and its proposals for personal
equity plans, the government has almost certainly stimulated interest in the potential for profitable equity investment, but in the process it is quite likely that further indirect
investment in equities through unit trusts and investment
trust companies has also been encouraged. Consequently,
the policy may have had disruptive effects on the flows of
funds into the more traditional repositories of personal
savings, and hence again had undesired side-effects on the
interest rate structure. Indeed, many intermediaries have
shown great willingness to exploit these trends by engaging
in a more aggressive marketing of their share purchase and
investment advice facilities. In fact, on a more general note,
the ultimate effects of government policy initiatives on the
development of the financial services industry depend
heavily upon the business strategy of the individual institu-

tions, including the desired composition of asset and liability portfolios and the range of non-intermediation services that they wish to offer.

Ongoing Structural Changes in the Financial Services Sector

Despite the important innovations in the provision of financial services, including the development of new forms of instruments and new techniques of operation, a very high proportion of the recent growth in financial services activity has been generated through an expansion of the traditional financial intermediation services. However, this growth has not been due merely to a raising of the volume of their activity by the long-established providers of specific services. Whilst this has occurred on a wide front, it must also be recognized that most financial markets have experienced the entry of new participant institutions, or at least have seen institutions of formerly negligible significance become important market forces in their own right. An excellent example in this context relates to the rapid increase in lending for house purchases by the clearing banks during the early 1980s. In 1980 the banks accounted for just 6 per cent of total mortgage loans in the UK; by the third quarter of 1982 they were supplying about 40 per cent of the market. Without doubt this action had a fundamental influence on the subsequent competitive environment both for mortgage lending and for retail deposits in general. The changing competitive environment, which was only in part due to the banks' desired portfolio adjustments, also generated substantial increases in outstanding consumer credit, foreign currency lending and leasing activities. The concurrent growth in the provision of fund management services and capital market activities during the first half of the 1980s has led to the widening of interest in longer-term savings media, and in particular in the possibilities for investment through pension funds, life assurance and unit trusts.

In recent years, within the overall growth of activity in the UK financial system, there has been a distinct shift towards the use of financial intermediaries by ultimate borrowers and lenders. As mentioned above, the direct holding of equity shares by the personal sector has given way to investment through financial institutions. The taxation gains available through institutional investment, and the wider recognition of the indirect portfolio diversification opportunities to be obtained, made this course of development almost inevitable. The existence of high nominal, and subsequently high real, rates of interest from the late 1970s onwards, together with the relatively poor stock market performance throughout much of the decade, had the effect of dissuading the company sector from raising funds through the issue of long-term fixed rate bonds and equities. In addition, diminishing rates of return on capital tended to reduce the flow of internally generated funds for British industry. In consequence, many companies were pushed towards bank financing, often on a short-term basis but with the view to rolling-over debt as necessary.

It is, therefore, hardly surprising that the banks, building societies, insurance companies and pension funds dominate the domestic UK financial system. Furthermore, the financial strength concentrated within these institutions has made their own portfolio decisions of crucial relevance to the other developments within the financial system. In particular, the growth in importance of investment in overseas company equities may be traced directly to the insurance companies and pension funds, as well as to unit trust and investment trust companies. Similarly, the trend towards the latter institutions holding a greater proportion of their claims on companies in the form of equity shares is quite compatible with the higher proportion of public sector debt held within their portfolios since the mid-1970s. The natural desire for portfolio diversification within the rapidly changing financial framework, interacting with the government's need to finance large public sector borrowing requirements and to undertake substantial debt funding operations in a non-inflationary manner, has obviously been of great significance in this respect.

It is important to recognize that, despite the shift towards the use of financial intermediaries by ultimate borrowers and lenders, the absolute growth of financial markets and the increasing sophistication of participants have been so great that those individuals and institutions providing advice, information and brokerage facilities in respect of direct investment opportunities have also become significantly more important in absolute terms. Initially, during the 1970s, the role of money brokers gained importance since corporate treasurers were often frustrated in the satisfaction of their financial requirements through the banking system due to the application of monetary controls by the authorities. The setting up of direct borrowing/lending transactions to bypass official controls consequently became increasingly popular. However, the providers of non-intermediary services (that is, those financial services which do not entail a direct effect on the providers' own assets and/or liabilities holdings) have continued to prosper even after the removal of monetary controls and the easing of restrictions on financial intermediation activities. The expansion of the financial services industry, and the complex array of facilities and services now available, has placed a premium on informed and impartial advice for prospective users of financial services. In fact, it is within this broader context of financial services that a number of the longer-established intermediaries have begun to offer advice and assistance to customers in respect of facilities which they may not offer themselves, but for which they may be willing to act as agents.

Underlying the above-mentioned changes in the UK financial services industry have been a number of quite fundamental longer-term structural adjustments within the framework of economic activity as a whole. One extremely important factor has been the steadily rising level of income and wealth, and in particular the resultant growing proportion of the population earning income and/or holding wealth at levels above the threshold at which the desire to acquire financial services tends to grow rapidly. This trend is supported by the fact that, for many individuals, an increasing proportion of income is saved as their absolute level of income rises. Furthermore, as asset portfolios increase in size, irrespective of whether they are held personally or through claims on financial intermediaries, the need for asset management services is also likely to grow, and the potential for introducing an international dimension into portfolio diversification becomes more apparent.

In relation to this issue the abolition of exchange controls in the UK, and the deregulation of overseas financial markets, did not merely provide the opportunity for wider portfolio diversification but also promoted the development of what many observers argue were crucial hedging activities in the face of an increasingly uncertain international trading and investment environment. Prior to 1973 most Western nations operated an adjustable peg exchange rate system, whereby each nation's monetary authorities would intervene in the foreign currency markets in order to ensure the stability of its currency's value relative to the US dollar. Thus, so long as the authorities were able to meet their commitments (through the use of official currency reserves and borrowing overseas), the risks from exchange rate movements for those engaged in international trade and investment were quite small. Once the floating exchange rate regime was introduced the individual participants in the international financial markets had to face a much higher risk in their transactions, and this provided a clear stimulus for financial institutions to design instruments and provide services to help ease this burden. Therefore, a potentially lucrative line of business was made available as a result of the official policy decision to abandon the adjustable peg exchange rate regime, although it was not until the abolition of exchange controls in respect of capital transactions that a full range of financial facilities could be considered.

The future development of UK financial intermediaries will depend heavily upon the evolving pattern of inter-sector and intra-sector flows of funds. Whilst it would seem reasonable to suggest that the personal sector will continue to be a (if not the) major surplus sector, with clear implications for the importance to financial intermediaries of maintaining their base of personal sector customers, the position of the corporate sector is much less certain. Since 1980 the levels of profitability in British industry, as well as its cash flow position, have improved markedly, and if these trends continue the corporate sector's external financing requirements are unlikely to grow at the rates experienced since the late 1970s. Furthermore, the renewed buoyancy of stock market activities, together with the somewhat more restrained sales of long-term government debt and the recently officially sanctioned facility for companies to issue short-term instruments, can only depress the prospects for continuing high levels of corporate sector borrowing from the banking sector. Nevertheless, the banks still provide important financial services in respect of the floatation of equity shares and marketable debt on the behalf of companies. However, a shift back by the corporate sector towards financing in the capital markets can only augur well for the major non-bank investment intermediaries.

A somewhat disturbing possibility for the retail deposit-taking institutions is that the increased financial sophistication of the personal sector may tend to diminish its propensity to hold immediately liquid assets (especially bank and building society deposits) due to the improved access available to credit facilities should the need for funds arise at short notice. Hence it is quite possible that an increasing proportion of surplus funds will be diverted into longer-term savings media. As a result, and somewhat ironically, the more effective and efficient that the retail intermediaries become in providing short-term borrowing facilities for customers, the harder it may become for them to raise funds through retail channels. Of course, the recycling of funds through the wholesale markets may allow the institutions to make good any shortfalls in their own financing requirements, but this is not without important implications for their costing structures and for the nature of financial risk embodied in their portfolios.

To the extent that financial institutions have become more diversified in the range of activities undertaken, future changes in the tax regime related to savings and investment decisions, and the application of official monetary controls, are likely to have a wider impact than in the past, although if the effects are more widely dissipated throughout the institutional system its development is perhaps less likely to be distorted. Indeed, the recent structural changes within the financial system may have strengthened individual groups of institutions' resistance to discriminating policy actions. Related to this issue is the possibility that official monetary control activities may have to be made more complex, or at least applicable to a wider range of institutions, as the provision of near-money assets by non-bank financial intermediaries renders the identification and control of private sector spending power more awkward.

Bank Financial Intermediaries

Since the beginning of the 1970s the purely domestic activities of UK banking institutions have tended to grow somewhat more slowly than those of the non-bank intermediaries, although once foreign currency denominated business is taken into account the broad rates of growth have been quite similar. In respect of domestic activities the commercial banks have often been subject to officially imposed restrictions for monetary control or prudential purposes, and until 1971 the clearing banks operated an interest rate cartel (with the condonation of the authorities). The abandonment of this cartel, as part of the package of Competition and Credit Control regulations introduced by the Bank of England in September 1971, was perhaps the first outward sign that the days were numbered for competitive restrictions within UK retail financial markets.

The opportunities opened up by the Competition and Credit Control regulations undoubtedly contributed to a new mood of optimism in UK banking circles during the early 1970s. Competition became more aggressive and the pressures grew to diversify away from the more traditional banking activities. It was during this period that banks turned increasingly to liability management techniques,[1] utilizing larger amounts of wholesale money market funds. However, this period of relatively unrestricted activity was only short-lived, for whilst banks had greater freedom in their business activities than during the 1960s, the requirements of monetary controls soon led to the re-imposition of direct controls to influence banks' portfolio structures.

414

Specifically, in September 1973, an interest rate ceiling of 9½ per cent per annum was applied to retail deposits with UK banks of less than £10,000,[2] and this restriction stayed in force for a period of 2 years. The implications for the banks' competitive position relative to building societies are obvious enough. In addition, between December 1973 and June 1980, the supplementary special deposits (corset) scheme was applied periodically to UK banks. This scheme set targets for the growth rate of banks' interest-bearing eligible liabilities (effectively interest-bearing sterling deposits with less than 2 years to maturity), with severe financial penalties being imposed upon institutions violating the targets. This proved to be a very powerful restraint on banks bidding for funds in both retail and wholesale markets, with consequent effects on interest rate structures and the levels of competition for funds. Indeed, throughout the period of the mid-to-late 1970s UK banks were not only often constrained on the liabilities side of their balance sheets, but also the Bank of England periodically issued qualitative lending guidelines which were intended to encourage the channelling of funds towards specific forms of economic activity (and in particular towards manufacturing investment and import substitution purposes). Therefore, whilst the Competition and Credit Control regulations had laid the framework for what should have been a much more competitive and dynamic banking sector in the UK, the authorities' more or less *ad hoc* monetary control requirements laid obstacles in the way of free competition, at least in respect of domestic sterling intermediation activities.

However, it must not be thought that this direct interference with banking activities stifled competition within the UK financial system, nor that it excluded banks from engaging in lucrative financial business. It must be recognized that most of the non-bank intermediaries were largely free to vie for a share in domestic personal sector savings and in the markets for overseas funds, although those institutions offering the closest substitutes for basic bank deposit facilities (in particular the building societies and the National Savings Bank) were endowed with a useful opportunity to consolidate their positions in the market for personal sector funds. In addition, the banks were not restricted in their off-balance-sheet activities, which meant that they were able to assist their customers to obtain funds indirectly.

Technically, the process whereby borrowing and lending transactions are squeezed from normal banking channels by the operation of direct monetary controls is known as 'disintermediation'.[3] To a certain extent this activity provided a safety valve for the competitive pressures simmering within the UK financial system during the 1970s. It also tended to frustrate the government's monetary controls, and was an important reason for the ultimate abolition of the distorting direct controls. Nevertheless, many commentators would argue that the monetary control regime was sufficiently effective to bottle up competitive pressures within the financial system and, in particular, to hold back desired portfolio adjustments by the banks. Moreover, it was suggested that the nature of the controls would inevitably lead to severe adjustments of banking activity once they were withdrawn. Indeed, almost as soon as the corset mechanism and the qualitative lending guidelines were abolished by the Bank of England, the banks launched into a period of rapid portfolio adjustment. An early manifestation of this activity was the reintermediation of large volumes of funds which had previously been driven from conventional banking channels.[4] A subsequent, and more significant, adjustment was the banks' foray into the market for mortgage loans. In relation to this action it was undoubtedly the operation of the building societies' interest rate cartel, which had tended to hold rates on mortgage loans below the market clearing level, which provided the commercial stimulus. Given the frustration of many would-be home buyers because of their difficulty in obtaining funds from building societies, and recognizing the premium rate charged by many societies on loans above a specified amount, the banks found a ready market for mortgage loans which they could offer without delay and at competitive rates of interest (especially where the larger-sized loans were concerned). For the first time the pre-eminence of the building societies in the provision of mortgage finance was not simply being challenged, it was being overwhelmed.

However, the belief that a fundamental shift had occurred in the provision of housing finance was short-lived, as by the end of 1982 the banks were pulling back from their assault on the mortgage market. At the time the banks were heavily criticized (particularly by the building societies) for having destabilized an important domestic financial market, but with hindsight the banks' behaviour was only to be expected. One of the banks' objectives was to make a delayed asset portfolio adjustment, rather than to raise substantially and permanently their flows of new mortgage loans. Nevertheless, there is some evidence to suggest that in their haste to attract business (and the more lucrative transactions) they may have overshot their target portfolio adjustments. In any event, doubts were raised about the wisdom of banks taking on to their books a rapidly expanding volume of illiquid assets. Furthermore, as mentioned above, many banks were also experiencing strong demands for funds from the corporate sector during the early years of the 1980s, and hence there was certainly no shortage of potentially profitable outlets for their available funds in areas other than the mortgage market.

Despite their general eagerness to challenge other UK financial intermediaries in areas where their expertise might not be at its strongest, UK banks were not without their own problems at the beginning of the 1980s. The earlier shift towards the internationalization of their lending activities had left a number of banks holding substantial claims against borrowers whose creditworthiness had become extremely suspect. In the late summer of 1982 the sovereign debt problem was thrown into sharp focus by Mexico's threat that it would default upon its debt servicing commitments. At the same time, domestic banks found that the challenge from overseas banks was arising on a wider front, and in a more aggressive form. The overseas banks began to pose a serious threat, especially in relation to corporate customers, being able to offer innovative financial packages at costs which the domestic banks found hard to match. Indeed, during the early 1980s, the pressure was also increasing from domestic non-bank financial intermediaries, particularly in respect of the retail deposits markets. This was, in fact, one of the major factors underlying the growing shift by the clearing banks towards liability management through the wholesale markets.

Since 1983, the apparently greater sensitivity of savings flows to interest rate movements, and the introduction by some non-bank financial intermediaries of interest-bearing accounts with money transmission facilities attached, would appear to have pushed domestic banks into the position where they had no alternative but to fight back (or else risk losing large portions of their traditional private sector business). Recognition of the importance of tapping the surplus funds of the personal sector has made the market for retail deposits the main battleground. Current accounts paying interest, 'free banking' for zero-interest current account holders remaining in credit, specially designed saving schemes for target groups, the intensive marketing of related retail financial services, and so on have become the norm for the major clearing banks. Related to this is the development of cash management facilities for small businesses, and a willingness to show more sympathy for the financial problems of the small unincorporated business. In addition, the marketing thrust of many banks has involved a revitalizing of their rather aloof image. They have become increasingly sensitive to the research findings that the non-bank institutions are often seen as being friendlier, more understanding and more accessible than banks. The introduction of open plan customer areas with modern décor, and the relegation of routine cash transactions to the background, often through the use of automated teller machines, is merely a part of the banks' response. The reopening of branches on Saturday mornings, and the establishment of outposts within department stores and shopping areas, is perhaps an even more important recognition of the need to satisfy customer requirements on their terms. A solid base of retail customers is now seen as being crucial to banks' efforts to market their wide range of services, many of which could be of use to the ordinary personal customer.[5]

It is widely accepted in banking circles and beyond that there can be no return to the earlier days when the average bank or building society personal customer showed almost surprising naïvety in the management of his financial affairs. Competition between financial institutions and a greatly improved consumer intelligence has raised the average level of financial sophistication within the financial system beyond recognition. In many respects, the textures of retail and wholesale business have become less distinct as the responsiveness of participants in retail markets has become much more sensitive to conditions in the financial environment in general.

Developments in Technology

The fundamental impact of advances in technology on the financial services industry is unquestionable. But what is far less certain is how the introduction of new technology will influence its evolving structure. An inherently destabilizing feature of the technological revolution is that it is fed by the very same competitive forces which it is itself intended to feed. Thus, for example, a basic form of automated teller machine (ATM) may be introduced by one bank as a means of holding down the growth of labour costs, with a view to allowing pricing structures for services to be set more competitively. But this action may be seen as a threat to the retail services of other institutions, which may then feel obliged to introduce a second generation of machines providing a wider range of facilities for their customers. At this point the ATMs may become the focus of competition between certain institutions, rather than simply a means of holding costs in check to the benefit of other services. Indeed, a possible irony of this occurrence is that once institutions begin to compete over technology, the direct costing issues may be pushed into second place behind marketing considerations, thus making the net benefit to customers extremely difficult to assess.

Notwithstanding the doubts which may exist as to the direct net gain to financial institutions and their customers of the introduction of advanced technology into everyday transactions, there is no question that it has now become a part of the established package of financial services expected from retail financial institutions. The ATMs, and in particular automated cash withdrawal facilities, are now taken for granted by most bank and many building society customers. Home banking and electronic funds transfer at the point of sale (EFTPOS)[6] have been much slower to take off in the UK, but the signs are that once their potential is recognized by a sufficiently large number of retail customers then the competition in these areas will become just as intense as for any other retail financial services.

An important implication of electronic funds transfer is that the optimal size of branch networks for financial intermediaries is brought into question. The reason is that advanced technology means that customers have less need to travel to their bank or building society in order to undertake financial transactions. Remote ATMs may be located in department stores, shopping precincts and public buildings. A unified EFTPOS network could extend to the majority of sales outlets, and home banking does not even require the customer to leave his own home. For institutions with large investments in branch networks, and in the commensurate staff complements, the issues raised are of the greatest importance. It would appear that, if widespread rationalization of branches is to be avoided, then the only option available is for institutions to diversify their range of services thereby allowing their branch networks to be used more intensively. The spreading of branch overheads is likely to become ever more crucial to the overall competitiveness of institutions, particularly as the capital costs of the new automated systems are often substantial.

The problems raised by technology are perhaps most severe for banks. Because they were at the forefront of the implementation of technology to the provision of financial services, many of their earlier systems rapidly became obsolete, and even second generation systems are currently looking decidedly out-of-date. Banks have often had to carry the expense of developing both hardware and software systems, only to see their work overtaken by the introduction of much more sophisticated products. The awakening of many other institutions to the potential of computer technology has been relatively recent, and hence they have often had the advantage of being able both to purchase tried and tested equipment 'off the shelf' and also to utilize the services of computer consultants whose numbers have also grown rapidly in recent years. This has not only meant that these financial institutions have been given a competitive edge in the use of certain forms of technology, it has also allowed installation and operation costs to be kept within manageable bounds. A related issue is that technological advances have placed within the reach of relatively small-sized financial institutions the prospect of being able to provide services (on a commercially viable basis) which were previously restricted almost exclusively to the large clearing banks. Moderately priced computer systems may now undertake data storage and processing functions which would formerly have required labour-intensive operations only viable for the largest institutions running a national branch network. Money transmission services have been especially amenable to such automation, and competition in this line of business is of great relevance to banks given the above-mentioned importance of securing the retail savings deposits of the personal sector.

Whether or not future technological advances will be of greater assistance to the development of small to medium-sized financial institutions than to the development of the larger institutions is an open question. There are undoubt-edly economies of scale to be obtained through the intensive use of expensive equipment, but with the advent of the microprocessor and the difficulties arising in attempts to interface the different computer systems which may exist within the component parts of a large organization, it may be that the net gains from large-scale operations are minimal. Indeed, the ability to use computer technology as the basis for offering tailor-made financial service packages to customers may provide efficient but small institutions with the chance to establish their own niche in particular markets. In addition, whatever the size of the institutions, the power of computers to store and process information on customers' personal financial characteristics provides an extremely useful aid to marketing activities. Targeting of specific groups of customers for the offer of new or revamped services may be both cost-effective and successful in pre-empting their defection to competing institutions. In short, computer technology may allow institutions to obtain the best return from their ongoing diversification of services.

The Internationalization of Financial Services

The internationalization of the UK financial services industry goes well beyond the provision of normal banking facilities in relation to the financing of international trade and payments. Certainly, there has been an upward trend in international trade during the postwar years (but with some retrenchment during the 1974/5 and 1979/81 world recessions), and payments imbalances have grown substantially. However, the more fundamental issue in respect of the development of UK financial intermediaries has been the general internationalization of outlook of their management strategy. With the exception of the building society sector and the National Savings movement, UK financial intermediaries have become increasingly involved with activities having an international dimension. Some institutions have established branches or subsidiaries overseas in a deliberate attempt to broaden their customer bases; others have begun trading in financial instruments originating overseas. UK insurance companies, pension funds, unit trusts and investment trust companies have raised significantly the proportion of their portfolios held in the form of foreign company and government securities. In addition, it must be recognized that the internationalization of financial activities has not simply been in one direction, for just as UK financial institutions and market participants have seen the benefits from a broader diversification of activities and portfolios, so too foreign institutions and investors have seen opportunities for profitable transactions in the UK. Branches and subsidiaries of foreign institutions have been established in the UK, and have posed competitive threats not only to UK banks but also to non-bank intermediaries with respect both to wholesale and retail business. Whether it be, for example, in relation to the provision of mortgage loans, of venture capital, or of life assurance facilities, there is generally foreign competition to be found in the market. The choice for the user of financial services is clearly improved, and the extra competition should help to maintain trading standards. However, it must never be forgotten that the introduction of new forms of risk may pose dangers for those market participants hitherto unfamiliar with international transactions.

In recent years, the official position on the internationalization of UK financial services has been one of broad encouragement. The Bank of England has openly welcomed foreign participants in the UK financial system, especially as a means of improving consumer choice and enhancing competition. But the Bank has also sounded warnings that foreign incursions must remain within acceptable limits. It would appear that the Bank (and by implication the government) would not be disposed to allow the take-over of important sectors of the UK financial system by overseas-based companies.[7] Furthermore it would seem to be probable that the official blessing for foreign participation in the UK financial system is directed largely towards wholesale activities, and towards securities transactions in particular. The political implications of having UK building societies or other savings institutions channel massive volumes of funds to the more prosperous regions of Western Europe, or even to the Far East and North America, have perhaps not yet been fully absorbed.

The Building Society Sector

The building society sector is an extremely important element of the UK financial system. This is not merely because of the absolute volume of funds under its control, but more critically as a result of its pivotal position in relation to the ongoing evolution of the financial system. It is perhaps testimony to the unique status of building societies in the UK, and to the inventiveness and skill of their managements, that they have been labelled as the main competitors of the banks on a retail level whilst at the same time being restricted to a very narrow range of activities by an outdated legislative framework. Indeed, it is perhaps trepidation with respect to the impact that the building societies may have on the financial system should they be given a freer regulatory environment that has led to the heated debate over the extent of the proposed changes in the legislative framework.

During the 1970s the building society sector grew rapidly, largely at the expense of the market share of National Savings, but also to some extent at the expense of the major clearing banks. Quite simply, the building societies were able to tap the growing financial surpluses of the personal sector by offering straightforward services easily understood by ordinary people. Interest rates paid on savings have also been relatively good, with the composite tax rate scheme meaning that most savers have had no worry about paying tax on their interest earnings. In addition, the prospect of home ownership has been made more attractive by the tax concessions on interest payments on mortgage loans, and by the fact that residential property has proven to be one of the best hedges against inflation.

In the main, UK building societies have an image of reliability, accessibility and friendliness towards their customers, and it is this image that most building societies are aiming to exploit as part of their development strategy following the enactment of the Building Societies Act 1986. The fundamental problem in this respect is that any shift in the nature of services offered and in the methods of marketing employed may undermine the reputation of societies for reliable, good quality service. It is perhaps for this reason that many senior building society managers have gone out of their way to emphasize that it is their intention that the emphasis of their business will not alter in the aftermath of the new legislation. Rather, they view the new freedoms to be gained as providing an opportunity for the consolidation of their existing services. Nevertheless, the possibility of being able to offer unsecured loans to customers (to furnish their new homes) has been welcomed by many building societies, as has the prospect of being able to provide other services required by the home buyer. Whilst the extent of such activities has been placed within strict limits in the Building Societies Act, the sheer scale of building societies' operations and their ready access to a large proportion of the adult population of the UK have generated visible concern in other sectors of the financial system and amongst the providers of certain related professional services.

. The implications of building societies offering services closer akin to those available from banks are undoubtedly important, but at the same time they must be kept within a proper perspective. For many years the volume of building society funds ultimately channelled towards expenditures not related to house purchase is believed to have been substantial. Quite simply, as home owners have moved house they have taken out larger mortgage loans than required, and consequently have released equity from their investment in property. Similarly, an increasing number of homes are being inherited by individuals who have no direct use for them, and hence when these properties are sold to people utilizing borrowed building society funds the original mortgage loans leave the housing market completely. Consequently, the real issue is not so much the ultimate use of building society funds but rather the security against which those funds are to be lent. A first mortgage on a residential property provides one of the best securities available for a financial institution. It is the prospect of massive amounts of unsecured lending that causes concern in some circles. Thus it is argued that if building societies are to maintain absolute confidence in their activities, they must cover adequately the risk associated with unsecured lending by holding appropriate levels of reserves. Unfortunately, the capital bases of many societies are not sufficiently strong when evaluated against the standard criteria applied to banks. Furthermore, in the absence of corporate status, the only way in which societies may build up their reserves is through the generation of surpluses, and this has recently been made more difficult by the increasingly competitive environment in both mortgage loan and retail deposit markets.[8] Therefore, any society wishing to diversify its services, especially in respect of on-lending, will most certainly have to look carefully at its operating efficiency, and will have to consider the role of computer technology and the justification for large branch networks. Indeed, the larger building societies are in a similar, though less extreme, position to the clearing banks in relation to this issue. The desire to utilize branch networks more intensively by offering a wider range of services is a natural reaction for societies, but the limitations they face in terms of the skills and experience of staff provide an obvious handicap. Consequently, the possibility of agency work for insurance companies, pension funds and the like may be an attractive proposition for some societies. Simply acting as retailers of financial products on behalf of other institutions, and collecting a fee or commission on sales made, may allow societies to improve their services to customers but without the business risks which may attend the direct provision of such facilities.

The belief that building societies will turn themselves into banks within the new legislative framework is probably quite unfounded. Certainly, some of the large societies will undoubtedly offer more facilities with a banking flavour, but even in respect of these it is widely accepted that individual institutions may be obliged to buy in the necessary expertise. To turn themselves into banks would not make commercial sense; existing skills and expertise would be wasted and their valuable public image would be placed in jeopardy. Societies may, of course, develop links with other types of financial intermediaries to a much greater extent than has been experienced in the past. At the extreme this could lead to mergers between societies and other (perhaps banking) institutions, but the more likely route in the shorter term is through collaborative arrangements. For example, societies might intermediate with other institutions by parcelling mortgages for sale in blocks, or by participating in the securitization of mortgage loans,[9] which would not only create a secondary market in mortgage loans but would also help building societies with their own cash flow management. This activity would also serve to transform retail claims on borrowers into wholesale financial instruments, which is perhaps not so unrealistic given the increasing use of wholesale funds by building societies to make retail mortgage loans.

A view held by many observers is that building society interest rates are likely to become more volatile in future as societies discover the need to react more quickly to changes in the financial environment. If this does come about then it is unlikely that queues for mortgage loans will return. Higher rates of interest on both deposits and loans will tend to attract increased inflows of funds, whilst at the same time choking off the demand for loans. Existing depositors will gain from this action, but existing borrowers will find their interest commitment increasing. A further consequence is that societies will have less need to hold high levels of liquid assets, and a higher proportion of funds attracted may therefore be on-lent. The tapping of the wholesale money markets (by the larger societies) would tend to support this trend. However, a countervailing force, which could push for higher rather than lower levels of liquidity, may arise if societies seek to offer additional services, perhaps related to money transmission activities.

There are several directions that the development of the building society sector may take. One commonly floated possibility is that the sector may divide into two or three subgroups. The relatively small number of very large societies (perhaps the top ten by asset size) may form one group which not only controls a large proportion of the total assets of the sector, but also is the focus for the major innovations in activities. These institutions are likely to make increasing use of wholesale funding sources and be at the forefront of the application of technology to the provision of retail financial services. Access to this particular group of societies might come about through a preliminary round of mergers between somewhat smaller institutions attempting to achieve the scale of operations thought to be necessary for the efficient provision of newer services. It should, however, be noted that recent experience has shown that mergers between societies which would have given their unified body unquestioned 'first division' status have not been easy to achieve.[10]

The second broad group of societies may contain the relatively small institutions dependent upon strong local connections. Their specialist local knowledge, and their ability to maintain the traditional characteristics of building societies, may perhaps ensure their continued survival as relatively narrow intermediaries servicing local needs. In this context it is the third group of societies which would appear to be most at risk from developments within the financial sector. These are the medium-sized institutions which lack a national base. Such institutions may be too large to benefit from the specialist niches available to local institutions, perhaps losing their individual identity in the process of competing for market shares whilst at the same time being too small to take advantage of the opportunities for new activities involving wholesale funding, unsecured lending, and so on. However, an important counter-argument is that advances in computer technology and developments within the financial system as a whole may have made the provision of certain facilities somewhat more viable for institutions which are not of the largest order. Nevertheless, operational efficiency is of crucial significance to all institutions. Without the interest rate cartel to offer protection to the weakest members of the sector, the competitive pressures are likely to cause inefficient institutions to be left behind, with their future prosperity placed in doubt.

A final, somewhat controversial issue, relates to the importance or role of building society managements in determining the future evolution of their sector. The mutual status of building societies, many of which have huge memberships caring little to become involved with the management decision-making of their organizations, effectively places the power to determine their strategic planning into the hands of their managers. Thus the managers of building societies are probably in a unique position in respect of their freedom of action. This obviously makes the supervisory framework of crucial importance in providing checks on the possible abuse of power by managers, including their taking of excessive risks with savers' funds. The higher levels of competition in the building societies' traditional markets make this issue all the more pertinent. However, the argument is sometimes heard that the organizational structure of societies is such as to foster excessively conservative decision-making: a satisficing approach to strategic decisions, particularly in respect of staffing issues, being favoured over a more aggressive style of management. This issue remains unresolved, and yet in many respects it is likely to be crucial to the future evolution of the building society sector, and ultimately to the structure of retail financial activity in the UK.

Notes

1 Liability management involves institutions in seeking out funds in order to meet commitments to on-lending. The more traditional approach to banking activity in the UK has been based upon asset management whereby suitable uses are sought for deposited funds already in hand.

2 It should be recognized that during the period 1973 to 1975 the UK was experiencing historically high rates of inflation, and hence the 9½ per cent interest rate ceiling represented a significantly negative real rate of interest.

3 An important form of disintermediation during the mid-to-late 1970s became known as 'the acceptance bill leak'. Quite simply, being unable to provide even the most creditworthy of corporate customers with the loans that they desired (due to the operation of monetary controls) banks would invite these customers to issue bills of exchange which they would then 'accept' for a fee. By doing this the banks guaranteed payment on the bills upon maturity, and hence turned the bills into 'bank bills' which are highly marketable on the money markets. The corporate customers would then sell the bills (have them discounted) at very fine rates, and hence would obtain funds through the money markets on reasonable terms. Thus the banks were able to help their customers to obtain funds without there being any impact upon their balance sheets. The bank earned a fee for the provision of the acceptance services, and the only risk carried by the bank was if the customer should have insufficient funds available to discharge the underlying debt through the bank upon the maturity of the bills.

4   An unfortunate side-effect of the reintermediation was that a significant boost was given to the growth rate of £M3 as banks returned to making loans (creating deposits) for corporate customers instead of facilitating the use of pre-existing funds through the money markets. But despite this it is believed that the process had little net effect on private sector purchasing power in aggregate, thus meaning that the interpretation of the £M3 statistics was distorted.

5   It was reported in the January 1985 edition of *Banking World* that the average branch manager of a UK clearing bank had approximately 120 different financial services available to offer to his customers. Since that time the number has undoubtedly grown.

6   Home banking relates to the facility for personal customers to initiate financial transactions as well as to access financial data from their own homes using a microcomputer with keyboard and visual-display screen linked to the financial intermediary's computer system through the British Telecom network. Such forms of electronic banking have been available to corporate customers of certain banks for several years. The large US banks based in London have been at the forefront of these developments. EFTPOS allows funds to be transferred instantaneously between customers' accounts (as the counterpart to purchases/sales of goods or services), again utilizing a simple processor unit at the vendor's place of business linked to the financial institution's computer system via the Telecom network.

7   On this issue see *Bank of England Quarterly Bulletin*, March 1985, p. 45.

8   Near the end of 1985 the Chief Registrar of Friendly Societies made public his worries that societies might not be sufficiently strong financially to meet the pressures which would be placed upon them by the development of new services. He expressed particular concern about societies' capital ratios. On this matter see *The Times, Special Report on Building Societies*, 14 April 1986.

9   Securitization means that marketable securities are floated which are backed by a bundle of mortgage loans. Individual borrowers from building societies could then effectively find the claims against them being traded in the open market. There are currently certain legal and technical problems related to this activity, but tentative steps have already been taken in this direction by the National Home Loans Corporation (an independent mortgage intermediary company floated in September 1985). Interestingly, the Building Societies Association has put forward proposals to the government for a code of practice in relation to securitization which, if accepted, would probably make it more difficult for other institutions to gain a

foothold in the market. It is proposed that individual borrowers would have to give their permission explicitly for their
mortgage debt to be transformed. Although this would not
affect the borrowers' legal position in respect of their commitments, it would seem to place the onus upon those wishing to
operate a securitization facility to convince individual borrowers of their case. On this issue see *The Times*, 8 May 1986.
10 See *Financial Times*, 10 July 1986.

CHAPTER TWELVE

The Regulatory Framework

The Regulatory Environment

The activities of all individuals and institutions within the UK are subject to limits established by the law of the land. The maintenance of the social framework and good order in the relationships between individuals and institutions requires that sanctions must be taken against those who would violate the requirements of the law in the pursuit of personal material gain, or as the result of wanton disregard of the welfare of others. However, in addition to the broad principles of justice which underpin the operation of the modern democratic state, it has been deemed necessary for specific regulatory frameworks to be formulated in respect of particular areas of business activity. In order to protect individuals and companies from exploitation, either through deliberate misrepresentation of the substance of transactions and activities or as a result of their lack of knowledge of the technicalities and commitments associated with transactions, the state has often introduced relevant legislation. The Sale of Goods Acts, the Trades Descriptions Act and the Companies Acts are just three of the better-known examples of action in this context. Through the common law, the judiciary has also established precedents concerning acceptable business behaviour. In addition, it has been traditional in many areas of activity for professional and trade associations to formulate rules of good conduct and codes of practice for their members, which, although lacking any legal basis, have provided powerful pressure for conformity and good behaviour.

432

The recognized importance of the financial system to the economic body of the nation has meant that the activities of participants in financial markets have tended to be subject to a disproportionate amount of regulation and supervision, through both the state legislative and judicial machinery and (extensively) through self-regulatory mechanisms. The complexity of many financial transactions, and the potentially serious consequences for both individuals and companies of entering into commitments which prove to be more onerous than was initially believed would be the case, has generated widespread pressures for the close supervision of activities.

Traditionally, the emphasis of supervision in the UK has been placed upon the honesty of the provider of financial services rather than upon his technical competence to provide the service. However, the issue of financial services supervision spreads well beyond the protection of the naïve from their own ignorance and the inept from their own greed. The complex interrelationships between financial institutions and between financial markets have placed the fear of chain-reaction defaults, widespread losses of confidence and unmanageable financial crises firmly into the minds of influential commentators, regulatory bodies and successive British governments. In short, the desire to maintain the stability of the financial system, and hence to support economic activity as a whole within the country, has tended to dominate the thoughts and actions of those with the power to influence the regulatory framework of the UK financial services industry.

Despite the amount of attention paid to the regulation of the financial services industry, the treatment of its component parts has been relatively uneven. The evolution of the regulatory framework in the UK has resulted in some activities being closely controlled with legal responsibility being vested with government departments (for example, the Department of Trade and Industry has been responsible for the insurance sector and for the activities of unit trusts); other financial institutions have been supervised by non-governmental public bodies operating with varying degrees of formality (the Bank of England in respect of the banking sector and the Registry of Friendly Societies in respect of the building societies are good examples of this form of supervision); and yet other areas of activity have effectively escaped specific formal controls. Furthermore, as the controls which have been operated have usually been applied to identified groups of institutions, it has been possible for very similar activities to be supervised in markedly different ways merely because they were undertaken by institutions placed within different categories for control purposes. The recent developments in relation to the supervision of financial services in the UK have tended both to formalize and to standardize the framework, with the objective being to strengthen the protection offered to the users of financial services whilst at the same time to make more equitable the requirements to be placed on the providers of financial services. There has also been a trend towards the removal or at least the reduction, of restrictive practices which might limit free competition within the financial system.

A fundamental dilemma facing all regulators in the process of formulating the rules and norms of acceptable behaviour for institutions within their remit is that the desire to construct adequate safeguards for the users of financial services may effectively result in a conservatism of institutional behaviour which stifles initiative and suppresses competitive forces. The supervisory framework may inadvertently legitimize barriers to entry for would-be participants in markets, and may foster inefficient working practices which can only be to the ultimate detriment of the users of the financial services. Recognition of this problem in recent years has led to a much greater emphasis upon the importance of competitive forces *per se* as a check on the exploitation of users of services. However, it must be stressed that other than in respect of the trustee savings banks and the building societies, the traditional demarcation of financial services in the UK was not due to statutory requirements. Rather, the financial structure evolved within the framework of informal guidelines for the 'appropriate' scope of business for specific institutions laid down by bodies such as the Bank of England, the Department of Trade and Industry, and the Stock Exchange. The attitude of many professional bodies, certain requirements of the Companies Acts and the fiscal privileges offered in relation to fairly narrowly defined financial services, merely served to consolidate the position. It was only after the mid-1960s that attitudes became somewhat more liberal in respect of the range of activities which were deemed to be acceptable for certain groups of institutions. But the fundamental shift of opinion has taken place only since the mid-1970s, with the increasing threat of international competition and the recognition of the business potential of diversified financial activities.

The arguments in favour of freer competition and the removal of restrictive practices within the financial system are logically sound and widely accepted. However, it must never be forgotten that without adequate safeguards free competiton may rapidly degenerate into a free-for-all, where the prospect for short-term profits attracts market participants whose credentials may be inappropriate to say the least. Thus there arises the rationale for the self-regulatory organization to oversee the activities of its members (who are engaged in the provision of a particular form of financial service), but operating within a formal legal regulatory framework. Quite simply, a self-regulatory organization which is run (and perhaps financed) by the institutions and/or individuals offering a particular class of financial service not only has available the expertise and technical skills to be able to scrutinize the applications of aspirant members of the group, but it also has a vested interest in maintaining the business standards and the confidence of potential customers. Nevertheless, there is always the danger that self-regulation may be viewed as little more than a number of 'clubs' for market participants which may pay only cursory attention to the rights of customers whilst seeking to protect the interests of members. Thus there must be adequate formal controls in order to ensure that the rules and operations of the self-regulatory organizations are themselves fair and effective, and that a satisfactory balance is struck between the needs of customer protection and those of efficient competitive provision of financial services. It is this form of financial services supervision which is currently being introduced in the UK. Nevertheless, this form of supervisory system is not without its faults, and the trend towards financial conglomerates will only aggravate the associated problems. In particular, the issue of overlap of supervisory responsibilities and the implications for the operations of an institution subject to the possibility of conflicting control requirements have yet to be confronted. There are also the difficulties in respect of identifying the institutions which may be classified as providing a particular service for the purposes of the control requirements, and in relation to the inequity of applying the same requirements to institutions with markedly different business profiles.

In respect of these problems the authorities have been adamant that providers of financial services must comply with the supervisory requirements even if it entails the restructuring of the legal form of the business. For example, the Governor of the Bank of England has stated that

> no one institution can simultaneously provide an array of financial services if the regulatory requirements applying to each are mutually incompatible. In some cases, the potential difficulties of overlapping jurisdiction could be solved by an appropriate degree of separation of each activity within the institution concerned. But in others, where different activities require different capital, liquidity or asset structures, the necessary degree of separation may well entail entrusting each of the activities in question to a separate company within a group.
>
> (*Bank of England Quarterly Bulletin*, March 1984, p. 43)

In the same speech he went on to emphasize that, on occasions, higher standards of behaviour might be expected of institutions than those which were implied by the formal legal requirements relating to its activities. In respect of the possible acquisition of banks by non-bank institutions he stated:

> We also need to be satisfied that any non-bank acquiror appreciates the extent of the moral commitment which we expect from the owners of a deposit-taking company, which may exceed the degree of commitment required by law. (p. 44)

A further problem faced by the regulators of the financial services industry is that of 'moral hazard'. That is, because of the possible risks to the stability of the financial system as a whole emanating from the collapse of a large deposit-taking or savings institutions, the regulatory body (and perhaps ultimately the state) might deem it to be necessary to provide some form of financial support for institutions facing liquidity pressures. This support might be financed by the state through the regulatory body, or it may be financed by an insurance or deposit protection scheme to which financial institutions are required to contribute. However, to the extent that individual institutions are effectively insured against failure, the issue arises as to whether this might not encourage risks to be taken in financial transactions which would otherwise be avoided. Clearly, the prospect of the ultimate sanction of bankruptcy being removed may distort financial decisions, and the free market mechanism cannot be said to be working effectively. The solution to this problem may lie in the adequacy of the supervisory framework and the requirements laid down in order to ensure that institutions are well managed and pursue their activities with prudence and caution. It is obviously inappropriate for the authorities to underwrite the solvency of all financial institutions in all circumstances.

It is often argued that, whilst the authorities should be willing to provide assistance to institutions which have done everything which could reasonably have been expected both within, and beyond, the requirements of the supervisory framework and which have nevertheless found themselves in difficulties due to quite unforeseeable circumstances, there is no reason why institutions consciously taking excessive risks in the pursuit of large profits should be bailed out if their calculations prove to have been unfounded. Nevertheless, the fear of the possible detrimental effects on the stability of the financial system may ultimately still force the hand of the authorities, in which case it might be suggested that as a condition of support the management of the institution is replaced, and that where ethically questionable practices have taken place their membership of relevant professional bodies be revoked. The prohibition of the incompetent and the reckless from financial markets would appear to be just as important to investor protection as the removal of the corrupt. Furthermore, the investor might be helped more effectively through the enforcement of rigorous disclosure requirements. If users of services are to make reasoned decisions in full knowledge of the type of risks they face, it is important that they should be be given access to information on the activities of institutions plying for their custom, and this should relate not just to variables such as liquidity, reserves, asset structures and so on, but should also cover information on the skills and experience of the management staff.

The Gower Report and the Background to the Financial Services Bill

In 1981 the British government commissioned Professor Jim Gower to investigate and report upon investor protection in the British financial system. An interim paper was published in January 1982 and the final report appeared in January 1984. The overall tone of the Gower Report was one of dissatisfaction with the supervisory arrangements for British financial institutions. The report highlighted the mixture of strong and weak supervision which was: inconsistent, complicated, uncertain, inequitable, tending to create elites and fringes, and involving an unnecessary diversity of regulations and regulators. Gower concluded that there were basically two approaches to dealing with the problems of the regulatory framework. On the one hand an official body might be created and vested with statutory powers to monitor, supervise and enforce the rules of behaviour thought to be appropriate to financial services institutions. On the other hand the pre-existing, largely informal, self-regulatory bodies might be formalized and given statutory backing to regulate the activities of their members within the scope of their competence. Ultimately, it was the latter proposal, with some amendments, which was accepted by the government as the model for financial services supervision in the UK. In particular the Securities and Investments Board (SIB) was established as the independent body to oversee the operation of the self-regulatory organizations (SROs), and to be responsible for the direct supervision of any relevant providers of financial services either unwilling or unable to join a recognized SRO. The Financial Services Bill, setting out the proposed legislation to establish the new regulatory framework, was laid before Parliament in December 1985.

It was Gower's recommendation that SROs should be considered for recognition by the authorities as legitimate regulatory agencies only if they met certain basic conditions. The most important of these conditions included the following: The SRO should only exist if there was a genuine need for its services, otherwise there could be a proliferation of unnecessary regulatory bodies; it was necessary that members of SROs should be willing automatically to disclose to their customers the possibility of conflicts of interest in their activities; the SRO must ensure that its members are professionally competent in respect of their chosen area(s) of activity; there should be no unnecessary restrictions on competition; investors should be protected through the establishment of compensation funds (where these were not already in existence); fund managers should maintain a separation between their clients' funds and their own; and SROs must be willing to make random checks on members to ensure that their agreed rules are being applied. There is still uncertainty as to how far the government is willing to pursue these conditions for SRO recognition as there has been substantial resistance to some of them from a number of important financial institutions.

It must be emphasized that the Financial Services Act, which vests powers in the Secretary of State for Trade and Industry to be delegated to the SIB and in turn to the SROs, is aimed at setting out a framework for the supervision of broad areas of financial activities, but it does not set out to establish a supervisory framework for the whole of the financial services industry (defined as the specific group of institutions involved in the provision of financial services). It is intended that the supervisory powers passing down through the SIB will relate to activities in the securities markets (but excluding the gilt-edged securities market), activities in futures and options markets, unit trust management, insurance broking, fund management, and the provision of investment advice and corporate finance advice. The Department of Trade and Industry will still maintain direct responsibility for the operations of insurance companies (within the terms of the Insurance Companies Act 1982), certain unit trust activities, and Lloyd's; it will also be responsible for monitoring compliance with the Companies Acts (as consolidated by the 1985 Act). The Bank of England maintains responsibility for the operations of all banking institutions as defined by the Banking Act 1979, as well as for activities on the gilt-edged securities market, the bullion market, wholesale money markets and the foreign exchange market. Responsibility for the building societies has passed to the new Building Societies Commission vested with powers under the Building Societies Act 1986. Finally, it must be presumed that the City Panel on Takeovers and Mergers will continue to function in relation to relevant financial services sector activity in this sphere, although its precise status has not yet been made clear.

Despite the criticisms which were directed towards the Financial Services Bill (and by August 1986 no less than 600 amendments to the original document had been tabled), the fact remains that it represented the first attempt at establishing a truly comprehensive supervisory framework for the provision of financial services in the UK. Across the broad range of investment and related activities, the Bill sought to apply formal regulated standards of investor protection and focused upon both the integrity and the competence of the providers of financial services. However, whilst dissatisfaction with the pre-existing regulatory framework made the proposed changes desirable, it was undoubtedly the changing structure of the financial services industry which made the proposals necessary. The tremendous growth of the industry in recent years, the diversification of activities within institutions, the increasing complexity of transactions, the growing competitiveness between institutions, and the trend towards internationalization of activities have been crucial factors in this respect. With the relaxation of restrictions on participation in financial service activities, and the increasing unwillingness of new entrants to domestic financial markets to accept the established norms and traditions or to react to the hints and veiled requests of the authorities, the formalization of the supervisory framework became inevitable.

An initial function of the SIB was to formulate codes of conduct and regulations for institutions and individuals involved in the provision of the relevant financial services. These codes and regulations form the basis of the SIB's rule book, and they establish the standards expected of the SROs' own rules.[1] The SIB's rule book had to be submitted to the Director General of Fair Trading, whose job it was to ensure that the rules embodied therein did not encourage or facilitate restrictive practices or anti-competitive behaviour in the financial services industry. The Director General reported back to the Secretary of State for Trade and Industry in April 1987, and in fact made several important criticisms of the likely effects of the SIB's proposed rules on competition between financial services businesses. However, the Director General also admitted that it would have been virtually impossible to formulate effective supervisory rules without having some effect on the free market mechanism. Consequently, and following a few minor amendments by the SIB, the rule book received the approval of the Secretary of State, and in April 1987 the formal powers of supervision of financial services businesses, as prescribed by the Financial Services Act, were transferred to the SIB. It is envisaged that during the second half of 1987 the various SROs will complete the preparation of their own rule books, which also must be vetted by the Director General of Fair Trading. They will then apply to the SIB for recognition, upon receiving which they will then be able to deal formally with applications from individuals and institutions wishing to take up membership with them.

An extremely controversial issue has been the amount of power which should be delegated to the SIB to control the SROs, to investigate alleged violations of supervisory requirements and to pursue prosecutions within the provisions of the Financial Services Act. As late as the summer of

1985 influential voices within the financial services establishment, supported by many MPs (from the government's own ranks), favoured only a minimal role for the SIB. Their fear was that a powerful independent regulatory board with sole responsibility for (and intimate technical experience of) the financial services sector might frighten away foreign participants, and drive activities to overseas centres where the control regime was less restrictive. However, more recently attitudes have been changing, not least because of the circumstances surrounding the collapse of Johnson Matthey Bankers and the continuing accusations of malpractice at Lloyd's Insurance Market (which interestingly is explicitly excluded from the financial services legislation). In addition, the government has become visibly anxious not only that the financial institutions should adhere to the rules of fair play in business transactions, but also that the policing of their activities should be seen to be effective and just. Political factors have clearly weighed heavily at a time of blatant prosperity for many of those working for City institutions. It now appears that the SIB will be given sufficient powers to allow it to carry out its initially desired functions effectively. It is proposed that the SIB will be able to order amendments to the rule books of the SROs, have substantial powers to investigate suspected wrongdoers, and that it will be delegated the power to prosecute individuals and firms caught providing financial services without appropriate authorization. Given that the SIB is to remain a private company without any support from public funds, the extent of these powers is all the more surprising.

A major problem still to be resolved is the nature of the relationship between the SIB, the SROs and other regulatory bodies, and the distribution of supervisory responsibility between them. It may be presumed that where an institution's activities fall within the remit of two or more regulators, one body will take on the role of 'lead regulator', but the formula for deciding which one that will be is uncertain. The issue is even more complex in respect of overseas regulatory bodies. International co-operation between regulators would appear to make sense, but where professional standards and legal requirements differ, and there is little precedent for the exchange of intelligence on the activities of financial institutions, the problems may be great. There are also ongoing arguments over the projected costs of running the supervisory mechanism (the whole of which has to be met by levies on the private sector members of the regulatory organizations)[2] and the nature of the proposed investor compensation funds.

The Financial Services Act

Speaking on the passage of the Financial Services Bill through Parliament, the Governor of the Bank of England was emphatic about the authorities' intention to strengthen market regulation and investor protection, as well as to establish a framework that had sufficient flexibility and sophistication to accommodate the rapidly changing structure of the UK financial system without compromising the standards of supervision:[3]

> During 1987, we should have in place a system of regulation that is firmly based on statute, but which is essentially run by practitioners. This combination should provide effective investor protection while being flexible to respond quickly to structural change. A practitioner-run system will, we believe, be better able to identify malpractice, and so be less bureaucratic . . . This will not be soft regulation. The measures are designed to bring the whole range of investment products within the scope of the law.

Formally, the Financial Services Act defines investments and investment businesses, requires persons carrying on investment business to be authorized and provides for their regulation. In this context investments include stocks and shares in British or overseas companies; debenture stock; loan stock; bonds; certificates of deposit; gilt-edged securities; local authority bonds; securities issued by foreign governments and international organizations; warrants; depository receipts for shares, bonds, or warrants; units in collective investment schemes; options on currency or on other investments; futures contracts for commodities; and insurance policies which constitute investments (such as endowment and unit-linked policies). A person will be deemed to be carrying on an investment business if he buys and sells investments, arranges for others to buy and sell investments, manages investments on the behalf of others, advises others on their investments, or operates a collective investment scheme. In addition, the trustees of occupational pension schemes will have to be authorized within the requirements of the Act unless the management of the scheme's assets is undertaken by a person who is himself authorized. However, trustees managing investments in an unpaid trustee capacity will not be obliged to seek authorization, and neither will individuals who give advice on investment matters purely as a consequence of selling advice on some other matter (for example, on taxation issues). The Act also embodies changes in the law relating to the listing of securities; offers of unlisted securities; collective investments; and insider dealing.[4]

It is now a criminal offence, punishable by fines and imprisonment, for any person to operate an investment business without prior authorization (unless otherwise exempted by the Act). Furthermore, the offending party will be unable to enforce his contracts and may be subject to a 'restitution order' requiring him to repay any profits made by the business, and to cover any losses incurred by others as a result of the operation of the business. The Act emphasizes the need to maintain confidence in the financial system in order to underpin its efficient operation. Indeed, the cost-effective provision of financial services to private businesses and individuals, as well as to the public sector, is seen as being an important influence on the formulation of the regulatory framework. It is argued that the need for a robust supervisory structure, capable of weathering the possibly rapid changes in the financial services industry, has to be balanced against the need to encourage free competition both domestically and internationally. The structure should stimulate financial innovation and responsiveness to customer demands rather than formalize restricted practices.

The appointment of the chairman and members of the SIB are at the discretion of the Secretary of State for Trade and Industry and the Governor of the Bank of England. These people are expected to play an extremely important role in the future development of UK financial services regulation as the Act leaves a large proportion of the detailed regulatory requirements to be established by the SIB. The initial composition of the eighteen-member board has not been without controversy, for whilst it is to be expected that the majority will have expertise in some areas of financial services activity, the fact that only one member is to be unconnected with the City establishment does not augur well for justice being seen to be done in respect of the misdemeanours of City practitioners.[5]

The Financial Services Act proposes that those wishing to undertake investment business may obtain authorization in one of five ways:

(1) The SIB will have the power to authorize directly 'fit and proper' persons.

(2) Membership of a practitioner-based SRO recognized by the SIB will be deemed as providing the required authorization. It is important to note that SROs will themselves only be granted recognition if it is believed that their own rules and procedures provide protection for investors of a level comparable to that offered by the SIB directly. Moreover, at any time, if the SIB has reason to believe that a recognized SRO is not performing its duties in the manner desired, it may apply for a court order directing the SRO either to undertake rule changes or to strengthen the application of its existing rules. Indeed, the SIB may restrict the scope of an SRO's regulatory discretion, and at the extreme may cancel its recognized status.

(3) Membership of a professional body which has been granted recognition by the SIB will be deemed to constitute authorization for an investment business.

(4) Insurance companies and insurance intermediaries involved in the provision of advice on endowment and unit-linked policies will continue to operate within the

general requirements of the Insurance Companies Act 1982, and hence will effectively obtain authorization through the Secretary of State for Trade and Industry who maintains responsibility for the supervision of insurance companies. However, whilst the Financial Services Act will not alter the position of the Insurance Companies Act 1982, it will extend the requirements placed on the above-mentioned insurance companies in respect of the marketing of investments, and hence it will strengthen the pre-existing regulatory framework and bring it more into line with the overall scheme as envisaged for other investment activity.[6] A similar arrangement will apply to friendly societies involved in the provision of insurance embodying an investment component.

(5) An investment business may be operated in the UK if the person or institution undertaking that business is duly authorized by another member state of the EEC, and where that state's requirements in respect of investor protection are judged to be at least as rigorous as those in force in the UK. Furthermore, this overseas authorization will only be available to businesses which do not have a permanent place of residence in the UK for purposes of providing their financial services. However, the Secretary of State for Trade and Industry will be empowered to prevent an overseas business from operating in the UK, irrespective of its domestic authorization, if British individuals and institutions are not given similar access to the domestic financial markets of the country from which that business originates.

Each SRO and professional body is expected to limit the scope of business which its members are entitled to undertake, although in theory any authorized person may undertake all forms of investment business. The implication of this position is that in practice the provision of an array of financial services by any individual or institution will probably necessitate membership of more than one SRO or professional body. The requirement for authorized businesses to adhere to the approved rules of their SRO or professional body (or the SIB itself in the case of a direct authorization) is to be underpinned by a provision in the Financial Services Act that it will constitute a criminal offence to make a false or misleading statement with intent to induce some other person or organization to enter into an investment agreement. This provision includes statements relating to the price or value of investments.

The sanctions available to the SIB are quite extensive. For example, it will be able to prohibit the employment in relation to investment business of any individual who has previously conducted his investment business affairs in a manner which is deemed not to be fit and proper. In respect of a directly authorized investment business the SIB will have the power to intervene in the running of the business, being able to restrict the scope of activities to be undertaken, require assets to be held within the UK, and even appoint a trustee to control the assets of the business. It is anticipated that recognized SROs will have similar powers of intervention in respect of the activities of their members. In addition, the SIB will be able to issue a public reprimand to an authorized business, withdraw or suspend its authorization, and apply for a court injunction in order to prevent a continued breach of rules. It may also apply to the court for an order of restitution requiring the repayment of profits made as a result of the breach of rules, and the making good of any losses incurred by investors in connection with that breach.[7] The SIB will be free to investigate the activities of any authorized or unauthorized investment business, having the power to obtain documents and question those people connected with the business. The Secretary of State for Trade and Industry will also be able to initiate investigations against any persons believed to be carrying out investment business, whether or not they are authorized to do so. In addition, the Secretary of State and the Director of Public Prosecutions will be able to instigate criminal proceedings within the provisions of the Act. The SIB is to be granted powers by the Secretary of State to prosecute alleged offenders only in certain circumstances.

Clearly, these regulatory powers are substantial, and given the serious implications which they generate for the livelihoods of individuals and those working in firms accused of breaching the rules of conduct, it is right to expect that there would be some form of independent appeals procedure against the stronger of the SIB's remedies for aberrant activities. Thus, other than in cases where court action is taken which offer the normal appeal procedures of the British legal system, it is intended that an appeals mechanism will operate in the form of an independent tribunal chaired by a lawyer (appointed by the Lord Chancellor) sitting with two other members (appointed by the Secretary of State), one of whom must be experienced in the practical operation of the financial services industry. The tribunal will investigate cases laid before it, and its decisions will be binding upon the SIB.

Finally, it should be noted that the Act exempts a number of bodies from authorization requirements. In particular, public bodies which undertake investment business in the course of their normal activities are to be exempt, as are the members of the Society of Lloyd's and its underwriting agents. In addition, tied agents working directly for authorized businesses will not be required to obtain authorization directly, as it is expected that their employers will take responsibility for their business conduct.

Conclusion

Some observers have been rather sceptical of the recent changes to the regulatory framework of the UK financial system, and have suggested that they may not even be sufficient to catch up with some of the more obvious structural changes which have occurred in the system since 1980. Indeed, the authorities' implicit condonation of diversification by financial institutions has been questioned at a time when the scandals at Lloyd's have brought forth the response of separating its functions more clearly and hence removing the potential for conflicts of interest to arise in the first place. However, it is difficult to see how the forces unleashed in the financial system in recent years could be reversed, or even if a reversal should be contemplated (assuming that one could be effected), given that many of the innovations experienced have resulted as a direct response to consumer demands.

The period since the mid-1970s has seen a massive increase in home ownership in the UK which has brought with it a corresponding expansion of building society activity, and naturally has thrown the societies into much more direct competition with the banking sector. The amounts of funds leaking from the housing finance market into normal consumer spending and investment activity is now believed to be substantial. The increasing affluence of the personal sector has been providing a growing amount of profitable opportunities for those institutions and individuals willing and able to offer attractive financial services to the ordinary saver. The investment dimension of life assurance and pension fund contributions, as well as the more obvious sources of collective investments with unit trusts and investment trust companies, have been marketed increasingly effectively and appear to have tapped an underlying willingness on the part of the general public to participate in equity investment at arm's length. The relative merits of direct equity investment are no longer so great for the individual, thus leaving the institutional shareholders to dominate the ownership of British listed companies.

The developments which have occurred within the UK financial system now provide opportunities for individuals to utilize their financial resources in an increasingly effective manner, and to plan for their future requirements at a level of sophistication which would have been almost unimaginable prior to 1980. For the corporate user of financial services the recent developments have been equally significant. New instruments and financial facilities have refined financial and risk management techniques beyond all recognition, and have helped companies as well as smaller businesses to cope with the ever changing and often unpredictable business environment.

The ultimate *raison d'être* of any financial system is to provide for the financial service needs of the individuals and businesses comprising the economy which it serves. The fundamental process of financial intermediation concerns

449

the channelling of funds between those with budget surpluses and those with deficits; and the nature of the money
transmission and payments facilities determine the ultimate
efficiency of business transactions at all levels. In this
context recent developments in the UK financial system
would appear to have made a positive contribution to the
well-being of the UK and its citizens. It must, however, be
recognized that as the nature of financial services becomes
ever more complex, so too do the risks they embody for the
user and for the provider. The authorities can offer some
protection for the naïve and the inexperienced, but the
ultimate safeguards against corruption and incompetence in
the financial services industry are a genuinely competitive
market environment and an increasingly well educated
population. Only then might there be an honest application
of the principle of *caveat emptor*.

Notes

1   By May 1987 five SROs had been formed, namely the Securities
    Association (TSA); the Association of Futures Brokers and
    Dealers (AFBD); the Financial Intermediaries, Managers and
    Brokers Regulatory Association (FIMBRA); the Investment
    Management Regulatory Organisation (IMRO) and the Life
    Assurance and Unit Trust Regulatory Organisation (LAUTRO).
2   The SIB itself has an initial budget of £6 million per annum and
    one estimate has put the cost of the entire supervisory
    mechanism in excess of £20 million per annum. See *The
    Economist*, 9 April 1986. To place these values in perspective it
    should be noted that the US Securities and Exchange Commis-
    sion has a budget of over $100 million per annum, financed
    entirely by the federal government.
3   See the governor's speech to the American Chamber of
    Commerce (UK), 21 January 1985, reported in *Bank of England
    Quarterly Bulletin*, March 1986, p. 72.
4   Insider dealing relates to the improper use for personal financial
    gain of information obtained in confidence during the normal
    course of business activities. The Act embodies amendments to
    the terms and definitions of the Company Securities (Insider
    Dealing) Act 1985.
5   Strictly, there are five lay members of the SIB, but three of these
    are senior managers of public companies (and hence are large-

scale users of the City's corporate financial services) and one is the Chief Executive of the SIB, although he is of civil service background.

6 Brokers acting as life assurance intermediaries, insurance consultants, and so on will be treated as any other investment business for the purposes of the Financial Services Act, and hence they will be required to obtain authorization through one of the normal channels.

7 The exercise of these powers in no way interferes with an investor's right to bring private action for damages against any business in breach of the approved rules of conduct.

Bibliography

Blanden, M. (1986), 'Point of sale or direct selling?', *The Banker*, April.

Cooper, J. C. B. (1980), 'Economies of scale in the UK building society industry', *Investment Analyst*, vol. 55.

Davies, G., and Davies, M. J. (1981), *Building Societies and their Branches – a Regional Economic Survey* (London: Franey).

Dickson, G. C. A., and Steele, J. T. (1984), *Introduction to Insurance*, 2nd ed. (London: Macdonald & Evans).

Drury, A. C. (1982), *Finance Houses* (London: Waterlow).

Franklin, P. J., and Woodhead, C. (1980) *The UK Life Assurance Industry* (London: Croom Helm).

Gilchrist, D., and Rothwell, S. (1980), 'Mergers of medium societies should mean more efficiency', *The Building Societies' Gazette*, no. 1350.

Gough, T. J. (1979), 'Building society mergers and the size–efficiency relationship', *Applied Economics*, June.

Gough, T. J. (1982), *The Economics of Building Societies* (London: Macmillan).

Gough, T. J., and Taylor, T. W. (1979), *The Building Society Price Cartel* (London: Institute of Economic Affairs).

Greaves, P. J. (1959), 'The banks and hire purchase', *National Provincial Bank Review*, February.

Keane, S. (1983), *Stock Market Efficiency* (Oxford: Phillip Allen).

Mabey, S., and Tillet, P. (1980), *Building Societies – the Need for Reform* (London: Bow Group).

Nellis, J. G., and Thom, R. (1983) 'The demand for mortgage finance in the United Kingdom', *Applied Economics*, August.

Parkin, J., and Ghosh, D. (1970), 'An econometric investigation of the portfolio and debt behaviour of building societies', Discussion Paper 24, University of Essex, Department of Economics.

Patrick, F. D., and Scobbie, A. (1969), 'Some aspects of withdrawals in ordinary life business', *Transactions of the Faculty of Actuaries*, vol. 21.

Price, S. J. (1958), *Building Societies: their Origins and History* (London: Franey).

Revell, J., and Moyle, J. (1966), *The Ownership of Quoted Ordinary Shares: a Survey for 1963* (London: Chapman & Hall).

Reynolds, N. (1984), 'Portfolio planning, risk and return', *Banking World*, November.

Stow, R. (1979), *Mortgage Finance in the 1980s – Report of the Working Party* (London: Building Societies Association).

Wilson, H. (1980), *Report of the Committee to Review the Functioning of Financial Institutions*, Cmnd 7939 (London: HMSO).

Winfield, R. G., and Curry, S. J. (1985) *Success in Investment*, 2nd ed. (London: John Murray).

Index

454